Don Harris (Ed.)

Engineering Psychology and Cognitive Ergonomics

Understanding Human Cognition

10th International Conference, EPCE 2013
Held as Part of HCI International 2013
Las Vegas, NV, USA, July 21-26, 2013
Proceedings, Part I

 Springer

Volume Editor

Don Harris
Coventry University
Faculty of Engineering and Computing
Priory Street
Coventry, CV1 5FB, UK
E-mail: don.harris@coventry.ac.uk

ISSN 0302-9743   e-ISSN 1611-3349
ISBN 978-3-642-39359-4   e-ISBN 978-3-642-39360-0
DOI 10.1007/978-3-642-39360-0
Springer Heidelberg Dordrecht London New York

Library of Congress Control Number: 2013941401

CR Subject Classification (1998): H.5, H.1, I.2, K.4, J.4, H.3, H.4, I.6

LNCS Sublibrary: SL 7 – Artificial Intelligence

Typesetting: Camera-ready by author, data conversion by Scientific Publishing Services, Chennai, India

Printed on acid-free paper

Springer is part of Springer Science+Business Media (www.springer.com)

Foreword

The 15th International Conference on Human–Computer Interaction, HCI International 2013, was held in Las Vegas, Nevada, USA, 21–26 July 2013, incorporating 12 conferences / thematic areas:

Thematic areas:

- Human–Computer Interaction
- Human Interface and the Management of Information

Affiliated conferences:

- 10th International Conference on Engineering Psychology and Cognitive Ergonomics
- 7th International Conference on Universal Access in Human–Computer Interaction
- 5th International Conference on Virtual, Augmented and Mixed Reality
- 5th International Conference on Cross-Cultural Design
- 5th International Conference on Online Communities and Social Computing
- 7th International Conference on Augmented Cognition
- 4th International Conference on Digital Human Modeling and Applications in Health, Safety, Ergonomics and Risk Management
- 2nd International Conference on Design, User Experience and Usability
- 1st International Conference on Distributed, Ambient and Pervasive Interactions
- 1st International Conference on Human Aspects of Information Security, Privacy and Trust

A total of 5210 individuals from academia, research institutes, industry and governmental agencies from 70 countries submitted contributions, and 1666 papers and 303 posters were included in the program. These papers address the latest research and development efforts and highlight the human aspects of design and use of computing systems. The papers accepted for presentation thoroughly cover the entire field of Human–Computer Interaction, addressing major advances in knowledge and effective use of computers in a variety of application areas.

This volume, edited by Don Harris, contains papers focusing on the thematic area of Engineering Psychology and Cognitive Ergonomics, and addressing the following major topics:

- Cognitive Issues in HCI
- Measuring and Monitoring Cognition
- Cognitive Issues in Complex Environments
- Productivity, Creativity, Learning and Collaboration

The remaining volumes of the HCI International 2013 proceedings are:

- Volume 1, LNCS 8004, Human–Computer Interaction: Human-Centred Design Approaches, Methods, Tools and Environments (Part I), edited by Masaaki Kurosu
- Volume 2, LNCS 8005, Human–Computer Interaction: Applications and Services (Part II), edited by Masaaki Kurosu
- Volume 3, LNCS 8006, Human–Computer Interaction: Users and Contexts of Use (Part III), edited by Masaaki Kurosu
- Volume 4, LNCS 8007, Human–Computer Interaction: Interaction Modalities and Techniques (Part IV), edited by Masaaki Kurosu
- Volume 5, LNCS 8008, Human–Computer Interaction: Towards Intelligent and Implicit Interaction (Part V), edited by Masaaki Kurosu
- Volume 6, LNCS 8009, Universal Access in Human–Computer Interaction: Design Methods, Tools and Interaction Techniques for eInclusion (Part I), edited by Constantine Stephanidis and Margherita Antona
- Volume 7, LNCS 8010, Universal Access in Human–Computer Interaction: User and Context Diversity (Part II), edited by Constantine Stephanidis and Margherita Antona
- Volume 8, LNCS 8011, Universal Access in Human–Computer Interaction: Applications and Services for Quality of Life (Part III), edited by Constantine Stephanidis and Margherita Antona
- Volume 9, LNCS 8012, Design, User Experience, and Usability: Design Philosophy, Methods and Tools (Part I), edited by Aaron Marcus
- Volume 10, LNCS 8013, Design, User Experience, and Usability: Health, Learning, Playing, Cultural, and Cross-Cultural User Experience (Part II), edited by Aaron Marcus
- Volume 11, LNCS 8014, Design, User Experience, and Usability: User Experience in Novel Technological Environments (Part III), edited by Aaron Marcus
- Volume 12, LNCS 8015, Design, User Experience, and Usability: Web, Mobile and Product Design (Part IV), edited by Aaron Marcus
- Volume 13, LNCS 8016, Human Interface and the Management of Information: Information and Interaction Design (Part I), edited by Sakae Yamamoto
- Volume 14, LNCS 8017, Human Interface and the Management of Information: Information and Interaction for Health, Safety, Mobility and Complex Environments (Part II), edited by Sakae Yamamoto
- Volume 15, LNCS 8018, Human Interface and the Management of Information: Information and Interaction for Learning, Culture, Collaboration and Business (Part III), edited by Sakae Yamamoto
- Volume 17, LNAI 8020, Engineering Psychology and Cognitive Ergonomics: Applications and Services (Part II), edited by Don Harris
- Volume 18, LNCS 8021, Virtual, Augmented and Mixed Reality: Designing and Developing Augmented and Virtual Environments (Part I), edited by Randall Shumaker
- Volume 19, LNCS 8022, Virtual, Augmented and Mixed Reality: Systems and Applications (Part II), edited by Randall Shumaker

- Volume 20, LNCS 8023, Cross-Cultural Design: Methods, Practice and Case Studies (Part I), edited by P.L. Patrick Rau
- Volume 21, LNCS 8024, Cross-Cultural Design: Cultural Differences in Everyday Life (Part II), edited by P.L. Patrick Rau
- Volume 22, LNCS 8025, Digital Human Modeling and Applications in Health, Safety, Ergonomics and Risk Management: Healthcare and Safety of the Environment and Transport (Part I), edited by Vincent G. Duffy
- Volume 23, LNCS 8026, Digital Human Modeling and Applications in Health, Safety, Ergonomics and Risk Management: Human Body Modeling and Ergonomics (Part II), edited by Vincent G. Duffy
- Volume 24, LNAI 8027, Foundations of Augmented Cognition, edited by Dylan D. Schmorrow and Cali M. Fidopiastis
- Volume 25, LNCS 8028, Distributed, Ambient and Pervasive Interactions, edited by Norbert Streitz and Constantine Stephanidis
- Volume 26, LNCS 8029, Online Communities and Social Computing, edited by A. Ant Ozok and Panayiotis Zaphiris
- Volume 27, LNCS 8030, Human Aspects of Information Security, Privacy and Trust, edited by Louis Marinos and Ioannis Askoxylakis
- Volume 28, CCIS 373, HCI International 2013 Posters Proceedings (Part I), edited by Constantine Stephanidis
- Volume 29, CCIS 374, HCI International 2013 Posters Proceedings (Part II), edited by Constantine Stephanidis

I would like to thank the Program Chairs and the members of the Program Boards of all affiliated conferences and thematic areas, listed below, for their contribution to the highest scientific quality and the overall success of the HCI International 2013 conference.

This conference could not have been possible without the continuous support and advice of the Founding Chair and Conference Scientific Advisor, Prof. Gavriel Salvendy, as well as the dedicated work and outstanding efforts of the Communications Chair and Editor of HCI International News, Abbas Moallem.

I would also like to thank for their contribution towards the smooth organization of the HCI International 2013 Conference the members of the Human–Computer Interaction Laboratory of ICS-FORTH, and in particular George Paparoulis, Maria Pitsoulaki, Stavroula Ntoa, Maria Bouhli and George Kapnas.

May 2013   Constantine Stephanidis
                                            General Chair, HCI International 2013

Organization

Human–Computer Interaction

Program Chair: Masaaki Kurosu, Japan

Jose Abdelnour-Nocera, UK
Sebastiano Bagnara, Italy
Simone Barbosa, Brazil
Tomas Berns, Sweden
Nigel Bevan, UK
Simone Borsci, UK
Apala Lahiri Chavan, India
Sherry Chen, Taiwan
Kevin Clark, USA
Torkil Clemmensen, Denmark
Xiaowen Fang, USA
Shin'ichi Fukuzumi, Japan
Vicki Hanson, UK
Ayako Hashizume, Japan
Anzai Hiroyuki, Italy
Sheue-Ling Hwang, Taiwan
Wonil Hwang, South Korea
Minna Isomursu, Finland
Yong Gu Ji, South Korea
Esther Jun, USA
Mitsuhiko Karashima, Japan

Kyungdoh Kim, South Korea
Heidi Krömker, Germany
Chen Ling, USA
Yan Liu, USA
Zhengjie Liu, P.R. China
Loïc Martínez Normand, Spain
Chang S. Nam, USA
Naoko Okuizumi, Japan
Noriko Osaka, Japan
Philippe Palanque, France
Hans Persson, Sweden
Ling Rothrock, USA
Naoki Sakakibara, Japan
Dominique Scapin, France
Guangfeng Song, USA
Sanjay Tripathi, India
Chui Yin Wong, Malaysia
Toshiki Yamaoka, Japan
Kazuhiko Yamazaki, Japan
Ryoji Yoshitake, Japan
Silvia Zimmermann, Switzerland

Human Interface and the Management of Information

Program Chair: Sakae Yamamoto, Japan

Hans-Jorg Bullinger, Germany
Alan Chan, Hong Kong
Gilsoo Cho, South Korea
Jon R. Gunderson, USA
Shin'ichi Fukuzumi, Japan
Michitaka Hirose, Japan
Jhilmil Jain, USA
Yasufumi Kume, Japan

Mark Lehto, USA
Hiroyuki Miki, Japan
Hirohiko Mori, Japan
Fiona Fui-Hoon Nah, USA
Shogo Nishida, Japan
Robert Proctor, USA
Youngho Rhee, South Korea
Katsunori Shimohara, Japan

Michale Smith, USA
Tsutomu Tabe, Japan
Hiroshi Tsuji, Japan

Kim-Phuong Vu, USA
Tomio Watanabe, Japan
Hidekazu Yoshikawa, Japan

Engineering Psychology and Cognitive Ergonomics

Program Chair: Don Harris, UK

Guy Andre Boy, USA
Joakim Dahlman, Sweden
Trevor Dobbins, UK
Mike Feary, USA
Shan Fu, P.R. China
Michaela Heese, Austria
Hung-Sying Jing, Taiwan
Wen-Chin Li, Taiwan
Mark A. Neerincx, The Netherlands
Jan M. Noyes, UK
Taezoon Park, Singapore

Paul Salmon, Australia
Axel Schulte, Germany
Siraj Shaikh, UK
Sarah C. Sharples, UK
Anthony Smoker, UK
Neville A. Stanton, UK
Alex Stedmon, UK
Xianghong Sun, P.R. China
Andrew Thatcher, South Africa
Matthew J.W. Thomas, Australia
Rolf Zon, The Netherlands

Universal Access in Human–Computer Interaction

Program Chairs: Constantine Stephanidis, Greece, and Margherita Antona, Greece

Julio Abascal, Spain
Ray Adams, UK
Gisela Susanne Bahr, USA
Margit Betke, USA
Christian Bühler, Germany
Stefan Carmien, Spain
Jerzy Charytonowicz, Poland
Carlos Duarte, Portugal
Pier Luigi Emiliani, Italy
Qin Gao, P.R. China
Andrina Granić, Croatia
Andreas Holzinger, Austria
Josette Jones, USA
Simeon Keates, UK

Georgios Kouroupetroglou, Greece
Patrick Langdon, UK
Seongil Lee, Korea
Ana Isabel B.B. Paraguay, Brazil
Helen Petrie, UK
Michael Pieper, Germany
Enrico Pontelli, USA
Jaime Sanchez, Chile
Anthony Savidis, Greece
Christian Stary, Austria
Hirotada Ueda, Japan
Gerhard Weber, Germany
Harald Weber, Germany

Virtual, Augmented and Mixed Reality

Program Chair: Randall Shumaker, USA

Waymon Armstrong, USA
Juan Cendan, USA
Rudy Darken, USA
Cali M. Fidopiastis, USA
Charles Hughes, USA
David Kaber, USA
Hirokazu Kato, Japan
Denis Laurendeau, Canada
Fotis Liarokapis, UK

Mark Livingston, USA
Michael Macedonia, USA
Gordon Mair, UK
Jose San Martin, Spain
Jacquelyn Morie, USA
Albert "Skip" Rizzo, USA
Kay Stanney, USA
Christopher Stapleton, USA
Gregory Welch, USA

Cross-Cultural Design

Program Chair: P.L. Patrick Rau, P.R. China

Pilsung Choe, P.R. China
Henry Been-Lirn Duh, Singapore
Vanessa Evers, The Netherlands
Paul Fu, USA
Zhiyong Fu, P.R. China
Fu Guo, P.R. China
Sung H. Han, Korea
Toshikazu Kato, Japan
Dyi-Yih Michael Lin, Taiwan
Rungtai Lin, Taiwan

Sheau-Farn Max Liang, Taiwan
Liang Ma, P.R. China
Alexander Mädche, Germany
Katsuhiko Ogawa, Japan
Tom Plocher, USA
Kerstin Röse, Germany
Supriya Singh, Australia
Hsiu-Ping Yueh, Taiwan
Liang (Leon) Zeng, USA
Chen Zhao, USA

Online Communities and Social Computing

Program Chairs: A. Ant Ozok, USA, and Panayiotis Zaphiris, Cyprus

Areej Al-Wabil, Saudi Arabia
Leonelo Almeida, Brazil
Bjørn Andersen, Norway
Chee Siang Ang, UK
Aneesha Bakharia, Australia
Ania Bobrowicz, UK
Paul Cairns, UK
Farzin Deravi, UK
Andri Ioannou, Cyprus
Slava Kisilevich, Germany

Niki Lambropoulos, Greece
Effie Law, Switzerland
Soo Ling Lim, UK
Fernando Loizides, Cyprus
Gabriele Meiselwitz, USA
Anthony Norcio, USA
Elaine Raybourn, USA
Panote Siriaraya, UK
David Stuart, UK
June Wei, USA

Augmented Cognition

Program Chairs: Dylan D. Schmorrow, USA, and Cali M. Fidopiastis, USA

Robert Arrabito, Canada
Richard Backs, USA
Chris Berka, USA
Joseph Cohn, USA
Martha E. Crosby, USA
Julie Drexler, USA
Ivy Estabrooke, USA
Chris Forsythe, USA
Wai Tat Fu, USA
Rodolphe Gentili, USA
Marc Grootjen, The Netherlands
Jefferson Grubb, USA
Ming Hou, Canada

Santosh Mathan, USA
Rob Matthews, Australia
Dennis McBride, USA
Jeff Morrison, USA
Mark A. Neerincx, The Netherlands
Denise Nicholson, USA
Banu Onaral, USA
Lee Sciarini, USA
Kay Stanney, USA
Roy Stripling, USA
Rob Taylor, UK
Karl van Orden, USA

Digital Human Modeling and Applications in Health, Safety, Ergonomics and Risk Management

Program Chair: Vincent G. Duffy, USA and Russia

Karim Abdel-Malek, USA
Giuseppe Andreoni, Italy
Daniel Carruth, USA
Eliza Yingzi Du, USA
Enda Fallon, Ireland
Afzal Godil, USA
Ravindra Goonetilleke, Hong Kong
Bo Hoege, Germany
Waldemar Karwowski, USA
Zhizhong Li, P.R. China

Kang Li, USA
Tim Marler, USA
Michelle Robertson, USA
Matthias Rötting, Germany
Peter Vink, The Netherlands
Mao-Jiun Wang, Taiwan
Xuguang Wang, France
Jingzhou (James) Yang, USA
Xiugan Yuan, P.R. China
Gülcin Yücel Hoge, Germany

Design, User Experience, and Usability

Program Chair: Aaron Marcus, USA

Sisira Adikari, Australia
Ronald Baecker, Canada
Arne Berger, Germany
Jamie Blustein, Canada

Ana Boa-Ventura, USA
Jan Brejcha, Czech Republic
Lorenzo Cantoni, Switzerland
Maximilian Eibl, Germany

Anthony Faiola, USA
Emilie Gould, USA
Zelda Harrison, USA
Rüdiger Heimgärtner, Germany
Brigitte Herrmann, Germany
Steffen Hess, Germany
Kaleem Khan, Canada

Jennifer McGinn, USA
Francisco Rebelo, Portugal
Michael Renner, Switzerland
Kerem Rızvanoğlu, Turkey
Marcelo Soares, Brazil
Christian Sturm, Germany
Michele Visciola, Italy

Distributed, Ambient and Pervasive Interactions

Program Chairs: Norbert Streitz, Germany, and Constantine Stephanidis, Greece

Emile Aarts, The Netherlands
Adnan Abu-Dayya, Qatar
Juan Carlos Augusto, UK
Boris de Ruyter, The Netherlands
Anind Dey, USA
Dimitris Grammenos, Greece
Nuno M. Guimaraes, Portugal
Shin'ichi Konomi, Japan
Carsten Magerkurth, Switzerland

Christian Müller-Tomfelde, Australia
Fabio Paternó, Italy
Gilles Privat, France
Harald Reiterer, Germany
Carsten Röcker, Germany
Reiner Wichert, Germany
Woontack Woo, South Korea
Xenophon Zabulis, Greece

Human Aspects of Information Security, Privacy and Trust

Program Chairs: Louis Marinos, ENISA EU, and Ioannis Askoxylakis, Greece

Claudio Agostino Ardagna, Italy
Zinaida Benenson, Germany
Daniele Catteddu, Italy
Raoul Chiesa, Italy
Bryan Cline, USA
Sadie Creese, UK
Jorge Cuellar, Germany
Marc Dacier, USA
Dieter Gollmann, Germany
Kirstie Hawkey, Canada
Jaap-Henk Hoepman, The Netherlands
Cagatay Karabat, Turkey
Angelos Keromytis, USA
Ayako Komatsu, Japan

Ronald Leenes, The Netherlands
Javier Lopez, Spain
Steve Marsh, Canada
Gregorio Martinez, Spain
Emilio Mordini, Italy
Yuko Murayama, Japan
Masakatsu Nishigaki, Japan
Aljosa Pasic, Spain
Milan Petković, The Netherlands
Joachim Posegga, Germany
Jean-Jacques Quisquater, Belgium
Damien Sauveron, France
George Spanoudakis, UK
Kerry-Lynn Thomson, South Africa

Julien Touzeau, France
Theo Tryfonas, UK
João Vilela, Portugal

Claire Vishik, UK
Melanie Volkamer, Germany

External Reviewers

Maysoon Abulkhair, Saudi Arabia
Ilia Adami, Greece
Vishal Barot, UK
Stephan Böhm, Germany
Vassilis Charissis, UK
Francisco Cipolla-Ficarra, Spain
Maria De Marsico, Italy
Marc Fabri, UK
David Fonseca, Spain
Linda Harley, USA
Yasushi Ikei, Japan
Wei Ji, USA
Nouf Khashman, Canada
John Killilea, USA
Iosif Klironomos, Greece
Ute Klotz, Switzerland
Maria Korozi, Greece
Kentaro Kotani, Japan

Vassilis Kouroumalis, Greece
Stephanie Lackey, USA
Janelle LaMarche, USA
Asterios Leonidis, Greece
Nickolas Macchiarella, USA
George Margetis, Greece
Matthew Marraffino, USA
Joseph Mercado, USA
Claudia Mont'Alvão, Brazil
Yoichi Motomura, Japan
Karsten Nebe, Germany
Stavroula Ntoa, Greece
Martin Osen, Austria
Stephen Prior, UK
Farid Shirazi, Canada
Jan Stelovsky, USA
Sarah Swierenga, USA

HCI International 2014

The 16th International Conference on Human–Computer Interaction, HCI International 2014, will be held jointly with the affiliated conferences in the summer of 2014. It will cover a broad spectrum of themes related to Human–Computer Interaction, including theoretical issues, methods, tools, processes and case studies in HCI design, as well as novel interaction techniques, interfaces and applications. The proceedings will be published by Springer. More information about the topics, as well as the venue and dates of the conference, will be announced through the HCI International Conference series website: http://www.hci-international.org/

General Chair
Professor Constantine Stephanidis
University of Crete and ICS-FORTH
Heraklion, Crete, Greece
Email: cs@ics.forth.gr

Table of Contents – Part I

Cognitive Issues in HCI

Measuring and Monitoring Cognition

Cognitive Issues in Complex Environments

Productivity, Creativity, Learning and Collaboration

Table of Contents – Part II

Driving and Transportation Safety

Cognitive Issues in Aviation

Military Applications

Cognitive Issues in Health and Well-Being

Part I
Cognitive Issues in HCI

Data Transmission Latency and Sense of Control

Bruno Berberian[1], Patrick Le Blaye[1], Christian Schulte[1],
Nawfel Kinani[1], and Pern Ren Sim[2]

[1] Systems Control and Flight Dynamics Department, ONERA, Salon de Provence, France
Bruno.Berberian@onera.fr
[2] DSO National Laboratories, Singapore
spernren@dso.org.sg

Abstract. Latency has been identified as a major bottleneck for usability of human-system interaction devices. However, the theoretical basis of the effect of latency on action control mechanisms remains weak. In this study, we aimed to investigate the cognitive implications of latency for Human-Computer Interaction. We proposed models of agency (i.e., mechanism underlying the feeling of control) as a possible interpretative framework on the nature of the transformation induced by latency. In a series of 3 experiments, we propose to tackle this problem by (1) characterizing the effects (performance and agency) of transmission delays on UAS camera control, and (2) designing and evaluating HMI solutions to mitigate these effects with regard to the agency principle. Our results showed that (1) latency decreases sense of agency and human performance, (2) models of agency could provide HMI solution for latency compensation. Interests of agentive experience accounts for better system design are discussed.

Keywords: Latency, Agency, Action Control, UAS, Cognition.

1   Introduction

Latency, or lag, is the time delay in device position updates [4]. Latency has been shown to dramatically degrade human performance in motor-sensory tasks with interactive systems as well as planning and performance in teleoperation scenarios [2; 8; 14; 15]). In general, the effect involves a reduction in control accuracy which ultimately drives the operator to adopt a "move and wait" strategy when latency exceeds about 300 ms (see [3; 11; 12; 13]). This problem of latency is particularly true when you consider Unmanned Aircraft System (UAS) operation, latency generally exceeding 300 ms in such system. Clearly, data transmission latencies between Unmanned Aerial Vehicles (UAVs) and control stations affect the effective operator control of these UAVs.

However, if lag is currently considered by User Interface Designers as a major bottleneck for usability of human-system interaction devices [8], the theoretical basis of the effect of latency on action control mechanisms remains weak. We assume that characterizing how latency impacts the cognitive processing involved in action

D. Harris (Ed.): EPCE/HCII 2013, Part I, LNAI 8019, pp. 3–12, 2013.
© Springer-Verlag Berlin Heidelberg 2013

control should provide guidelines to User Interface Designers for latency compensation. A possible interpretative framework on the nature of the transformation induced by latency can be tracked back to the mechanism of agency. When we act, we usually have a clear feeling that we control our own action and can thus produce effects in the external environment. This experience of oneself as the agent of one's own actions has been described as "the sense of agency" (for reviews, see [5]). Models of agency suggest that the experience we have of causing our own actions arises whenever we draw a causal inference linking our thought (or intention) to our action. This inference occurs in accordance with principles that follow from research on cause perception and attribution (see [5; 6; 9; 10]). Interestingly, temporal contiguity is central for sense of agency: immediate cause–effect pairings are generally privileged [18; 17; 19] and task-meaningful temporal windows introduced between a cause and its effect is necessary [1]. So that, to perceive a sense of control, the effect cannot start too soon or start too late; it has to be on time just after the action.

In this context, we hypothesized that (1) the data transmission latency directly impacts the sense of agency, (2) designing HMI solutions offering the maximal agency could compensate the negative effect of latency on a teleoperation control task. In a series of 3 experiments, we propose to tackle this problem by (1) characterizing the effects (performance and agency) of transmission delays on UAS camera control, and (2) designing and evaluating HMI solutions to mitigate these effects with regard to the agency principle.

2   Experiment 1: Latency and Agency in Simple Paradigm

The first experiment was designed to characterize the link between agency and latency. To address this issue, we used the classical Fitts' task in a discrete version. In this paradigm, participant had to move a cursor as quick and as accurate as possible, toward a target from a home position (one-dimensional movement). Latency was introduced between the initiation of the physical movement of the device (stylus) and the time the corresponding update appears on the screen (movement of the visible cursor). Effect of input device latency on human performance and sense of agency were computed. As showed by), we hypothesized that the latency directly impacts (1) human performance in such pointing task (see [8]) and (2) the sense of agency (see [19]).

2.1   Method

Participants. Nine right-handed from the French Aerospace lab volunteered to participate in this experiment. All had normal vision and were naïve as to the hypothesis under investigation. Their mean age was 24 (range = 21–32 years).

Materials and Apparatus. We used an interactive graphics system using targets displayed on a LCD (Dell P2210, 22") and a cursor manipulated by an input device (graphic tablet WACOM Intuos 4 XL + stylus). Stylus movements over a graphics tablet motion of a vertical green line cursor. A vertically elongated white bar on the screen represented the target against a grey background. The stylus' position was sampled at a frequency of 150 Hz. An adjacent monitor (17'' touch screen) showed two horizontal lines used for agency measures recording (see later).

Procedure. The participants' task was to move a cursor as quick and as accurate as possible, toward a target from a home position (one-dimensional movement). The sequence of events on each trial is described in Figure 1. (1) Participants' cursor is situated at the central position. (2) After a short interval, a sound got the signal for the beginning of the movement. (3) The participant moved the cursor as quick as possible towards the target. (4) The cursor reached the target. (5) After a controlled temporal delay, an acoustic feedback concerning the success of the target was given. (6) After each trial, measures of agency were computed (details in *Measure of agency* section). In order to test the effect of latency on agency, a temporal gap was introduced between the initiation of the physical movement of the device (stylus) and the time the corresponding update appears on the screen (movement of the visible cursor). Four different levels of latency were tested (0, 250, 750 or 1500ms). In a last condition, called control condition, the movement of the cursor was externally produced (i.e., participant only observed). Task difficulty was also manipulated by using two different target sizes (30 mm for *ID2* versus 10 mm for *ID3*).

Measure of Agency. If the sense of agency has been proved to be difficult to quantify, it is now accepted that different aspects has to be considered, conscious and unconscious aspects. Conscious aspect refers to the explicit judgement of causal control. In contrast, unconscious aspect refers to change involved in voluntary action (i.e., agentive situation), particularly perceptual change. An interesting one relates to the perceived duration of intervals between actions and effects. Recent research has shown that human intentional action is associated with systematic changes in time perception: the interval between a voluntary action and an outcome is perceived as short as the interval between a physically similar involuntary movement and an outcome. This phenomenon called intentional binding [7] offers an implicit measure of the sense of agency. Relative to these two aspects of agency, two measures were collected for each trial. Unconscious aspect of agency was evaluated by the temporal delay perceived between action and effect. Participant had to estimate on a scale from 0s to 1s the temporal delay perceived between the entrance in the target and the appearance of the success feedback. If they were told that the possible range of delays was between 1 ms and 1000 ms, only three Action/Effect delays (250 ms, 500 ms, and 750 ms) were presented, in a random order. Conscious aspect of agency was evaluated by judgement of agency. Participants has to report how strongly they felt that they controlled the pointing movement, using a scale from 0 (no causal involvement) to 1 (strong causal involvement).

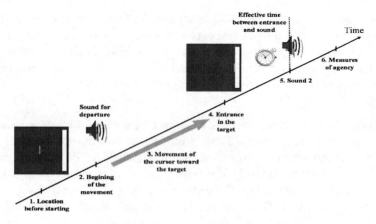

Fig. 1. Typical sequence of events for one trial

To summarize, we have (1) five conditions of *latency*, (2) two index of *difficulty* (ID2 versus ID3) and (3) three effective *Action/Effect delays*. Each participant made two trials for each combination of *Latency*, *Difficulty* and *Action/Effect Delay*, being in total sixty trials per participants. The trials were tested in random order.

2.2   Results and Discussion

In this study, our primary concern is the relationship between latency and sense of agency, at both unconscious and conscious levels. The impact of latency on performance is also computed.

Unconscious Aspect of Agency: Temporal Judgement. The first measure of agency collected concerns the perceived duration of intervals between actions and effects. As previously introduced (see Intentional binding effect), if latency reduces the sense of agency, action/effect interval estimation should increase with the level of latency. To test this hypothesis, we performed a 5*2*3 ANOVA with *Latency* (0, 250, 750, 1500ms, control condition), *Difficulty* (ID2, ID3) and *Action/Effect delay* (250, 500, 750 ms) as within subject factors. Our results (see Figure 2A) show a significant effect of *Latency* on interval estimation ($F(4,68)= 11.91$, $p<.01$). Post-hoc analysis revealed that interval estimates increased monotonically with the level of latency: the more the cursor movement was delayed, or the less it relied on participant's actual movement, the longer the action-effect interval was perceived, and this even if the actual action/effect delays are completely independent of the latency introduced in the system. Interestingly, no significant difference ($p>.01$) was observed between the conditions with large latency (750 and 1500 ms) and the control condition (movement externally produced). These results indicate that the unconscious aspect of agency is sensitive to the latency, with increasing latency leading to a higher interval estimate, which we interpret as a gradual decrease in sense of agency.

Conscious Aspect of Agency: Explicit Judgement of Agency. The second measure of agency collected concerns the judgement of agency: How much do you feel in control? As for the unconscious aspect of agency, this feeling of control should decrease with latency. Our results (see Figure 2B) confirm such hypothesis, since a significant effect of *Latency* on verbal reports was observed ($F(3, 51) = 60.76$, $p<.01$). Post hoc analysis shows that judgement of causality decreased monotonically with the level of latency (all ps,.01). These results indicate that the conscious aspect of agency is sensitive to the latency, with increasing latency leading to a gradual decrease in judgement of agency. A significant effect of *Difficulty* is also observed ($F(1,17) = 25.96$, $p<.01$). Post-hoc analysis for *Difficulty* reveals that subject have larger sense of control for easier task (ID2), results not observed for time estimation ($F(1,17)= 1.32$, n.s.). More particularly, conscious aspect of agency seems more sensitive to performance than unconscious aspect. A possible explanation could be found regarding the relation between performance and judgement of agency.

Performance: Movement Time. Finally, we computed the effect of the latency on movement time. As previously observed by MacKenzie and Ware [8], we observe a significant effect of *Latency* on movement time ($F(3,51) = 51.37$, $p<.01$) (see Figure 2C). Post-hoc analysis reveals a progressive decrease in movement time in regard to the latency. These results indicate that the performance is sensitive to the latency, with increasing latency leading to a poorer performance (i.e., a larger movement time).

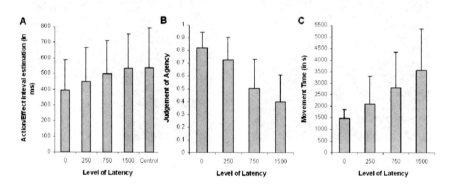

Fig. 2. Modulation of (A) Interval Estimates, (B) Judgement of Agency, and (C) Movement Time by actual level of *Latency*

3   Experiment 2 and 3: Wegner Principle for Latency Compensation

Our first experiment indicates that latency (1) decreases conscious and unconscious aspects of agency, (2) impacts human performance. It clearly demonstrates that increase in latency is correlated to a decrease in sense of agency. Such decrease is congruent with models of agency (see [18; 17]). Indeed, as claimed by priority principle, to perceive a sense of control, the effect cannot start too soon or start too late; it has to be on time just after the action. In this context, we hypothesized that designing HMI solutions that enhance agency (particularly in regard to priority principle) could compensate the negative effect of latency. To tackle this question, we focused on teleoperation control task. The aim was to propose human-machine interface (HMI) solutions that reduce the effects (oscillatory behaviour) of latency on an operator's performance.

The HMI solution developed was a predictive cue called the "Payload Director". The goal of this help is to provide immediate feedback to the operator about the predicted position of the payload due to the user input. The aim of the design is to satisfy the condition of temporal contiguity for sense of agency. Indeed, by presenting an anticipated effect of the action, we decrease the gap between the command sent by the operator and the perceived effect of this action, even if action is really effective only several seconds after. Figure 3 is the screen shot of the payload director. The circle indicates the position which the crosshair will centre on as a result of the user input. The position of the circle is calculated using the known control function of the payload controller. Figure 4 illustrates the function of the Payload Director.

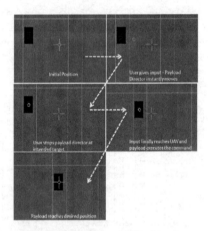

Fig. 3. Payload Director (PD)   **Fig. 4.** Illustration of PD's function

Two experiments were designed to evaluate this HMI solution in a complex setting involving controlling a UAS camera for target acquisition. Particularly, two groups of participants performed respectively a pointing task (acquire a fixed target as quick as possible) and a tracking task (track a moving target). These two experiments were conducted using ONERA's remote piloted system simulator. This simulator comprises a UAS pilot station which includes payload control sticks (for camera command) and video screen (for camera control, i.e. visualization of the camera's image). Delays were introduced between the stick command input and the movement of the camera and their effects on agency and performance were observed with or without the Payload Director.

3.1   Method

Participants. Eight and ten right-handed from the French Aerospace lab participated respectively in the pointing and the tracking tasks. All had normal vision and were naïve as to the hypothesis under investigation. Their mean age was 26 (range = 22–31 years) for the pointing task, 27 (range = 23–34 years) for the tracking task.

Procedure for the Pointing Task. The participants' task was to move a cursor as quick and as accurate as possible, toward a target from a home position (two-dimensional movement). The sequence of events on each trial was as follows (see Figure 5). At the beginning of each trial, participants' cursor is situated at the central position (home position). (2) After a short interval, a target appeared. There were 6 different target positions at equi-distance from the crosshair of the payload (see Figure 6). (3) The participant moved the camera as quick as possible towards the target. (4) The cursor reached the target (visual feedback for target acquisition). (5) After each trial, measures of agency were computed. Relative to the two aspects of agency (conscious and unconscious), two different measures were collected. Unconscious aspect of agency was evaluated by the temporal delay perceived between action and effect. Particularly, participant had to estimate on a scale from 0s to 2s the latency perceived between their action on the stick and the movement of the camera. Conscious aspect of agency was evaluated by verbal reports. Participants made an explicit judgement of agency, by reporting how strongly they felt that they controlled the pointing movement, using a scale from 0 (no causal involvement) to 1 (strong causal involvement). In order to test the effect of latency on agency, four different levels of *Latency* were tested (0, 250, 750 or 1500ms). Finally, each level of latency was performed with or without help. Altogether, each participant performed 32 trials (4 repetitions for each combination *Latency/Help*). The trials were tested in random order.

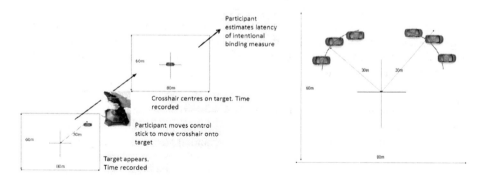

Fig. 5. Typical sequence of events for one trial   **Fig. 6.** Equi-distant targets

Procedure for the Tracking Task. The participants' task was to keep the payload cursor on a moving target from a moving UAV (two-dimensional movement). The sequence of events on each trial was as follows (see Figure 5). At the beginning of each trial, participants' cursor is situated at the central position (home position). (2) After a short interval, a moving target appeared. There were 24 different paths made up of repeatable components in different order for similar difficulty. Frequency and sharpness of turns are controlled. Path time was of 50 seconds. (3) The participant moved the camera to keep crosshair in the moving target. (4) After each trial, measures of agency were computed in the same way than in the pointing task. Three different levels of *Latency* were tested (0, 500, or 1000ms). Finally, runs were performed for each level of latency with or without help. Altogether, each participant performed 24 runs (4 repetitions for each combination *Latency/Help*). The trials were tested in random order. The measure of agency was computed at both unconscious (temporal estimation of latency) and conscious (explicit judgement of control) levels.

3.2   Results and Discussion

As observed in our first experiment, latency reduces the sense of agency at both unconscious and conscious levels, but also human performance. In this study, we aimed to propose an HMI solution to compensate these negative effects. If efficient, our help should increase sense of agency and performance in presence of latency. In other words, for a same level of *Latency*, we anticipated better performance and sense of control in presence of the help proposed (the Payload Director) than without.

Unconscious Aspect of Agency: Temporal Judgement. At the unconscious level, a decrease in agency leads to a larger estimation of the temporal delay between my action and its effect (Action/Effect interval). We hypothesized that the Payload Director could partially mitigate this effect. To test this hypothesis, we compared the effect of Latency on Action/Effect delay estimation with and without the Payload Director in the two tasks. Whatever the target, fixed or moving, we observed a significant difference in Action/Effect delays estimation with or without the Payload Director (with $F(1,7) = 52.15$, $p<.01$ for fixed target and $F(1,19) = 45.62$, $p<.01$ for moving target) (see Figure 7A). Post-hoc analysis reveals that the Action/Effect delays are estimated shorter with the Payload Director for the two experiments. These results indicate that the HMI solution proposed partially mitigates the effect of Latency in regard to the unconscious aspect of agency.

Conscious Aspect of Agency: Explicit Judgement of Agency. At the conscious level, a decrease in agency leads to a decrease in the judgement of control. As hypothesized for unconscious aspect of agency, we anticipated that the Payload Director could partially mitigate this effect. To test this hypothesis, we compared the effect of Latency on judgement of agency with and without the Payload Director in the two tasks. Our results (see Figure 7B) showed a significant difference in judgement of agency with or without the Payload Director (with $F(1,7) = 29.33$, $p<.01$ for fixed target and $F(1,19) = 25.16$ $p<.01$ for moving target). Post-hoc analysis reveals that subjects have larger sense of control with the Payload Director than without for the two tasks. These results indicate that the HMI solution proposed partially mitigates the effect of Latency in regard to the conscious aspect of agency.

Performance. Concerning the performance measure, we used the time for acquisition in the pointing task, and the percentage of time the payload cursor is on the moving target (Ratio of time Crosshair-Over-Target or COT Ratio) for the tracking task. In the two tasks, we observed an increase in performance with the Payload Director. In the pointing task, our results showed a significant difference between time for acquisition with and without the Payload Director ($F(1,7) = 55.92$, $p<.01$). Post-hoc analysis reveals shorter time for acquisition with the Payload Director (see Figure 7C). The same effect was observed in the tracking task. Wilcoxon Signed Rank Test shows that the overall difference in performance between Payload Director and No Help condition were statistically significant ($p<.01$). Particularly, the time over the target is larger with the Payload Director than without. These results indicate that the HMI solution proposed partially mitigates the effect of Latency in regard to the operator performance.

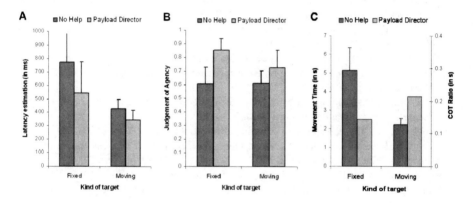

Fig. 7. Modulation of (A) Latency Estimates, (B) Judgement of Agency, and (C) Performance (Movement Time or COT ratio) by the HMI solution proposed (i.e., the Payload Director)

4   Conclusion

In the current context of continue increase in complexity, latency problem becomes a major human factors question. This is particularly true considering the use of UAS. In this context, we aimed to investigate the cognitive implications of latency for Human-Computer Interaction. Our study yielded two important results. First, we showed that the sense of agency evolves as a function of latency. Particularly, increase in latency leads to a decrease in sense of agency. Second, we showed that the Wegner formal framework of agency (for a review, see [16]) provides principles to design Human-Machine Interfaces capable of compensate the negative effects of latency on action control. By this way, we show that psychological ideas about the self, and particularly the concept of agency, can help to (1) understand the theoretical basis of the effect of latency on action control mechanisms, (2) propose HMI solutions to mitigate latency effect on action control. More generally, we consider that accounts of agentive experience could provide guidelines for better system design.

References

1. Berberian, B., Sarrazin, J.C., Le Blaye, P., Haggard, P.: Automation Technology and Sense of Control: A Window on Human Agency. PLoS ONE 7(3), 34075 (2012)
2. Chung, G.K.M., So, R.H.Y.: Manual control with time delays in an immersive virtual environment. In: McCabe, P.T. (ed.) Contemporary Ergonomics 2011. Taylor & Francis (2011)
3. Ferrell, W.R.: Remote manipulation with transmission delay. IEEE Trans. on Human Factors in Electronics, HFES 6(1) (1965)
4. Foxlin, E.: Motion tracking requirements and technologies. In: Stanney, K.M. (ed.) Handbook of Virtual Environments: Design, Implementation and Applications, pp. 163–210. Lawrence Erlbaum, Mahwah (2002)
5. Gallagher, S.: Philosophical concepts of the self: implications for cognitive sciences. Trends in Cognitive Sciences 4, 14–21 (2000)
6. Gilbert, D.T.: Attribution and interpersonal perception. In: Tesser, A. (ed.) Advanced Social Psychology, pp. 98–147. McGraw-Hill (1995)
7. Haggard, P., Clark, S., Kalogeras, J.: Voluntary action and conscious awareness. Nature Neuroscience 5(4), 382–385 (2002)
8. MacKenzie, S., Ware, C.: Lag as a determinant of Human performance in interactive systems. In: Proc. ACM Conference on Human Factors in Computing Systems (INTERCHI), ACM SIGCHI, pp. 488–493 (1993)
9. McClure, J.: Discounting causes of behavior: Are two reasons better than one? Journal of Personality and Social Psychology 74(1), 7–20 (1998)
10. Michotte, A.: The perception of causality. Basic Books, New York (1963) (trans. T. R. Miles, E. Miles); Pavlovych, A., Stuerzlinger, W.: The tradeoff between spatial jitter and latency in pointing tasks. In: Proc. EICS 2009, pp. 187–196. ACM Press (2009)
11. Poulton, E.C.: Tracking skill and manual control. Academic, New York (1974)
12. Sheridan, T.B.: Musings on telepresence and virtual presence. Presence 1(1), 120–125, 212–227 (1992)
13. Smith, K.U., Smith, W.M.: Perception and action, pp. 247–277. Saunders, Philadelphia (1962)
14. So, R.H.Y., Chung, G.K.M.: Sensory Motor Responses in Virtual Environments: Studying the Effects of Image Latencies for Target-directed Hand Movement. IEEE Engineering in Medicine and Biology Society, 5006 5008 (2005)
15. Ware, C., Balakrishnan, R.: Target acquisition in fish tank VR: The effects of lag and frame rate. In: Graphics Interface 1994, pp. 1–7. Canadian Information Processing Society, Toronto (1994)
16. Wegner, D.M.: The illusion of conscious will. MIT Press (2002)
17. Wegner, D.M.: The mind's best trick: How we experience conscious will. Trends in Cognitive Sciences 7, 65–69 (2003)
18. Wegner, D.M., Wheatley, T.: Apparent mental causation: Sources of the experience of will. American Psychologist 54(7), 480–492 (1999)
19. Young, M.E., Rogers, E.T., Beckmann, J.S.: Causal impressions: predicting when, not just whether. Mem. Cogn. 33, 320–331 (2005)

Towards a Model for Predicting Intention in 3D Moving-Target Selection Tasks

Juan Sebastián Casallas[1,3], James H. Oliver[1], Jonathan W. Kelly[1,2], Frédéric Merienne[3], and Samir Garbaya[3]

[1] Virtual Reality Applications Center, Iowa State University
1620 Howe Hall, Ames, Iowa, USA
[2] Department of Psychology, Iowa State University
W112 Lagomarcino Hall, Ames, Iowa, USA
[3] Institut Image, Arts et Métiers ParisTech
2 rue Thomas Dumorey, Chalon-sur-Saône, France
{casallas,oliver,jonkelly}@iastate.edu, frederic.merienne@ensam.eu,
samir.garbaya@gmail.com

Abstract. Novel interaction techniques have been developed to address the difficulties of selecting moving targets. However, similar to their static-target counterparts, these techniques may suffer from clutter and overlap, which can be addressed by predicting intended targets. Unfortunately, current predictive techniques are tailored towards static-target selection. Thus, a novel approach for predicting user intention in moving-target selection tasks using decision-trees constructed with the initial physical states of both the user and the targets is proposed. This approach is verified in a virtual reality application in which users must choose, and select between different moving targets. With two targets, this model is able to predict user choice with approximately 71% accuracy, which is significantly better than both chance and a frequentist approach.

Keywords: User intention, prediction, Fitts' Law, moving-target selection, perceived difficulty, decision trees, virtual reality.

1 Introduction

Selection of moving targets is a common task in human–computer interaction (HCI) and more specifically in virtual reality (VR). Unfortunately, most of the HCI studies on selection, based on Fitts' Law [4], have focused on static targets (for a compendium, see, for example [6]). Recently, however, new performance models [1] and interaction techniques [8] have been proposed to address the specificities and difficulties of moving-target selection.

Novel moving-target selection techniques, such as *Comet* and *Ghost* [8], enhance pointing by expanding selectable targets or creating easier-to-reach proxies for each target, respectively. Nevertheless, these techniques may suffer from clutter and overlap when the number of selectable objects is increased [8]. A possible solution to these limitations, also present in static selection, is to predict

D. Harris (Ed.): EPCE/HCII 2013, Part I, LNAI 8019, pp. 13–22, 2013.
© Springer-Verlag Berlin Heidelberg 2013

the intended targets [8,15]. Unfortunately, to the authors' knowledge, current predictive techniques are tailored towards static-target selection.

Current static-target prediction techniques are based on the trajectory and velocity profiles of the pointer [13,17,21,15]. The peak accuracy rates for prediction using these techniques require a wide window of user input—at least 80% of the pointing movement—but some of them are intended to predict endpoints [13,21], rather than intended targets [17,15].

In contrast with static-target prediction techniques, this study explores the feasibility of predicting intended moving targets based only on the initial physical states of both the user and the targets, namely initial hand position, target position and target size, in a 3D selection task. To exclude factors, other than size and position, that may bias these predictions, the targets in the analyzed 3D task are kept identical in every other aspect, such as color and speed.

1.1   Identical Choices, Mental Effort and Fitts' Index of Difficulty

In the mid 90's, Christenfeld [3] conducted a series of real-life studies in which he found the middle position to be up to 75% predictive of people's choices when selecting among otherwise identical options, such as items from the same product in a supermarket or restroom stalls. In the same series of studies, he also explored route selection and found participants tended to choose based on the initial segment of the route and not on the optimal route—this was posteriorly named the *Initial Segment Strategy* [2]. Christenfeld suggested that these outcomes are consistent with the principle of minimizing *mental effort*, although he did not formalize this notion.

From a human-performance standpoint, selecting the middle choice among identical objects minimizes Fitts' Law's *Index of Difficulty* [4] (ID, see Equation 1 for its so-called Shannon Formulation [14]), since middle objects have the smallest distance (D) relative to the person and thus the smallest ID. Recent research also suggests that Fitts' ID can be related to perceived difficulty [5,12,20]. Thus, in Christenfeld's studies, people may have minimized their perceived effort by choosing the objects with the minimum ID.

$$ID = \log_2(D/W + 1) \tag{1}$$

This research explores the hypothesis that this relationship between ID and perceived effort can be used to predict user intention in 3D selection tasks. To do so, however, the influence of target distance (D) *and* width (W) on such predictions must be evaluated; as opposed to distance only, the common factor in Christenfeld's item selection studies. More importantly, it is possible that the correlation between ID and perceived effort will decrease with the addition of target motion, since the correlation between ID and selection time is reduced in moving-target selection relative to static selection [10]. Regardless, we hypothesize that ID, or another function of target size and initial distance may be predictive of user intention in moving-target selection tasks. Additionally, in accordance with the Initial Segment Strategy, we hypothesize that in the case of a sequential selection task, the first target's ID will be more predictive of user intention than the sum of IDs in the sequence.

2   Methods

2.1   Participants

Twenty-six unpaid participants, from the city of Chalon-sur-Saône, France aged 23 to 47, participated in the study. There were eighteen males and eight females; only two participants were left-handed.

2.2   Apparatus

The experiment was developed in VR JuggLua [18], a Lua wrapper for VR Juggler and OpenSceneGraph. The application was deployed in the "MoVE", a 4-surface CAVE-like virtual environment with three walls and a floor. The $3\times3\times2.67$ m environment was projected using passive, Infitec stereo [11] at 1160×1050 pixels per face. Four infrared ART cameras tracked the pose (position, P, and orientation, Q) of each participant's head and wand, using reflective markers mounted on Infitec stereo glasses and an ART Flystick2, respectively. This allowed each participant to have an adequate 3D perception and interact with the virtual world.

2.3   Procedure

Each participant was asked to stay in the middle of the MoVE ($x = 0, z = 0$) facing the front wall and was instructed to complete a series of target selection tasks. In each trial, they were presented with a horizontal array of virtual spheres of different sizes, starting in front of them and flying towards them in z. All of the spheres had the same texture, scaled accordingly to the sphere's size. Each participant was instructed to touch each sphere by extending their arms only to reach the spheres—as opposed to wait for the spheres with their arms already extended. If a sphere was touched, or if it got 0.5 m past the participant's head in z, it disappeared. Each trial ended when the participant had touched all of the spheres, or when the remaining spheres got past their head.

Visual and auditory feedback were used to indicate participant's performance. A virtual counter was placed in front of the participant at $(0, 0, -5)$, which would show the number of missed spheres during each block; the counter would be reset to zero at the beginning of each block of trials. When a participant hit a sphere, a spatialized sound would be played, co-localized with the wand position; a different spatialized sound would be played, co-localized with the overall centroid of the remaining spheres, when the spheres got past the participant's head.

At each frame of the application, the elapsed time, head pose (P_h, Q_h), wand pose (P_w, Q_w), sphere positions (P_i) and possible collisions between the wand and the spheres were recorded in a log file. The experimental setup is depicted in Fig. 1.

Fig. 1. Experimental setup with an array two spheres

2.4   Design

A within-subjects, factorial design was used, with two blocks of trials, each with a different number of conditions presented in a random order. In every trial, all of the spheres appeared 0.3 m below the participant's head and 5 m in front of them ($P_{i,y} = P_{h,y} - 0.3, P_{i,z} = -5$).

In the first block each trial had only one sphere, moving at a constant speed of 2.5 m/s in z. Factors were sphere radius ($r_1 = [0.1, 0.2]$) and sphere position (*left*: $P_{1,x} = 0.5$, *center*: $P_{1,x} = 0$, and *right*: $P_{1,x} = 0.5$). Each of the six conditions was presented to the participant in a random order until completing five trials per condition (30 total). The first block was intended only for training, so that users could become familiar with the environment and the task.

After completing the first block, the number of spheres was increased to two and velocity was decremented to 1.5 m/s in z. The spheres were positioned 0.5 m apart in x but the pair could appear offset to the *right* ($P_{1,x} = -0.5, P_{2,x} = 0$), *left* ($P_{1,x} = -0.5, P_{2,x} = 0$), or *centered* ($P_{1,x} = -0.25, P_{2,x} = 0.25$) with respect to the user (see Fig. 2). Factors were sphere radius ($r_i = [0.1, 0.2]$) and row position (*left, center* and *right*). Each of the 12 conditions was presented to the participant in a random order until completing five trials per condition (60 total).

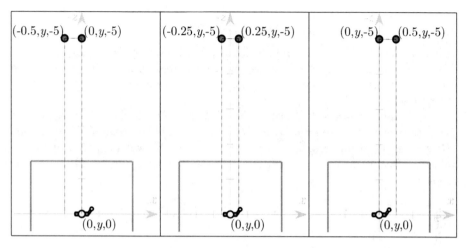

Fig. 2. Possible row positions—*left, center* and *right*—with respect to the user in the two-sphere block

3   Analysis

Trials in which a participant did not touch any sphere were discarded. Based on the initial wand position (P_w), sphere diameter (W_1,W_2) and initial sphere position (P_1,P_2), different values were calculated, including wand–sphere distances,

$$D_1 = |P_w - P_1| \tag{2}$$

$$D_2 = |P_w - P_2| \tag{3}$$

wand–sphere indices of difficulty,

$$ID_1 = \log_2(D_1/W_1 + 1) \tag{4}$$

$$ID_2 = \log_2(D_2/W_2 + 1) \tag{5}$$

inter–sphere distance,

$$D_{sph} = |P_2 - P_1| \tag{6}$$

inter–sphere indices of difficulty,

$$ID_{1,2} = \log_2(D_{sph}/W_2 + 1) \tag{7}$$

$$ID_{2,1} = \log_2(D_{sph}/W_1 + 1) \tag{8}$$

and total indices of difficulty

$$ID_{T1} = ID_1 + ID_{1,2} \tag{9}$$

$$ID_{T2} = ID_2 + ID_{2,1} \tag{10}$$

Using the Weka machine-learning suite [7], feature-sets $\{ID_{T1}, ID_{T2}\}$, $\{ID_{1,2}, ID_{2,1}\}$, $\{ID_1, ID_2\}$ and $\{D_1, D_2, r_1, r_2\}$ were evaluated with the J48 classifier, an open source implementation of the C4.5 decision tree algorithm [19], to predict the first selected sphere.

The classifier chooses its decision nodes recursively, based on the feature that yields the greatest *Information Gain* (I)—a measure of the diminution of entropy $(H$, a measure of uncertainty) on the training set (S) when splitting it by the values of feature (A). In this experiment, the equations for I and H are the following:

$$I(S, A) = H(S) - H(S|A) \tag{11}$$

$$H(S) = -p_1 \log_2 p_1 - p_2 \log_2 p_2 \tag{12}$$

$$H(S|A) = \sum_{v \epsilon Values(A)} \frac{|S_v|}{|S|} H(S_v) \tag{13}$$

where p_i is the relative frequency (see Equation 14) of sphere i (sph_i) within set S and S_v corresponds to the subset obtained by splitting S with the value v of feature A. The advantage of this classifier is that it produces easy to interpret rules, choosing the simplest decision tree from the input attributes. In this study's scope, the decision trees allowed representation and analysis of the possible participant strategies to solve each task. To avoid over-fitting to the experimental data, 10-fold cross validation was used on the generated tree models.

Finally, data were also analyzed using a frequentist approach, by calculating the relative frequency of choosing either sphere:

$$p_i = n_i/N \tag{14}$$

where n_i corresponds to the number of trials in which sph_i was chosen and N is the total number of trials. This approach allows generating a simple, one-node decision tree with an empty feature-set $(\varnothing)$ that always predicts the sphere with the highest frequency.

4   Results

Participants showed an overall preference for the right sphere. The decision tree generated using the frequentist approach always predicted sph_2 as the selected sphere with approximately $64\% \pm 2.4\%$ accuracy, with a 95% confidence level (see last row of Table 1).

Decision trees generated with the J48 algorithm from feature-sets 1–4 (see Table 1) yielded approximately $71\% \pm 2.26\%$ accuracy on predicting the selected sphere, with a 95% confidence level, which is significantly better than both chance and a frequentist approach. Statistically, none of the tested feature-sets seemed to perform significantly better (or worse) than each other; however, the generated tree for feature-set 1 is more complex than those generated for feature-sets 2–4, making it less practical and perhaps over-fitted to the data [16] considering that the 5 non-leaf nodes were generated from only 2 attributes.

Table 1. Accuracy and 95% confidence intervals for the evaluated feature-sets

	Feature-set	Tree Size	Number of Leaves	Accuracy	95% Confidence Interval
1	ID_{T1}, ID_{T2}	9	5	70.5577%	±2.27491%
2	$ID_{1,2}, ID_{2,1}$	5	3	71.2062%	±2.26003%
3	ID_1, ID_2	5	3	70.9468%	±2.26605%
4	D_1, D_2, r_1, r_2	5	3	71.2062%	±2.26003%
5	∅	1	1	63.8132%	±2.39848%

Interestingly, the fact that feature-sets 2 and 4 had the same accuracy, 95% CIs and a similar tree configuration (3 leaves out of 5 nodes) implies that they are equivalent. This may seem surprising, since the only relevant factors in the inter–sphere indices of difficulty, which compose feature-set 2, are sphere diameters (W_1, W_2)[1] (see Equations 7 and 8), whereas feature-set 4 is composed not only of sphere radii (r_1, r_2), but also of wand–sphere distances (D_1, D_2). A closer look at the generated decision tree for feature-set 4 (Fig. 3), however, shows that the decision tree included only sphere radii; wand-sphere distances (D_1, D_2) were probably ignored by the J48 algorithm on the basis of low information gain. Thus, it is safe to conjecture that the radii provide an equivalent information gain not only to feature-set 2, but also to feature-set 3, since their generated trees had similar configurations and yielded an equivalent accuracy.

The overall tendency for choosing the right sphere (sph_2) first is most likely due to the majority of the participants being right-handed; unfortunately, there weren't enough left-handed participants to evaluate the effects of handedness on the generated models. According to the decision tree generated from feature-set 4 (see Fig. 3), participants would only choose sph_1 first if sph_2 was smaller; if both spheres had the same radius, or if sph_2 was bigger, sph_2 would be selected first.

5 Discussion

Considering that decision trees were built based only on the initial position of the user's wand and the initial size and position of the spheres, predictions bore a very high accuracy. It is likely, however, that the accuracy will decrease if the number of targets is increased, but it is expected that the accuracy will still be better than chance.

---

[1] Inter-sphere distances are equal for all of the trials $(D_{sph} = 0.5)$, annulling their influence on $ID_{1,2}$ and $ID_{2,1}$ and, thus, on feature-set 2.

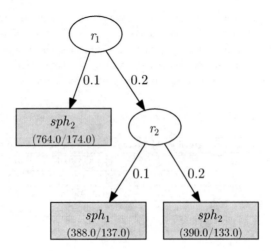

Fig. 3. Decision tree for feature-set 4, suggesting that participants based their decisions only on sphere size, with a preference for the right sphere. Leaves represent prediction outcomes (sph_1 or sph_2), while the other nodes represent tested attributes (r1 or r2). The numbers in parenthesis within the leaves represent the total number of instances that fall into that leaf, over the number of incorrectly predicted instances among these instances.

Considering that the decision tree for feature-set 4 consisted only of radii, quantities from which every other feature-set is derived (see Equations 4–10) and apparently equivalent in terms of information gain to the features in other feature-sets (see the results section), suggests that size is more predictive of intended targets than every measure of Fitts' ID evaluated. This may be due to the fact that the spheres get closer to the user throughout each trial, eventually annulling the z-component of the target's distance, this corroborates Jagacinski's findings on 1D selection times on moving targets [10]. The fact that absolute horizontal sphere positions ($P_{i,x}$) did not affect user choices may suggest that users prepared their hands horizontally, while waiting for the target, or that it was more comfortable for them to reach for the right sphere first, followed by the left sphere, which seems reasonable considering that most participants were right handed.

In any case, this result suggests that participants did not have an optimal global strategy to execute their reaching tasks. Yet, this does not imply that participants optimized the initial segment either, at least as hypothesized in terms of Fitts' ID.

6   Conclusion and Future Work

The feasibility of predicting user intention in a very simple moving-target selection task was demonstrated. This approach revealed the practicality and power of using decision trees to predict user intention. Although Fitts' ID served as a good predictor of intended target selection, sphere radius seemed to yield equivalent accuracy. This suggests a very basic strategy from the users in which distance does not play an important role for choosing targets. Because the targets were moving and there was some waiting time while the target arrived, it is possible that users prepared the starting position of their wands prior to executing the pointing task.

Future work should include a greater number of spheres with different vertical positions, as well as different movement directions. Beyond size, distance and movement, this approach could be extended to consider other factors such as target semantics, if any, as well as user behaviors and gestures. The potential of using other "indices of difficulty," formulated specifically for moving-target selection [1,9,10], to predict user intention should also be explored. Finally, it should also be possible to refine decision trees in real time, to adapt the generated models to each user.

References

1. Al Hajri, A., Fels, S., Miller, G., Ilich, M.: Moving target selection in 2D graphical user interfaces. In: Campos, P., Graham, N., Jorge, J., Nunes, N., Palanque, P., Winckler, M. (eds.) INTERACT 2011, Part II. LNCS, vol. 6947, pp. 141–161. Springer, Heidelberg (2011)
2. Bailenson, J.N., Shum, M.S., Uttal, D.H.: The initial segment strategy: a heuristic for route selection. Memory & Cognition 28(2), 306–318 (2000)
3. Christenfeld, N.: Choices from identical options. Psychological Science 6(1), 50–55 (1995)
4. Fitts, P.M.: The information capacity of the human motor system in controlling the amplitude of movement. Journal of Experimental Psychology: General 121(3), 262–269 (1954)
5. Grilli, S.M.: Perceived Difficulty in a Fitts Task. PhD thesis, Cleveland State University (2011)
6. Guiard, Y., Beaudouin-Lafon, M.: Fitts' law 50 years later: applications and contributions from human-computer interaction. International Journal of Human-Computer Studies 61(6), 747–750 (2004)
7. Hall, M., National, H., Frank, E., Holmes, G., Pfahringer, B., Reutemann, P., Witten, I.H.: The WEKA Data Mining Software: An Update. SIGKDD Explorations Newsletter 11(1), 10–18 (2009)
8. Hasan, K., Grossman, T., Irani, P.: Comet and Target Ghost: Techniques for Selecting Moving Targets. In: Proceedings of the SIGCHI Conference on Human Factors in Computing Systems, CHI 2011, Vancouver, BC, Canada, pp. 839–848. ACM (2011)
9. Hoffmann, E.R.: Capture of moving targets: a modification of Fitts' Law. Ergonomics 34(2), 211–220 (1991)
10. Jagacinski, R.J., Repperger, D.W., Ward, S.L., Moran, M.S.: A Test of Fitts' Law with Moving Targets. Human Factors: The Journal of the Human Factors and Ergonomics Society 22(2), 225–233 (1980)
11. Jorke, H., Simon, A., Fritz, M.: Advanced Stereo Projection Using Interference Filters. In: 3DTV Conference: The True Vision - Capture, Transmission and Display of 3D Video, Istanbul, Turkey, pp. 177–180. IEEE (2008)

12. Kourtis, D., Sebanz, N., Knoblich, G.: EEG correlates of Fitts's law during preparation for action. Psychological Research 76(4), 514–524 (2012)
13. Lank, E., Cheng, Y.-C.N., Ruiz, J.: Endpoint prediction using motion kinematics. In: Proceedings of the SIGCHI Conference on Human Factors in Computing Systems, CHI 2007, San Jose, CA, USA, pp. 637–646. ACM (2007)
14. MacKenzie, I.S.: A Note on the Information-Theoretic Basis for Fitts' Law. Journal of Motor Behavior 21(3), 323–330 (1989)
15. McGuffin, M.J., Balakrishnan, R.: Fitts' law and expanding targets: Experimental studies and designs for user interfaces. ACM Transactions on Computer-Human Interaction (TOCHI) 12(4), 388–422 (2005)
16. Mitchell, T.M.: Machine learning. McGraw-Hill, Boston (1997)
17. Noy, D.: Predicting user intentions in graphical user interfaces using implicit disambiguation. In: CHI 2001 Extended Abstracts on Human Factors in Computing Systems, Seattle, Washington, USA, pp. 455–456. ACM (2001)
18. Pavlik, R.A., Vance, J.M.: VR JuggLua: A framework for VR applications combining Lua, OpenSceneGraph, and VR Juggler. In: 2012 5th Workshop on Software Engineering and Architectures for Realtime Interactive Systems (SEARIS), Singapore, pp. 29–35. IEEE (2012)
19. Quinlan, J.R.: C4.5: Programs for Machine Learning. Morgan Kaufmann, San Mateo (1993)
20. Slifkin, A.B., Grilli, S.M.: Aiming for the future: prospective action difficulty, prescribed difficulty, and Fitts' law. Experimental Brain Research 174(4), 746–753 (2006)
21. Wonner, J., Grosjean, J., Capobianco, A., Bechmann, D.: SPEED: Prédiction de cibles. In: 23rd French Speaking Conference on Human-Computer Interaction, IHM 2011, Sophia Antipolis, France, pp. 19:1–19:4. ACM (2011)

Image Quality Assessment Using the SSIM
and the Just Noticeable Difference Paradigm

Jeremy R. Flynn, Steve Ward, Julian Abich IV, and David Poole

University of Central Florida, 4000 Central Florida Boulevard, Orlando, FL, USA
{jflynn,jabich}@ist.ucf.edu, steve@iqatest.com,
mr.david.a.poole@gmail.com

Abstract. The structural similarity index (SSIM) has been shown to be a superior objective image quality metric. A web-based pilot experiment was conducted with the goal of quantifying, through the use of a sample of human participants, a trend in SSIM values showing when the human visual system can begin to perceive distortions applied to reference images. The just noticeable difference paradigm was used to determine the point at which at least 50% of participants were unable to discern between compressed and uncompressed grayscale images. For four images, this point was at an SSIM value of 96, while for two images it was at 92, for an average of 95. These results suggest that, despite the wide differences in the type of image used, the point at which a human observer cannot determine that compression has been used hovers around an SSIM value of 95.

Keywords: Applied cognitive psychology, Designing for pleasure of use, Display design, Formal error prediction techniques, Human error, Human Factors / System Integration, Psychophysics for display design.

1 Introduction

The Internet is rich with images and media consumption is at an all-time high. According to a Pew report on online usage of photos and videos, 56% of the internet users sampled either created and uploaded photos to the internet or took existing images and reposted them to image sharing websites [1]. Websites that cater to this behavior are wildly popular. Tumblr.com has a blogging service where users primarily post images and videos, and has ranked the 36th most visited website in the world, followed closely by Pinterest.com, an online pin board that essentially has a wall of images from all over the Internet, which has ranked 38th [2]. Imgur.com is ranked 97th globally [2], and its only function is for users to share and display uploaded images. In an average month, there are over 61 million photos uploaded, 33 billion image views, and over 4 petabytes of bandwidth used by Imgur alone [3]. With such a large amount of traffic, it becomes important to optimize bandwidth usage and load times which requires the compression of images. Imgur's policy is to automatically compress, resize, and adjust the quality of images that are otherwise too large in an effort to make them more easily viewable online and to save space [4], but this may

D. Harris (Ed.): EPCE/HCII 2013, Part I, LNAI 8019, pp. 23–30, 2013.
© Springer-Verlag Berlin Heidelberg 2013

noticeably decrease the image quality. The objective of our work was to reveal whether an image quality index can be used to determine the point in which human observers cannot tell the difference between compressed and uncompressed images. This metric could then be applied to all compressed visual media, but here the focus is online image databases due to the potential impact in this domain. Online image database services could use the metric as a part of an automated image adjustment procedure to ensure that image compression does not noticeably detract from perceptual quality.

Images are not stored as raw source signals, instead they are compressed into a format. According to Shen and Kuo, the quality of the compressed image depends on the data source, coding bit rates, and the compression algorithm [5]. For lossy compression, which includes JPEG, the researchers state that there is a trade-off between lower bit rates at the cost of increased distortion in image quality. JPEG is an acronym for Joint Photographic Experts Group and is formally defined by a joint ISO/ITU-T standard, ISO/IEC IS 10918-1 or the ITU-T Recommendation T.81 [6]. Raw digital images compressed in the JPEG format are ubiquitous on the internet, in presentations, and in documentation. JPEG images, even at the lowest compression, are smaller in storage size than many other types of image formats [7].

Small storage size is important when dealing with large servers which contain, in some cases, millions, or even billions, of images. In this situation, it is advantageous to minimize image file sizes while maintaining sufficient image quality, such that an average human observer cannot perceive a distortion or loss of image quality due to compression of the original image. Since the JPEG format is very common on the internet and with digital imagery, it was chosen as the type of distortion to be applied to the reference images used in this study.

Having a large sample of subjects available to quickly and efficiently determine the quality of an image, or determine when an image reaches a level of distortion that is detectable, is not practical or feasible. To address this need, there are a range of different methods of analyzing images compression as it relates to the perceptual capabilities of the human visual system (HVS), ranging from mathematical algorithms to complex models that seek to analyze and quantify elements of an image based on features pertinent to the HVS, such as contrast, masking, and summation [8]. In light of the multiple different methods available, the most useful would be an analysis metric that could quickly quantify the image. Traditional methods to achieve this include the mean squared error (MSE) or peak signal-to-noise ratio (PSNR). The usage of MSE, for example, may be problematic as it does not always provide an adequate evaluation of image quality as it would be perceived by the HVS [9]. Rather than a simple measurement of error between signals, an algorithm that accounts for structural similarity between images would better model how the HVS perceives distortion. The structural similarity approach depends on the assumptions that natural images are highly structured and the HVS is suited for extracting structural information from scenes. It then follows that an accurate approximation of perceived image quality should be the measurement of structural similarity. Research has shown that an algorithm based on a structural similarity approach, such as the Structural SIMilarity (SSIM) index, more closely resembles the way humans perceive structural distortions in an image and thus assess image quality [9].

The purpose of this study was to collect and analyze subjective responses from human participants to determine if the point at which a compressed image is noticeably different from the uncompressed original aligns with a particular SSIM value, which can then be used to predict the point at which the average human can begin to perceive distortion due to compression in an image.

2   Method

2.1   Reference Images

We initially planned on using images from a common image database such as the University of Southern California's SIPI database [10]. However, we discovered that many of these images lacked the necessary requirements that were desired in a set of reference images, which includes high quality and a variety of subjects. Additionally, most of the images in that database were under some form of copyright protection or the copyright status was unknown. It was decided that the reference images used in the web-based survey would be of high quality and be free of any copyright issues.

The six images chosen to be reference images in this study were selected from the Wikimedia Commons [11] website because they all met the criteria of being high quality and of varied subject matter. They were all freely licensed under the Creative Commons Attribution-Share Alike 2.5 Generic license [12]. The images exhibited various characteristics, including a public domain image of Albert Einstein, a landscape of the Arnisee region in Switzerland, a bald eagle, a complex pattern of cracks in desiccated sewage, an apple, and a windmill.

ImageMagick [13], an open-source image processing utility, was used to convert the original color reference images to grayscale, resize them to have maximum dimensions of 384 pixels, and apply the various degrees of JPEG compression. This was done in an effort to systematically control how all of the images were processed. The value of 384 pixels was chosen due to the limitations of small screen resolutions that could possibly be used by some of the participants. Octave [14], an open-source numerical computation tool, was used to calculate the SSIM values for all the distorted images. Figure 1 shows how various degrees of distortion affect image quality, as measured by the SSIM, where lower values translate to lower image quality.

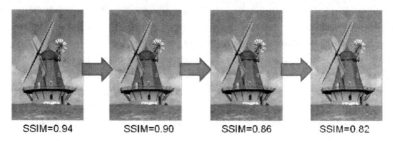

SSIM=0.94   SSIM=0.90   SSIM=0.86   SSIM=0.82

Fig. 1. Increasing degrees of distortion and associated SSIM values

2.2   Participants

A total of 30 participants, comprised of 24 females and 6 males, completed the online experiment and submitted results. They were recruited through word-of-mouth requests and online postings. No compensation was given for participation in this study. Participants were also informed of their ability to withdraw from the study at any time, in which case none of their biographical data or results would be submitted. The mean age of the participants was 34 years ($SD = 15$).

2.3   Biographical Questionnaire

If participants agreed to participate in the experiment, they were directed to a biographical questionnaire. The questionnaire collected biographical data such as the participant's age, sex, primary language, quality of vision (normal or corrected-to-normal), experience with photo editing or image processing, and computer and video game proficiency.

2.4   Image Comparisons

After completing the questionnaire, participants were presented with an instructional page that described the task they would be performing. A practice image comparison session was then given to familiarize participants with the task. The image used was of the Giza Necropolis, which was also selected from the Wikimedia Commons and processed in the same manner as the six reference images. This particular image was not used as a part of the actual experimental task. Participants were presented with the following instructions: "These images are different. One of them has severe distortion. Severe distortions are noticeable by their blockiness. A distorted image may appear on either the left side or the right side. These messages will not be shown during the actual experiment. They are only instructional." Participants were presented with two buttons to click, "Identical" and "Different." They were then given feedback about the decision they made in the practice session, but it was made known that no feedback would be given to participants during the actual task.

For each of the 6 reference images, 10 degrees of JPEG compression were applied. The reference image and its distorted versions comprised an image set. To each image, different levels of JPEG compression were applied until the image reached the following specific SSIM values: 82, 84, 86, 88, 90, 92, 94, 96, 98, 99.9. This resulted in 10 different versions of each of the six images in addition to the original reference with varying levels of distortion as quantified by the SSIM.

Within an image set, the reference image was compared to itself 10 times and compared once per distorted version of the reference. Consequently, in each image set, 20 image comparisons were made. The sets were presented in a random order, as were the distorted and reference images in each set. The reference image was placed randomly on either the right or left side of its counter image. Every comparison was made one at a time.

On each page, participants were presented with the two images. Participants were also given the following instructions: "If you can perceive a difference in the images, select Different. If you cannot perceive a difference in the images, or you are unsure if they are different, select Identical." One of the images was the original reference while the other was the same image with some level of distortion applied. Participants then clicked one of the two buttons, "Identical" or "Different."

After a selection of "Identical" or "Different", the images disappeared for a brief inter-stimulus interval to reduce any visual artifacts, and the buttons were disabled to prevent accidental double-clicking. The next pair of images appeared 300ms after the previous pair had disappeared. The buttons were enabled 500ms after the new image pair appeared. While the buttons were disabled, no selection could be made. All the images were pre-loaded to avoid any delay in the image presentation.

Participants were given the opportunity to take as many breaks as they liked. They could work at their own pace and were not restricted to complete the task in a particular amount of time. The client-side code was written in JavaScript. When the last image comparison was made, the result data and the biographical information were serialized from a JavaScript object into a string using the JavaScript Object Notation (JSON) library. The JSON-formatted string was submitted automatically without user interaction. The server-side code that processed and stored the results was written in PHP. Results could be downloaded for further analysis in a spreadsheet.

3   Results

Based on the answers to the biographical questionnaire, 28 participants reported having normal or corrected-to-normal vision, with only 2 reporting they did not. Sixty-seven percent of the participants had some type of prior image processing or photo editing experience, while 33% had no such experience. On average, participants spent about 32 hours per week using a computer for various tasks. Twenty-six participants reported spending little to no time playing video games. Four participants played video games more than 20 hours per week, which raised the average of video game use to about 7 hours per week ($SD = 15.75$).

Seventy-seven percent of the participants felt they were above average in computer proficiency, 13% felt they were average, and 10% felt they were below average. Thirty-two percent of the participants felt they were above average in video game proficiency, 46% felt they were average, and 22% felt they were below average.

The data were scanned in an effort to remove those participants who may not have been completing the task, but rather were simply clicking buttons. As noted previously, for each of the six images the participant was presented with an image set ten times where both images were the uncompressed, original reference image. If they responded more than 50% of the time that the identical images were different, this indicates that they may have not been actually completing the task. We conducted the analysis in both the original and cleaned datasets, and while some of the averages were different between the two, ultimately the results were the same. We decided to retain the cleaned data as it is more accurate.

The just noticeable difference (JND) paradigm was utilized in this study. The JND is the point in which half of the participants report perceiving a difference between two stimuli. Eckert and Bradley [8], citing the previous work of Watson et al., suggested that utilizing JND is an effective method of determining the point at which an individual is able to perceive the visual difference between compressed and uncompressed images. Therefore, we examined the data across SSIM values for each image to determine the point at which at least 50% of participants were unable to discern between compressed and uncompressed images. See Figure 2 for a visual representation of the percentage of participants who perceived the compressed and uncompressed image as being identical by SSIM value for each of the six images used in this study, and see Table 1 for the actual values with the JND SSIM value highlighted.

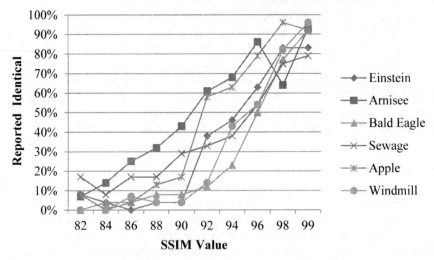

Fig. 2. Percentage of participants that reported that the uncompressed and compressed images were identical by SSIM value for all six images

Table 1. Percentage of participants that reported that the uncompressed and compressed images were identical by SSIM value for all six images with JND point highlighted

SSIM	82	84	86	88	90	92	94	96	98	99
Einstein	8%	4%	0%	4%	4%	38%	46%	63%	83%	83%
Arnisee	7%	14%	25%	32%	43%	61%	68%	86%	64%	93%
Eagle	0%	4%	4%	8%	8%	12%	23%	50%	77%	92%
Sewage	17%	8%	17%	17%	29%	33%	38%	54%	75%	79%
Apple	8%	0%	4%	13%	17%	58%	63%	79%	96%	92%
Windmill	0%	0%	7%	4%	4%	14%	43%	54%	82%	96%

For four images, the JND was at an SSIM value of 96, while for two images it was at 92, for an average of 95. These results suggest that the point at which a human observer cannot determine that compression has been used hovers around an SSIM value of 95.

4   Discussion

Using the just noticeable difference paradigm, we examined the data across SSIM values for each image to determine the point at which at least 50% of participants were unable to discern between compressed and uncompressed grayscale images. Our results suggest that, despite the wide differences in the type of image used, the point at which a human observer cannot determine that compression has been used hovers around an SSIM value of 95. This is useful since the SSIM can be used to analyze images after compression to predict whether the decrease in quality will be perceptible by the user.

It is important to note that two images (the landscape of the Arnisee region and the apple) reached the JND at an SSIM value of 92, while participants reported the JND for the other four images at 96. This may indicate that the content of the image itself affects the JND point from either a bottom-up or a top-down processing perspective. Regarding bottom-up visual perception, the HVS processes visual information by analyzing structures, which is why techniques such as SSIM are so apt at predicting visual perception of distorted images [15]. Future research efforts could focus on how different types of features that are perceived by the HVS, as represented in a wide variety of images, affect the JND as quantified by the SSIM. This would allow for parsing the components of human vision against which the SSIM algorithm can be tested. An alternative method would be to examine the top-down approach of visual perception and examine how the content, meaning the actual subject, of images affect the JND. For example, previous research has suggested that some images, such as faces, are processed in different areas of the brain as compared to other objects [16]. In the present study, the face of Albert Einstein was not perceived any differently with respect to the JND point from an image of an eagle, a windmill, or the complex pattern of cracks in desiccated sewage. Replicating this study that combines both processing perspectives with a wide variety of images that focus on familiar and un-familiar faces and objects, as well as images that manipulate the type and complexity of HVS features, may reveal a different pattern of results.

This study had some limitations. The results only pertain to grayscale images. One potential avenue of future research involves replicating this study using the same images displayed in full color to determine if the JND point changes. This is especial-ly pertinent as it seems that the majority of images on the internet are in color, not grayscale.

Another limitation of this study was the sample size. The purpose of this work was to develop a method of quantifying image compression perception based on SSIM utilizing the JND paradigm. As a pilot experiment, it revealed that this method does yield meaningful results. Replication using these methods on a large scale by compa-nies that deal in image hosting services would allow for a far-greater sample size. A company could embed the survey within their website through a pop-up message that offers the user a chance to complete a survey--this is essentially a crowd-sourcing technique for data collection and a method already employed by some companies to gather customer feedback [17]. This would provide the company with information based on their own image set as how to best automate the compression of their images based on SSIM, utilizing the JND paradigm or even selecting their own criterion (e.g., a website specializing in art may wish to determine the SSIM value at which 90% of users cannot discern between compressed and uncompressed images). Hopefully these steps provide additional evidence and guidance for the ways that the SSIM index value can be used to determine optimal image compression.

5   Author's Note

The experiment address is `http://iqatest.com`. The source code may be downloaded from Google Code at `https://code.google.com/p/iqatest`. It is released under the GNU General Public License v3, copyrighted 2010 Steve Ward.

References

1. Rainie, L., Brenner, J., Purcell, K.: Photos and videos as social currency online (2012), `http://pewinternet.org/Reports/2012/Online-Pictures.aspx`
2. Alexa Top Sites, `http://www.alexa.com/topsites`
3. Imgur Site Stats, `http://imgur.com/stats/month`
4. Imgur FAQ, `http://imgur.com/faq#quality`
5. Shen, M.Y., Kuo, C.C.J.: Review of Postprocessing Techniques for Compression Artifact Removal. J. Vis. Commun. Image Represent. 9, 2–14 (1998)
6. Skodras, A., Christopoulos, C., Ebrahimi, T.: The JPEG 2000 Still Image Compression Standard. IEEE Signal Process. Mag. 18, 36–58 (2001)
7. Richardson, G.: Jpeg Compression (2003), `http://photo.net/learn/jpeg/`
8. Eckert, M.P., Bradley, A.P.: Perceptual Quality Metrics Applied to Still Image Compression. Signal Process. 70, 177–200 (1998)
9. Wang, Z., Bovik, A.C., Sheikh, H.R., Simoncelli, E.P.: Image Quality Assessment: From Error Visibility to Structural Similarity. IEEE Trans. Image Process. 13, 600–612 (2004)
10. University of Southern California's SIPI Image Database, `http://sipi.usc.edu`
11. Wikimedia Commons, `https://commons.wikimedia.org`
12. CC BY-SA 2.5 Generic License, `https://creativecommons.org/licenses/by-sa/2.5/`
13. ImageMagick, `http://www.imagemagick.org`
14. GNU Octave, `https://www.gnu.org/software/octave/`
15. Wang, Z., Bovik, A.C., Lu, L.: Why is Image Quality Assessment So Difficult? In: IEEE International Conference on Acoustics, Speech, and Signal Processing, pp. IV-3313–IV-3316. IEEE Press, New York (2002)
16. Kanwisher, N., McDermott, J., Chun, M.M.: The Fusiform Face Area: A Module in Human Extrastriate Cortex Specialized for Face Perception. J. Neurosci. 17, 4302–4311 (1997)
17. Chan, S.: That popup survey tool for Fresh & New feedback (2011), `http://www.freshandnew.org/2011/01/that-popup-survey-tool-for-fresh-new-feedback/`

Presenting a Fire Alarm Using Natural Language: The Communication of Temporal Information

Yan Ge, Xianghong Sun, and Li Wang

Institute of Psychology, CAS
16 Lincui Road, Chaoyang District, Beijing, 100101, China
{gey,sunxh}@psych.ac.cn

Abstract. Language comprehension is an important issue in fire alarm systems. This study focuses on the expression of temporal information in a fire situation. Both absolute time and relative time were designed to compare the expression types of temporal information. The time sequence and spatial sequence were designed to explore the expressions of a complicated fire that has more than one point of origin. A 5-point Likert scale and ranking task were used to evaluate the comprehensibility of different presentation forms. The results show that using absolute time to describe the point of origin of the fire and its spreading state aided better comprehension. The mechanism and potential reasons are also discussed. In addition, some suggestions for future designs of fire alarm systems are proposed.

Keywords: fire alarm, temporal information, comprehensibility.

1 Introduction

Based on modern information technology, Automatic Fire Alarm Systems could present any fire situation based on information from the smoke detectors. Communicating the spread of fire efficiently and effectively will help firefighters save lives and property. When a fire alarm is received, firefighters need to first evaluate the fire situation as quickly and accurately as possible. How to represent a fire alarm in natural language was an important issue in the design of fire alarm systems. Most research has focused on speech intelligibility[1—4] but the human factors in a fire alarm system have rarely been studied[5]. There are still some psychological issues, such as working memory capacity and language comprehension, that need to be studied.

The comprehension of natural language is one of the crucial issues in human—computer interaction. Stevens conducted some research about intelligibility, naturalness, and preference of text-to-speech synthesis[6]. The issue of content expression of the message was not explored much. Based on this status and practical needs, we conducted some research about information presentation of fire alarm systems from a psychologist's perspective. The manners of information presentation were compared, and we found that information presented by audio and text simultaneously was the best method for an En Route display of Fire Information [7, 8], confirming the results of Le

D. Harris (Ed.): EPCE/HCII 2013, Part I, LNAI 8019, pp. 31–38, 2013.

Bigot et al.[9]. We also conducted some research about the structure of language in the communicating the spread of fire[10] but we were unable to determine how to organize the specific information, such as temporal information, to present a fire alarm in natural language.

This study investigates how to present the temporal information about a fire effectively. Two questions need to be answered in this respect. First, how can the temporal information of a fire's point of origin and the status of the fire's spreading be presented? Absolute time and relative time were designed to evaluate both conditions. Furthermore, how can the temporal information about a fire with more than one point of origin be presented? We examined the case of a fire with two points of origin and designed two forms—time sequence and spatial sequence—to explore the comprehensibility of communication for a complicated fire situation.

2   Method

2.1   Participants

Twenty firefighters from two fire brigades participated in this study. All were males, aged from 22 to 29 years. Each of them was paid for participation.

2.2   Materials

Scenarios
Six fire scenarios were used in this research, including four scenarios with one point of origin and two scenarios with two points of origin.

Presentation Forms
Absolute time vs. Relative time
There are two time points that should be present in a fire scenario—time referring to the point of origin and the time referring to the spread of the fire. Firefighters estimate the state of fire based on this information. The temporal information can be presented by an absolute or a relative reference. So four combination forms were designed in this study, as given below:

— OASR: Origin using absolute time, spreading using relative time.
— ORSR: Origin using relative time based on current time spreading also uses relative time based on current time
— OASA: Origin using absolute time, spreading also using absolute time.
— ORSO: Origin using relative time based on current time and spreading using relative time based on origin time.

Each scenario can be presented in these four forms. Below is an example for one scenario (Table 1). In total, there were 24 descriptions used in this study. The room type and number were modified in order to avoid repetition and to guarantee the consistency of complexity of each scenario.

Table 1. Examples of four time presentation forms

Form	Origin time	Point of fire	Spread time	Spread state
OASR	*At 14:22*	Smoke was first	*3 minutes later*	Smoke then
ORSR	*9 minutes ago*	detected on the	*6 minutes ago*	spread to the First
OASA	*At 14:22*	Ground Floor in	*At 14:25*	Floor, near Room
ORSO	*9 minutes ago*	Break Room 026.	*3 minutes later*	130.

Time sequence vs. Spatial sequence

For scenarios with two points of origin, the presentation of each origin was also studied. There are two forms to describe the alarm information:

— Time sequence (TS): In this form, all events, including the point of origin of the fire and state of spreading, are strictly described in time sequence.
— Spatial sequence (SS): In this form, all events associated with one floor were described, followed by another floor.

The two scenarios with two points of origin were presented in both forms. See Table 2 for examples. So, there were eight additional descriptions for scenarios with two points of origin. The room type and number were also modified. In total, there were 32 descriptions used in this study.

Table 2. Examples of presentation for a fire with two points of origin

Form	Example
Time sequence (TS)	At 16:10, smoke was first detected on the second floor in MECHANICAL ROOM 208 and on the tenth floor in the JANITOR'S Room 1006. Smoke quickly spread to the second floor CORRIDOR 207. Smoke also quickly spread into the tenth floor CORRIDOR 1007. By 16:15, smoke was detected in the second floor STAIRWELL 2 and the third floor STAIRWELL 2. By 16:20, smoke had spread to the eleventh floor CORRIDOR 1100.
Spatial sequence (SS)	At 16:10, smoke was first detected on the second floor in MECHANICAL ROOM 208. Smoke quickly spread into the second floor CORRIDOR 207. By 16:15, smoke was detected in the second floor STAIRWELL 2 and the third floor STAIRWELL 2. At 16:10, smoke was first detected on the tenth floor in the JANITOR'S Room 1006. Smoke quickly spread into the tenth floor CORRIDOR 1007. By 16:20, smoke had spread to the eleventh floor CORRIDOR 1100.

2.3 Questionnaires

Questionnaires were used in this study to investigate how to present information relating to the fire alarm. Two measurement methods were used in this questionnaire: a 5-point Likert scale and a ranking task.

- *5-point Likert scale.*

The Likert scale is the most widely used psychometric scale in survey research. A 5-point scale was used in this study to evaluate the comprehensibility of every description subjectively. Five ordered response levels were chosen to represent the different comprehensibility levels (1 = Very hard to understand; 2 = Hard to understand; 3 = Neutral; 4 = Easy to understand; 5= Very easy to understand).

- *Ranking task.*

The ranking task directly investigates the participants' preference. For four different temporal presentations, the participants were asked to rank the order according to their ease of understanding. For two forms that described alarm information for a fire with two points of origin, the participants were asked to choose which one was easier to understand.

2.4   Procedure

We recruited volunteers from two fire brigades to participate in this study. First, we introduced this study to firefighters and answered their queries about the questionnaire. Then, the firefighters filled in the questionnaires individually. In the first part of the questionnaire, participants had to evaluate all 32 descriptions of the fire situation on the 5-point Likert scale. It included four time presentation forms and two sequence presentation forms. However, the participants were not informed about the differences in this part of the questionnaire; all they had to do was rate these descriptions according to the ease or difficulty of understanding. In the second part of the questionnaire, the differences between the presentation forms were explained directly after each example. Participants had to rank them from easy to hard, based on their comprehensibility. Demographic information was also collected. It took 10 minutes for the firefighters to complete this questionnaire.

3   Results

The data were analyzed with SPSS 17.0.

Time Presentation Forms
The data of subjective evaluation scores for the four time presentation forms were analyzed using repeated measure with one within-subjects factor. The main difference in the time presentation forms was significant, $F(3, 57) = 10.01$, $MSE = .20$, $p < .001$. Paired comparisons reflected that the differences between other three forms and Form OASA were significant. Form OASA was much easier to understand for the firefighters. The descriptive data are shown in Fig. 1.

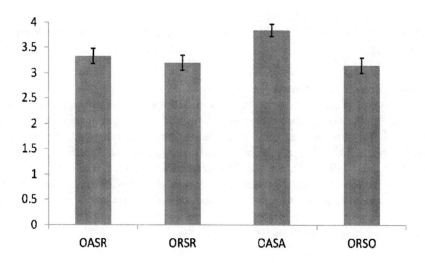

Fig. 1. Subjective evaluation of the four time presentation forms

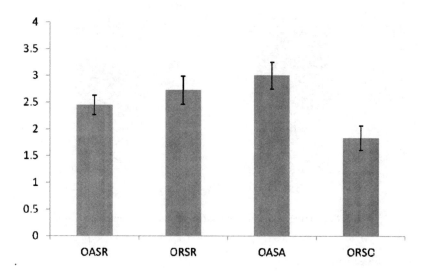

Fig. 2. Ranking results of the four time presentation forms

Data from only 18 participants were collected in the ranking task because two participants did not complete this task. The data were transformed at first. Participants' results were scored based on the weighting factor for the ranking order: 4 for the first one, 3 for the second, 2 for the third, and 1 for the fourth. Then, the data were also analyzed using repeated measure of ANOVA. The analysis revealed a significant difference among the four presentation forms, $F (3, 51) = 2.99$, $MSE = 1.5$, $p < .05$. Paired comparisons showed that the differences between Forms ORSO and OASA, and Forms ORSO and ORSR were significant. Form OASA fared better than Form ORSO, while Form ORSO fared the   worst in the last three forms. The details are shown in Fig. 2

Sequence Presentation Forms
For description of alarm information for fires with two points of origin, two   tasks were also applied to measure their comprehensibility. The data of subjective evaluation points for the two sequence presentation forms were entered into a Paired-Samples T-test. The difference between time sequence and the spatial sequence was not significant, t (19) = .72, p = .48. The descriptive statistics results are shown in Fig.3. For the ranking task, 18 participants answered the questionnaire. Ten of them chose the spatial sequence to present fire scenarios with two points of origin, while the other eight participants preferred the time sequence. No difference was found between the two forms by using the chi-square test.

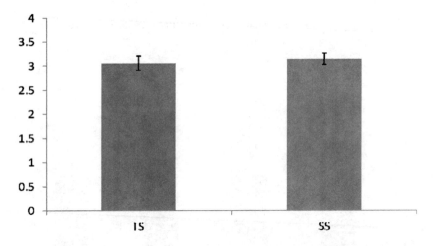

Fig. 3. Subjective evaluation of the two sequence presentation forms

4   Discussion

The main findings show that Form OASA is the best method to use in time presentation forms for better comprehension. Besides, no significant difference was found between the sequence presentation forms.

For the time presentation forms, subjective evaluation and a ranking task were used to measure the comprehensibility of each description. A 5-point Likert scale was used as subjective evaluation to compare the differences among the forms. The score of Form OASA was much higher than the other three forms. For the ranking task, Form OASA was significantly better than Form ORSO. The differences between Form OASA and OASR, and Form OASA and ORSR were not significant, but there was a noticeable trend where Form OASA was better than Form OASR (3.00 vs. 2.44) and

Form ORSR (3.00 vs. 2.72). Form ORSO not only used relative time but also used two base points, which were hard to understand. Combining the results from the two tasks, it was concluded that using absolute time to describe a fire situation is better than using relative time. In firefighting, the fire conditions change quickly. A one-minute delay could lead to great risk. Using absolute time could provide specific information. This information could reduce people's mental workload, especially in the case of firefighters. They could process this information more quickly and react faster and more effectively. Besides, absolute time supplied a fixed time point, and firefighters could refresh their situation awareness conveniently. This is important in emergency situations.

For the sequence presentation forms, the same tasks were used to measure the comprehensibility of each description. There was no significant difference detected between the two forms in the two tasks, but a trend was seen in the data. The score of the spatial sequence form was higher than the time sequence form (3.14 vs. 3.05) in subjective evaluation. More firefighters thought spatial sequence was easier than time sequence in the ranking task. For fire scenarios with more than one point of origin, they were the key factor to describe the fire clearly. To describe a fire in time sequence could lead to ambiguity in people's minds. Describing a fire in spatial sequence helps build a cognitive map of the fire conditions. It is then easier to infer the distribution and spread of a fire situation. The mission of firefighters is to put out a fire, so the spatial information is more important. Fire scenarios with more than one point of origin were too complicated to be described under these two methods. Further research could consider other options to study this issue.

There are still some limitations in our research. First, we only used questionnaires to study the effect of temporal information. Simulation experiments and field studies could provide more method and data support for this research question. Second, a fire situation with more than one point of origin is very complicated but very common in everyday life. Describing a fire of this kind is an open question and deserves to be explored in depth. Finally, this study focused only on firefighters opinion. A fire alarm system should satisfy the need of the occupants, too. Thus, the scope of future research should extend to all kinds of people.

5   Conclusion

In sum, using absolute time to describe a fire's point of origin and its spreading state was found to be better for comprehension. So, we recommend the use of absolute time in the future design of fire alarm systems. For a complicated fire with more than one point of origin, presenting the points of origin in a spatial sequence may be easier for people to understand.

Acknowledgement. This work was supported by NSF China (31100750, 91124003). We thank Thomas Plocher, Henry Chen, and Jian-geng Du for technology support.

References

1. Geoffroy, N.A.: Measuring Speech Intelligibility in Voice Alarm Communication Systems. Thesis, Worcester Polytechnic Institute (2005)
2. Jacob, K.: Understanding Speech Intelligibility and the Fire Alarm Code. Paper presented at the National Fire Protection Association Congress (2001)
3. Steeneken, H.J.M.: Standardisation of Performance Criteria and Assessments Methods for Speech Communication. In: The Sixth European Conference on Speech Communication and Technology (Eurospeech 1999), Budapest, Hungary, Session Slot2. OR3 (2006)
4. Stepnitz, R., Shields, W., McDonald, E., Gielen, A.: Validity of smoke alarm self-report measures and reasons for over-reporting. Injury Prevention 18(5), 298–302 (2012)
5. Proulx, G., Richardson, J.: The human factor: building designers often forget how important the reactions of human occupants are when they specify fire and life safety systems. Canadian Consulting Engineer 43(3), 35–36 (2002)
6. Stevens, C., Lees, N., Vonwiller, J., Burnham, D.: On-line experimental methods to evaluate text-to-speech (TTS) synthesis: effects of voice gender and signal quality on intelligibility, naturalness and preference. Computer Speech & Language 19(2), 129–146 (2005)
7. Qu, W., Sun, X., Plocher, T., Wang, L.: A Study of Information Retrieval of En Route Display of Fire Information on PDA. In: Jacko, J.A. (ed.) HCI International 2009, Part III. LNCS, vol. 5612, pp. 86–94. Springer, Heidelberg (2009)
8. Sun, X., Qu, W., Plocher, T., Wang, L.: A Study of Fire Information Detection on PDA Device. In: Jacko, J.A. (ed.) HCI International 2009, Part III. LNCS, vol. 5612, pp. 105–113. Springer, Heidelberg (2009)
9. Le Bigot, L., Rouet, J.F., Jamet, E.: Effects of speech- and text-based interaction modes in natural language human-computer dialogue. J. Hum. Factors 49, 1045–1053 (2007)
10. Ge, Y., Wang, L., Sun, X.: Application of Natural Language in Fire Spread Display. In: Harris, D. (ed.) Engin. Psychol. and Cog. Ergonomics, HCII 2011. LNCS (LNAI), vol. 6781, pp. 365–373. Springer, Heidelberg (2011)

Using Cognitive Work Analysis to Drive Usability Evaluations in Complex Systems

Aren Hunter and Tania Randall

Defence R&D Canada – Atlantic, Dartmouth, Nova Scotia, Canada
{Aren.Hunter,tania.Randall@drdc-rddc.gc.ca}

Abstract. This paper describes how Cognitive Work Analysis (CWA) can be utilized to support a system-level usability analysis. Overall, we suggest that CWA-derived work tasks should be considered as useful in guiding the development of scenario-based usability questions. We also suggest that usability practitioners be mindful of the importance of time consistencies in developing scenarios and in the appropriate timing of questions throughout the scenario. When evaluating the results of a system level usability experiment it is useful to view the results in light of cognitive and attentional biases.

Keywords: Attention, Biases, Cognitive Work Analysis, Mental Models, System, Usability, Work Tasks.

1 Introduction

1.1 Overview

The intent of this paper is to profile the use of Cognitive Work Analysis (CWA) as a tool in performing a system level analysis. Although the primary objective of this research project was to assess the usability and functionality of an Integrated Information Display (IID), this particular paper addresses the process we undertook to perform the usability assessment. This paper is an attempt to fill the notable gap in the literature with respect to system level usability evaluations. As such, we believed that the use of CWA to inform our assessment was unique, generalizable and worth reporting. We also believed that there was value in reporting on the use of mental models and cognitive biases when evaluating a design. This paper will also shed light on the valuable aspects of CWA and the challenges in using it to define system level usability parameters. The process we describe is generalizable and valuable for researchers in various domains.

1.2 Background

Time-sensitive military missions often require operators to incorporate and process data that are distributed and presented in a variety of formats. In an attempt to understand and reduce demands on "information analysis" (p.65) [1] in submarines,

D. Harris (Ed.): EPCE/HCII 2013, Part I, LNAI 8019, pp. 39–48, 2013.

Defence R&D Canada – Atlantic (DRDC Atlantic) designed an IID to aid the warfighting capabilities of the Officer of the Watch (OOW) [2]. This IID is the focus of the following usability analysis.

As part of the IID design process a CWA was completed [2]. The CWA allowed for an analysis of the OOW's work domain. In general, CWA is used in these contexts to expose work restrictions that define decision making [3, 4]. The majority of researchers use CWA to gather information to aid the design of an interface for a complex system [5]. CWA extracts information requirements that are needed by operators to make effective decisions. In essence, the information requirements provide an explanation of what information is important in the work domain [2]. Once this is complete, the second step in display design is to determine how the information should be presented. The challenge at this point becomes translating hundreds of information requirements into meaningful graphics that support operator decision making to complete various work goals. To do this effectively the information needs to be integrated in a way that defines the limits of the work system [4] and minimizes pressure on cognitive and attentional resources. Unfortunately, CWA techniques have not been optimized to easily turn information requirements into a usable design [5].

Information from the IID was categorized in the following eight categories: Date and Time Group, Primary Ownship Status, Sound Velocity Profile, Tactical Picture, Contact Management, Schedule of Events, Alerts/Alarms, and Dynamic Information Area [6]. The layout of the categories on the IID are depicted in Figure 1. Due to issues related to intellectual property we are not able to present the readers with a fully mocked up display. However, certain isolated components of the display will be presented in this paper.

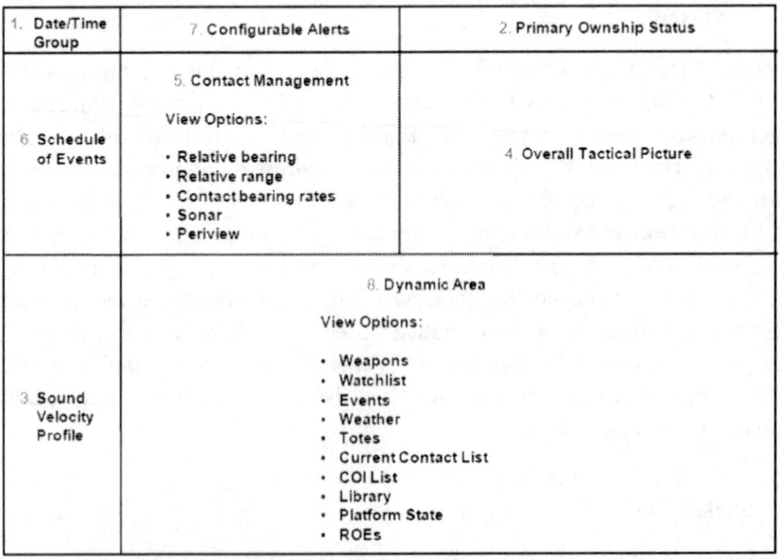

1. Date/Time Group	7. Configurable Alerts	2. Primary Ownship Status
6. Schedule of Events	5. Contact Management View Options: • Relative bearing • Relative range • Contact bearing rates • Sonar • Periview	4. Overall Tactical Picture
3. Sound Velocity Profile	8. Dynamic Area View Options: • Weapons • Watchlist • Events • Weather • Totes • Current Contact List • COI List • Library • Platform State • ROEs	

Fig. 1. Represents the layout of information in the IID and the titles assigned to each [2]

Following the initial design layout an independent team conducted usability testing to assess usability and functionality prior to implementing the completed display. For this assessment, each of the areas depicted in Figure 1 was evaluated by submariner subject matter experts (SMEs) for issues related to their functionality and usability. To simulate the "dynamic" aspects of the display a series of five IID screenshots (scenes) were developed. Each of the screenshots included time relevant changes to the IID to mimic what would happen if the IID was fully functional. The scenes were manipulated by the researcher using a button press at the appropriate time in the evaluation. For example, Figure 2 depicts the change in tactical information in area four in the display from scene three (time 12:57) to scene four (time 14:06) [6]. This was an effective way to implement some level of dynamic fidelity without having to feed real data into the display. At each new "scene" we asked the user specific questions about the content of each display area, the functionality and usability of each display area, the anticipated content changes in the elements and the expectations for change in the next scene.

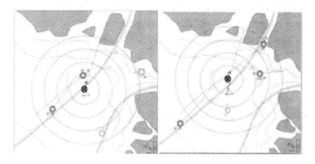

Fig. 2. Scenario for the tactical picture at 12:57 (scene 3) and 14:06 (scene 4) which depicts the movement of contacts across time periods [6]

2 System Level Evaluation

Often a newly designed display is built to replace an outdated one allowing for a baseline evaluation between the old system and the new system [7, 8, 9]. However, since the IID is a new concept there was no old display available for comparison. As such, the display was evaluated based on these three criteria: CWA derived requirements, mental models, and attention biases. In the sections to follow we will give examples of tests using each of these criteria. It should be noted that traditional usability testing is efficient when evaluating the one-to-one relationship between elements, but these techniques are not easily applied to complex integrated displays. The complexity of integrated displays requires both an evaluation of individual components (i.e., a particular gauge) and a "holistic" evaluation of the system (i.e., the integration of information) [10]. The remainder of this section will outline how we tested this new system. It also outlines what portions of the available CWA were most effective in supporting our evaluation.

Roth and Eggleston [7] indicate that complex system usability needs to be driven by a "work-centered evaluation" (p.204) to determine the value of the display in supporting work functions and work tasks. These types of evaluations require an understanding of specific work tasks and contexts, cognitive and attentional resources, task complexity, and performance expectations which matches well to the outputs of CWA [7]. This requires that scenario appropriate metrics and questions be designed for use in the usability evaluation [11]. Understanding when, and under what conditions, the display supports and overwhelms cognitive and attentional resources is also vital in determining the limitations of the display [11].

3   CWA Derived Requirements

3.1   Scenario Development

The first task, prior to beginning the evaluation, was to develop a detailed scenario with enough complexity to allow for realistic work centered decisions [9, 11]. The literature is vague on guidelines for developing these types of scenarios, but we found that scenarios or storyboards used during the CWA were sufficient enough in detail to support "work-centered" decision making. Dynamic scenarios, regardless of domain, require realistic timelines and event sequences. Our experience suggests that users are particularly sensitive to deviations in time and the progression of elements across time. As such, maintaining predictability across time are key factors in scenario realism. When inconsistent patterns, such as slight target movement (jumping too far ahead or not far enough) are present in a scenario then the SME's mental model becomes unreliable. This becomes particularly important for scenarios that require users to maintain awareness and predict the future status of the system as is often the case with dynamic displays [12]. Another important aspect comes from the naturalistic decision making literature which suggests that realistic time constraints are key to encouraging users to make realistic decisions. When testing a new system the researcher should ensure that realistic time constraints are in place to force SMEs to make decisions that provide a reasonable solution [13]. Providing them with too much time is not realistic and does not accurately reflect the way real world decisions are made. In effect, time is one way that researchers can induce ecological validity into scenario-based decision-making.

3.2   Question Development

Once the scenario was established a series of questions were developed. Questions were required as part of the system level analysis to assess if the IID supported the level of decision making that was intended. It is important to note that question development was one of the most challenging phases involved in the system level evaluation. It was also the phase of the analysis that leveraged the most from the CWA. In order to design system relevant questions we utilized the work functions that were extracted from the CWA design work [6]. In total, ten work functions were assessed for their applicability to question design. For each of the work functions a list of high-level and low-level work tasks were also identified. From these we narrowed down the list of work functions and tasks to a set of scenario relevant functions and tasks. In the end, we had four relevant work functions, four high-level work tasks, and 22 low-level work tasks. A sample of the scenario relevant work functions and tasks are presented below in Table 1.

Table 1. Outline of work functions extracted from the CWA with high and low level work tasks [6]

Work Functions	Work Tasks	High Level Work Tasks	Low Level Work Tasks
Overall tactical picture interpretation	Work Task 1	Integrate information related to tactical picture	
	Work Task 2		Acquire information related to the tactical picture
	Work Task 3		Update understanding of the tactical picture as required
	Work Task 4		Understand relevance of tactical picture to safety covertness and mission
Contact Management	Work Task 1		Classify Contact
	Work Task 2		Establish best Target Motion Analysis (TMA) solution (range, course, speed)
	Work Task 3		Monitor bearing rates of contacts
	Work Task 4	Track Contact of Interest (COI)	

We found that low-level work tasks, in comparison to high-level work tasks, were most suitable for constructing questions with measurable outcomes. While CWA results were useful for determining what tasks need to be completed to achieve a particular work function, they provided no indication as to when these tasks need to be performed. For example - is a low-level target motion analysis (TMA) task best made at the beginning, middle, or end of the scenario? ; is it best made before or after a particular event occurs? For this reason, we had to review the availability of task related information at each point in the scenario to ensure that the questions were being posed at an optimal time in the scenario. Posing questions too early or too late would not provide an adequate representation of the system's ability to support the work task in question.

To answer these types of questions, we had an SME review the scenario and construct subtasks that could be asked as lead-up questions to the low-level work tasks. This allowed us to gauge how early in the scenario users began gathering information and what information sources on the display were most helpful in gathering this information. We also had the SME evaluate which areas of the display were most likely to support this question so that we could compare the user's extraction of data to that of the SMEs. An example of this process is provided in Table 2 below.

Table 2. Link between low-level work tasks, scenes (time), subtasks and display area

CWA Work Functions	Low Level Work Tasks	Scene	Subtask related usability questions	Relevant IID Areas
Contact Management	Classify Contact	1	Not enough detail for scenario specific questions. Is there anything currently happening that would affect your mission goals?	All
		2	Not enough details for scenario specific questions. Utilizing the information presented on the IID, please give us your interpretation of the current tactical situation, noting any changes for the previous scene. Is this information consistent with your expectations? Could you have anticipated these changes?	Tactical Picture
		3	Utilizing the information presented on the IID please give us your interpretation of the current tactical situation, noting any changes from the previous scene. Is this information consistent with your expectations? Could you have anticipated these changes? New contacts entered the scenario and these questions are based on a correct recognition of these contacts. If the user did not recognize the new contacts then point them out. Follow-up Questions What information did you use to determine there are new contacts? If you wanted to find out if the contacts have characteristics of your Contact of Interest (COI) what display information would you use? What are the propulsion characteristics of your COI? What are the weapons characteristics of your COI?	Tactical Picture Range Information Information Area

4   Mental Models

4.1   Mental Models and the IID

While CWA derives various useful information requirements there is still a need to evaluate how the information requirements should be integrated and how they support user decision making. A "mental model" is essentially what drives users to perform in certain ways and to make certain decisions, and is representative of their expectations. A display that supports the user's mental model reduces uncertainty and aids the decision making processes of the user [14]. We found it useful to assess the user's mental model in an attempt to understand how users use the display and what information in the display best supports their decision making.

As an example, we assessed the user's mental model of motion. From the literature we know that mental representations of motion differ from static information [15]. As such, we believed there to be value in testing both static and dynamic forms of the gauges, especially since some of the dynamic gauges are slow moving and therefore have more static characteristics than dynamic ones. To start we isolated the static gauges from the whole display (Figure 3) and we asked users questions such as- "how do you expect this gauge to change as fuel level decreases?" "which way do you expect the dashed line to move over time?" "what do you think will happen when the line reaches the darker colour?" [16]. These questions forced the users to verbalize their mental model so we could compare their mental model to the actual movement of the gauge.

Fig. 3. Fuel gauge. Dashed line represents current fuel with 82% available

Once we obtained an understanding of the user's static mental model we used dynamic sliders and dropdown menus to simulate movement and changes to the system as they would happen in the dynamic display. The sliders and drop-down menus, presented underneath of the gauges in Figure 4, were adjusted to manipulate the lines depicted in the graphic. This allowed us to follow-up on the user's expectations and to clarify confusing elements. We found this strategy particularly helpful for graphics that were less obvious. Speed (Figure 4 right graphic), was a particularly difficult graphic for the users to delineate because it had three separate colour coded lines. The meaning of these lines in the static condition was not apparent to the users. Motion was introduced by changing the numbers in the dropdown menus and by manipulating the slider. In doing this it became clear which line represented current speed (black dashed) and which one represented planned speed (blue line). We believe that testing elements in their static and dynamic form adds value to the assessment by tapping into both the static and dynamic mental models of the user.

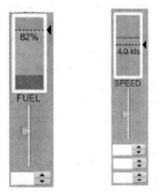

Fig. 4. Fuel and speed gauges with dropdown menus and sliders used to induce motion

As a second example the IID had a new design for ownship spatial orientation based upon common aerospace displays (Figure 5). While CWA provided information requirements, there was still a need to determine how, and what, information should have been integrated. We found it useful to assess mental models to determine the "how" for the newly integrated graphics. Properly integrated information should be less effortful to evaluate than the components that make up the integrated concept. Again, we assessed the user's mental model to determine how separate concepts may be integrated and what the spatial representation of those elements should be. In doing this we found that our user's mental model of "ownship" was from a "side-view" which made the new graphics with "look through" perspectives difficult for them to understand. The OOWs view of their submarine had an impact on how they integrated information related to the spatial orientation of ownship. As a result of this we redesigned the graphic in Figure 5 for a more simplistic integration from a "side-view" perspective. As such, we suggest that mental models that include an understanding of spatial representations be used to assess integrated concepts.

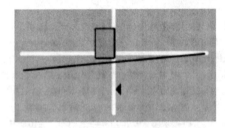

Fig. 5. Ownship attitude indicator with depth, trim, roll, pitch, rudder angle information

5   Attention

5.1   Attentional Factors in the IID

One of the main difficulties with CWA for use in display design is that it assigns equal priority to all information requirements as a way to support all possible decision making tasks. This makes it difficult to determine how information should be oriented, sized, arranged, and integrated in the display. In order to support the user and aid the design, it is imperative that priorities be assigned and accurately reflected in the display layout. While understanding the expectations of the user is important, there is also a need to understand the cognitive and attentional resources required to process the relevant information. Part of our assessment evaluated user behaviours and outcomes with respect to perceptual and cognitive biases. In doing this, we are better able to predict the potential shortfalls of the display in high-stress and high-workload conditions.

As an example, it is known that display logistics (i.e., arrangement, size, and proximity of information) directs attention and display viewing patterns [17]. Display sampling refers to the sequence of gaze patterns, which is driven by attention, to areas on the display [14, 17]. Ideally more important or vital areas of the display will be sampled more frequently than areas of low importance. With respect to the IID we found that some of the areas did not hold enough real-estate to reflect the importance of the information. Of course, this is likely a reflection of the fact that priorities were not assigned to the information extracted from the CWA. For example, we found that SMEs used Area 4 more than Area 5 (see Figure 1), yet the two areas were of equal size. Had priorities been assigned to the information areas we would have known that the tactical picture was of high importance and required more screen real-estate.

While we noted that the users gathered a lot of their information from the tactical picture we also have concerns that making the tactical picture too large would promote attentional tunneling [17]. By making one area of the display larger we run the risk of directing the user's attention to this area at the expense of other vital information in the display. To combat this bias we suggest that scanning techniques, such as scanning the display in a particular pattern, be presented to users to maximize the amount of information they retrieve from the display. This would also help combat "event rate" [17] (p.73) biases which direct attention to quickly changing areas at the expense of more static areas in the display [17, 18]. Ideally, the recommended sampling technique would mimic the OOWs current data extraction mental model to allow the user to spend more time and resources evaluating the acquired information and making decisions.

6   Conclusion

We believe that usability professionals can minimize the ambiguity of system level testing by utilizing CWA derived work tasks. In the current assessment, we found that both the work functions and high-level work tasks were too general to adequately formulate questions. We did find that the CWA derived low-level work tasks were useful in guiding the development of scenario based usability questions. However, it was necessary to break the low-level work tasks into subtasks. The subtasks allowed us to formulate time relevant specific questions with measurable outcomes. We also recommend that priorities be assigned to the CWA derived information requirements to aid the design of the system-level display. Furthermore, we found the consideration of mental models and attentional biases in our assessment valuable in identifying ways to improve design and decrease attentional load.

References

1. Zelik, D.J., Patterson, E.S., Woods, D.D.: Measuring attributes of rigor in information analysis. In: Patterson, E., Miller, J.E. (eds.) Macrocognition Metrics and Scenarios: Design and Evaluation for Real-World Teams, pp. 65–83. Ashgate, Aldershot (2010)
2. Chalmers, B.A.: Developing an Information Integration Display for Submarine Command and Control. Presented at Undersea Human Systems Integration Symposium 2011. American Society of Naval Engineers (2011)
3. Xiao, T., Sanderson, P.M.: Developing and evaluating the organizational constraints analysis (OCA) approach to analysing work coordination via resource allocation case studies. Presented at the Human Factors and Ergonomics Society 56th Annual Meeting, pp. 373-377 (2012)

4. Vicente, K.J.: Cognitive Work Analysis: Toward Safe, Productive, and Health Computer-Based Work (eds). Lawrence Erlbaum Associates Inc., Mahwah (1999)
5. Read, G., Salmon, P., Lenne, M.: From Work Analysis to Work Design: A review of Cognitive Work Analysis Design Applications. Presented at the Human Factors and Ergonomics Society 56th Annual Meeting, pp. 368–372 (2012)
6. Rehak, L., Karthaus, C., Lee, B., Matthews, M., Taylor, T.: Human Systems Integration (HSI) Personal Communication
7. Roth, E.M., Eggleston, R.G.: Forging new evaluation paradigms: Beyond statistical generalization. In: Patterson, E.S., Miller, J. (eds.) Macrocognition Metrics and Scenarios: Design and Evaluation for Real-World Teams, pp. 203–219. Ashgate Publishing (2010)
8. O'Hara, J.: A quasi-experimental model of complex human machine system validation. International Journal of Cognition, Technology, and Work 1, 37–46 (1999)
9. Redish, G.: Expanding Usability Testing to Evaluate Complex Systems. Journal of Usability Studies 2, 102–111 (2007)
10. Pfautz, J., Roth, E.: Using cognitive engineering for system design and evaluation: A visualization aid for stability and support operations. International Journal of Industrial Ergonomics 5, 389–407 (2006)
11. Patterson, E.S., Roth, E.M., Woods, D.D.: Facets of complexity in situated work. In: Patterson, E.S., Miller, J. (eds.) Macrocognition Metrics and Scenarios: Design and Evaluation for Real-World Teams, pp. 1–10. Ashgate Publishing (2010)
12. Rousseau, R., Tremblay, S., Lafond, D., Vachon, F., Breton, R.: Assessing temporal support for dynamic decision making in C2. Presented at the 51st Annual Meeting of the Human Factors and Ergonomics Society Baltimore, MD, pp. 1259–1262 (2007)
13. Bryant, D.J., Webb, R.D.G., McCann, C.: Synthesizing two approaches to decision making in command and control. Canadian Military Journal 4, 29–34 (2003)
14. Bellenkes, A.H., Wickens, C.D., Kramer, A.F.: Visual scanning and pilot expertise: The role of attentional flexibility and mental model development. Aviation, Space, and Environmental Medicine 68, 569–579 (1997)
15. Freyd, J.J.: Dynamic Mental Representations. Psychological Review 94, 427–438 (1987)
16. Lamoureux, T., Pasma, D., Kersten, C.: CAE PS Personal Communication
17. Wickens, C., Hollands, J.: Engineering Psychology and Human Performance. Prentice Hall, Upper Saddle River (2000)
18. Donk, M.: Human Monitoring behavior in a multiple-instrument setting: Independent sampling, sequential sampling or arrangement-dependent sampling. Acta Psychologica 86, 31–55 (1994)

Effect of Transliteration on Readability

Sambhav Jain, Kunal Sachdeva, and Ankush Soni

Language Technologies Research Centre, IIIT Hyderabad, Iran
sambhav.jain@research.iiit.ac.in,
{kunal.sachdeva,ankush.soni}@students.iiit.ac.in

Abstract. We present our efforts on studying the effect of transliteration, on the human readability. We have tried to explore the effect by studying the changes in the eye-gaze patterns, which are recorded with an eye-tracker during experimentation. We have chosen Hindi and English languages, written in Devanagari and Latin scripts respectively. The participants of the experiments are subjected to transliterated words and asked to speak the word. During this, their eye movements are recorded. The eye-tracking data is later analyzed for eye-fixation trends. Quantitative analysis of fixation count and duration as well as visit count is performed over the areas of interest.

Keywords: Eye Tracking, Transliteration, Readability.

1   Introduction

Readability can be technically accounted as the ease with which the text can be read and understood. There are various factors that can be explored to measure the readability such as "speed of perception," "perceptibility at a distance," "perceptibility in peripheral vision," "visibility," "the reflex blink technique," "rate of work" (e.g., speed of reading), "eye movements," and "fatigue in reading" (Tinker, Miles A. 1963).

The early research on readability date back to 1880's when English professor L. A. Sherman, pointed out that average sentences length is getting shorter with time and attributed the fact to ease of reading shorter sentences than the longer one by common mass(Sherman, L.A. 1893). The first psychological study in the field was (Kitson, Harry D. 1921), which observed that each type of reader bought and read their own type of text and the respective text types differ in sentence length and word length trend, showing that sentence length and word length are the best signs of being easy to read.

The research on readability since then has been explored extensively in the field of psycholinguistics. Major research methodologies that are employed here include Behavioral Tasks, Language Production Errors, Neuroimaging and Eye Movements. A typical behavioral task would include presenting the subject with linguistic stimuli and ask to perform an action in response (e.g. articulating a given word). The response to the stimuli is recorded and measured (if required). Often this is also complemented by "priming effect" where the earlier linguistic stimuli is provided along with a supporting or disaccording linguistic stimuli and the effect of it is compared with the earlier observation. Language production error methodology analyzes error patterns and investigates a systematic process responsible for it. Neuroimaging take advantage of medical techniques like positron emission tomography (PET), functional magnetic resonance imaging (fMRI),

D. Harris (Ed.): EPCE/HCII 2013, Part I, LNAI 8019, pp. 49–57, 2013.

event-related potentials (ERPs) in electroencephalography (EEG) and magneto encephalography (MEG), and Trans cranial magnetic stimulation (TMS). Eye tracking make use of a device called eye-tracker which can determine and record the point of gaze (where one is looking) or the motion of an eye relative to the head.

Research on readability is not limited to single language but various studies engaging multiple languages have been performed with multilingual readers (Caramazza&Brones, 1979, Soares&Grosjean, 1984).

Language pairs with different writing scripts gave a new angle to the research on readability with an additional factor of orthographical complexity getting introduced. India, with more than a hundred languages and almost each having a different writing script from other, provides great research opportunities.

Kumar et. al. 2010 performed fMRI study of phrase reading for Hindi-English bilinguals and observed left putamen activation for the less fluent language (English). Das et al. 2011, also employed neuroimaging to reveal dual routes to reading in simultaneous proficient readers of English-Hindi orthographies.   Rao, et al. 2011 have targeted Hindi – Urdu orthographies and did behavioral analysis on the readability of the two. They observed a relatively faster orthographic characteristics speed in Hindi word naming as compared to that in Urdu.

The advent of digital communication mediums have given rise to the use of transliterated text where the text is written in different script, generally English in most of the cases. However, there is no major readability study yet on the transliterated text.   This has motivated us to study the effect of transliteration on human readability. We have tried to explore the effect by analyzing the eye movement of the subject while reading.

In past, eye-tracking has been explored by linguistic researchers to investigate the human reading patterns in language (Rayner 1998). However, there are no studies on the readability research of transliterated text using eye-tracking.

More recently, eye tracking has also been applied to experimental studies in translation process research (Jakobsen and Jensen 2008, Pavlovicand Jensen 2009, Alves, Pagano and Silva 2010, Hvelplund 2011, Carl and Kay 2011, Carl and Dragsted 2012, among others). In most of these works, eye-tracking data have provided input for quantitative analyses of fixation count and duration in areas of interest in texts.

Eye-tracking studies have also contributed to the investigation of the lexical retrieval of words and the processing of syntax, semantics, and discourse. In reading studies, the movements of the eyes are recorded as sentences are read. Typical dependent variables are word-based duration measures such as the time the eyes dwell on a word before proceeding to the next word or the probability to move backwards from a word. Increased in this times and rates of regressions on a specific word are commonly interpreted as posing difficulty to process that word or one of the previous words (Rayner, 1998; Clifton et al., 2007; Vasishth et al., 2013).

2   Span and Scope of Transliteration

In this research, we have studied the effect of transliteration on human readability by analyzing the eye-movement of the participants subjected to reading stimuli.

Transliteration is the process of converting a text from one writing script to another by substituting the alphabets. For example in Chinese, the text '母亲' means 'mother' and pronounced 'mouchan'; to represent it in text as 'mouchan' instead of '母亲' is transliteration. Here the substitution is done from Chinese alphabets (source script) to Latin alphabets (target script). Across transliterations, the pronunciation of the lexicon however remains unaltered. Off late, transliteration is quite frequently seen especially in case of digital communication like email, chat, blogs etc. The target language in majority of the cases is observed to be English. This is due to that fact that there is an ease to type in English given Latin layout keyboard. The reverse is also seen in practice where an English word is observed in a different script other than Latin. This is majorly seen in case of borrowed vocabulary words. Globalized use of English as official language is accounted as the main reason for it.

The abundant use of transliteration in digital communication has introduced a need for better design of text input mediums and product designers are now considering factors effecting readability, to come up with better display devices. However these are challenging issues as investigating the factors that contribute to better reading or writing experience are not straight forward as writing and reading are not just physical but also a unique cognitive ability of humans, and cognitive aspects are tough to be directly articulated, identified or answered.

Here we have made an effort towards identify such factors, by exploring the eye-tracking technique. Eye-tracking has been extensively explored in past for readability research to investigate the human reading patterns (Rayner 1998). Except here we are having transliterated text instead of the regular text. We have chosen Hindi and English languages, written in Devanagari and Latin scripts respectively, due to high availability of Hindi-English bilingual speakers in the neighborhoods.

3   Experiment

3.1   Objective

The objective of the experiment is to report the changes in the human reading pattern when the text is transliterated. The independent variables in our experiment were as follows:

- Fixation Count
- Fixation Duration
- Visit Count
- First Fixation Duration

3.2   Participants

The experiment is conducted at IIIT Hyderabad which is a deemed university in South India, with two major streams of Computer Science and Electronics & Communication. The university has ample number of students from North India where Hindi is the majorly spoken language. Twenty-four proficient biliterate readers of Hindi-English volunteered from the campus. They included 17 male and 7 female students, aged 20–28 years approximately. All except one claimed Hindi as their native language, but all of them agreed to have received formal education in Hindi during schooling. The participants were given small incentive in form of chocolates for being part of the experiment.

3.3   Stimulus Material

Our stimuli consisted of 8 slide shows. Each slide show comprised of three kinds of slides (Fig1).

a) Instruction Slide.

This slide contains the general information about the experiment.

b) Fixation Slide.

This slide just had a star figure in the middle of the slide. This slide appeared between any two consecutive word slides so that the first fixation landing position could be captured more effectively. The fixation screen is important to minimize the chances of subject already looking at the position where a stimulus is to appear.

c) Word Slide.

This slide contains a single word in one of the quadrant of the slide which is selected randomly.

We establish a baseline with one pair of slideshow, having words in Hindi and English with their respective scripts. The other three pair of slides contains transliterated text with English words in Devanagari and Hindi words denoted in Latin. The words are automatically selected from 'Gyannidhi Corpus' (*Arora et. al. 2003*). We only considered words having more than three syllables (approximately greater than 8 characters) to have ample eye movement for a word. On the basis of their frequency of occurrence (Low, Medium and High) in the corpus, 10 words are randomly selected from each frequency class and for each language, giving us the three pair of slides mentioned earlier.

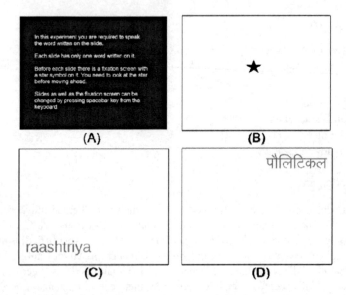

Fig. 1. (A) Instruction slide (B) Fixation Slide (C) Transliterated Hindi word in Latin (D) Transliterated English word in Devanagari

3.4   Procedure

We employ eye tracking machine Tobii X120. Tobii X120 eye tracker is widely used for research in the academic community, and to conduct usability studies and market surveys. The stimuli are loaded in the eye tracker and each participant's response is recorded on the same. We maintained a random order for the above mentioned slide shows so that any kind of bias can be avoided .The internal order of slides in a slide show is also randomized. For analysis, each word is enclosed in a rectangular boundary and the resulting rectangle is partitioned in four equal parts (fig.2) for area of interest analysis, over selected parameters viz. number of fixation points, duration of fixation and number of visits. It is important to divide the word in areas of interest as we want to know which part does subject focuses on. This approach provides an advantage of increased statistical power over a normal whole-volume analysis approach.

3.5   Task

Each participant was subjected to above mentioned eight slide shows .They were asked to enunciate the word occurring on the screen thereby ensuring that they read the complete word. During the process their eye movements are captured with the eye tracker.

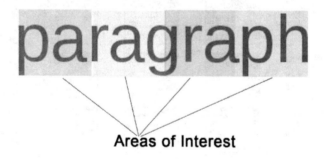

Fig. 2. Four rectangular regions of *Area of Interest* analysis

3.6   Results

We performed the Area of Interest (AOI) analysis for the independent variables in our experiments. The readings recorded by the eye-tracking apparatus are processed via Tobii AOI analysis application. The results for visit count and fixation duration are shown below in Table1 and Table2 respectively. The heat maps for fixation duration are shown in Fig 3. The detailed results for first fixation duration and fixation count are not shown due to space constraint.

4   General Discussions

Our experiment results show an increase in the average reading duration for the transliterated text over the baseline. The average fixation time in case of English written in Devanagari is noted to be greater than that in the case of Hindi written in Latin. This reinforces the observation by (Rao et. al. 2011) that the readability depends on the complexity of the orthography. A high concentration of fixations is seen in the second and the third partitions of the boundary as compared to the first and the fourth partition. The observation can be accounted for, from the study of peripheral vision and central vision by (Legge et. al. 2001). There is an increase in the number of visits in the AOIs over the baseline for both English and Hindi. Also, for both, the languages, the transliterated text, showed a subtle increase in the average fixation number and average fixation count for low frequency words as compared to their medium and high frequency counterparts.

Table 1. ExperimentResults for Visit Count per word averaged over 24 participants. (N=Visit Instances, Mean =Avg. visits, Sum=Total visits, Sdev= Standard deviation)

	Rectangle 1		Rectangle 2		Rectangle 3		Rectangle 4		Total	
Baseline English	N	8.7	N	18.9	N	17.6	N	7.7	N	529
	Mean	1.471	Mean	2.111	Mean	2.085	Mean	1.247	Mean	1.871
	Sum	12.8	Sum	39.9	Sum	36.7	Sum	9.6	Sum	990
	Sdev	0.468	Sdev	1.054	Sdev	0.944	Sdev	0.515	Sdev	1.05
Baseline Hindi	N	8.4	N	18.9	N	17.8	N	7.9	N	530
	Mean	1.595	Mean	2.101	Mean	1.949	Mean	1.354	Mean	1.858
	Sum	13.4	Sum	39.7	Sum	34.7	Sum	10.7	Sum	985
	Sdev	0.684	Sdev	0.964	Sdev	1.234	Sdev	0.493	Sdev	1.22
High English	N	10.5	N	19.6	N	19.1	N	8.7	N	579
	Mean	1.752	Mean	2.444	Mean	2.005	Mean	1.345	Mean	2.009
	Sum	18.4	Sum	47.9	Sum	38.3	Sum	11.7	Sum	1163
	Sdev	0.992	Sdev	1.123	Sdev	1.045	Sdev	0.471	Sdev	1.1
High Hindi	N	13.2	N	19.9	N	19.9	N	13.1	N	661
	Mean	1.538	Mean	2.724	Mean	2.523	Mean	1.634	Mean	2.21
	Sum	20.3	Sum	54.2	Sum	50.2	Sum	21.4	Sum	1461
	Sdev	0.673	Sdev	1.333	Sdev	1.274	Sdev	0.7	Sdev	1.33
Mid English	N	13.5	N	19.8	N	19.8	N	10.5	N	636
	Mean	2.252	Mean	3.096	Mean	2.495	Mean	1.638	Mean	2.489
	Sum	30.4	Sum	61.3	Sum	49.4	Sum	17.2	Sum	1583
	Sdev	1.26	Sdev	1.483	Sdev	1.199	Sdev	0.806	Sdev	1.61
Mid Hindi	N	13.5	N	19.3	N	19.1	N	12	N	639
	Mean	1.704	Mean	2.642	Mean	2.215	Mean	1.433	Mean	2.089
	Sum	23	Sum	51	Sum	42.3	Sum	17.2	Sum	1335
	Sdev	0.916	Sdev	1.261	Sdev	1.171	Sdev	0.561	Sdev	1.38
Low English	N	12.8	N	19.2	N	19.5	N	12.6	N	6
	Mean	2.008	Mean	3.089	Mean	2.944	Mean	1.802	Mean	2.5
	Sum	25.7	Sum	59.3	Sum	57.4	Sum	22.7	Sum	15
	Sdev	0.999	Sdev	1.562	Sdev	1.687	Sdev	0.756	Sdev	2.26
Low Hindi	N	12.6	N	19.3	N	19.3	N	11	N	622
	Mean	1.841	Mean	3.114	Mean	2.233	Mean	1.582	Mean	2.312
	Sum	23.2	Sum	60.1	Sum	43.1	Sum	17.4	Sum	1438
	Sdev	0.911	Sdev	1.688	Sdev	1.242	Sdev	0.687	Sdev	1.71

Table 2. Experiment Results for Fixation Duration per word averaged over 24 participants. (N=Avg. fixations, Mean =Avg. fixation time per fixation (in sec.), Sum=Total fixation time (in sec.), Sdev= Standard deviation (in sec.))

		Rectangle 1	Rectangle 2	Rectangle 3	Rectangle 4
Baseline English	N	12,8	39,9	36,7	9,6
	Mean	0,216	0,269	0,3	0,309
	Sum	2,762	10,719	11,015	2,965
	Sdev	0,085	0,116	0,137	0,138
Baseline Hindi	N	13,6	39,9	35,2	11
	Mean	0,291	0,292	0,339	0,332
	Sum	3,962	11,641	11,937	3,655
	Sdev	0,115	0,166	0,181	0,169
High English	N	18,4	47,9	38,3	11,7
	Mean	0,283	0,274	0,311	0,322
	Sum	5,204	13,132	11,903	3,762
	Sdev	0,136	0,137	0,16	0,158
High Hindi	N	20,3	54,2	50,2	21,4
	Mean	0,26	0,254	0,282	0,289
	Sum	5,283	13,763	14,154	6,187
	Sdev	0,127	0,109	0,126	0,163
Mid English	N	30,4	61,3	49,4	17,2
	Mean	0,3	0,264	0,311	0,319
	Sum	9,119	16,169	15,35	5,486
	Sdev	0,17	0,127	0,155	0,153
Mid Hindi	N	23	51	42,3	17,2
	Mean	0,289	0,255	0,299	0,292
	Sum	6,647	12,981	12,63	5,025
	Sdev	0,127	0,113	0,136	0,163
Low English	N	25,7	59,3	57,4	22,7
	Mean	0,283	0,259	0,298	0,32
	Sum	7,273	15,342	17,111	7,263
	Sdev	0,121	0,12	0,166	0,155
Low Hindi	N	23,2	60,1	43,1	17,4
	Mean	0,275	0,254	0,289	0,301
	Sum	6,379	15,255	12,449	5,234
	Sdev	0,118	0,11	0,135	0,153

Fig. 3. Heat Maps for Fixation Duration

5   Conclusion and Future Work

The increase in the statistics of fixation duration and visit count indicates that there is an extra effort required on the part of a reader to process and to speak the transliterated text. Thus, our results conclude that the familiar word forms are quickly perceived by the mind rather than the unfamiliar forms and thus readability is not just the mere process of identifying the constituent alphabets but more of a cognitive process.

For simplicity, here we have assumed that each character takes an equal effort in reading on the part of the reader. In future we wish to relax this assumption and investigate the effect over transliterated texts. Also, existing quantitative readability measures (Sinha 2012, Benjamin, 2012) can be explored for selecting the stimuli text.

References

1. Rayner, K.: Eye movements in reading and information processing: 20 years of research. Psychological Bulletin Journal (1998)
2. Arora, K.K., Shukla, S.A.V.G.V.N., Agrawal, S.S.: Gyannidhi: A parallel corpus for Indian languages including nepali. In: Proceedings of Information Technology: Challenges and Prospects (ITPC-2003), Kathmandu, Nepal (May 2003)
3. Rao, C., Vaid, J., Srinivasan, N., Chen, H.C.: Orthographic characteristics speed Hindi word naming but slow Urdu naming: evidence from Hindi/Urdu biliterates. Springer Reading and Writing Journal (2011)
4. Legge, G.E., Mansfield, J.S., Chung, S.T.L., et al.: Psychophysics of reading. XX. Linking letter recognition to reading speed in central and peripheral vision. Citeseer Vision Research Journal (2001)
5. Tinker, M.A.: Legibility of print, vol. 1. Iowa State University Press, Ames (1963)
6. Sherman, L.A.: Analytics of literature: A manual for the objective study of English prose and poetry. Ginn (1893)
7. Kitson, H.D.: How to use your mind; a psychology of study. JB Lippincott Company (1921)
8. Soares, C., Grosjean, F.: Bilinguals in a monolingual and a bilingual speech mode: The effect on lexical access. Memory & Cognition 12(4), 380–386 (1984)

9. Alves, F., GonçAlves, J.L., Szpak, K.: Identifying Instances of Processing Effort in Translation Through Heat Maps: an eye-tracking study using multiple input sources. In: 24th International Conference on Computational Linguistics, p. 5 (December 2012)

10. Von der Malsburg, T., Vasishth, S.: What is the scanpath signature of syntactic reanalysis? Journal of Memory and Language 65(2), 109–127 (2011)

11. Kumar, U., Das, T., Bapi, R.S., Padakannaya, P., Joshi, R.M., Singh, N.C.: Reading different orthographies: an fMRI study of phrase reading in Hindi–English bilinguals. Reading and Writing 23(2), 239–255 (2010)

12. Das, T., Padakannaya, P., Pugh, K.R., Singh, N.C.: Neuroimaging reveals dual routes to reading in simultaneous proficient readers of two orthographies. Neuroimage 54(2), 1476–1487 (2011)

13. Carl, M., Jakobsen, A.L., Jensen, K.T.: Studying human translation behavior with user-activity data. In: Proceedings of the 5th International Workshop on Natural Language Processing and Cognitive Science, NLPCS 2008, Barcelona, Spain, pp. 114–123 (June 2008)

14. Pavlović, N., Jensen, K.T.: Eye tracking translation directionality. Translation Research Projects 2, 93 (2009)

15. Hvelplund, K.T.: Allocation of Cognitive Resources in Translation: an eye-tracking and key-logging study (Doctoral dissertation, Københavns Universitet Københavns Universitet, Det Humanistiske Fakultet Faculty of Humanities, Institut for Engelsk, Germanskog Romansk Department of English, Germanic and Romance Studie) (2011)

16. Carl, M., Kay, M.: Gazing and Typing Activities during Translation: A Comparative Study of Translation Units of Professional and Student Translators. Meta: Journal des Traducteurs 56(4) (2011)

17. Carl, M., Dragsted, B.: Inside the monitor model: Processes of default and challenged translation production. Translation: Computation, Corpora, Cognition 2(1) (2012)

18. Clifton, C., Staub, A., Rayner, K.: Eye movements in reading words and sentences. Eye Movements: A Window on Mind and Brain, 341–372 (2007)

19. Vasishth, S., von der Malsburg, T., Engelmann, F.: What eye movements can tell us about sentence comprehension. Wiley Interdisciplinary Reviews: Cognitive Science 4(2), 125–134 (2013)

20. Benjamin, R.G.: Reconstructing Readability: Recent Developments and Recommendations in the Analysis of Text Difficulty. Educational Psychology Review, 1–26 (2012)

21. Sinha, M., Sharma, S., Dasgupta, T., Basu, A.: New Readability Measures for {B}angla and {H}indi Texts. In: Proceedings of COLING 2012: Posters (2012)

The Effects of User Involvement in Online Games, Game-Playing Time and Display Duration on Working Memory

Fang-Ling Lin[1], Tai-Yen Hsu[2], Tung-Shen Wu[1], and Chih-Lin Chang[1]

[1] College of General Education, Hsiuping University of Science and Technology,
Taichung City, Taiwan
{fingling,wu1096}@mail.hust.edu.tw, salamen.sa@msa.hinet.net
[2] Department of Physical Education, National Taichung University of Education,
Taichung City, Taiwan
hsu@ntcu.edu.tw

Abstract. College students spending too much time on online games every week tend to suffer from worsened learning ability, concentration problems, poor academic performance, and decreased interactions with other people. This study's author conducted a questionnaire-based survey to examine how many hours college students from central Taiwan spend on online games per week, in order to find out their average daily involvement in such games. Using proportionate stratified sampling, the survey respondents were selected to examine the weekly involvement in online games among college students from central Taiwan, who were divided into low-, medium- and high-involvement groups in a cluster analysis. Results of the survey were tested using a self-developed evaluation system based on working memory and response time. Totally 36 college students, or 12 students from each of the low-, medium- and high-involvement groups, were randomly selected from the population to test how involvement in online games, game-playing time and display duration affected their working memory. Findings from this study include: I. The low, medium and high levels of online game involvements are defined as an average 1.34 hours, 4.84 hours and 10.27 hours spent on online games every day. 30.9% of the survey respondents said they spent more than 4 hours on online games, which suggests that online games may be the reason why college students stay up all night so often. II. This testing discovers that the levels of involvement in video gaming ($p < 0.05$), display duration ($p < 0.05$), and the interaction of the two factors will all have an impact on visual working memory ($p < 0.05$).

Keywords: Online games, involvement in online games, Display duration, game-playing time, Attention.

1 Introduction

1.1 Research Background

According to the estimation made by the Institute for Information Industry in Taiwan in 2009, there are as many as 350 million broadband users worldwide. Video games have also gradually transformed to grow beyond the stereotypical ideas of gambling

D. Harris (Ed.): EPCE/HCII 2013, Part I, LNAI 8019, pp. 58–67, 2013.
© Springer-Verlag Berlin Heidelberg 2013

and unhealthy leisure activity. Due to economic recession, many people face the problem of losing their jobs, being forced to retire, and being forced to be dismissed. As a result, another form of economy, "stay-at-home economy" (otaku economy), has been formed. The increase of online population, speedy fiber internet, and the popularity of home computers has led to the emergence of "video gaming addiction", a behavior pattern developed by individuals and video games[11]. The after effects of being overly involved in internet gaming, including alienation, tendency toward violence, behavioral disorder, anxiety, loss of concentration, and low learning efficiency have not only become personal problems of the users but major social issues[8]. Although there are many studies focusing on middle school and elementary school students, there is very little research done on college students.

The surveys are conducted through stratified sampling to understand college students' level of involvement in video games each week in central Taiwan[11][15]. This study uses surveys as research tools and the survey structure is divided into three parts: first, variables of personal background; second, usage behavior of video games; third, mental and physical state. Four thousand college students from different departments are surveyed. According to the sampling curve proposed by [9], when the population is 4,000, at least 351 people must be sampled and the conservative estimation of the survey response rate is 80%. As a result, the number of survey should be at least 439. This research uses surveys to study the amount of time that college students spend each week on video games in colleges in central Taiwan to understand the background and behavioral pattern of video game involvement, which is one of the research motivations of this study.

Early studies focused on the negative effects caused by internet addiction[11] but very few focused on working memory of the video game addicts. Therefore, the impact of video games on visual working memory is the second research motivation of this study. The examination of video gaming and visual concentration is conducted with self-designed and self-developed visual code testing tools[3]. Subjects are randomly selected from the video gaming groups of low, middle, and high levels of involvement to test the level of involvement and the impact of time length toward working memory. The dependent variables of working memory generate the accuracy rate.

1.2   Research Objectives

Therefore, there are two purposes of research in this study. The first purpose is to study the behavioral pattern of college students' involvement in video gaming and the research subject are students in the colleges in central Taiwan. The second purpose is to, based on the survey analysis from the first stage of the study, adopt cluster analysis to divide the subjects into video gaming groups of low, middle, and high levels of involvement based on their average time spent on video games and to analyze the impact on working memory caused by the levels of involvement, time length of involvement, and code display duration[2].

2   Research Methods

2.1   Survey of the Background and Behavioral Pattern of College Students' Involvement in Video Gaming in Colleges in Central Taiwan

Three sections of the surveys used by [5]are selected to be the survey tool for this study. College students were surveyed to study the different level of involvement in video gaming and their behavioral patterns. Stratified sampling is conducted and the survey time is approximately 30 to 35 minutes. The first part of the survey is "Basic Information" to understand background factors such as personal variables and recreational resources. The second part is "Experience in video gaming" to examine the type of game played by the subject, the environment of playing, the motivation of playing, the time of playing, feeling and evaluation for playing. The third part is "Video Gaming Addiction Chart."

In order to understand the influence of college students' levels of involvement in video gaming and their behavioral pattern, survey structures of past literatures have been studied to summarize and generate the survey structure of this study. The survey structure is divided into three sections: first, variables of personal background; second, usage behavior of video gaming; third, mental and physical state. The survey design is completed based on the above structure. Three sections of the survey used by [5] are selected to be the survey tool for this study.

Lee [10] once applied less than one SD of the sample mean and it is 15.87% after the application in the group with lower level of involvement in video gamming while it is 15.87% before the application in the group with higher level of involvement, more than one SD of the sample mean. The group with middle level of involvement is within plus or minus one SD, 68.26%, which is the middle of the sample scores. This research applies cluster analysis toward the study of the groups with high, middle, and low levels of involvement in video gaming.

2.2   The Impact Caused By Different Levels of Involvement in Video Gaming and Different Time Length on Working Memory

Based on the analytical result of the surveys, experiment participants are divided into three groups of high, middle, and low levels of involvement in video gaming. Twelve people are randomly selected from each group and a total of 36 people from the three groups are tested on their visual attention to compare the difference in working memory caused by the time of video gaming, level of video gaming, and display duration[2].

(1)   Research subject
      Twelve people are randomly selected from the three groups of high, middle, and low levels of involvement in video gaming and there are a total of 36 subjects.
(2)   Research tool
      (A)A self-designed "Visual Code working Memory Evaluation System" is used and the software function includes the setting of the background color,

code color, font size, font, code number, display duration, the number of questions, inspection duration, total inspection duration, calculating the correct number of questions and the time required.

(B) Equipment and environment setting: ambient light illumination is set at 350 lx, PC parameter setting. Please refer to Table 1[3].

Table 1. The settings of Visual Code working Memory Evaluation System

VDT pixels	Background color	Code color	Font size	Display duration	Code number	Font	Inspection duration
1152×864	White	Black	72	0.3 & 0.4 Sec.	7	Arial	10 Minutes

(3) Design of the experiment

This experiment offers the video game Runes of Magic to the participants and each participant must have more than five hours of experience in playing Runes of Magic. The variables of the experiment are three levels of involvement degree (high, middle, and low); two levels of code display duration (0.3 second and 0.4 second); two levels of video gaming time (two hours and three hours). During the experiment recording process, each set of experimental time is ten minutes and the dependant variables are the accuracy rate. The experiment adopts a repeated measure design. Random grouping experiments are conducted with the groups of high, middle, and low involvement levels. Within three minutes after the participants finished playing the video games, the participants are tested in 3 minutes.

(4) Experiment Process

A. Before the experiment, explain to the participants the purpose, the precautions, and the operation method of the experiment. Each participant has two practices with ten questions each time before playing the video game. The testing lasts approximately ten minutes.

B. Setting of the testing system (please refer to Table 1).

C. The participants play the video game Runes of Magic for a random of two (or three) hours and take the test within three minutes after playing the game.

D. Testing of the participants:

(A) Start by pressing any button.

(B) Codes are displayed randomly (Arabic numerals 0-9, each number is one code; seven numbers will be randomly displayed at the same time, the number of the code might repeat).

(C) The participants key-in the seven code numbers they remember in five seconds.

(D) The participants complete the test when ten minutes has passed or 100 sets of random codes have been finished.

(E) Calculate and analyze the accuracy rate of the set of codes entered by the participants, including all correct in 1-7 codes, 1-6 codes, 1-5 codes, 1-4 codes, 1-3 codes, and 1-2 codes.

3   Results and Discussion

3.1   Survey of the Background and Behavioral Pattern of College Students' Involvement in Video Gaming in Colleges in Central Taiwan

The survey includes six aspects and a total of 104 questions. The survey for each class was conducted through stratified sampling; therefore there are some samples from each class. Deducting the surveys with missing values, the Cronbach α reached 0.944 after correction, demonstrating good validity.

Table 2. Cluster analysis chart of the time spent on video gaming

	Cluster		
group	1	2	3
Time spent on video gaming	33.9	72.4	9.4

Table 3. Cluster analysis of the time spent on video gaming ANOVA summary

	Cluster		Deviation		F-value	P
	MS	df	MS	df		
Time of playing	72433.88	2	63.556	492	1139.679	.000

$^*P < 0.05$

3.2   The Impact on Working Memory Caused by Different Involvement Levels In Video Gaming and Time of Usage

Table 4. Summary chart of the MANOVA testing of the involvement levels, involvement time in video gaming and display duration.

Effect terms	Numeric	F-value	df of Assumed	df of error	p
Involvement level (A)	.240	22.050	12.000	254.000	.000
Display duration (B)	.886	2.713	6.000	127.000	.016
A*B	.802	2.462	12.000	254.000	.005

$^*P < .05$; A= Involvement level, B= Display duration; A*B=Interaction of between A and B.

Table 5. Summary chart of the testing of effect terms among the involvement levels of video gaming of the subjects.

Source	variables	SS of Type III	df	MS	F-value	p
	The 2nd code	732.347	2	366.174	5.552*	.005
	The 3rd code	1279.847	2	639.924	9.268*	.000
Involvement	The 4th code	5591.625	2	2795.812	28.623*	.000
level	The 5th code	31918.347	2	15959.174	148.518*	.000
	The 6th code	47723.181	2	23861.590	154.734*	.000
	The 7th code	59062.181	2	29531.090	157.320*	.000

$*p < 0.05$

Table 6. Summary chart of the effect term testing among the duration time of the participants

Source	variables	SS of Type III	df	MS	F-value	p
	The 2nd code	2.250	1	2.250	.034	.854
	The 3rd code	5.444	1	5.444	.079	.779
Duration	The 4th code	14.694	1	14.694	.150	.699
Time	The 5th code	403.340	1	403.340	3.754	.055
	The 6th code	1040.063	1	1040.063	6.744*	.010
	The 7th code	427.111	1	427.111	2.275	.134

$*P < 0.05$

4   Discussion

4.1   Survey of the Background and Behavioral Pattern of College Students' Involvement in Video Gaming in Colleges in Central Taiwan

As of July 2003, there were more than 3.51 million households enjoying the internet and the internet penetration rate in general households were as high as 54%. The estimated internet user was approximately 11,750,000, about half of the total population of Taiwan. According to the estimation of the Institute for Information Industry in 2009, there were as much as 350 million global broadband users. There are 521 effective samples in this survey. Analytical study of the surveys indicates that 35.5% of the college students in central Taiwan play video game more than eight times each week. On average, men are involved in video gaming for 25 hours each week, higher than the 13 hours of women. There are 308 men who have been involved in video gaming for over three years, which is 59.18% of the surveyed population. According to the daily time of usage of the high-risk group is four hours, approximately 24.5

hours a week[5]. The standard for heavy users set by Canadian scholars is seven hours and above per week, which indicates that 59.18% of the college students have become heavy users and even high-risk users in college or even in their high school years. During non-weekends and non-holidays, 30.9% of the students are involved in video gaming for more than 4 hours a day; as high as 42.8% are involved in video gaming for more than 4 hours a day on weekends and holidays. As the time for video gaming increases, sleeping time decreases and might cause poor school grades. Cluster analysis of the surveys discovers that the average number of hours spent on video gaming each week from the groups of middle and high levels of involvement are several times higher than the research result of 12.5 hours per week discovered by Harn[7].

In addition to the fact that video gaming causes poor school work, the research result of Huang [8]discovers that more boy students have played online game and have a higher percentage of online gaming addictions. In terms of years of experience, moreover, the highest percentage of students are those with three and more years of experience; the higher the frequency and the longer the time spend in video gaming each week, the higher the tendency for game addiction. Research shows that video gaming can fulfill the users' need for self-fulfillment and social interaction yet it poses the potential threat of addiction[15], leading to negative psychological responses of anxiety and a sense of emptiness. When the act of video gaming is suspended, the person becomes anxious and hard to control his or her impulsive behavior, neglecting the interactive relationship between people and matters in the surrounding. Studies show that the important variables of video gaming addictions include certain personality traits such as a tendency of depression, anxiety, low self-esteem, type A personality, and alienation in interpersonal relationship[6]. Previous studies show that obsession in video gaming might lead to addiction problems and it may cause a great impact of mental damage on the young students. Although research literatures also mention that the experience of playing video games can improve visual concentration[11], this study discovers that some college students have become heavy user, and even users of high-risk group, with their over-involvement in video gaming. Psychological damages might have been caused; how to correct or adjust their life style will be a major challenge in future education.

Past researches show that obsession with video gaming might cause addiction issues, causing psychological damage to the young students. This study also discovers that as many as 88.8% of college students play online games at home. Therefore, parents should establish good communication channels with the children, understanding their children's online activities. It would be best if the parents can regulate their children's time and behavior online, educating them about the correct concept in internet use to avoid the damages caused by the internet on the children and avoiding the students' indulgence in the world of online gaming.

Information security company Norton commissioned opinion polling firm StrategyOne to conduct a survey in more than 14 countries including America, England, and Canada about internet behaviors and experiences. The survey included 2,800 children aged 10 to 17 and more than 7,000 adults. The survey discovered that children in Taiwan spend an average of 15 hours per week online, preceded only by Brazil's 18.3 hours, showing that the children in Taiwan are overly indulged in the internet. A research done in 1998 with 2,249 students from 12 high schools and vocational high schools shows a high 85% of the students goes online[4]. According to the analytical study of the "Internet Addiction Clinic" at the Kaohsiung Medical University Chung-Ho Memorial Hospital, the level of seriousness of internet addiction in Taiwan is the third in the world, closely following Singapore and Korea[12]. How do we educate the children to have correct concepts in computer usage, how do we restrict the time for computer games and internet use, how do we divert the children's attraction to video games and the internet, and how do we develop alternative leisure activities are all pending issues and action items for the future.

4.2   The Impact on Short-Term Memory Caused by Different Levels of Involvement in Video Gaming and Different Time of Usage

This testing discovers that the levels of involvement in video gaming ($p < 0.05$), display duration ($p < 0.05$), and the interaction of the two factors will all have an impact on visual working memory ($p < 0.05$). There are many testing methods for visual concentration. For the vision, concentration is a very important information processing mechanism; without concentration, recognition, learning and memorization will become impossible. Psychologist Berlyne[1] once pointed out that human beings and animals are usually most interested in things that are not too easy and not too complicated.

Therefore, the goal of this study is to test if visual concentration will be influenced by the length of time involved in video gaming, the length of time for code display, the number of code displayed, and level of involvement in video gaming in the past (the average time spend on video gaming each day). The result shows that the experiment participants, no matter which group of involvement level, demonstrate better post-test scores than pre-test scores($p < 0.05$). The results also proved experiences of playing video gaming can promote the ability of working memory[3]. And another reason the phenomenon is caused by the learning effect from using the visual code working memory evaluation system one more time.

A person is focused on doing requires more resources, the ability to monitor surrounding messages will become worse[13]. The well-known "Posner paradigm" has become the model for studying visual spatial selective attention. Posner utilizes the length of gap between cue time and the appearance of the target to discover that visual attention can be divided into covert shift of attention (a shift of attention without moving the eye sight) and sustained attention (attention is kept at the cue spot). Covert shift of attention include the process of disengage, move, and engage, which are mostly complete by the parietal lobe in the brain. This process provides the frontal lobe with the command of priority management, managing and strengthening the level of the attention. Normally people who the average of working memory are 7±2 [14]. The later process is the so-called sustained attention. The study result also discovers that the level of involvement in video gaming has significant impact on the accuracy rate of the display codes. Display duration will influence the accuracy rate

($p < 0.05$) for the six codes.   There is no significant difference ($p > 0.05$) when there are seven codes, maybe because the number of codes is beyond the working memory capacity of the subjects.

This study adopts visual working memory evaluation system, which is based on the important features of visual attention mentioned by many of the scholars mentioned above.   Sanders and McCormick[14] make the following suggestions on the screen color: do not use too many colors; avoid using extreme colors such as red or blue, avoid using color combinations such as red and blue, red and green, and blue and green; increase the color contrast between the text and the background. Zhu and Tsao [16] point out in their study on the pairing of the target and background color that the best result is achieved with a combination that has a greater contrast: white target and black background, yellow target and black background, green target and black background.   Research results show that there are no significant differences ($p > 0.05$) when the involvement time in playing the video games is two hours and three hours. While analyzing the reason, it is shown that the subject of experiment had a daily average of at least 1.34 hours playing video games in the past, with the highest average time 10.34 hours. It is understandable that significant differences were not reached since the number of hours is much higher than the 2 hours or 3 hours adopted in this experiment.

5   Conclusion and Suggestion

Due to the popularity of the internet, computers and the World Wide Web have become indispensable tools of living for today's families.   Video games and the internet have also become major items in the lives and leisure activities of teenagers and college students.   The quality of leisure life and the level of concentration, which is most crucial to learning, have gradually been corroded by video games and the internet.   It is important to contemplate how we can help children develop correct concepts in computer usage, how do we regulate appropriate time length for computer usage to avoid traits of video game addiction such as tendency of depression, anxiety, low self-esteem, type A personality, and alienation in interpersonal relationship. Some students even try to fulfill their goal of self-realization through the virtual reality world of the video games, causing negative psychological damage such as anxiety, sense of emptiness, and behavioral impulses beyond control.   This study discovers that as high as 88.8% of the college students play internet video games at home. The development of parent-and-child activities in the family as a replacement for playing video games will effectively reduce the time spent on video games and avoid the potential threat caused by over-involvement.

References

1. Berlyne, D.E.: Structure and direction in thinking, New York; Chen, S.H., Wong, L.Z., Su, Y.R., Wu, H.M., Yang, P.F.: Development of a Chinese Internet Addiction Scale and Its Psychometric Study. Chinese Journal of Psychology 45, 279–296 (2003)

2. Chang, C.L., Li, K.W., Jou, Y.T., Hsu, T.Y.: The Study of the Impact of Environmental Illuminance on the Visual Codes Working Memory during a Fencing Game. In: 2009 IEEE International Conference on Networking, Sensing and Control, pp. 318–324 (2009)
3. Chang, C.-L., Hsu, T.-Y., Lin, F.-L., Huang, C.-D., Huang, I.-T.: Leisure Activities for the Elderly–The Influence of Visual Working Memory on Mahjong and Its Video Game Version. In: Stephanidis, C. (ed.) Posters, Part I, HCII 2011. CCIS, vol. 173, pp. 358–362. Springer, Heidelberg (2011)
4. Chen, S.H., Wong, L.Z., Su, Y.R., Wu, H.M., Yang, P.F.: Development of a Chinese Internet Addiction Scale and Its Psychometric Study. Chinese Journal of Psychology 45, 279–296 (2003)
5. Feng, J.Y.: A study of the video gaming *experience, addictive tendencies, and the perceived health status of junior high school students*. Taiwan Journal of Public Health, National Taiwan Normal University (2005)
6. Griffiths, M.: Computer game playing in early adolescence. Youth Soc. 29, 223–238 (1997)
7. Harn, P.L.: The Impact of Internet Users' Characteristics, Behaviors, and Psychological Traits on Internet Addiction for Taiwanese High School Students, Taipei: unpublished master's thesis at the National Taiwan Normal University Department of Educational Psychology and Counseling (2000)
8. Huang, Y.L.: A Relational Study of On-line Game Addiction, Behavior, and Leisure Satisfaction for Fifth and Sixth Graders of Elementary School, Changhua: unpublished master's thesis of the EMBA Classes at the Da-Yeh University Department of Leisure, Recreation, and Tourism Management (2006)
9. Krejcie, R.V., Morgan, D.W.: Determining Sample Size or Research Activities. Educational and Psychological Measurement 30(3), 89 (1970)
10. Lee, G.S.: A Study of using Data Mining techniques to explore relationship of long-latency auditory evoked potentials P300 and IQ, Tainan: unpublished master's thesis at the National University of Tainan Graduate Institute of Technology Education (2004)
11. Lin, F.L., Chang, C.L., Jou, Y.T., Pan, S.C., Hsu, T.Y., Huang, C.D.: Effect of the Involvement Degree of Playing Video Games on Brain waves for an hour. In: IEEE 17th International Conference on Industrial Engineering and Engineering Management, vol. 2, pp. 1043–1047 (2010)
12. Peng, Y.H.: Research on teenagers internet usage behavior and addiction during leisure time, Taipei: unpublished master's thesis at the National Taiwan Normal University Graduate Institute of Sport, Leisure and Hospitality Management (2003)
13. Pomplun, M., Reingold, E.M., Shen, J.: Investigating the visual span in comparative search: The effects of task difficulty and divided attention. Cognition 81(2), 57–67 (2001)
14. Sanders, M.S., McCormick, E.J.: Human factors in engineering and design, 7th edn. McGraw-Hill, New York (1993)
15. Young, K.S.: What Makes the Internet Addictive: Potential Explanations for Pathological Internet Use. In: The 105th Annual Conference of the American Psychological Association (1997)
16. Zhu, Z.H., Tsao, L.R.: The impact on *CRT display efficacy* caused by target - *background color with color*. Acta Psychologica Sinica 2, 128–134 (1994)

An Approach to Optimal Text Placement on Images

Gautam Malu and Bipin Indurkhya

International Institute of Information Technology,
Hyderabad, India
gautam.malu@research.iiit.ac.in, bipin@iiit.ac.in

Abstract. In deciding where to place a text block on an image, there are two major factors: aesthetic of the design composition, and the visual attention that the text block naturally attracts. We propose a computational model to address this problem based on the principles of visual balance and the diagonal method of placing emphasis. A between-subject study with seven participants was conducted to validate our model with subjective ratings. Eight color photographs were used to generate a set of text-overlaid images as the stimuli. Participants rated the stimuli for aesthetic appeal on a seven-point likert scale. Results show that the participants preferred text-overlaid images generated by our method of text placement over random text placement.

Keywords: Computational aesthetics, Interface design, Visual Balance, Diagonal Method.

1 Introduction

Some previous studies in the field of computational aesthetics have focussed on layouts containing text blocks and images on a solid color background [1,2], but these studies do not address the aesthetics of text-overlaid images. Sandhaus *et al* [3] have dealt with the same but on an image background. These studies are concerned with the arrangement of multiple elements on a single background. Lai *et al.* 2010 [4] have proposed a computational model for overlaying a single text element on a background image. However, their approach only works for images with homogeneous backgrounds.

In this paper, we propose a computational model for optimal text placement on images using the principles of visual balance. We also used the diagonal method to improve the overall aesthetics of text-overlaid images.

Visual balance is a key principle in the study of design and composition [5,6]. In his book, *Art and Visual Perception,* Rudolf Arnheim [7] articulates visual balance in terms of perceived *visual weights.* In recent years, there have been several studies on computational modeling of visual balance using different kinds of visual weights: for example, contrast for grayscale images [2], visual saliency [8], and color contrast for colored images [4]. It is generally agreed that in a balanced composition the visual weight is equally distributed in every directions.

D. Harris (Ed.): EPCE/HCII 2013, Part I, LNAI 8019, pp. 68–74, 2013.

The diagonal method [9] suggests that the objects an artist wants to emphasize are often found at one of the bisecting diagonals of the frame. A bisecting diagonal is one that bisects a corner angle [Figure 1]. Arnheim [7] also stated that objects when placed at the diagonals appear *visually heavier* than any other location. Following this principle, text can be emphasized if placed at one of the bisecting diagonals.

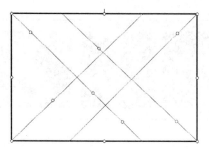

Fig. 1. Bisecting diagonals of a rectangle

2   Approach

We followed two approaches to position text on an image:
- Based on Visual Balance (VB)
- Based on Visual Balance and Diagonal Method (VB + DM)

2.1   Approach Based on Visual Balance (VB)

2.1.1   Visual Weight We defined the visual weight in terms of visual saliency values, as follows:

$$W(x, y) = \begin{cases} S(x, y), S(x, y) > T \\ 0, otherwise \end{cases} \tag{1}$$

Here, T is the threshold obtained using Otsu's method[10].

2.1.2   Saliency Algorithm We used a graph-based saliency model that also incorporates face detection along with low-level saliency features of color, intensity, and orientation [11]. Voila Jones algorithm was used for face detection [12]. This saliency algorithm does not incorporate the saliency of text; so we made a text conspicuity map by using delta functions at the center of the text block with 2D Gaussian with the standard deviation equal to the minimum of the sides of the text block. We added this conspicuity map to the existing saliency map. Now, the saliency map is the uniform linear combination of all five normalized conspicuity maps: Color(C), Intensity(I), Orientation(O), Face(F) and Text(T) [Figure 2].

$$S = \frac{1}{5}[N(\overline{C}) + N(\overline{I}) + N(\overline{O}) + N(\overline{F}) + N(\overline{T})] \tag{2}$$

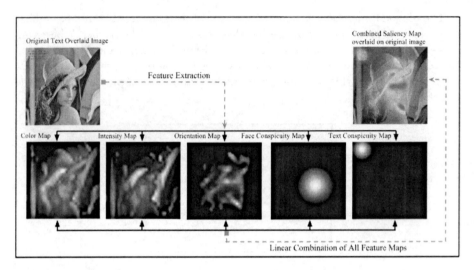

Fig. 2. Modified saliency model: An image is processed through standard color, orientation and intensity multi-scale channels [13], along with face detection channel and text detection channel. All five maps are normalized to the same range, and added with equal weights to a final saliency map.

2.1.3   Text Placement The center of mass (x_c, y_c) was computed from $W(x, y)$, as follows:

$$x_c = \frac{\sum_{j=1}^{h} \sum_{i=1}^{w} W(i,j) \times i}{\sum_{j=1}^{h} \sum_{i=1}^{w} W(i,j)} \tag{3}$$

$$y_c = \frac{\sum_{i=1}^{w} \sum_{j=1}^{h} W(i,j) \times j}{\sum_{i=1}^{w} \sum_{j=1}^{h} W(i,j)} \tag{4}$$

Here, $w=$ Width of the image $h=$ Height of the image

For a balanced composition, the center of mass should be at the minimal distance from the center of the frame. We find the quadrant in which the center of mass was located. To minimize the distance between the center of mass and the center of the image, the text block should be placed in a quadrant opposite to the quadrant in which the center of mass was located. We gridded this quadrant, with each grid cell being equal to the size of the text block. The text block was placed at each grid cell and the center of mass was calculated again. We calculated the Manhattan distance between the center of mass and the center of the image. The grid cell with the least distance was selected for placement of the text block.[Figure 3]

2.2   Visual Balance and Diagonal Method (VB+DM) Approach

This method was an extension of the visual balance method. Diagonal method states that the salient objects should be placed at one of the bisecting diagonals, but it does not specify the diagonal or the location of the diagonal. After computing the text location by VB method (section 2.1), the text block was moved perpendicularly to the bisecting diagonal of the nearest corner. [Figure 3]

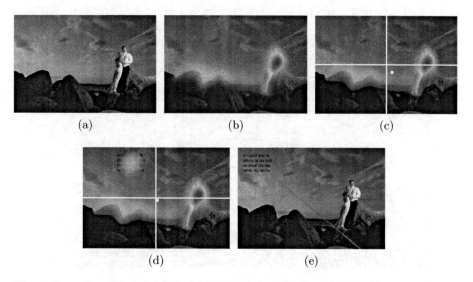

Fig. 3. Overview of the approach: (a) Input Image, (b) Saliency map, (c) Visual weights and center of visual weight (d) Text placement using VB model (red line indicates the bisecting diagonal), (e) Text placement using VB+DM method; red lines are for illustration only

3   User Evaluation

To evaluate the performance of our method, we conducted user evaluation study in which we compared both models against random placement of text blocks as well as with each other.

Seven university students (three females and four males; mean age: 23.2; age range 20 -26) took part in the evaluation study. None of the participant had any formal art education. Art naive participants were selected to avoid any possible background effect of expertise in art.

Eight colored photographs were selected from http://photo.net/. All photpgraphs were rated at least six on a seven point scale by Photo.net users. Three variants of each photograph were prepared by placing a text block on them using the following methods [Figure4]:

- random placement excluding the salient regions and a 10 pixel margin on all sides.
- VB Approach (section 2.1).
- VB+DM Approach (section 2.2).

The only difference between the variants was the location of the text. The text block was devoid of any semantic meaning, as we are not considering the semantics of the text while finding its optimal position.

Each participant was shown all three variants of each photograph simultaneously and was asked to rate each variant on a seven-point scale for aesthetic quality. The photographs and variants were presented in random order. Their responses were normalized per image per participant between 0 and 1. A total of 168 (3x8x7) responses were gathered.

(a)   (b)   (c)

Fig. 4. Examples of the stimuli used in user evaluation study (a) Random placement of text,(b) Based on VB model, (c) Based on VB+DM model

4   Results and Discussion

A one-way between-subject ANOVA test revealed that the mean aesthetic scores were significantly different for all three models at $p < 0.01$ level$[F(2,165) = 28.455, p = 0.000]$. Post-hoc comparison using Tukey HSD test indicted mean aesthetic scores for both VB model ($M = 0.3343, SD = 0.0745$) and VB+DM model($M = 0.3891, SD = 0.0771$) are significantly better than random placement ($M = 0.2741, SD = 0.0896$). The results also indicated that the mean aesthetic score for VB+DM model is significantly higher than VB model at $p < 0.01$ level.

Taken together, these results suggest that our approach using both visual balance and diagonal method performed better than random placement of text on images. It is noteworthy that the diagonal method further significantly increased the overall aesthetics of the text-overlaid image.

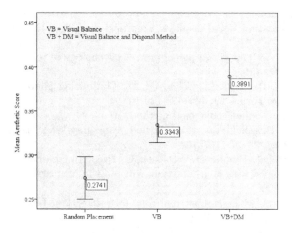

Fig. 5. Mean aesthetic scores for all three methods

5 Applications and Future Work

There are many websites that allow users to share their photographs in public domain, for example *Photo.net*.One example is a portal for online greeting cards (e-cards), where the user supplies a message which is overlaid on the selected image. Existing systems simply place the text message on the top of the image and send it as an e-card. In our model, the text color is defined by the user, but it could also be decided automatically using different color harmony schemes[14]. Different color evokes different emotional reactions [15,16]; so according to the emotional content of the message different color harmonies could be used.

References

1. Ngo, D.C.L., Teo, L.S., Byne, J.: A mathematical theory of interface aesthetics. Visual Mathematics 2 (2000)
2. Lok, S., Feiner, S., Ngai, G.: Evaluation of visual balance for automated layout (2004)
3. Sandhaus, P., Rabbath, M., Boll, S.: Employing aesthetic principles for automatic photo book layout. In: Lee, K.-T., Tsai, W.-H., Liao, H.-Y.M., Chen, T., Hsieh, J.-W., Tseng, C.-C. (eds.) MMM 2011, Part I. LNCS, vol. 6523, pp. 84–95. Springer, Heidelberg (2011)
4. Lai, C.Y., Chen, P.H., Shih, S.W., Liu, Y., Hong, J.S.: Computational models and experimental investigations of effects of balance and symmetry on the aesthetics of text-overlaid images. International Journal of Human-Computer Studies 68(1), 41–56 (2010)
5. Locher, P.J., Jan Stappers, P., Overbeeke, K.: The role of balance as an organizing design principle underlying adults' compositional strategies for creating visual displays. Acta Psychologica 99(2), 141–161 (1998)

6. Locher, P., Cornelis, E., Wagemans, J., Stappers, P.: Artists' use of compositional balance for creating visual displays. Empirical Studies of the Arts 19(2), 213–228 (2001)
7. Arnheim, R.: Art and visual perception: A psychology of the creative eye. Univ of California Press (1954)
8. Liu, L., Chen, R., Wolf, L., Cohen-Or, D.: Optimizing photo composition. Computer Graphics Forum 29, 469–478 (2010)
9. Westhoff, E.: Westhoff's diagonal method
10. Otsu, N.: A threshold selection method from gray-level histograms. Automatica 11(285-296), 23–27 (1975)
11. Cerf, M., Harel, J., Einhäuser, W., Koch, C.: Predicting human gaze using low-level saliency combined with face detection. Advances in Neural Information Processing Systems 20 (2008)
12. Viola, P., Jones, M.J.: Robust real-time face detection. International Journal of Computer Vision 57(2), 137–154 (2004)
13. Itti, L., Koch, C., Niebur, E.: A model of saliency-based visual attention for rapid scene analysis. IEEE Transactions on Pattern Analysis and Machine Intelligence 20(11), 1254–1259 (1998)
14. Cohen-Or, D., Sorkine, O., Gal, R., Leyvand, T., Xu, Y.Q.: Color harmonization. ACM Transactions on Graphics (TOG) 25, 624–630 (2006)
15. Valdez, P., Mehrabian, A.: Effects of color on emotions. Journal of Experimental Psychology: General 123(4), 394 (1994)
16. Kaya, N., Epps, H.H.: Relationship between color and emotion: a study of college students. College Student Journal 38, 396–405 (2004)

Visuospatial Processing and Learning Effects in Virtual Reality Based Mental Rotation and Navigational Tasks

Thomas D. Parsons[1], Christopher G. Courtney[2], Michael E. Dawson[2], Albert A. Rizzo[2], and Brian J. Arizmendi[2]

University of North Texas, Denton, Texas
University of Southern California, Los Angeles, California
Thomas.Parsons@unt.edu

Abstract. Visuospatial function and performance in interactions between humans and computers involve the human identification and manipulation of computer generated stimuli and their location. The impact of learning on mental rotation has been demonstrated in studies relating everyday spatial activities and spatial abilities. An aspect of visuospatial learning in virtual environments that has not been widely studied is the impact of threat on learning in a navigational task. In fact, to our knowledge, the combined assessment of learning during mental rotation trials and learning in an ecologically valid virtual reality-based navigational environment (that has both high and low threat zones) has not been adequately studied. Results followed expectation: 1) learning occurred in the virtual reality based mental rotation test. Although there was a relation between route learning and practice, a primacy effect was observed as participants performed more poorly when going from the first zone to the last.

Keywords: Visuospatial Processing, Learning, Virtual Reality, Mental Rotation: Navigation.

1   Introduction

Visuospatial function and performance in interactions between humans and computers involve the human identification and manipulation of computer generated stimuli and their location. A number of neuropsychological studies have found that visuospatial tasks activate different cortical areas such as the Broadmann area V5, superior parietal lobule, parieto-occipital junction and premotor areas [1]. One measure of visuospatial processing in the human-computer-interaction literature is performance on virtual reality based mental rotation [2], which can be enhanced through practice [3]. The impact of learning on mental rotation has been demonstrated in studies relating everyday spatial activities and spatial abilities. Newcombe, Bandura, and Taylor [4] found a substantial positive relationship between a visuospatial relations test and a number of daily spatial activities. Quaiser-Pohl and Lehmann [5] found significant relationships among visually mediated sport activities, computer activities, and mental rotation. Quaiser-Pohl et al [6]

D. Harris (Ed.): EPCE/HCII 2013, Part I, LNAI 8019, pp. 75–83, 2013.

also found a relationship of action-and-simulation-playing with MRT performance. These studies point to the malleability of visuospatial abilities and their relation to both experimental practice and everyday (non-laboratory) learning.

1.1   Virtual Reality Based Navigation

Assessment of navigation-based learning and memory has been of interest to neuropsychologists for many years and has been broadly studied over the past four decades by researchers concerned with the neurobiological bases of learning and memory [7]. A great deal of this research has focused on assessing the navigation performance of rats and mice in the Morris water navigation task (MWT; [8], [9]). While immersed in the MWT animals are trained to locate a hidden escape platform submerged in a circular pool of opaque water. A virtual reality version of the Morris water task (VMWT) has been developed for assessment of human navigational ability [10-12]. Of note, the VMWT has proven useful in studying spatial learning theories [11], [12]. Virtual reality based navigation has been suggested as representative of real-world functioning [13-15]. Navigation, like mental rotation, has been shown to be impacted by learning. Walker and Lindsay [16] assessed the visuospatial domain through the use of virtual reality based navigation with a virtual auditory display—finding an overall improvement in performance from one navigation map to the next. This learning or practice effect mimics the sort of learning effects found in mental rotation performance.

1.2   Impact of Threat on Cognitive Performance within Virtual Environments

An aspect of visuospatial learning in virtual environments that has not been widely studied is the impact of threat on learning in a navigational task. Stress related responses to threat are important because associations have been found among increased stress, cortisol, and poor learning/memory in both rodents [17] and humans [18]. When a user is immersed in a virtual environment, they can be systematically exposed to specific feared stimuli within a contextually relevant setting [19], [20]. Further, virtual reality environments allow for optimal arousal identification and classification [21]. This modality of virtual reality exposure comports well with the emotion-processing model, which holds that the fear network must be activated through confrontation with threatening stimuli and that new, incompatible information must be added into the emotional network [22], [23].

1.3   Research Aims

To our knowledge, the combined assessment of learning during mental rotation trials and learning in an ecologically valid virtual reality-based navigational environment (that has both high and low threat zones) has not been adequately studied. Our aims were to 1) attempt to replicate prior findings that learning occurs in a virtual reality based mental rotation test; 2) assess whether navigational learning occurred in a virtual simulation of a Middle Eastern city; and 3) assess the impact of threatening stimuli presented while subjects navigated a three dimensional virtual environment.

2   Methods

2.1   Participants

Subjects included 49 undergraduate students (18 males and 31 females) between the ages of 18 and 25 took part in the University of Southern California's Institutional Review Board approved study. Strict exclusion criteria were enforced so as to minimize the possible confounding effects of additional factors known to adversely impact a person's ability to process information, including psychiatric (e.g., mental retardation, psychotic disorders, diagnosed learning disabilities, attention-deficit/hyperactivity disorder, and bipolar disorders, as well as substance-related disorders within 2 years of evaluation) and neurologic (e.g., seizure disorders, closed head injuries with loss of consciousness greater than 15 minutes, and neoplastic diseases) conditions.

2.2   Procedure

Virtual reality spatial rotation: After informed consent was obtained, basic demographic information, computer experience and usage, and spatial activities history were recorded. Next, a previously validated (see Parsons et al., 2004 [2]) neuropsychological measure of virtual reality spatial rotation (VRSR) was used. The VRSR assessment and training system was designed to present a target stimulus (TS) that consists of a specific configuration of 3D blocks within a virtual environment. The stimuli appear as "hologram-like" three-dimensional objects floating above the projection screen (see Figure 1).

Fig. 1. Virtual reality spatial rotation

After presentation of TS, the participant is presented with the same set of blocks (working stimuli; WS) that needs to be rotated to the orientation of the target and then superimposed within it. The participant manipulates the WS by grasping and moving a sphere shaped "cyberprop" which contains a tracking device. The motion of the sphere is imparted upon the WS. Upon successful superimposition of the WS and TS a "correct" feedback tone is presented and the next trial begins. The new WS appears attached to the sphere (user's hand), and a new TS appears. In this mode of interaction, users do not need to press any buttons or select objects. The WS simply appears attached to the sphere for users to manipulate [2].

Virtual Reality Navigation Task: The virtual navigation task utilized herein was that of a virtual Middle Eastern city, which included a route-learning and navigation simulation to assess landmark and route knowledge of the newly experienced VE. Participants were led along a predefined path through a virtual Middle Eastern city by a group of virtual military service personnel serving as guides. The guides led participants through six zones alternating between high and low environmental threat levels. During the high threat zones, participants experienced an ambush situation in which bombs, gunfire, screams and other visual and auditory forms of threat were present, whereas none of these stimuli were presented in the low threat zones. Upon reaching the end of this initial tour through the city, participants were instructed to navigate back to the starting point following the same path taken during the initial tour. Participants were to pass through each zone in reverse order until reaching the original starting point. If the participant strayed too far from the path, which was quantified as the distance it would take to walk for 10 seconds in a perpendicular direction from the original path, an arrow appeared in the corner of the screen that assisted the participant in finding his or her way back to the original path. During the navigation task, there were no longer any threatening stimuli presented in the high threat zones. The navigation task ended when the participant crossed the zone 1 marker.

The virtual environment depicting an Iraqi city was presented to participants with use of an eMagin Z800 head mounted display complete with head tracking capabilities to allow the participant to explore the environment freely. The virtual environment was created using graphic assets from the Virtual Reality Cognitive Performance Assessment Test [24], [25], using the Gamebryo graphics engine to create the environment. A tactile transducer floor was utilized to enhance the ecological validity of the VE by making explosions and other high threat stimuli feel more lifelike [26]. Auditory stimuli were presented with a Logitech surround sound system. Participants experienced the VE while residing in an acoustic dampening chamber, which had the added benefit of creating a dark environment to remove any peripheral visual stimuli that were not associated with the VE, resulting in increased immersive qualities of the simulation.

Fig. 2. Examples of high (left) and low (right) threat zones

3   Results

As expected, learning occurred in the virtual reality based mental rotation test. There was a significant learning curve with an attendant difference in performance from Trial 1 to Trial 24 (t=5.27; p<.01). Responses elicited by the variations in threat were

Table 1. Descriptives for Virtual reality navigation task

	Minimum	Maximum	Mean	SD
Seconds in Zones				
High Threat				
Zone 1	53.01	186.65	71.48	25.28
Zone 2	12.56	186.71	76.67	24.90
Zone 3	53.59	147.85	80.82	23.52
Low Threat				
Zone 1	55.54	111.45	64.30	11.04
Zone 2	42.29	138.18	75.42	16.99
Zone 3	21.30	183.10	67.74	23.97
Route Deviations				
High Threat				
Zone 1	.24	97.73	31.98	23.16
Zone 2	.22	410.77	57.31	80.02
Zone 3	1.43	358.14	71.8830	80.68
Low Threat				
Zone 1	.25	204.17	32.92	32.49
Zone 2	.17	869.85	71.90	137.21
Zone 3	.14	485.34	58.99	91.86
#Arrow Prompts				
High Threat				
Zone 1	0.00	42.00	10.87	11.68
Zone 2	0.00	35.00	8.89	8.97
Zone 3	0.00	100.00	20.85	23.56
Low Threat				
Zone 1	0.00	71.00	7.44	13.72
Zone 2	0.00	56.00	15.91	14.93
Zone 3	0.00	74.00	12.93	21.41

used to predict an outcome measure related to participants' performance navigating along the newly learned route in the novel virtual Middle Eastern city. Specifically, we looked at: 1) Time in zones; 2) Number of route deviations; and 3) Number of computer-generated prompts (arrows) to reorient the user (see Table 1).

Although there was a relation between route learning and practice, a primacy effect was observed as participants performed more poorly when going from the first zone to the last:

1. Time in Zones: comparing the first and last zone (Mean = 13.26; Standard Deviation = 17.61; Standard Error of the Mean = 2.51; t=4.36; p<.01)
2. Route Deviations (Mean = 38.95; Standard Deviation =93.18; Standard Error of the Mean = 13.59; t=2.87; p<.01)
3. Computer Reorientations (Mean = 13.40; Standard Deviation = 31.31; Standard Error of the Mean = 4.47; t=2.98; p<.01).
4. The impact of threat level on learning was most notable for its impact on Time in Zones: This was evidenced by the fact that subjects had decreased learning in the high threat zones (Mean = 21507; Standard Deviation = 59476; Standard Error of the Mean = 8496; t= 2.53; p<.01).

4   Discussion

A primary focus of this study was upon visuospatial function and performance in interactions between humans and computers that involve the human identification and manipulation of computer generated stimuli and their location. Our goal was to combine assessment of learning during mental rotation trials and learning in an ecologically valid virtual reality-based navigational environment (that has both high and low threat zones).

We were able to replicate prior findings that learning occurs in a virtual reality based mental rotation test. A number of researchers have found that repeat exposures to even a two-dimensional test leads to a rather marked increase in performance [27], [28], [29]. [30]. The learning effects have practical and theoretical implications. The practical aspect, in terms of experimental design, is best illustrated by reference to Hampson's observation that the expected effect of period phase on spatial performance did not materialize in a within-subject design, as opposed to a between subjects design [29]. Hampson attributed this to the learning effects for tasks and this concern can be extended to the MRT as well. It should be pointed out that the extreme responsiveness of MRT performance to learning contrasts sharply to some other behaviors in which sex differences between males and females have been found, such as a fine motor task. No gender differences were found for the VRSR. From our theoretical perspective, VRSR stimuli represent an increase in the complexity of a stimulus (from 2D to 3D) and results in an increase in the cognitive load (working memory) of the task. We consider our data on a perceptual continuum with stimuli and tasks increasing in complexity to match "spatial conditions." As a result, working memory load seems to increase steadily with stimulus complexity, due to task demands. Therefore we assert that the relation between stimulus complexity and task demand reflects a functional relationship between stimulus complexity and the load of working memory for these stimuli. We argue that stimulus complexity provides a parsimonious theoretical framework for understanding the differences between these tasks with full realization that interpretations are variegated by one's working heuristics.

Although there was a relation between route learning and practice, a primacy effect was observed as participants performed more poorly when going from the first zone to the last; and the impact of threat level on learning was most notable for its impact on Time in Zones. These findings are consistent with findings that emphasize that stress related responses to threat are important because associations have been found among increased stress, cortisol, and poor learning/memory in both rodents [17] and humans [18] can be well expressed in a virtual environment with varying levels of threat. Given the fact that when a user is immersed in a virtual environment, they can be systematically exposed to specific feared stimuli within a contextually relevant setting [19], [20].

In sum, results followed expectation: 1) learning occurred in the virtual reality based mental rotation test. Although there was a relation between route learning and practice, a primacy effect was observed as participants performed more poorly when going from the first zone to the last.

References

1. Strauss, E., Sherman, E., Spreen, O.: A Compendium of Neuropsychological Tests: administration, norms and commentary, 3rd edn. Oxford University Press, New York (2006)
2. Parsons, T.D., Larson, P., Buckwalter, J.G., Rizzo, A.A.: Sex Differences in Mental Rotation and Virtual Reality Spatial Rotation. Neuropsychologia 42(4), 555–562 (2004)
3. Feng, J., Spence, I., Pratt, J.: Playing an action video game reduces gender differences in spatial cognition. Psychological Science 18, 850–855 (2007)
4. Newcombe, N., Bandura, M.M., Taylor, D.G.: Sex differences in spatial ability and spatial activities. Sex Roles 9, 530–539 (1983)
5. Quaiser-Pohl, C., Lehmann, W.: Girls' spatial abilities: Charting the contributions of experience and attitudes in different academic groups. British Journal of Educational Psychology 72, 245–260 (2002)
6. Quaiser-Pohl, C., Geiser, C., Lehmann, W.: The relationship between computer-game preference, gender, and mental-rotation ability. Personality and Individual Differences 40, 609–619 (2006)
7. D'Hooge, R., De Deyn, P.P.: Applications of the Morris water maze in the study of learning and memory. Brain Res. Brain Res. Rev. 36(1), 60–90 (2001)
8. Morris, R.G.M.: Spatial localization does not require the presence of local cues. Learning and Motivation 2, 239–260 (1981)
9. Morris, R.G., Garrud, P., Rawlins, J.N., O'Keefe, J.: Place navigation impaired in rats with hippocampal lesions. Nature 297, 681–683 (1982)
10. Astur, R.S., Ortiz, M.L., Sutherland, R.J.: A characterization of performance by men and women in a virtual Morris water task: a large and reliable sex difference. Behav. Brain. Res. 93, 185–190 (1998)
11. Hamilton, D.A., Sutherland, R.J.: Blocking in human place learning: evidence from virtual navigation. Psychobiology 27, 453–461 (1999)

12. Hamilton, D.A., Driscoll, I., Sutherland, R.J.: Human place learning in a virtual Morris water task: some important constraints on the flexibility of place navigation. Behav. Brain Res. 129, 159–170 (2002)
13. Nadolne, M.J., Stringer, A.Y.: Ecologic validity in neuropsychological assessment: Prediction of wayfinding. Journal of International Neuropsychological Society 7, 675–682 (2000)
14. Waller, D., Hunt, E., Knapp, D.: The transfer of spatial knowledge in virtual environment training. Presence: Teleoperators and Virtual Environments 7(2), 129–143 (1998)
15. Parsons, T.D.: Neuropsychological Assessment using Virtual Environments: Enhanced Assessment Technology for Improved Ecological Validity. In: Brahnam, S. (ed.) Advanced Computational Intelligence Paradigms in Healthcare: Virtual Reality in Psychotherapy, Rehabilitation, and Assessment, pp. 271–289. Springer, Germany (2011)
16. Walker, B., Lindsay, J.: Navigation Performance With a Virtual Auditory Display: Effects of Beacon Sound, Capture Radius, and Practice. Human Factors 48, 265–278 (2012)
17. Shors, T.J., Dryver, E.: Stress impedes exploration and the acquisition of spatial information in the eight-arm radial maze. Psychobiology 20, 247–253 (1992)
18. Lupien, S.J., de Leon, M., de Santi, S., Convit, A., Tarshish, C., Nair, N.P., Thakur, M., McEwen, B.S., Hauger, R.L., Meaney, M.J.: Cortisollevels during human aging predict hippocampal atrophy and memory deficits. Nat. Neurosci. 1, 69–73 (1998)
19. Parsons, T.D., Rizzo, A.A.: Affective Outcomes of Virtual Reality Exposure Therapy for Anxiety and Specific Phobias: A Meta-Analysis. Journal of Behavior Therapy and Experimental Psychiatry 39, 250–261 (2008)
20. Rizzo, A.A., Pair, J., Graap, K., Treskunov, A., Parsons, T.D.: User-Centered Design Driven Development of a VR Therapy Application for Iraq War Combat-Related Post Traumatic Stress Disorder. In: Proceedings of the 2006 International Conference on Disability, Virtual Reality and Associated Technology, pp. 113–122 (2006)
21. Wu, D., Courtney, C., Lance, B., Narayanan, S.S., Dawson, M., Oie, K., Parsons, T.D.: Optimal Arousal Identification and Classification for Affective Computing: Virtual Reality Stroop Task. IEEE Transactions on Affective Computing 1, 109–118 (2010)
22. Macedonio, M., Parsons, T.D., Rizzo, A.A.: Immersiveness and Physiological Arousal within Panoramic Video-based Virtual Reality. Cyberpsychology and Behavior 10, 508–516 (2007)
23. Courtney, C.G., Dawson, M.E., Schell, A.M., Iyer, A., Parsons, T.D.: Better than the real thing: Eliciting fear with moving and static computer-generated stimuli. International Journal of Psyhophysiology 78, 107–114 (2010)
24. Parsons, T.D., Rizzo, A.A.: Initial Validation of a Virtual Environment for Assessment of Memory Functioning: Virtual Reality Cognitive Performance Assessment Test. Cyberpsychology and Behavior 11, 17–25 (2008)
25. Parsons, T.D., Cosand, L., Courtney, C., Iyer, A., Rizzo, A.A.: Neurocognitive Workload Assessment Using the Virtual Reality Cognitive Performance Assessment Test. In: Harris, D. (ed.) EPCE 2009. LNCS (LNAI), vol. 5639, pp. 243–252. Springer, Heidelberg (2009)
26. Parsons, T.D., Rizzo, A.A., Courtney, C., Dawson, M.: Psychophysiology to Assess Impact of Varying Levels of Simulation Fidelity in a Threat Environment. Advances in Human-Computer Interaction 5, 1–9 (2012)
27. Casey, M.B., Brabeck, M.M.: Exceptions to the male advantage on a spatial task: Family handedness and college major as factors identifying women who excel. Neuropsychologia 27, 689–696 (1989)

28. Baenninger, M., Newcombe, N.: The role of experience in spatial test performance: A meta-analysis. Sex Roles 20, 327–344 (1989)
29. Hampson, E.: Variations in sex-related cognitive abilities across the menstrual cycle. Brain and Cognition 14, 26–43 (1990)
30. Kail, R.: The impact of extended practice on rate of mental rotation. Journal of Experimental Child Psychology 42, 378–391 (1986)

Error Analysis for Tablet User Interface Transfers Based on Operational Knowledge Interference

Kazutoyo Takata[1,2], Koji Morikawa[2], and Tsukasa Hirashima[1]

[1] Department of Information Engineering, Hiroshima University,
1-4-1 Kagamiyama, Higashihiroshima-shi, Hiroshima 739-8527, Japan
[2] Advanced Technology Research Laboratory, Panasonic Corporation,
3-4 Hikaridai, Seika-cho, Soraku-gun, Kyoto 619-0237, Japan
{takata,tsukasa}@lel.hiroshima-u.ac.jp,
{takata.kazutoyo,morikawa.koji}@jp.panasonic.com

Abstract. Operational errors were collected and analyzed with regard to the use of different tablet UIs. The effects of previous operational knowledge upon the use of new devices were clarified through user experiments in which forty subjects participated. A comparison was made of three different types of tablet UIs that were equipped with three different operating systems: iOS 5, Windows 8 (release preview), and Windows 7. The results showed the user's dependence upon previous operational knowledge when using a new tablet PC. This dependency was demonstrated both in the ratio of the users' accurate operation, and in their process of exploring an unknown operation.

Keywords: knowledge transfer, tablet PC, mental model, error analysis, gesture.

1   Introduction

In recent years tablet PCs have rapidly achieved widespread use, providing a variety of applications, such as music players, email, maps, and camera. To maximize the utility of these applications, users must know how to select a desired application and execute the related tasks, as well as know how to switch to other applications. One of the problems of tablet PCs is that they have different touch or gesture operations because each one is equipped with its own operating system (OS), whose operations are designed based on their different policies. To take one example, iOS features the metaphor of real world interaction in the elements of its gesture design, such as flipping a sheet of paper [1]. Windows 8, on the other hand, focuses on the redesign of optimal touch operation, as shown in features such as its dynamic menu bar, which is based on the idea that simple physical interactions alone are not sufficient to realize flexible operations [2].

Users often make mistakes with new tablet PCs because they tend to operate them based on their previous experience of similar devices [3]. Therefore, from the perspective of Human–Computer Interaction (HCI) it is important to analyze such common operational errors [4], identify the effects of previous experience, and apply the results to the operations of new tablet PCs.

D. Harris (Ed.): EPCE/HCII 2013, Part I, LNAI 8019, pp. 84–93, 2013.

A number of experimental research efforts on tablet PCs have focused upon the domain of HCI. Li et al. [4] reported that the adoption of buttons that can be pressed by the non-writing hand offers the fastest performance with a pen tablet interface. Bragdon et al. [5] presented bezel-initiated gestures, which offered the fastest performance with smart phones, and mark-based gestures, which were the most accurate. These studies provide a framework of general knowledge for the design of touch operation, but they do not consider the differences in knowledge or experience among users. As regards the effects of previous knowledge upon the operation of a new device, we have conducted several previous user tests that involved switching to a new DVD recorder. Our results showed that there are specific operational error patterns that depend upon the user's previous experience using DVD recorders of individual manufacturers [6][7]. The results also indicated that operational errors can be used for estimating user intention and for generating adaptive help.

A similar phenomenon of a prior-knowledge effect is common in the operational errors users make when using a new tablet PC, because the touch operations are designed with variations in the origin, direction, and number of fingers used. In our DVD recorder experiments, we observed that this led to users making multiple guesses as to how they would operate a new device. The aim of this study is to clarify the effects of previous knowledge during the use of a new tablet PC, and analyze the resulting error patterns in order to provide improved usability via adaptive operational support. The experimental results showed that dependency upon previous knowledge could be observed both in the users' ratios of accurate operation, and in their process of exploring unknown operations.

2   Operation Model for Tablet PCs

2.1   Definition of Operation Model

We differentiate a tablet PC's model of operation in terms of two perspectives: the operation model of the user, and the operation model of the device. The operation model of the user is a set of rules that the user knows about how the device works, in terms of its internal structure and processes [9]. The operation model of the device is a set of rules about the device-side functions, and how they are programmed to perform in response to the user's operation. In this paper, we refer to the operation model of the user as the "operation model," and the operation model of the device as the "device model." The influence of the operation model upon a user using a new device is shown in Figure 1.

As shown in the figure, user A has an operation model A, and user B has an operation model B, which is different from operation model A. When users A and B begin to use a new device C, each user operates it based upon the operation model they already know (in this case, as model A and model B, respectively). If their previously known operation model does not enable them to correctly operate device model C, the device interprets operation A and/or operation B as an error operation. In general, operation A is not always equivalent to operation B because they are based

upon
different operation models.

In addition, two processes take place before a function is executed. The first process is the user's internal prediction of the procedure, based upon that individual's operation model. The second is an action process, based upon looking at the device's surface design. According to this model, an error operation occurs when the operation model and device model are not in agreement, or when the user cannot find the appropriate button after scrutinizing the surface design of the new device.

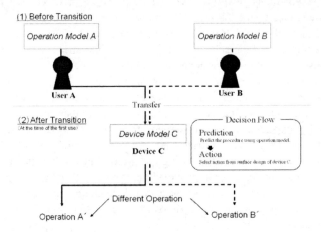

Fig. 1. Interpretation of user's operation according to the device model

2.2 Operation Model of a Tablet PC

A tablet PC is characterized by a flat menu structure and touch operation. Application icons are evenly arranged on the home screen, and the user touches the desired application icon in order to execute the application. Figure 2 shows a conceptual diagram of the selection of an application on a tablet PC. The application icons are displayed on the home screen, and the selected application occupies the entire screen. This simple procedure of application selection dramatically improved the usability of the tablet as compared with the conventional mobile phone, PC, and DVD recorder, which had complicated menu structures. However, switching applications still presented a difficulty, because one application occupies the entire screen, and all the buttons on the screen are intended for the current application.

A conceptual diagram of the transition between applications is shown in Figure 3. As shown in the figure, the screen is used to display home, each application, and the settings of the OS. The transitions between screens are usually operated using a physical button that is outside the tablet screen. However, every OS provides a touch operation for switching between screens by bypassing the home screen without pressing the physical button. In summary, the operation of tablet PCs can be separated into four categories: (i) transitions between home and applications, (ii) transitions between applications, (iii) operations in a single application, and (iv) transitions between

OS settings and home/applications. To examine the effects of previous experience of an operation model, we prepared an operational test that included the operational categories (i), (ii), and (iii) shown in Figure 3. A comparison of user manuals of tablet PCs showed that there are often operational differences in categories (i) and (ii), and therefore, error analysis could be profitably performed for these categories by matching an operation model and a device model.

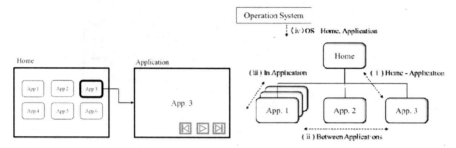

Fig. 2. Screen usage in a tablet PC   **Fig. 3.** Application transitions in a tablet PC

3   Experiment

3.1   Purpose

The purpose of this experiment was to verify the effects of the user's prior operational knowledge when using a new tablet PC.

We selected iOS and Windows 8 tablet PCs for the experiment, based on their availability at the time of this experiment (August 2012). The models of the devices for switching applications were different from each other. Figure 4 shows a conceptual diagram of the application switching method of the two OSs. The menu buttons explicitly displayed in the screen are only for inside applications, and no information about the switching application is displayed. The switching operations were called a "four-finger pinch" gesture, whose design imitates the real-world movement used in turning up a sheet of paper. On the other hand, no menu buttons for the inside applications and switching application are displayed in Windows 8, as the interactive menu bars are hidden outside the screen (bezel gesture). Hidden menu bars can be displayed by sliding the right bezel to the inside of the screen, and tapping one of the icons, just as one does on a conventional PC.

We therefore set the switching control shown in Figure 3 as the experimental task, because the method of switching between applications was different for each OS. In order to compare the original gesture operation for each OS, users were not permitted to use the physical home button installed on the tablet body. Furthermore, thirteen common applications were arranged in the same order on the home screen, in order to eliminate any possible effect of the arrangement of the application icons.

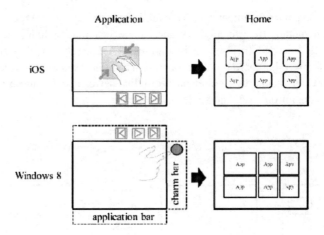

Fig. 4. Switching operations in iOS 5 and Windows 8

3.2   The nside the nsl of ed by , ng Applicationtion is Displayede Operation Model Point of View and from the Decation, (ii) transitiMethod

Subjects. Forty subjects participated in the experiments, all of them were university students. The experiments were performed from August 16 to November 5, 2012. Each participant provided a written informed consent.

Apparatus. Three different types of tablet PCs were used: Apple iPad running iOS 5.1 (iOS), Acer ICONIA TAB running Windows 8 release preview (win8), and Acer ICONIA TAB running Windows 7 (win7). The presentation of tasks was performed by a PC monitor. The experimenter stood behind the subjects in order to execute the task presentation and operation of the test apparatus.

Procedure. The experiment was conducted in three steps: learning, confirmation, and testing. First, the subjects were divided into four groups, as listed in Table 1. In the learning step, subjects learned the operation method of one tablet PC of these three OSs. The same testing task was then provided on a new tablet PC. Groups G3 and G4 were a control group that learned conventional Windows 7, whose operation is almost the same as that of a PC mouse. The experiment time was a maximum of 45 min.

Table 1. Instruction Group

Group	Number	Learning	Testing
G1	10	iOS	win8
G2	10	win8	iOS
G3	10	win7	win8
G4	10	win7	iOS

Step1: Learning (10 min). The subject learned the tablet operation in an OS, which is specified in the 'Learning' column in Table 1. Since the task sheet of this step contains a combination of the task statement and correct operation, the subject can learn how to operate the tablet for each task. At the same time, the operation model could

be acquired through this learning step. Seven learning tasks (Q1–Q7) were prepared, as shown in Table 2, which covered the transitions (i–iv) shown in Figure 3. An example of a task sheet that was used for learning win8 is shown in Figure 5. The answer operation was designated by the drawing.

Table 2. The learning tasks

Learning and testing tasks			Testing tasks		
	Task Statement	Class		Task Statement	Class
Q1	Start Internet Explorer (IE).	(i)	Q8	Select music from the application list.	(i)
Q2	Back to the home screen.	(i)	Q9	Play the music.	(iii)
Q3	Start music.	(i)	Q10	Stop the music.	(iii)
Q4	Change from music to IE.	(ii)	Q11	Go back to the home screen	(i)
Q5	Open a tab on IE.	(iii)	Q12	Start map.	(i)
Q6	Back to the home screen.	(i)	Q13	Change a display to an aerial photograph.	(iii)
Q7	Display an application list.	(iv)	Q14	Change from map to music.	(ii)
			Q15	Display an application list.	(iv)

Step2: Confirmation (5 min). A confirmation test was conducted to determine whether the operations in step 1 had been performed correctly. Error operations were learned again until all tasks were performed correctly. We assumed that the users acquired an understanding of the operation model during Steps 1 and 2.

Step3: Testing (maximum 30 min). Each group performed an experiment using a different tablet (the column 'Testing' in Table 1). Fifteen operational tasks were prepared, as shown in Table 2. The testing tasks Q8–Q15 shown in Table 2 were the same kind of tasks as tasks Q1–Q7. These tasks were added in order be able to analyze the user's process of operation discovery via exploratory interaction. The maximum time for one task was set at 2 min, and the subject could give up the search at any time. During the testing step, the users' operation sequences were recorded by a video camera, and the number and types of operations they performed were analyzed.

3.3 Results

Accuracy Rates for All Tasks. The mean accuracy rates for all tasks for all subjects are shown in Figure 6. The arrows indicate the users' movement from the learning tablet to the testing tablet, while the percentages indicate the accuracy rate. As can be seen in the figure, the accuracy rate of each group was more than 56%. This rate includes the tasks that were unknown to the subjects, and thus shows that the interface of each tablet was well designed for beginners. As regards the differences in accuracy, the rates for groups that tested Windows 8 (G1:85%, G3:86%) were approximately 20% higher than those for groups that tested iOS (G2:60%, G4:56%). These results show that Windows 8 makes it easier to discover the correct operation via exploratory interaction.

Accuracy Rates for Each Task. The mean accuracy rates for each task for all subjects are shown in Figure 8. The tasks that received ratios of less than 30%, which are grayed out in Figure 8, were Q2, Q4, Q6, Q7, Q11, Q14, and Q15, all of which were related to application switching. The remaining tasks involved application selection or operation (classes (i) and (iii) in Tables 2 and 3). These results show that operation error tends to occur most in the switching between applications. Moreover, the rates of these tasks differed, depending upon the tablet being used. For example, in Q4, even though G1 and G3, which operated win8, showed a rate of 80%, G2 and G4, which operated iOS, showed low rates of 20% and 0%, respectively. These results suggest that the design concept of each OS influenced its usability in a user's initial use of a new tablet PC.

Q4 Change from music to Internet Explorer.
A.4 Swipe from the left frame.

Fig. 5. Example of a task sheet

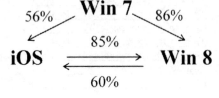

Fig. 6. Accuracy ratio for all tasks

The Influence of Previous Knowledge. On all 15 tasks, all users made their first operational error on Q2. Detailed analysis was then performed on the operational records for Q2 ("Return to home screen"), in which we expected to observe the effects of learned knowledge. The task of returning to the home screen is difficult because the screen is occupied by the current application, and no information is displayed for application switching or returning to the home screen.

Table 3. Accuracy ratio for each task

	G1:iOS→win8	G2:win8→iOS	G3:win7→win8	G4:win7→iOS
Q1	100	100	100	100
Q2	60	0	50	10
Q3	100	100	100	100
Q4	80	20	80	0
Q5	100	100	90	100
Q6	70	20	90	10
Q7	10	20	30	0
Q8	100	100	100	100
Q9	100	100	100	100
Q10	100	100	90	100
Q11	100	20	90	10
Q12	100	100	100	100
Q13	100	80	100	90
Q14	100	20	100	20
Q15	50	20	70	0
Q1-15	85	60	86	56

The frequencies and ratios in the operational records for Q2 are shown in Figure 7(a). The operational records included the number of fingers used, the starting point gesture on the screen, and the type of action used (e.g., tap, swipe, pinch). The records were classified into three categories: (a) the bezel gesture, as a starting point gesture on the outer frame, which was peculiar to Windows 8 (bezel); (b) the use of four fingers, which was peculiar to iOS (four-finger); and (c) other operations (other). The ratio for the bezel gesture was 45% in G2, who learned using Windows 8, a ratio that was more than 1.5 times those of the other groups (19–31%). The ratio for the four-finger gesture was 20% in G1, who learned using iOS, whereas the ratio was 0% in the other groups who did not learn using iOS. These results show that the user's previous knowledge interferes with his initial operation of a new tablet PC.

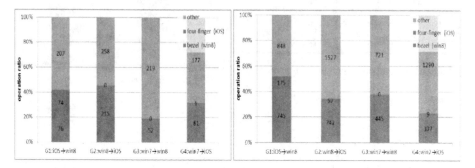

(a) Q2 "Move from application to home"   (b) Q1-Q15

Fig. 5. Frequencies and ratios for operations

The frequencies and ratios in the operational records for all tasks are shown in Figure 7(b). Compared with Q2, the ratio of bezel operation increased from 20% to 40% in G1 and G3. On the other hand, the four-finger operation hardly changed, showing a movement from 0% to 3% in G2 and G4. These results suggest that the exploratory operation as related to the number of fingers was more difficult than the search as related to the starting point or action.

3.4   Analysis of the Error Factor

We then analyzed the factors involved in error tasks whose accuracy rates were less than 30%. Error tasks were collected for Q2, Q4 and Q7 after the same task was summarized. The correct operation of these three tasks is shown in Table 5. The boxes with bold lines show the operation of error tasks. In Q2 and Q4, the menu search tasks, such as the menu tapping of win8, had a high accuracy rate (50–80%), whereas gesture search tasks, such as the pinching and swiping of iOS had a low accuracy rate (0–20%). Similarly, on Q7, the gesture search tasks had a low rate (0–30%).

These results show that operating errors occurred during tasks that required a gesture search other than a menu search. Figure 9 shows the mean accuracy rate for tasks that required both menu search and gesture search. The accuracy rate of the menu search tasks was 95%, whereas that of the gesture search tasks was 18%. This suggests that it is difficult for users to find a new gesture even if the design of the correct gesture is based on a real world action. Gesture search was one of the factors that reduced the immediate usability of tablet PCs.

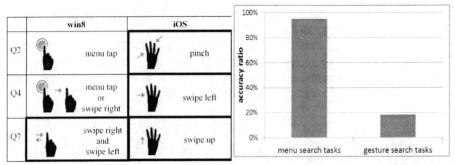

Fig. 8. Correct answer operation for error tasks.

Fig. 9. Accuracy ratios for menu search tasks and gesture search tasks.

4   Discussion

Application to Operational Support. Our first main finding is that users' previous knowledge of a tablet PC has a strong influence on their degree of operational error when first using new tablet PC, especially when switching applications. This means that it is necessary to provide optimum support according to the user's experience, in addition to improving usability by standardizing the device's interface design, to prevent operational errors. In order to realize such optimum support, estimation of a personal operation model for each user is needed. If a device has a database of the operational error pattern based on a user's previous experience, a personalized operation model can be inferred when they make certain errors (e.g., the four-finger error is presumed to be an iOS model in Q2), and adaptive support can then be offered to each user. Our second main finding is that more participants completed menu search tasks than completed gesture search tasks. This suggests that menu manipulation is easier for an initial search than a gesture operation that imitates a real world operation. For a search using a gesture operation, feedback on different search strategies (e.g., alerting the user as to the number of fingers used in iOS) becomes an effective approach to improving usability.

Scope of Observation. The observations acquired in this study are applicable to the switching of applications when users first use a new tablet, based upon our initial users test. In addition, we need to test a greater variety of users in order to verify the broader validity of our results, since we did not test users who have little experience using electronic devices, such as children or the elderly.

Restrictions on Experiment Implementation. Most tasks given in this test can be done using the physical home button attached to the tablet body, which is what users generally tend to use. Although operation of the home button is easier, the switching task is faster when it is performed using a gesture on the screen.

Future Work. Touch operation commands are made and impacted by the number of fingers used by the user, the starting point, the gesture on the screen, and the type of action being performed. However, the results of our analysis of the operation log show that subjects did not try to change the number of fingers they used. Clarifying the gesture operations that are required during search processes is still necessary in order to facilitate optimal gesture design in tablet PCs.

5 Conclusion

In this paper, we analyzed the effects of previous knowledge in relation to the factors that cause user error when users first use a new tablet PC. According to the results obtained, we found that there are several operational error patterns that depend upon the users' operation model, which is the product of their previous experience. It was found that these errors occurred most frequently in switching applications. Furthermore, an analysis of the operational records showed that the gesture search is one of the factors that reduced the initial usability of tablet PCs. It is necessary for us to gain further understanding of the user's exploration of new gesture operations in order to produce better design of the operations of tablet PCs.

References

1. Apple Inc., iOS Human Interface Guidelines – Human Interface Principles (2012), https://developer.apple.com/library/ios/#documentation/UserEx perience/Conceptual/MobileHIG/Principles/Principles.html#//ap ple_ref/doc/uid/TP40006556-CH5-SW1
2. Hofmeester, K., Wolfe, J.: Self-revealing gestures: teaching new touch interactions in Windows 8. In: CHI 2012 Extended Abstracts on Human Factors in Computing Systems, pp. 815–829 (2012)
3. Norman, D.A.: Cognitive engineering. In: Norman, D.A., Draper, S.W. (eds.) User-Centered System Design, pp. 31–61. Lawrence Erlbaum, Hillsdale (1986)
4. Fischer, G.: User modeling in human-computer interaction. User Modeling and User-Adapted Interaction 11, 65–86 (2001)
5. Li, Y., et al.: Experimental analysis of mode switching techniques in pen-based user interfaces. In: CHI 2005 Proceedings of the SIGCHI Conference on Human Factors in Computing Systems, pp. 461–470 (2005)
6. Bragdon, A., et al.: Experimental analysis of touch-screen gesture designs in mobile environments. In: CHI 2011 Proceedings of the SIGCHI Conference on Human Factors in Computing Systems, pp. 403–412 (2011)
7. Takata, K., Morikawa, K.: Transfer of operational knowledge influenced by experienced appliances. Transactions of Information Processing Society of Japan 52(4), 1475–1484 (2011)
8. Takata, K., et al.: Analysis of exploratory interaction under the conceptual instruction during finding the operation sequence of appliances. The Transactions of the Institute of Electronics, Information and Communication Engineers J95-A(1), 97–106 (2012)
9. Kieras, D.E., Bovair, S.: The role of a mental model in learning to operate a device. Cognitive Science 8, 255–273 (1984)

Multitasking: Digital Natives' Interaction with New Media

Tuba Uğraş[1] and Sevinç Gülseçen[2]

[1] Yildiz Technical University, Istanbul, Turkey
tubaugras@yahoo.com
[2] Istanbul University, Istanbul, Turkey
sevincg@yahoo.com

Abstract. We aimed to analyze multitasking behaviors of digital natives in Turkey while interacting with new media, within the scope of the following questions: What kind of multitasking behaviors do digital natives exhibit? How does being a multitasker influence digital natives' interaction with new media? We used dominant-less dominant, quantitative-qualitative sequential mixed research method. The target group is teenagers, aged from 13 to 17 as being digital natives. The sample size is 494 in the quantitative part; 10 in the qualitative part. According to the results, the rate of being a multitasker among digital natives is very high. Multitaskers think multitasking is a very natural behavior and they feel very comfortable with it. On the other hand, there are some negative issues regarding multitasking, such as losing attention.

Keywords: Digital natives, Multitasking, New media, Cognitive load, Interaction.

1   Introduction

By the pioneer developments in computer technologies, especially with the emergence of the Internet, digitalization has started in all the areas in the information age that we live in. Digital culture has become an inseparable part of the information society [1]. A new generation, who was born and has been raised in the world of such a society, appeared. There is plenty of naming for this new generation but in this study we will use Prensky's [2] term: "digital natives". He defines digital natives as "native speakers of the digital language of computers, video games and the Internet". They are the people born after 1980's and surrounded by digital media and other digital technologies.

Digital natives differ in characteristics and express their needs in ways that are different from the previous generations. As stated by Prensky [2], for example, they "like to parallel process and multi-task". Multitasking behavior is influential on individuals' lives in various extents, such as in terms of their interaction with technological tools, especially considering the information age that we live in. In fact, information and communication technologies in the world of digital natives are no more based on traditional media. Manovich [3] said that media turned into new media as a

D. Harris (Ed.): EPCE/HCII 2013, Part I, LNAI 8019, pp. 94–103, 2013.

result of enormous developments, especially in 1990's. Lister et al. [4] listed the properties of new media as digital, interactive, hypertextual, virtual, networked, and simulated. This is the media by which digital natives are surrounded.

The term multitasking originally belongs to computer sciences. It is defined as "the running of two or more programs (sets of instructions) in one computer at the same time" [5]. While the term belongs to computer sciences, however, it has been used by various disciplines other than computer sciences such as media and human sciences as well. When it comes to humans, multitasking is defined as "the ability to conduct two or more tasks at the same time both requiring attention and various advanced cognitive processes" [6].

Multitasking behavior has come into prominence in the last decades. The research done by Rideout et al. [7] shows that in the USA, multitasking proportion among youths aged 8-18 increase gradually; multitasking proportion is 16% for 1999, 26% for 2004, and 29% for 2009. They define multitasking proportion as "the proportion of media time that is spent using more than one medium concurrently". This finding is very important because it implies that the rate of multitasking behavior of young people is raising in parallel to the developments in technology. On the other hand, according to some research, doing or attempting to do more than one task at a time overloads the capacity of the human information processing system [8, 9]. Cognitive overload may be a barrier to some activities, such as learning. In this case, Hembrooke and Gay [10] say that multitasking may have a negative impact on learning due to cognitive overload. While designing human-computer interfaces, optimum use of working memory should be taken into consideration in order to balance the cognitive load [11]. Therefore, the relation between multitasking and cognitive load for digital natives has a value to be investigated within the context of human-computer interaction.

Then, it becomes more of an issue to examine on multitasking behavior of digital natives; especially in the present days when new media become dominant by the use of Web 2.0 technologies and social media in our lives, and in such a world that multitasking behavior becomes widespread. In this respect, we aimed to analyze multitasking[1] behaviors of digital natives in Turkey while interacting with new media, within the scope of the following questions: What kind of multitasking behaviors do digital natives exhibit? How does being a multitasker influence digital natives' interaction with new media? Research questions related to the former are: Do digital natives exhibit multitasking behaviors? How are multitasking behaviors of digital natives distributed with regard to age, gender, and socio-economic status (SES)? Research questions related to the latter are: Why (or not) do digital natives do more than one activity while online? How do digital natives do more than one activity while online? How do digital natives feel doing more than one activity while online?

---

[1] While multitasking is valid for any activity, here, it is addressed to new media usage, focusing on the Internet.

2   Method

In the study, we used dominant-less dominant and quantitative-qualitative sequential mixed research method. First, we conducted the less dominant, quantitative part and then the dominant, qualitative part.

2.1   Participants

The target group is teenagers, aged from 13 to 17 as being digital natives. The universe of the study is teenagers of 13-17 years old in Turkey; study universe is teenagers of 13-17 years old in Istanbul. In the quantitative part, study sample was determined by disproportional group sampling method; and stratified according to age, gender, and socio-economic status (SES). Total size of participants is 494 (age 13: 103, age 14: 101, age 15: 82, age 16: 101, and age 17: 107; females: 240 and males: 254; low-SES: 267 and high-SES: 227) [12]. In the dominant qualitative part, the focus group consists of 10 participants selected by extreme or deviant case sampling of purposive sampling methods, with regard to being a multitasker or not. We chose the participants of the qualitative part based on the findings about being a multitasker, from the first part. Half of these participants are multitaskers, and the other half are non-multitaskers. Also, we took into consideration that there were one multitasker and one non-multitasker at each age.

2.2   Design

We used descriptive model in the quantitative part; and case study model in the qualitative part.

2.3   Materials

In the quantitative part, a questionnaire was used as the data collection tool in order to determine the multitasking behaviors of digital natives as well as their demographic information [12]. In the qualitative part, focus group interviews were carried out in order to have detailed information about multitasking behaviors of digital natives, by using semi-structured interview questions.

2.4   Analysis

Findings from the quantitative part were analyzed by using percentage frequency distributions. Findings from the qualitative part were analyzed using descriptive analysis method. Before descriptive analysis, interviews were transcribed into text. Then, descriptive analysis was performed through four stages. At the first stage, a thematic framework was constructed. At the second stage, transcripts were annotated and organized for each theme. At this stage, participants were labeled with their age and multitasking behavior, such as 13-M where 13 stands for the age and M stands for being a multitasker or 13-nonM where 13 stands for the age and nonM stands for being a non-multitasker. At the third stage, findings were obtained. At the last stage, findings were discussed and interpreted.

3   Results

In order to answer research questions, data from both quantitative and qualitative parts were analyzed. The results are given below, respectively.

3.1   What Kind of Multitasking Behaviors Digital Natives Exhibit

In the quantitative part, we tried to answer the following research questions within the scope of the question of "What kind of multitasking behaviors do digital natives exhibit?":

- Do digital natives exhibit multitasking behaviors?
- How are multitasking behaviors of digital natives distributed with regard to age, gender, and socio-economic status (SES)?

Multitasking behavior of digital natives were analyzed in terms of: (1) Using more than one technological tool while online, (2) Using more than one program on computer while online. The former was asked as "Do you do more than one activity at the same time while you are online? For example watching TV, listening to music, or talking on the cell phone while searching the Web for your homework..." The latter was asked as "Do you do more than one activity on the computer at the same time while you are online? For example checking your e-mails, posting to your Facebook profile, or doing chat while searching the Web for your homework..." The purpose of emphasizing "while searching the Web for your homework" in the example given in the questions is to mention an activity that is not automatic, but requires attention. Table 1 shows the distribution of affirmative answers addressing to these cases.

Table 1. Distribution of multitasking behaviors

	f (N=494)	%
Using more than one technological tool while online (a)	388	79%
Using more than one program on computer while online (b)	412	83%
Doing both	356	72%
Doing at least one of "a" or "b"	444	90%
Doing neither	50	10%

From Table 1, we see that the rate of digital natives who use more than one technological tool while online is 79%; that of digital natives who use more than one program on computer while online is 83%; that of digital natives who behave in both ways is 72%. It can easily be seen that the rate of digital natives who behave at least one of these ways is 90%; and that of digital natives who behave in neither one of these ways is 10%.

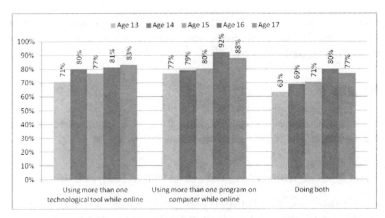

Fig. 1. Distribution of multitasking behaviors with regard to age

The distribution in Figure 1 is obtained by analyzing multitasking behavior of digital natives with regard to age.

As we see from Figure 1, the rates of multitasking behavior for each age group are almost the same and close to each other. The highest rate among digital natives who use more than one technological tool while online belongs to 17 year olds (83%). The highest rate among digital natives who use more than one program on computer while online belongs to 16 year olds (92%). The highest rate among digital natives who behave in both ways belongs also to 16 year olds (80%).

The distribution in Figure 2 is obtained by analyzing multitasking behavior of digital natives with regard to gender.

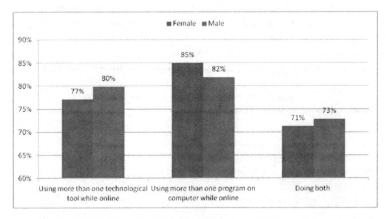

Fig. 2. Distribution of multitasking behaviors with regard to gender

As we see from Figure 2, the rates of multitasking behavior for females and males are close to each other. The rate of using more than one technological tool while online is higher among males (80%) than females (77%). The rate of using more than one program on computer while online is higher among females (85%) than males (82%). The rate of behaving in both ways is higher among males (73%) than females (71%).

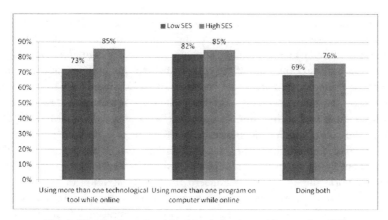

Fig. 3. Distribution of multitasking behaviors with regard to SES

The distribution in Figure 3 is obtained by analyzing multitasking behavior of digital natives with regard to SES.

As we see from Figure 3, the rates of multitasking behavior among digital natives from high-SES are higher than those from low-SES. The rate of using more than one technological tool while online is higher among high-SES (85%) than low-SES (73%). The rate of using more than one program on computer while online is higher among high-SES (85%) than low-SES (82%); but those rates are close to each other. The rate of behaving in both ways is higher among high-SES (76%) than low-SES (69%).

3.2   How Being a Multitasker Influences Digital Natives' Interaction with New Media

In the qualitative part, we tried to answer the following research questions within the scope of the question of "How does being a multitasker influence digital natives' interaction with new media?":

- Why (or not) do digital natives do more than one activity while online?
- How do digital natives do more than one activity while online?
- How do digital natives feel doing more than one activity while online?

Thematic framework was developed in parallel to these research questions, respectively: (1) Reasons for being a multitasker (or non-multitasker), (2) Multitasking style, (3) Feelings while multitasking.

The first theme is "reasons for being a multitasker (or non-multitasker)". The theme was analyzed within the scope of participants' answers to the following questions: "You reported that you (don't) use more than one technological tool while online, why?" "You reported that you (don't) use more than one program on computer while online, why?" According to the results, multitasker participants agreed that multitasking is *a natural behavior* of them. For example, the participant coded as 13-M stated "I don't do otherwise" about using more than one technological tool at the same time. Similarly, 15-M said "in general, I already behave like that" about using more than one program on computer at the same time. On the other hand, non-multitasker participants have a common feature: *not having enough opportunity to get experience* in multitasking. One of the reasons behind this is to use new media rarely or never. For example, the participant coded as 13-nonM stated "We have no computer. I don't use the Internet much." Another reason is not to have access to more than one technological tool to use simultaneously. For example, 16-nonM said "There is no TV in the room which I do my homework, there is a desktop computer only." There is another common feature of non-multitaskers: *prejudice* against possible negative effects of being a multitasker. When they think of multitasking, especially while doing homework, they assert their concern for losing attention or concentration, or wasting time; thus having lower points at school. For example, 15-nonM stated "I don't do multitasking since I think I can lose my concentration." Similarly, 14-nonM said that "I don't use the Internet. I don't have any Facebook account because I don't want to get lower points at school."

The second theme is "multitasking style". The theme was analyzed within the scope of participants' answers to the following questions: "You reported that you use more than one technological tool while online, how?" "You reported that you use more than one program on computer while online, how?" Naturally, we asked these questions only to multitasker participants. When we examine on the records for these questions, we saw that this theme should be analyzed under two conditions: (1) at least one of the tasks, such as doing homework, requires attention (2) that doesn't require much attention. Although there is no big problem with the second case to mention, the first case needs to be examined. Results show that some multitaskers have developed some strategies in order to diminish the possible negative effects. For example, 14-M stated "I don't bother, if all the programs I was using are related to my homework." about using more than one program on computer at the same time. 13-M stated "While I am doing homework, I rather listen to music." about using more than one program on computer and/or more than one technological tool at the same time. In other words, 13-M prefers such an activity that requires less attention while he is doing homework at the same time. 16-M said "While doing homework, if the other programs related to my homework are open on my computer, there is no problem. But if they are not related to my homework, then I work with them in a sequence." On the other hand, one of the multitaskers, 15-M, has trouble because of losing concentration or has some concerns about wasting time with multitasking. 15-M stated "I don't use any other technological tool while I am doing my homework since I lose my concentration. I use more than one program while online but it is such a waste time. Those times I am worrying about my school life."

The third theme is "feelings while multitasking". The theme was analyzed within the scope of participants' answers to the following questions: "How do you feel when you are using more than one technological tool while online, especially while studying?" "How do you feel when you are using more than one program on computer while online, especially while studying?" We asked these questions only to multitasker participants as well. According to the results, we saw that all the multitasker participants' views about multitasking behavior were in a positive way. For example, 17-M said "I am feeling very comfortable while doing it." 14-M said "It is funny to multi-task. Indeed, the Internet is not fast enough for me. If it would be faster multitasking would be funnier." One of them, 13-M, even said "I love to behave like that so much."

4   Discussion

The rate of multitasking behavior among digital natives in Turkey is very high. Al-though the rates of those regarding to age, gender, and SES differ, it can easily be seen that all those rates are very high as well. In other words, it is common among digital natives to use more than one technological tool or more than one program on computer simultaneously while online. Similarly, as a result of their study with people aged from 14 to 65+ in Britain, Helsper and Enyon [13] found that multitasking beha-vior was observed with the significantly highest rate at 14-17 age range (%87) among all the age ranges. Also, Rideout et al. [7] found that only 13% of 13-18 aged youths were not computer multitasker in the USA in 2009. Computer multitasker means who "use a totally different medium while he/she is also using the computer –for example, watching TV, reading, or text messaging". Another 40% of that age group said they use another medium or text message most of the time while they are using computer; another 26% said they do so some of the time; another 17% said they do so a little of the time. In the project of Media Habits of MENA (Middle Eastern and North African) Youth, participants aged 13-28 stated their choices about other activities they usually engaged in while watching TV, as follows: 53% send and receive cell phone text messages, 50% talk on the phone, 41% send and receive email, 39% listen to music, 36% browse online, 35% do their homework or work, 19% play video games, and 17% read [14]. All those findings together with the findings of this study show that multitasking behavior among digital natives are very widespread all over the world.

In case of the effects of multitasking behavior on digital natives, we saw that multi-tasking digital natives think that multitasking is a very natural behavior and they feel very comfortable with it. Non-multitaskers, however, think in a negative way about multitasking behavior. The main two reasons behind this are: not having enough ex-perience in multitasking, and having prejudice against multitasking as it causes to lose concentration. These are very reasonable. It can be expected to make prejudice about a behavior related to using new media for one who doesn't have enough oppor-tunities to have access and use new media. Indeed, we saw that the common point of non-multitaskers is that they all use new media few and far between when we ex-amine the records of those participants [12]. The rate of using computer or Internet among them is at most weekly; the rate of using mobile phone is at most weekly (ex-cept one who uses daily); no one possesses tablet computer; no one have personal web site or blog; only one of them has a Facebook account but he uses it rarely. Thus we cannot expect them to get experience in multitasking. On the other hand, one of the multitaskers thinks that multitasking behavior may have a negative effect on their academic success since it can lead to lose concentration. Therefore, there appears a relation between multitasking and concentration obviously. Correspondingly, there are some research which state that attempting to do more than one task at a time overloads the capacity of the human information processing system [8, 9]. Additionally, we cannot be sure that the strategies, which were developed by some multitaskers to diminish the possible negative effects of multitasking, are really effective.

5   Conclusion

It becomes important to examine on behaviors of digital natives interactions with new media, especially in the present days when new media has become dominant in our lives and in such a world that multitasking behavior becomes widespread. From this point, we conducted this research which is about multitasking behaviors of digital natives in Turkey.

According to the results, it is observed that the rate of being a multitasker among digital natives in Turkey is very high. Also, according to the detailed analysis with regard to age, gender, and SES, those rates are very high and close to each other. According to multitaskers, multitasking is a very natural behavior and they feel very comfortable while doing it. On the other hand, non-multitasker participants have a common feature that they didn't have enough opportunity to get experience in multitasking. Although all the multitasker participants said they were doing more than one activity at the same time when online, we observed that their multitasking behavior may differ if at least one of the tasks requires much attention. In that case, some multitaskers pay special attention deciding on which activity to do simultaneously; some prefer doing activities in a sequence. Losing concentration is a very common obstacle, for both multitasker and non-multitasker digital natives, to do multitasking.

New media offer more than one possibilities to interact with simultaneously, i.e. multitasking. As new media bring new interaction ways, human behaviors change as well. Besides, human factors change as digital natives have different characteristics. Although human is the most complicated aspect of human-computer interaction, there are some cooperative disciplines such as psychology and cognitive sciences to deal with such a complicated factor [11]. Therefore, we suggest that there should be more interdisciplinary investigations especially on cognitive load while executing multiple tasks. Because the findings of this study relay on the self-reporting of participants on both questionnaire and interviews, there is the need for empirical data in order to get deeper findings to discuss about positive and negative issues on multitasking. Thus it could be possible to apply knowledge from cognitive neuroscience to achieve more effective human-computer interaction designs for the digital natives. Human-computer interaction offers more design opportunities, while there is a tendency to user-centered designs [15]. It becomes more of an issue that human-computer interaction designers and user experience designers should use the opportunity to reduce cognitive load.

In conclusion, the results provide valuable information for getting to know digital natives in Turkey by presenting the nature of their multitasking behaviors. Therefore, the study is worth in terms of providing information to apply on the related fields as well as providing some starting points for future research.

Acknowledgments. This work was supported by Scientific Research Projects Coordination Unit of Istanbul University. Project number 21411.

References

1. Türkoğlu, T.: Dijital Kültür (Digital Culture). Beyaz Yayınları, İstanbul (2010)
2. Prensky, M.C.: Digital Natives Digital Immigrants. On the Horizon 9(5), 1–6 (2001)
3. Manovich, L.: The Language of New Media. MIT Press, USA (2001)
4. Lister, M., Dovey, J., Giddings, S., Grant, I., Kelly, K.: New Media: A Critical Introduction. Routledge, Great Britain (2009)
5. Encyclopedia Britannica. Multitasking. britannica.com (2012), http://www.britannica.com/EBchecked/topic/397270/multitaskin g (retrieved April 05, 2012)
6. Van Schalkwyk, G.J.: Multi-Tasking. In: Caplan, B., DeLuca, J., Kreutzer, J.S. (eds.) Encyclopedia of Clinical Neuropsychology, pp. 1685–1686. Springer, New York (2011)
7. Rideout, V.J., Foehr, U.G., Roberts, D.F.: Generation M2 Project: Media in the Lives of 8- to 18-Year-Olds. A Kaiser Family Foundation Study (2010), http://www.kff.org/entmedia/upload/8010.pdf (retrieved October 08, 2011)
8. Koch, I., Lawo, V., Fels, J., Vorländer, M.: Switching in the cocktail party: Exploring intentional control of auditory selective attention. Journal of Experimental Psychology. Human Perception and Performance 37(4), 1140–1147 (2011)
9. Tombu, M.N., Asplund, C.L., Dux, P.E., Godwin, D., Martin, J.W., Marois, R.: A unified attentional bottleneck in the human brain. Proceedings of the National Academy of Sciences of the United States of America 108(33) (2011)
10. Hembrooke, H., Gay, G.: The Laptop and the Lecture: The effects of multitasking in Learning Environments. Journal of Computing in Higher Education 15(1), 46–64 (2003)
11. Çağıltay, K.: İnsan Bilgisayar Etkileşimi ve Kullanılabilirlik Mühendisliği: Teoriden Pratiğe (Human Computer Interaction and Usability Engineering: from Theory to Practice). ODTÜ Geliştirme Vakfı Yayıncılık, Ankara (2011)
12. Uğraş, T.: A Descriptive Analysis on New Media Usage Habits of Digital Natives in the Context of Information Society in Turkey (Unpublished master's thesis). Istanbul University, Turkey (2012)
13. Helsper, E., Enyon, R.: Digital Natives: Where is the Evidence? British Educational Research Journal, 1–18 (2009), http://eprints.lse.ac.uk/27739 (retrieved February 20, 2012)
14. Melki, J.: Media Habits of MENA Youth Project. Working Paper Series #4, American University of Beirut (2010), http://www.aub.edu.lb/ifi/public_policy/arab_youth/Documents/working_paper_series/ifi_wps04_ay_Melki.pdf (retrieved February 02, 2012)
15. Zhang, T., Dong, H.: Human-Centred Design: An Emergent Conceptual Model. In: Include 2009 Proceedings (2008)

The Use of Timed Directional Link Analysis to Improve User Interaction during Universal Remote Control Setup Procedures

Robert J. Youmans[1], Bridget Lewis, Ivonne J. Figueroa[1], and Jesus Perez[2]

[1] George Mason University, Department of Psychology, Fairfax, Virginia, USA
[2] Universal Electronics, Inc., San Mateo, California, USA
ryouman2@gmu.edu

Abstract. The universal television remote control is one of the most common pieces of household technology in the industrialized world. In spite of the ubiquity of the television remote, the complexity of the device often means that consumers find universal remotes to be confusing to operate, particularly when programming the remote to operate a new device or piece of technology. The present study employed an advanced version of a technique called link analysis in order to decompose how a typical user would go about programming a remote control in order to better understand where users might become confused during a standard setup procedure. Next, the authors worked with a project development team at Universal Electronics Incorporated (UEI) to produce a new model of the remote that was easier to use. Finally, the setup procedures of the new version of the remote control were tested against the previous version in a short usability test. The results of the study confirmed that programming new devices using the redesigned remote was faster, less error prone, and subjectively rated by users as easier to accomplish. These findings suggest that timed directional link analysis may be a viable technique that designers and human factors psychologists can utilize to improve the user experience of consumer electronics.

Keywords: Remote Control; Usability Testing; Link Analysis; Product Design.

1   Introduction

Developed in 1956 by Eugene Polly and Robert Adler, the television remote is a special type of technology, one that has become truly ubiquitous in the homes of industrialized societies. The success of the television remote control led to the development of additional remote controls for other types of home entertainment (e.g., the stereo receiver, the DVD player). As home entertainment systems grew in scope and complexity, many consumers realized that having a different remote control for each device confusing. In the wake of the influx of numerous specialized remote controls, demand grew for a 'universal' remote control, one that could control many different devices regardless of their function or manufacturing origin [1]. Consumers and electronics manufacturers alike thought that by replacing multiple

D. Harris (Ed.): EPCE/HCII 2013, Part I, LNAI 8019, pp. 104–113, 2013.
© Springer-Verlag Berlin Heidelberg 2013

dedicated remote controls with just one device, they could make user interactions with home entertainment systems faster, easier, and more intuitive.

Universal remotes have certainly accomplished some of the goals of their many developers set out. Not only have universal designs helped to unclutter coffee tables everywhere, but they have also allowed consumers to learn how to operate one remote rather than the many that may accompany each component of a complex home entertainment system. The 'Atlas' universal remote, developed by Universal Electronics Inc. (UEI), can be programmed to control several hundred models of home entertainment equipment regardless of their manufacturer or year of production. Because of its reliability and relatively low cost, the Atlas has become one of the most common universal remote controls available in the Unites States.

Fig. 1. Universal Electronics' Atlas universal remote control model

Although universal remote controls are commonplace, users do not always find remote controls to be user friendly. The Duke of Edinburgh, a famous advocate for usability in technology, quipped in 2009 that "to work out how to operate a TV set you practically have to make love to the thing," and an online search will quickly yield reviews, blogs, and even designers' personal websites that point to remote control designs as very good examples of very poor human factors. One of the major barriers that seems to limit designing user friendly universal remotes is that the remotes, by definition, are intended to control an incredible variety of different products that have been developed by other product design teams. As a consequence, universal remote control designers must try to balance the demands of supporting a great many products and systems with the demands of creating user-friendly products.

The work reported here represents one attempt by one of the world's leading manufacturers to strike a better balance between product support and ease of use while redesigning one of their most popular universal remote controls, the Atlas. To improve the human factors of the Atlas remote, the product development team employed multiple task analysis techniques, but this paper focuses specifically on a technique called *link analysis*, a technique that is particularly useful for analyzing the links between parts of a system as a person shifts her focus of attention between them [2]. Specifically, the link analysis reported here investigated how people shift their attention between printed instructions and the button clusters of the remote control while programming the device to control new products and systems.

1.1   Link Analysis

Link analysis is a task analysis method that identifies patterns of interactions between a human and systems ranging from small handheld interfaces to large-scale work environments. The "links" in the analysis represent one of three types of actions: mental shifts in operator attention, physical movements in operator behavior, or verbal communications between multiple operators (see [2]). In a traditional link analysis, the analyst tallies the sequential shifts in actions between these three types of interactions during normal system operation, and in doing so, he or she learns how an operator interacts with a system during a given procedure. Connection frequency data is then typically displayed on a resulting 'link table,' which forms a tabular representation of the task in a way that highlights areas of frequent system-user interaction. While link analysis is a useful task decomposition method in many domains, link analyses are perhaps most useful when link tables of the interactions allow the analyst to consider complicated interactions in a tabular format that may highlight frequent actions that are potentially complicated or frustrating for a user. In doing so, those interactions may be flagged for redesign when a product or system is upgraded, modified, or redesigned.

In spite of link analysis' usefulness, researchers have recently addressed limitations in this task decomposition method by modifying the traditional link analysis technique itself. For example, some researchers have developed computer-based link analysis techniques that allow algorithms for describing user interactions to optimize an interface layout for maximum efficiency [3]. Other researchers have noted that traditional link tables lack both directionality, information about whether a link represents an action that is moving towards or away from a given part of a system, and weighting, information about how relatively complicated or time consuming any given action is to complete.

Lin and Wu [3] addressed the lack of directionality and timing data by developing a directional link analysis, a technique whereby the direction of actions are recorded by an analyst and used to populate a modified link table [4]. As shown in Figure 3, a directional link analysis table represents system sub-areas along the side and top of the table, but the starting points of user interactions are always represented on the left vertical column, while the targets that the user's actions move towards are represented in the top horizontal row. Lin and Wu also addressed the issue of how different actions can affect usability by proposing a system whereby computer modeling is used to establish weighting variables that are assigned to links, although this process also requires that the analyst use a computerized version of link analysis.

Because link analysis was initially designed to be a relatively simple task decomposition method that can be achieved with paper and a pencil [2], we devised a simpler method in the study reported here called Timed Directional Link Analysis (TDLA), a link analysis technique that combines the directionality of the link tables used by Lin and Wu [3] with basic time information about each action sequence similar to those used during keystroke level modeling techniques [5]. By measuring or estimating the average time it would take a user to complete an action, essentially the time it takes for them to move from a start position to a target position, each link in the bi-directional table can be weighted with time information which will allow an analyst to determine which actions may be most burdensome to the user. As a result, the analyst can make recommendations to designers to either decrease the frequency of a cumbersome action, decrease the time it takes to complete a cumbersome action, or both, thereby improving the human factors considerations of the product or system.

2 Methods

To complete a TDLA of the Atlas remote, it was first necessary to define specific areas of the remote control and instruction manual. We identified four main areas used during new product setup: 1) the 'Setup' located at the top of the remote that consisted of the mode keys and setup button, 2) the numeric keypad located near the bottom of the remote control, 3) the step-by-step instructions found in the user manual, and 4) the list of numerical codes printed in the back of the user manual that corresponded to the hundreds of programmable brands and models that were supported by the universal remote. We reasoned that these were the major areas that a typical user would be required to successfully setup a new product that could be controlled by the Atlas remote (see Figure 2).

Fig. 2. The numeric keypad (rectangle) and setup (oval) portions of the remote, plus the instructions and an example of a code page from the instruction manual. Shifts between these four areas are represented by 'links' on the TDLA table shown in Figure 3.

Using the instructions and estimated action times, we then populated a TDLA table to illustrate orders of actions and the times necessary to complete them. We made two assumptions about how a user would interact with the product in order to complete the link analysis. First, we assumed that the average user would need to look up 2 codes before they found the code that correctly controlled his or her device. Second, we assumed that the user would not make any mistakes during the setup process. In reality, we note that both assumptions may be too optimistic – certainly users make errors or own products that cannot be controlled by the first or second code supplied by UEI. Reasonable assumptions made by the analysts that are held constant across product comparisons are necessary for an analyst to make while completing TDLA tables and many other task decomposition techniques [2]. With these assumptions in mind, we developed the TDLA table shown in Figure 3 representing the actions of a typical user who is using the Atlas instruction manual and remote to setup a new device that succeeds after the second code and makes no errors.

	T_{SETUP}	$T_{NUMBERS}$	$T_{INSTRUCTIONS}$	T_{CODES}
S_{SETUP}			2 (1.2 sec.)	...
$S_{NUMBERS}$	2 (1.2 sec.)		...	
$S_{INSTRUCTIONS}$	1 (1.2 sec.)	2 (6.7 sec.)		2 (37.6 sec.)
S_{CODES}		...	2 (1.2 sec.)	

Fig. 3. A TDLA table representing an average user as they attempt to program the Atlas remote while making no errors and cycling through two possible remote codes

2.1   Interpreting the TDLA Table

Two primary user-interaction observations were made following the TDLA of the Atlas remote. First, the Atlas redesign team realized that there were a total of 11 action links, a relatively large number, representing the various interactions that a user needed to make in order to setup a new device. Second, the team realized that one directional action link, users who finished reading the instruction and went to look up a code, was taking users much longer than they had anticipated. As shown in the grey cell in Figure 4, users took approximately 37.6 seconds to shift their attention away from the instruction set to the proper code listed in the back of the instruction manual. The problem was made worse because of the large numbers of codes that the user needed to search through, and because the codes were listed on multiple pages of the manual.

2.2   Redesigning the Atlas Remote

Data from the TDLA task decomposition method was provided to designers at Universal Electronics, who were also given the results of some past usability tests that suggested that users frequently committed errors while attempting to setup new products using the Atlas remote control. On the basis of this feedback, the designers were tasked with incorporating these findings into a large Atlas redesign effort. Virtual and physical prototypes were created based on the results of the TDLA and other forms of user testing, but the designers placed an emphasis on improving the setup functions of the remote. As shown in Figure 4, the result of the redesign effort was a new universal remote control named 'Champion,' which was released publically in June of 2011.

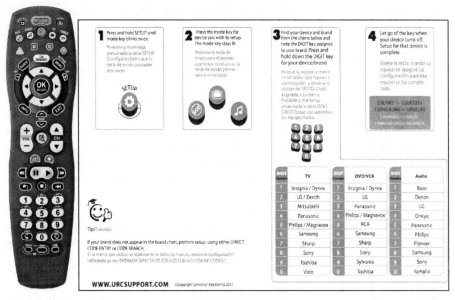

Fig. 4. The Champion universal remote (left) and the simplified 'Popular Brands' instruction set (right). Both were created to eliminate problems with Atlas setup found via TDLA.

Many new features have been included in the Champion, but two were specifically designed to improve on some of the problems during the setup procedure that the TDLA had identified. First, the designers recognized that a setup procedure that required fewer user action links (i.e., fewer shifts in action or attention) might make the setup procedure less overwhelming to the user. Second, the designers recognized that the time involved in looking up codes from the back of the Atlas manual should somehow be reduced. The primary solution that the designers reached was to develop a shortcut method for programming most new devices, which the designers called the 'Popular Brand' method. Using the Popular Brand setup method, users followed a greatly simplified procedure that required fewer actions (see Figure 4). Users were much less likely to need to look up codes because 10 of the most popular television, DVD player, and audio receiver brands were pre-programmed into the remote.

A second change made by UEI designers addressed situations where users needed to still use codes because a device was not among the 10 most popular brands. The original Atlas instruction manual was a small 59-page booklet, which created large delays when users flipped through pages to look up codes listed in the back of the manual. To address this, the designers decided that the Champion's user manual would be printed on one large double-sided 13 x 18 inch instruction sheet. The resulting instructions were much larger, but users did not have to flip between pages to look up codes using the new manual.

2.3   Comparison Testing of the Existing and New Remotes

Participants. Fifty-nine students from George Mason University volunteered to participate in a new usability test comparing the setup procedure of the Atlas and Champion remote controls. Participants ranged in age between 18 and 50 years of age, with a mean age of 20.8 years. Forty-seven percent of the participants in the sample identified themselves as female.

Design and Procedure. Participants in this study were randomly assigned to use either the Atlas or Champion, and their accompanying instructions, to complete a series usability tests. In the first usability test, participants programmed their remote to control a 2011 model LG television. The television model used in the first test was selected because it appeared on the Champion's list of the 10 most popular brands, and therefore was an appropriate test of whether the UEI designers' improvements to the setup procedure had been effective.

In the second usability test, participants programmed the remote to control an audio receiver. The audio receiver used in the second test was selected because it did not appear on the Champion's list of the 10 most popular brands, and was therefore a test that focused on the Champion's redesigned code-based setup procedure.

Measures. During usability testing, participants sat in a small laboratory in a comfortable chair facing a table that held the television and audio receiver. When the participant was ready to begin, he or she programmed the remote to control the television or audio device, and the experimenter timed how long it took participants to do so successfully. The experimenter also made note of any overt errors that the participants made, and these were tallied for later comparisons. At the conclusion of each usability test, participants were asked 'now that you have completed this task, please rate how easy you felt it was to accomplish using the remote control and instructions that you were provided?' Participants answered on a 7-point Likert like scale. A response of 1 indicated the procedure was 'not very easy,' 4 indicated that the procedure's ease was 'average,' and 7 indicated the procedure was 'easy to accomplish.' The rating procedure was adopted from those outlined by Lewis (1995).

3   Results

Two multivariate analysis of variance tests (MANOVAs) were conducted to test for reliable differences between the time, number of errors, and participants' ease-of-use ratings when participants were using the Atlas or Champion remotes. The first

MANOVA tested whether the 'Major Brands' setup procedure that was incorporated into the Champion remote setup procedure had resulted in a faster and more error-free setup procedure. As shown in Figure 5, the MANOVA revealed an overall significant effect of the remote condition, $F(58, 2) = 5.65$, $p < .01$. Champion users completed the setup procedure more quickly, $F(58, 2) = 17.07$, $p < .001$, and with fewer errors, $F(58, 2) = 10.68$, $p < .01$.

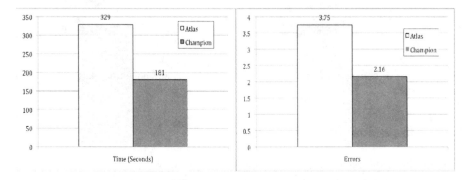

Fig. 5. Time to complete setup and error data, split by remote condition

The second MANOVA tested whether the simplification of the Champion instructions would improve the code-based setup procedure that had to be used when programming the remote to control a non-major brand. But before we could do so, we needed to address a large heterogeneous practice effect that was discovered in the Atlas condition. Because participants in the Atlas condition had already been asked to setup a television using coded entry during their first usability test, Atlas testers had already 'practiced' the coded entry method in the previous round of testing. Although they were being asked to find a new code that matched the audio receiver in the second test, we found that they were completing the task much more quickly, likely because they had memorized some of the procedure from the previous round of testing. This made direct comparisons against Champion users problematic because they were using coded entry procedures for the first time. Because of the practice effects, we decided that best test of whether the coded entry method was improved on the Champion remote was to compare the data we had gathered during the first round of Atlas testing against the data from the second round of Champion testing. In doing so, we more accurately compared how a new user would react to the different coded entry procedures the first time they used them, which was the focus of the testing.

As shown in Figure 6, the second MANOVA revealed an overall significant effect of the remote condition, $F(58, 2) = 5.92$, $p < .001$. Champion users again completed the setup procedure more quickly, $F(58, 2) = 18.37$, $p < .001$, and with fewer errors, $F(58, 2) = 7.49$, $p < .01$.

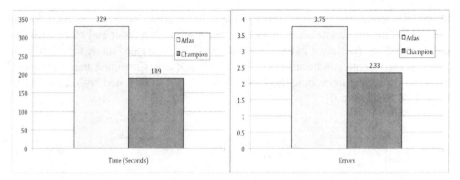

Fig. 6. Time to complete setup and error data, split by remote condition, during the second usability test

4   Discussion

The results of the usability tests revealed that the changes that UEI designers made to improve the user experience of programming the remote to control a new device were largely successful. Champion users completed the major brand setup procedure more quickly and with fewer errors than Atlas users, and Champion users anecdotally indicated that they felt that it was easy to operate the when using the major brands procedure. The designers were also successful at improving the time and error rates for using coded-based setup procedures.

Remotes that are produced at UEI are designed to control literally hundreds of manufactured products, and can be programmed to support thousands of different product models produced by those manufacturers. In a competitive marketplace, the adaptability of these remotes is clearly paramount. But companies like UEI who are committed to improving their products' human factors properties may indicate a shift in the remote control market, one where human factors will play a greater role. For example, as the technology behind home entertainment equipment continues to evolve, many products will gain Internet connectivity, an advance that will allow remote control systems to connect to devices regardless of their make or model. Given a market where all remote control systems are truly 'universal,' the adaptability of remotes may become something that users simply assume, making the human factors of remote controls just as important as they have become in the cellular telephone, gaming, and personal computer industries.

We believe that the choice whether or not to invest time and resources towards human factors considerations may make the difference between those companies that succeed and those that diminish as the marketplace for home entertainment electronics continues to evolve. UEI shipped an astonishing 200 million remote controls worldwide in 2011. We hope that our work with UEI will add human factors value to their product line, and also that it will decrease a few of the headaches that customers will experience as they program them to operate their home entertainment equipment.

Irrespective of remote control design, this project highlights the utility of link analysis as a useful task decomposition method for human factors analysts who are working to improve interactive technology. The technique requires relatively little training, and requires few resources to employ beyond detailed access to a product or system and a stopwatch. The modifications that we have introduced here to basic link analysis also should allow an analyst to recognize that not all actions, or even directions of actions, are created equal. In this study, our participants took longer to look up codes than to return to the instructions after finding them, but this same principle extends to many other domains where link analysis would be made more effective if weighting and directionality were taken into account. Employees take longer to go up stairs than to go down them, baggage screeners use more effort to begin visual searches than to complete them, and doctors can leave an operating room in seconds, but are required to complete a lengthy 'scrub in' procedure before they can return. These and many other interactive tasks can therefore be better analyzed when the analyst has the directional and weighting abilities that TDLA affords.

References

1. Zimmermann, G., Vanderheiden, G., Gilman, A.: Prototype implementations for a Universal Remote Console Specification. In: Proceedings of Human Factors in Computing Systems: CHI 2002 Extended Abstracts, Minneapolis, MN, April 20-25, pp. 510–511 (2002)
2. Kirwan, B., Ainsworth, L.K.: A guide to task analysis. Taylor & Francis, Abington (1992)
3. Lin, C.J., Yu, W., Wu, C.: Improving link analysis method in user interface design using a new computational optimization algorithm. In: Proceeding of the Human Factors and Ergonomics Society Annual Meeting Proceedings, pp. 1112–1116. Human factors and Ergonomics Society, Santa Monica (2008)
4. Lin, C.-J., Yu, W., Wu, C.: Improved link analysis method for user interface design – modified link table and optimization-based algorithm. Behaviour & Information Technology 29, 199–216 (2010)
5. Kieras, D.: Using the keystroke-level model to estimate execution times. Unpublished report. Ann Arbor: Department of Psychology, University of Michigan (2001); Lewis, J.R.: IBM computer usability satisfaction questionnaires: Psychometric evaluation and instructions for use. International Journal of Human-Computer Interaction 7, 57–78 (1995)

Part II

Measuring and Monitoring Cognition

Automatic Classification of Eye Blink Types
Using a Frame-Splitting Method

Kiyohiko Abe[1], Hironobu Sato[1], Shogo Matsuno[2],
Shoichi Ohi[2], and Minoru Ohyama[2]

[1] College of Engineering, Kanto Gakuin University, 1-50-1 Mutsuura-higashi, Kanazawa-ku,
Yokohama-shi, Kanagawa 236-8501, Japan
[2] School of Information Environment, Tokyo Denki University, 2-1200 Muzaigakuendai,
Inzai-shi, Chiba 270-1382, Japan
{abe,hsato}@kanto-gakuin.ac.jp

Abstract. Human eye blinks include voluntary (conscious) blinks and involuntary (unconscious) blinks. If voluntary blinks can be detected automatically, then input decisions can be made when voluntary blinks occur. Previously, we proposed a novel eye blink detection method using a Hi-Vision video camera. This method utilizes split interlaced images of the eye, which are generated from 1080i Hi-Vision format images. The proposed method yields a time resolution that is twice as high as that of the 1080i Hi-Vision format. We refer to this approach as the frame-splitting method. In this paper, we propose a new method for automatically classifying eye blink types on the basis of specific characteristics using the frame-splitting method.

Keywords: Eye blink, Voluntary blink, Interlaced image, Natural light, Input interface.

1   Introduction

Recently, input interfaces that use information derived from a user's eye blinks have been reported [1-5]. Users can input text or commands into PC systems via these interfaces. The systems only require user eye blinks as inputs. These systems were used to develop communication aids for people with severe physical disability such as amyotrophic lateral sclerosis (ALS). In general, eye blinks are detected by performing image analysis on moving images of the area surrounding the eye [1-5]. The moving images are recorded by a video camera. However, it is difficult for standard video cameras (such as NTSC and 1080i Hi-Vision) to measure the detailed temporal changes that occur during the eye blink process because eye blinks are relatively rapid (a few hundred milliseconds).

Therefore, a high-speed camera is required for detailed eye blink measurements [2]. Previously, we developed an eye blink detection method that utilizes split interlaced images [6]. These split images are odd- and even-numbered field images in the 1080i Hi-Vision format, which are generated from interlaced images. We refer to this approach as the frame-splitting method. The detailed temporal changes that occur during the eye blinking process can be detected using this method.

D. Harris (Ed.): EPCE/HCII 2013, Part I, LNAI 8019, pp. 117–124, 2013.

Human eye blinks can be classified into three types: involuntary blinks, voluntary blinks, and reflex blinks. Involuntary blinks occur unconsciously, whereas voluntary blinks are generated consciously by a cue. Reflex blinks are induced by stimuli such as loud sounds or bright lights. If voluntary blinks could be detected automatically, then it would be possible to develop a more user-friendly interface. We have confirmed the feature parameters of involuntary and voluntary eye blinks, which can be used to distinguish these two types of blinks from each other. In this paper, we present the frame-splitting method and the feature parameters of voluntary and involuntary eye blinks.

2   Eye Blink Measurement by Frame-Splitting Method

If the entire process of an eye blink is captured, the wave pattern of the eye blink can be generated. We have developed a new method for measuring the wave pattern of an eye blink. This method can be used with common indoor lighting sources such as fluorescent or LED lights, and it can measure the wave pattern automatically [6]. The experiments described below are conducted using this method. In this method, eye blinks are detected by measuring the pixels of the open-eye area [6]. The open-eye area is extracted from the eye images using the color information imbedded in their pixels.

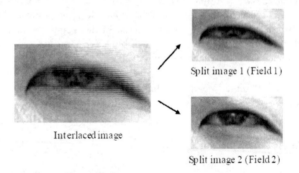

Split image 1 (Field 1)

Interlaced image

Split image 2 (Field 2)

Fig. 1. Overview of frame splitting method

1080i Hi-Vision video cameras output interlaced images. If one interlaced image is split by scanning even- and odd-numbered lines separately, two field images are generated. These field images are captured at 60 fields/s, and the 1080i interlaced moving images are captured at 30 frames/s; therefore, this method yields a time resolution that is twice as high as that of the 1080i Hi-Vision format. By using the frame-split images, the entire process of an eye blink can be captured. The overview of the frame-splitting method is shown in Fig. 1; the left-hand side shows the blinking eye image (interlaced), and the right-hand side shows the two field images split by the scan line. To describe this phenomenon clearly, the image on the left has been captured at a low resolution (145 × 80 pixels).

3   Classification of Eye Blink Types by Its Wave Pattern

3.1   Automatic Extraction for Wave Pattern of Eye Blink

Moving images of the eye include images of the blinking eye and those of the open eye. Thus, the contiguous data of the estimated open-eye area include the samples with these mixed situations. If we want to classify the eye blink types, we need to extract the data only for the blinking eye. Then, the parameters of eye blinks are estimated in order to classify the different types of eye blinks. To estimate the threshold for the extraction of the wave pattern of eye blinks, we utilize the difference wave pattern of eye blinks. A sample of the wave pattern of an eye blink and its difference wave pattern are shown in Fig. 2 and Fig. 3, respectively. In these figures, the x-axis indicates the sampling point (interval = 1/60 s), and the y-axis indicates the open-eye area pixels and its difference value, respectively.

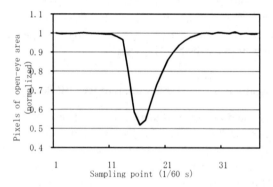

Fig. 2. Wave pattern of an eye blink

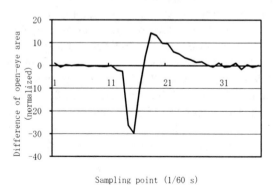

Sampling point (1/60 s)

Fig. 3. Difference wave pattern of an eye blink

These plots were normalized relative to the pixels in the open-eye area in the first field image. From Fig. 3, it is evident that the difference value for the blinking eye is greater than that for the open eye. In other words, the fluctuation in the difference value for the open eye is smaller than that for the blinking eye. Thus, we can use statistical information to distinguish between data for the open eye and that for the blinking eye. In particular, we estimate the average and standard deviation of the difference value of the open-eye area when the eye is open. By using these values, the threshold is estimated automatically. The thresholds for the discrimination of data when the eye is open, Th_1 and Th_2, are determined by the formulae

$$Th_1 = E_{avg} + 2\sigma \tag{1}$$

$$Th_2 = E_{avg} - 2\sigma, \tag{2}$$

where E_{avg} is the average difference value of the open-eye area when the eye is open, and sigma is its standard deviation. If the sample of the open-eye area is greater than Th_1, it indicates that the eye is opening. Similarly, if the sample of the open-eye area is smaller than Th_2, it indicates that the eye is closing. The part between these two results is the wave pattern for the blinking eye.

3.2   Feature Parameters for Classification of Eye Blink Types

If voluntary blinks could be detected automatically, then it would be possible to develop a more user-friendly interface. Thus, users could employ this interface to input commands to their PC consciously [3-5]. Many input interfaces that utilize the information of voluntary blinks have been developed. Users can input text to PCs by using these interfaces. However, these interfaces utilize specific patterns of eye blinks. For example, they use the method for classifying voluntary blinks on the basis of duration [4], [5] or the occurrence of multiple blinks [3].

To relax these conditions, we are developing a new interface. If users close their eyes firmly, the new interface captures an input command. In other words, the constraint when users utilize the interface by means of an eye blink is alleviated. To classify the eye blink types, we need to scrutinize the feature parameters of an eye blink. Eye blink patterns can be extracted automatically from the detection results using the method described in section 3.1. The feature parameters are estimated from the eye blink pattern. It is reported that there is a large difference in the duration of voluntary and involuntary blinks [4], [5]. We conduct metering experiments to confirm the parameters. The outline of an eye blink pattern is shown in Fig.4; we define the feature parameters on the basis of duration (T_d) and maximum amplitude (A_m) of an eye blink.

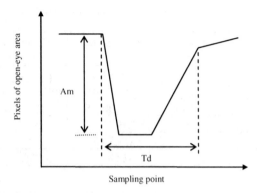

Fig. 4. Feature parameters of an eye blink

4   Metering Experiments

We confirmed the feature parameters of the eye blink types by conducting two experiments, both of which involved five subjects. In experiment 1, the subjects blinked unconsciously without any instructions from the researcher, i.e., involuntary blinks were measured. In experiment 2, the subjects blinked consciously, i.e., the subjects closed their eyes firmly when they heard a beep sound emitted by a PC. The beep sound generated at random, these intervals are 5 to 7 seconds. These experiments were conducted using the methods described in sections 2 and 3.

In these experiments, the thresholds for the extraction of the wave pattern of eye blinks were calculated using the contiguous data of the open-eye area. In particular, the subjects kept their eyes open for 3 s at the beginning of these experiments, and the thresholds were estimated using images captured when the eye was open. The experimental setup includes a 1080i Hi-Vision video camera (Sony HDR-HC9, for home use), and a PC (OS: Microsoft Windows 7; CPU: Intel® Core™ i7, 2.8-GHz clock frequency). The PC analyzes sequenced eye images captured by the video cameras.

4.1   Measurement of Feature Parameters of Eye Blink

We measured the feature parameters of the eye blink types using the method described in sections 2 and 3. The durations and the maximum amplitudes of the eye blinks are shown in Fig. 4. We also estimated the occurrence interval of involuntary blinks. These parameters were calculated from the successful results of automatic extraction of wave patterns of eye blinks.

Table 1 lists the parameters of involuntary blinks that are measured in experiment 1. Table 2 and Table 3 list the parameters of involuntary blinks and voluntary blinks that are measured in experiment 2, respectively. Tables 1–3 also list the average values of the durations, the maximum amplitudes, and the occurrence intervals. In addition, the standard deviations are listed in parentheses. The open-eye area varies widely among individuals. Therefore, the maximum amplitudes of eye blinks are normalized relative to the pixels in the open-eye area in the initial sample.

Table 1. Feature parameters of involuntary blinks (experiment 1)

Subject	Counts	Numbers of extraction	Duration (ms)	Maximum Amplitude	Occurrence interval(ms)
A	6	6	363.9(141.2)	0.394(0.130)	2783.3(965.8)
B	10	10	381.7(50.0)	0.355(0.029)	1170.4(731.6)
C	11	10	300.0(69.8)	0.329(0.048)	1142.9(453.2)
D	7	7	281.0(45.6)	0.329(0.049)	2322.2(1246.2)
E	4	4	237.5(16.0)	0.463(0.043)	3794.4(2508.9)
Average	-	-	312.8	0.374	2242.6

Table 2. Feature parameters of involuntary blinks (experiment 2)

Subject	Counts	Numbers of extraction	Duration (ms)	Maximum Amplitude	Occurrence interval(ms)
A	8	8	250.0(247.6)	0.410(0.047)	1490.9(1031.9)
B	6	6	258.3(20.4)	0.237(0.023)	1944.4(1236.8)
C	9	9	238.9(45.6)	0.274(0.037)	1216.7(422.1)
D	5	5	303.3(41.5)	0.281(0.039)	2336.1(1943.8)
E	3	2	216.7(0.0)	0.211(0.006)	2755.6(2348.4)
Average	-	-	253.4	0.283	1948.7

Table 3. Feature parameters of voluntary blinks (experiment 2)

Subject	Counts	Numbers of extraction	Duration (ms)	Maximum Amplitude
A	4	4	716.7(102.7)	0.575(0.015)
B	4	4	508.3(141.7)	0.354(0.022)
C	4	3	1038.9(265.8)	0.418(0.020)
D	4	3	794.4(34.7)	0.399(0.005)
E	4	3	516.7(44.1)	0.264(0.007)
Average	-	-	715.0	0.402

Table 1 indicates that the average duration and maximum amplitude of involuntary blinks are 312.8 ms and 0.374, respectively. We confirmed that the duration and maximum amplitude of involuntary blinks depend on the subject. Table 2 and Table 3 show that the average duration of involuntary blinks and voluntary blinks are 253.4 ms and 715.0 ms, respectively. In addition, these tables show that the average of the maximum amplitudes of involuntary blinks and voluntary blinks are 0.283 and 0.402, respectively. From the results of experiment 2, it is evident that the duration and the maximum amplitude of an involuntary blink are smaller than those of a voluntary blink. In addition, these values vary among individuals.

From Tables 1–3, we confirmed that the parameters of eye blinks depend on the experimental conditions. Therefore, if these parameters are utilized for an input interface that uses the classification of eye blink types, this system needs to be calibrated.

In addition, in experiments 1 and 2, the average intervals of involuntary blink occurrence are 2.2 s and 2.0 s, respectively. Considering the standard deviation of each subject, an involuntary blink occurs, at most, approximately every 6 s. From this result, if several involuntary and voluntary blinks are used for the calibration, then the calibration will take approximately 30 s.

4.2   Classification of Eye Blink Types

The feature parameters of eye blink were described in section 4.1. We confirmed that there is large difference in the duration of voluntary and involuntary blinks. Therefore, we classify the eye blink types by using the duration of the eye blinks as a feature parameter. Methods for classifying voluntary blinks on the basis of duration have been proposed [4], [5]. These methods use a fixed threshold. However, we confirmed that the threshold duration varies significantly and that it depends on the subject and the experimental conditions. These points are evident from the data in Tables 2 and 3. To classify the eye blink types with certainty, we focused on these points and developed a new method for estimating the threshold automatically. The threshold is calculated using the formula

$$Th_c = \frac{Tdv_{avg} - Tdiv_{avg}}{2} + Tdiv_{avg}, \tag{3}$$

where Tdv_{avg} and $Tdiv_{avg}$ are the average duration of voluntary and involuntary blinks, respectively. If the duration of an eye blink is greater than the threshold Th_c, this eye blink is classified as a voluntary blink. Otherwise, the eye blink is classified as an involuntary blink. The classification rates of eye blink types are listed in Table 4.

Table 4. Classification rates of eye blink types (experiment 2)

Subject	Counts		Passed Classifications		Classification rates (%)		
	Voluntary	Involuntary	Voluntary	Involuntary	Voluntary	Involuntary	Total
A	4	8	0	0	100	100	100
B	4	6	1	0	75	100	90
C	3	9	0	0	100	100	100
D	3	5	0	0	100	100	100
E	3	2	0	0	100	100	100
Average	-	-	-	-	95	100	98

The Th_c value utilized in Table 4 is calculated using the average durations of voluntary blinks and involuntary blinks listed in Table 2. In addition, the classification rates of eye blink types are estimated using the same experimental data.

Using our proposed method, the average rate of successful classification of voluntary eye blinks is approximately 95% for the experimental sample of five subjects (see Table 4). In addition, one passed classification occurs for a voluntary blink with subject B. However, we believe that this passed classification of a voluntary blink is not a major problem. If these passed classifications occur, the input can be attempted again through an intentional repetition of the voluntary blink.

5   Conclusions

We proposed a frame-splitting method that detects eye blinks using split interlaced images. These split images are odd- and even-numbered field images in the 1080i Hi-Vision format. This method also yields a time resolution that is twice as high as that of the 1080i Hi-Vision format. Using this method, the feature parameters of eye blinks can be detected automatically. We conducted experiments to measure the feature parameters that can be used to classify eye blink types. From the results, we confirmed that there is large difference in the duration of voluntary and involuntary blinks. We also confirmed that the threshold duration varies significantly and that it depends on the subject and the experimental conditions.

We developed a new method for classifying eye blink types, which utilizes the duration of the eye blinks. Using this method, voluntary blinks can be extracted from eye images that include involuntary blinks. This method also yields a high degree of accuracy. In our experiments with five different subjects, the average accuracy was 95%.

In the future, we plan to conduct additional experiments in order to confirm the accuracy of our calibration method. We also plan to develop a more user-friendly interface for using the information from voluntary eye blinks.

Acknowledgment. This work was supported by JSPS KAKENHI Grant Number 24700598.

References

1. Morris, T., Blenkhorn, P., Zaidi, F.: Blink Detection for Real-Time Eye Tracking. J. Network and Computer Applications 25(2), 129–143 (2002)
2. Ohzeki, K., Ryo, B.: Video Analysis for Detecting Eye Blinking using a High-Speed Camera. In: Proc. of Fortieth Asilomar Conf. on Signals, Systems and Computers, Pacific Grove, CA, pp. 1081–1085 (2006)
3. Gorodnichy, D.O.: Second Order Change Detection, and Its Application to Blink-Controlled Perceptual Interfaces. In: Proc. of the International Association of Science and Technology for Development Conf. on Visualization, Imaging and Image Processing, Benalmadena, Spain, pp. 140–145 (2003)
4. Krolak, A., Strumillo, P.: Vision-Based Eye Blink Monitoring System for Human-Computer Interfacing. In: Proc. on Human System Interaction, HIS 2008, Kracow, Poland, pp. 994–998 (2008)
5. MacKenzie, I.S., Ashitani, B.: BlinkWrite: Efficient Text Entry Using Eye Blinks. Universal Access in the Information Society 10, 69–80 (2011)
6. Abe, K., Ohi, S., Ohyama, M.: Automatic Method for Measuring Eye Blinks Using Split-Interlaced Images. In: Jacko, J.A. (ed.) HCI International 2009, Part I. LNCS, vol. 5610, pp. 3–11. Springer, Heidelberg (2009)

The Experimental Research of Task Load Quantitative Analysis Based on the Pupil Diameter

Xueli He, Lijing Wang, and Yingchun Chen

Fundamental Science on Ergonomics and Environment Control Laboratory
School of Aeronautic Science and Engineering
Beihang University, Beijing, China, 100191
15210988283@163.com

Abstract. The aim of this paper is to do experimental research of task load quantitative analysis based on the pupil diameter. Two sets of experiments were designed from several task elements: (1) Visual Tracking, Visual - Cognitive, Visual - Cognitive – Response; (2) Auditory-Cognitive, Auditory - Cognitive - Respond. In the experiment, the pupil diameter was obtained by eye tracker. From the experimental results, the change of pupil size in visual tracking experiment is the same as in visual cognition experiment, which can indicate the load of these two tasks being the same. The increasing size of the pupil diameter aroused by task of responding, in the experiments of Visual-Cognitive-Respond and Auditory-Cognitive-Respond, is also in the same. The results showed that pupil diameter can be used as the index for task load quantitative analysis.

Keywords: pupil diameter, task elements, eye tracker.

1 Introduction

While a precise definition of a workload is elusive, a commonly accepted definition is the hypothetical relationship between a group or an individual human operator and task demands. Relative aspects of workload seem to fall within three broad categories: the amount of work and the number of things to do; time and the particular aspect of time one is concerned with; and, the subjective psychological experiences of the human operator (Lysaght, Hill et al. 1989[1]). Hart and Staveland (1988) [2] describe workload as "the perceived relationship between the amount of mental processing capability or resources and the amount required by the task". Cognitive task analysis is to systematically define the decision requirements and psychological processes used by expert individuals in accomplishing demands [3]. "Mental workload refers to the portion of operator information processing capacity or resources that is actually required to meet system demands." (Eggemeier et al., 1991) [4]. Most of the definitions, workload, metal workload, cognitive workload represent the same meaning. The definition of Task Load is resources required to meet demands [5], which is one of the factors to construct workload, combining with individual skills and experience. The task load is just the resource requirements based on task nature. Task Load

D. Harris (Ed.): EPCE/HCII 2013, Part I, LNAI 8019, pp. 125–133, 2013.

Prediction is a critical aspect of design; it is a construct related to performance measures and subjective workload ratings that may help spot design defects.

Kevin M. Corker in NASA[6] established the MIDAS, which includes the workload assessment model, predicting the workload through the establishment of the task load. Bierbaum(1987)[7] has also established a workload prediction model and applied it to the design of the UH-60 aircraft with task load. Johnson (1990) [8] used the same method to establish a workload prediction model, and did a compare analysis of the aircraft design between MH-47E and CH-47D on operator workload in 1991[9], and applied to predict pilot operation workload of AH-64A aircraft. The studies above have established the workload assessment and prediction method by analyzing the task load value from subjective evaluation.

A lot of researches have been done on physiological measurements of workload (eye movement measurement, ECG measurement). We found that the pupil diameter is one of the most sensitive indices to workload. Ahlstrom (2006) [11] has studied different cognitive activity, eye movement parameters with sensitivity to mental workload changes; Van Orden[12] applied eye activity measures, and accurately estimated changes in sustained visual task performance. In the process of our experimental researches, we found that the pupil diameter can change between the task units with little task difficulty difference. It is feasible to use the eye movement technique as the task unit load measurement in this research program.

In the beginning of the design of man-machine interface, workload can only be evaluated by analyzing the tasks, so the measurement of workload is very important. However, usually the measurement is carried out by subjective estimates. The question is: could workload be quantitative measured by physiological measurement?

Eye tracking is an effective method, which could show the changes of tasks sensitively; especially when the task load is low or its changes are not obvious. In the circumstances, could eye tracking be used as a method of quantitative measurement of task load?

Therefore, this article researches by the two questions above. The design of the eye tracking experiments is based on the processing stages (perception, cognition, responding) of resources model [13, 14] to obtain the pupil sizes under different tasks.

2   Experiments

The four dimensions of four- dimensional multiple resource model includes: (1) processing stage: perception, cognition, responding; (2) perceptual modalities: visual, auditory; (3) visual channels: focal and ambient vision, and (4) processing codes: spatial and verbal.

The experiment was designed based on the above classification. This paper intends to use two simple sets of experiments to accomplish the quantitative analysis of the workload by pupil diameter. The first set included three different basis tasks: Visual Tracking, Visual - Cognitive, Visual - Cognitive – Response. The second set of experiments included two different basis tasks: Auditory-Cognitive, Auditory - Cognitive - Respond.

2.1 Experimental Contents

(1) The First Set of Experiments
Visual Tracking: The cursor "+"was shown on the computer screen randomly. The switching interval of two "+" can be set. In this experiment, there are four trials the time interval "2000ms" "1000ms", "600ms", "300ms", the total duration of each trial is 60 s. Subjects were required to do visual tracking "+" cursor on screen.

Visual - Cognitive: Letters were shown on the computer screen randomly. In this experiment, there are four trials with the time interval "2000ms" "1000ms", "600ms", "300ms", the total duration of the each trial is 60 s. Subjects were required to see the letters and try to recognize them.

Visual - Cognitive - Respond: Letters were shown on the computer screen randomly. In this experiment, there are four trials with the time interval "2000ms" "1000ms", "600ms", "300ms", the total duration of each trial is 60 s. The subjects were required to see the letters and cognitive and respond on the keyboard with the right keys.

(2) The Second Set of Experiments.
Auditory - Cognitive: Subjects were required to recognize after hearing the letters via sound. The experiment included three trials with interval time of "2000ms" "1000ms", "600ms". The experimental requirements were based on hearing letters and to identify them.

Auditory - Cognitive - Respond: Subjects were required to respond after hearing the letters via sound. The experiment included three trials with interval time of "2000ms" "1000ms", "600ms". The experimental requirements were based on hear letters to identify them. Subjects were required to see the letters and respond on the keyboard with the right keys.

2.2 Apparatus and Environment

Apparatus: two pieces of black paper, Eyelink II eye movement measurement system(shown in Fig. 1).

Experimental environment: experiment required to keep the light environment unchanged with illumination about 120 LUX.

2.3 Subject

10 students (undergraduate and graduate) participated in this experiment, male, age 19-25, visual acuity 1.0-1.5.

Fig. 1. Eyelink II eye movement measurement system

3   The Real Value of Pupil Diameter

Since the design theory of Eyelink II eye tracker is optical reflection and the units of pupil size Recorded is in pixels, the relative position of the collecting equipment in eye instrument and the pupil will affect the pupil diameter size recorded. Every time put on the eye tracker, the relative position between pupil-infrared of the head and eyes are different. So pupil diameter values recorded in difference experiments cannot be analyzed together. Therefore, only the pupil diameter recorded by eye tracker is translated into real size, which can provide the possibility of analysis between pupil diameter data of different experimental tasks.

3.1 Calculation of Ratio

After subjects closed their eyes, two eyelids of the subject are pasted on two black-round pieces with the diameter known after, the real diameter defined as dz. The diameter measured value of two black-round pieces by eye tracker is defined as dc. Then the ratio is defined as the division of measuring value and real value of black-round piece, as in:

$$r = dc / dz \tag{1}$$

This ratio value is just the same with the current measurement position, the relative position between the infrared camera and eyes unchanged.

3.2 Conversion Method

After measuring the diameter of black-round piece, with the relative position the infrared camera of the head and eyes being unchanged, it can be measured with eye tracker. The pupil diameter under the task experiment recorded by eye tracker is

Dc .So the real pupil diameter value(D) can be obtain through the value of ratio and measuring value, as in:

$$D= Dc/r \qquad (2)$$

4   Data Processing

The pupil diameter collected by eye tracker was processed through formulas (1), (2), mentioned above. The result of one subject was shown in Table 1and Table 2.

As the size of the pupil diameter varies with light intensity, little position change of stimulator can arouse the change of pupil. In order to analyze the various value of pupil diameter due to the task load, it is a must to control other factors affecting the pupil size. Thus, we need to record and analysis the pupil diameter in the natural state in the current task (the current light and distance to the pupil) when processing the data. For a different task, when their data of natural state is different, we need to amend the data with the pupil diameter of natural state, as shown in Table 1.

Table 1. Data processing results of on subject of the first set experiment

	natural state	Trial 1 (2000ms)	Trial 2 (1000ms)	Trial 3 (600ms)	Trial 4 (300ms)
Visual tracking	3.313	3.322	3.375	3.358	3.273
Visual cognition	3.292	3.506	3.516	3.449	3.355
Visual cognitive operations	3.684	4.265	4.303	4.354	4.357
Difference between natural state	0.383				
Visual cognition (as amended)	3.300	3.881	3.919	3.970	3.973

Taking the experimental data of one subject as example, the results of the first set experiment are shown in Fig.2, the amending data shown in Fig.3. The experimental data amended of the second set experiment are shown in Fig.4.

Table 2. Data processing results of on subject of the second set experiment

	Natural state	Trial 1 (2000ms)	Trial 2 (1000ms)	Trial 3 (600ms)
Auditory-cognitive	3.645	4.155	4.307	4.381
Auditory-cognitive-operation	3.519	4.708	5.295	5.454

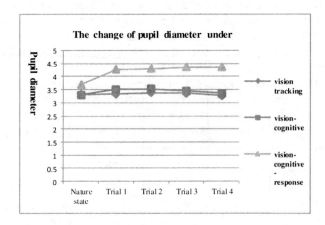

Fig. 2. The change curve of pupil diameter of the first set experiment of one subject

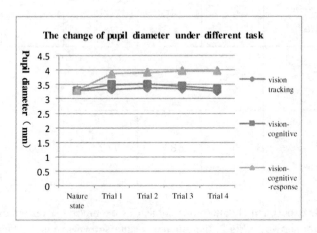

Fig. 3. The change curve of pupil diameter of the first set of experiments of one subject (having mended)

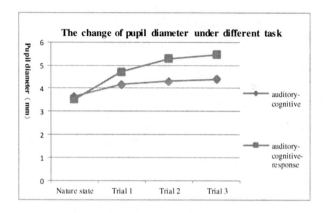

Fig. 4. The change curve of pupil diameter of the second set of experiments of one subject

The experimental data of other nine subjects were processed by the same method, and then average all the data of each task. The processing results are shown in Figure 5 and Figure 6.

As shown in Figure 5, we know that when the interval was set to 600ms and 300ms, with the increase of time pressure, pupil size stays in a relatively stable size.

Shown in Figure 6, the pupil diameters in Auditory-cognitive and Auditory-Cognitive-Respond tasks are increasing very obviously with the time pressure, and very regularly.

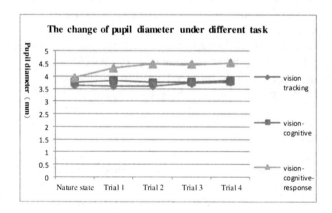

Fig. 5. The average value of pupil diameter of the first set of experiments of 10 subjects

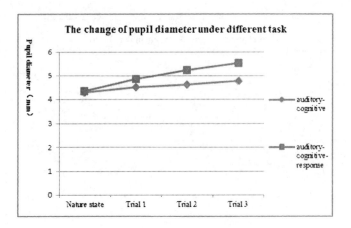

Fig. 6. The average value of pupil diameter of the second set of experiments of 10 subjects

5   Conclusion

In visual tracking experiments and visual cognition experiments, pupil size changes did not differ much from the results, which can determine the load of these two tasks being the same. Visual-Cognitive and Visual-Cognitive-Respond tasks caused by the pupil diameter changes were about 0.7mm or so.

For the tasks of Auditory-cognitive and Auditory-Cognitive-Respond tasks, both the slope of the curve and change size value can be used to represent the task load. The change values of pupil diameter between the two tasks are 0.75 mm.

The respond task of operation can be expressed by the value $(0.7 + 0.75) / 2 = 0.725$ mm of the pupil diameter changes.

The result shows that pupil diameter can be used as a good index to study task load quantitative analysis. There are some difficulties to establish the principle for giving task value, so the research for the task load quantitative analysis by pupil diameter has to continue for a long time.

6   Discussions

In the process of our experiment, we used three methods to measure task load, including subjective measurement, ECG measurement, and eye tracker measurement. From the measurement results, we found that subjective measurement and ECG measurement can't change accurately with the change of task load. So we can't to verify the experimental data by another method. So this paper has not presented the verification of the result. However, in the experiment, we can verify the data by doing different task by the subjects and doing the same experiment by the same subject in different time.

There are some difficulties to establish the principle for giving task value, so the research for the task load quantitative analysis by pupil diameter has to go on for a long time.

Acknowledgment. This research was under the strong support of the 973 Project of National Technological Department (2010CB734103).

References

1. Lysaght, R.J., Hill, S.G., et al.: Operator workload: comprehensive review and evaluation of operator workload methodologies. Fort Bliss, Texas, U.S. Army Research Institute for the Behavioural and Social Sciences: 262 (1989)
2. Hart, S.G., Staveland, L.E.: Development of a multi-dimensional workload rating scale: Results of empirical and theoretical research. In: Hancock, P.A., Meshkati, N. (eds.) Human Metal Workload, pp. 139–183 (1988)
3. WBI Evaluation Group, Cognitive task analysis. Needs assessment knowledge base (2007)
4. Eggemeier, F.T., Wilson, G.F., et al.: Workload assessment in multi-task environments. In: Damos, D.L. (ed.) Multiple Task Performance, pp. 207–216. Taylor & Francis, Ltd., London (1991)
5. Staveland, L.: Man-Machine Integration Design and Analysis System (MIDAS)Task Loading Model (TLM) Experimental and Software Detailed Design Report. Ames Research Center. CONTRACT NAS2-13210 (1994)
6. Corker, K.M.: An Architecture and Model for Cognitive Engineering Simulation Analysis Application to Advanced Aviation Automation. Presented at the AIAA Computing in Aerospace 9 Conference, San Diego, CA (1993)
7. Bierbaum: For developing a uh-60 workload prediction model, vol. IV: segment decision rules appendixes h and i. AD-A201 317 (1987)
8. Johnson, E.M.: Task Analysis/Workload (TAWL) User's Guide Version 3.0. U.S. Army Research Institute for the Behavioral and Social Sciences. AD-A221 865
9. Bierbaum, C.R., Hamilton, D.B.: Task Analysis and Workload Prediction for the MH-47E Mission and a Comparison with CH-47D Workload Predictions, vol. I: Summary Report. AD-A210 763 (1991)
10. Hamilton, D.B., Bierbaum, C.R.: Operator Workload Predictions for the Revised AH-64A Workload Prediction Model, vol. I: Summary Report. AD-A254 198 (1996)
11. Ahlstrom, U., Friedman-Berg, F.J.: Using eye movement activity as a correlate of cognitive workload. International Journal of Industrial Ergonomics 36, 623–636 (2006)
12. Van Orden, K.F., Jung, T.-P., Makeig, S.: Combined eye activity measures accurately estimate changes in sustained visual task performance. Biological Psychology 52, 221–240 (2000)
13. Wickens, C.D.: Multiple resources and performance prediction. Theoretical Issues in Ergonomics Science 3(2), 159–177 (2002)
14. Wickens, C.D., McCarley, J.S.: Applied Attention Theory, pp. 129–137. CRC Press (2008)

Analyzing Deceptive Speech

Christin Kirchhübel[1], Alex W. Stedmon[2], and David M. Howard[1]

[1] Audio Laboratory, Department of Electronics, University of York, UK
{ck531,david.howard}@york.ac.uk
[2] Cultural Communications and Computing Research Institute (C3RI),
Sheffield Hallam University, UK
a.stedmon@shu.ac.uk

Abstract. This current work explored the speech-based attributes of participants who were being deceptive in an experimental interrogation setting. In particular, the study attempted to investigate the appropriateness of using temporal speech cues in detecting deception. Deceptive and control speech was elicited from nineteen speakers and the data was analyzed on a range of speech parameters including Speaking Rate (SR), Response Onset Time (ROT) and frequency and duration of Hesitation markers. The findings point to a significant increase in SR, a significant decrease in ROT and a reduction in hesitation phenomena in the deceptive condition suggesting an acceleration of overall speaking tempo. The potential significance of temporal parameters for detecting deception in speech is recognized. However, the complex and multifaceted nature of deceptive behaviour is highlighted and caution is advised when attempting veracity judgments based on speech.

Keywords: Deception, Speaking Rate, Response Onset Time, Hesitations.

1 Introduction

Early research into characteristics of deception tended to focus on specific cues or behaviours that would reliably indicate that a deception was taking place. This has proved particularly problematic and more recently researchers have begun to investigate the emotional, cognitive and communicative processes that tend to accompany deception. Following this a number of theoretical frameworks have been developed to predict and account for the behaviour liars may display (De Paulo et al. 2003, Ekman, 1985, Miller & Stiff, 1993, Vrij, 2008). One such approach is the Cognitive Theory of deception that considers lying to be cognitively more demanding than truth-telling and empirical evidence supporting this line of thought can be found in the work of Walczyk et al. (2003, 2005).

From a speech analysis perspective, it has also been established that filled and unfilled pauses in speech are reactions associated with cognitive processes (Goldman-Eisler 1968). Based on this it may be hypothesised that the increase in cognitive load required for deception may lead to specific speech dependent measures of deception that would manifest themselves in the temporal domain, specifically, in an overall slowing down of speech.

D. Harris (Ed.): EPCE/HCII 2013, Part I, LNAI 8019, pp. 134–141, 2013.
© Springer-Verlag Berlin Heidelberg 2013

This current study explored the speech-based attributes of participants who were being deceptive in an experimental interrogation setting. Specific data were taken from audio recordings of the interrogation sessions that were part of a broader research study investigating a number of human deception responses across biological, physiological, psychological and behavioural dimensions. This paper presents an overview of the methodology that was relevant to the speech analysis and focuses specifically on the deceptive participants. More detailed descriptions of this research are contained in (Eachus et al. 2012).

2   Method

A total of 19 male participants were drawn from the staff and student population at the University of Nottingham where the experiment was conducted. All participants were native British English speakers and none had any self-reported voice, speech or hearing disorders.

A scalable interrogation paradigm was developed specifically for this study in which participants progressed from a baseline interview through two levels of interrogation (e.g. Baseline, Interview 1 and Interview 2). Participants were given a 'token' containing pictorial and verbal information that they had to conceal from the interviewers during the scaled interrogations. The Baseline interview contained neutral and relaxation based questions, designed to elicit control data and non-deceptive speech data. Both the interviews aimed to increase participant arousal by asking more probing and penetrating questions. Interview 1 provoked a low level of emotional involvement by posing general questions about social desirability and information concealment, whereas Interview 2 was more provocative by directly challenging participants about their truthfulness.

The questions for the three conditions were pre-recorded as audio files and presented via loudspeaker from a standard laptop computer to ensure that they remained constant across participants. For the most part, the questions were of a yes/no format resulting in the generation of short answer/monosyllabic responses. The three conditions contained 20 questions but in order to avoid participants anticipating the end of the interviews, the questions were not numbered in a serial fashion. The order of the conditions (e.g. Baseline, Interview 1 and Interview 2) was kept the same for all participants. Overall, the experiment took approximately 75 minutes to complete after which participants were debriefed and received a £30 participation reward.

3   Parameters Analysed

Every speaker provided 1 file for each of the three speaking conditions, resulting in 54 files for analysis. Given the nature of the data only a selected number of temporal parameters could be investigated. Amongst these were Speaking Rate (SR), Response Onset Time (ROT) and frequency as well as duration of filled pauses.

4   Apparatus

'Sound Forge TM Pro 10' software (Sony Creative Software) was used for initial editing of the speech files. The temporal analysis was performed using Praat 5.1.44 speech analysis software (Boersma & Weenink 2005). SR measurements were based on the number of phonetic syllables in each participant's speaking turns. ROT was measured as the time in between the end of a question and the beginning of the participant's response. With regards to hesitation markers, the frequency and duration of the 'vocalic' [ɛ] as well as 'vocalic + nasal' [ɛm] variants were taken into account. In order to control for differences in length of speaking time across conditions and speakers, the frequency aspect was conveyed in the form of a Hesitation Rate (HR) measurement calculated as number of hesitations per minute. Textgrids generated by Praat facilitated easy access to durational calculations which were then transferred into Microsoft Excel for a more accessible examination.

5   Results

The following section presents the results for all 19 speakers. Repeated Measures ANOVAs were employed to assess the significance of the inter- and intra-speaker comparisons for SR, ROT and frequency of hesitations. In cases where Mauchly's test indicated that the assumption of sphericity had been violated degrees of freedom were corrected using Greenhouse-Geisser estimates of sphericity. Post-hoc tests, if applicable, are reported using Bonferroni correction. Not every speaker employed hesitation markers which resulted in a lack of durational measures for some and, consequently, a reduction in sample size. Therefore, in order to account for the relatively small sample of durational measures, the non-parametric Friedman's ANOVA test was chosen.

5.1   Speaking Rate (SR)

Mean SR appeared to be affected by the different interview conditions. About half of the speakers tended to decrease their mean SR in Interview 1 while the other half showed an increase. Irrespective of the direction of change, the extent of change was similar ranging from 4.1%/-2.9% at the lower end to 29.5%/-31.2% at the upper spectrum. The results of Interview 2 were more coherent with 15 out of 19 speakers showing a higher mean SR compared to the Baseline. This increase spanned from 4.3% to 48.2%. A decrease was only noteworthy for 3 out of the 4 speakers covering a smaller range from -9.8% to -18.4%. Not only was there a traceable increase in mean SR in Interview 2 when compared to the Baseline, the effect was also evident, perhaps even more so, when contrasting the two interviews against each other. Almost all speakers exhibited a faster mean SR in Interview 2 than Interview 1 with values ranging from a 5.7% increase to a substantial 56.1% increase. At the inter-speaker level, mean SR changed significantly across the three conditions ($F (2, 36) = 7.271$, $p \leq .01$). Pairwise comparisons revealed that mean SR did not change significantly between Baseline (mean = 3.8 syll/sec) and Interview 1 (mean = 3.7 syll/sec) but that there was a significant increase in mean SR between Baseline and

Interview 2 (mean = 4.2 syll/sec) and between the two interviews. The observed trend of an increase in mean SR in Interview 2 also held true at the intra-speaker level. Post-hoc comparisons revealed a significant difference in mean SR between Baseline and Interviews for 7 out of the 19 participants. For the remaining 12 participants the change in mean SR between the three conditions was not significant ($p \geq .05$).

5.2   Response Onset Time (ROT)

Results from the ANOVA illustrated that mean ROT differed significantly between the three experimental tasks (F (1.316, 23.689) = 5.802, $p \leq .01$). Post hoc tests revealed that there was a significant decrease in ROT in Interview 1 (mean = 171ms) as compared to Baseline (mean = 228ms) and Interview 2 (mean = 196ms) ($p \leq .05$). Although no statistically significant change was observed between Baseline and Interview 2, a similar pattern of a reduction in ROT in the latter as compared to the Baseline was apparent. The majority of speakers showed a decrease in ROT for interview 1 which varied from 0.2 % to 63.7%. The magnitude of change for the four participants who increased their ROT in interview 1 only spanned from 1.7 % to 32.4% so the amount of maximum decrease in ROT was considerable larger than the amount of maximum increase. More participants increased their ROT in Interview 2 than Interview 1. The range of the increase in ROT displayed by seven participants was from 3.4% to 43.9%. The range of the reduction in ROT for the remaining 12 participants extended from 0.9% to 60.5%. Once again, the magnitude in decrease (227.6 ms) is greater than the magnitude in increase (146.9 ms). In terms of the intra-speaker analysis, seven of the participants showed a significantly lower ROT in one or both of the interview conditions when compared to the Baseline. Only one participant showed a significant difference in ROT between the two interview conditions.

5.3   Hesitations

Hesitations were analysed according to frequency and duration. As the calculation of HR resulted in only one numerical result per speaker per condition, statistical testing could only be performed on the inter-speaker level. The change in frequency of hesitations between the Baseline and two interview conditions was characterized by a decrease. A repeated-measures ANOVA illustrated that this change was statistically significant (F (1.185, 21.326) = 4.598, $p \leq .05$) and post-hoc comparisons identified that there were significantly less hesitations in Interview 2 (mean = 6.831 Hes/min) as compared to the Baseline (mean = 11.861 Hes/min). Although not statistically significant, the trend of a decrease in hesitations could also be observed for Interview 1 (mean = 7.750 Hes/min) as opposed to the Baseline. While a hesitation measure was obtained for all participants in the Baseline condition, the interview conditions often featured no hesitations at all. This was the case for 9 participants in Interview 1. 8 of the remaining 10 speakers decreased their HR by an average of 55.1%. Merely two participants employed more hesitations in Interview 1 as compared to the Baseline but for one of these the increase was striking reaching a doubling in HR from 30.18 Hes/min to 61.34 Hes/min. Similarly to interview 1, 7 participants did not produce any hesitations in interview 2 and 9 showed a decrease in HR averaging 55.4%. Three participants illustrated an increase in HR from Baseline to Interview 2 but the magnitude of increase was only noteworthy for one of the speakers reaching 57.6% as compared to 6% and 12% for the other two. 6 participants had no hesitations in either of the interviews. Thirteen participants demonstrated changes in hesitation frequency between the interviews but the direction of change varied amongst them with an equal number increasing and decreasing. While the range of decrease spanned from -0.7% to -33.4%, the increase was more remarkable stretching from 21% to 106.4%. Statistical examination confirmed no difference between Interview 1 and Interview 2 (p $\geq$.05). Only 9 out of the 19 speakers offered hesitation markers in all three conditions and even then the number of occurrences tended to be very low sometimes merely reaching 1 per condition. Therefore, it was decided to limit statistical testing to the inter-speaker level once again only using this subset of 9 participants. Duration of hesitations was significantly affected by the interviews ($x2$ (2) = 8, p $\leq$ .05). Wilcoxon Sign Ranked tests were used to follow up on this finding and it appeared that duration was no different between Baseline (mean = 43.9ms) and Interview 1 (mean = 41ms) or between Interview 1 and Interview 2 (mean = 36ms). However, for Interview 2, duration of hesitations was significantly lower compared to the Baseline (T = 0, p $\leq$ .01, r = -.63). None of the participants showed longer durations in Interview 2 when compared to the Baseline and for 5 out of the 9 participants this durational drop was particularly noticeable averaging around 30ms. For the remaining 4 participants the decrease was less striking ranging from 0.2ms to 3.2ms. While 6 participants also showed a reduction in hesitation length in Interview 1 ranging from 3.5ms to 17.1ms, we find that 3 participants produced longer hesitation markers as compared to the Baseline.

6   Summary and Discussion

A summary of the results is presented in Table 1. A significant increase in mean SR was observed for Interview 2 when contrasted with the Baseline and Interview 1. Mean ROT appeared to be decreasing across the two interview conditions compared to the Baseline but this reduction was only significant for Interview 1. Number of hesitations significantly declined in both interviews compared with the Baseline, but duration was only affected in Interview 2 which was characterized by a significant shortening in length of hesitation markers when compared against the Baseline values.

   For the majority of parameters examined the experimental effect manifested itself between the Baseline and either or both of the interview conditions. There tended to be little difference between the two interviews themselves despite the heightened interrogative pressure.The increase in mean SR in the interviews corresponds with the observed reduction in the number of hesitation pauses. In addition to this, the shorter ROTs would further indicate a general acceleration of speaking tempo when being deceptive.

Table 1. Summary of the results for all parameters investigated

Parameter	Interview 1	Interview 2
Speaking Rate (SR)	• Mixed results	• Significant increase compared to Baseline and Interview 1
Response Onset Time (ROT)	• Significant decrease compared to Baseline and interview 2	• Tendency for a decrease compared to Baseline
Frequency of Hesitations (HR)	• Significant decrease compared to Baseline • No change to Interview 2	• Significant decrease compared to Baseline • No change to Interview 1
Duration of Hesitations	• No significant change to Baseline or interview 2	• Significant decrease compared to Baseline

When probing the available literature, it appears that research into the temporal aspects of deceptive speech has resulted in conflicting observations. Indeed, the majority of studies tended to observe an overall slowing down of speaking tempo and, in particular, an increase in hesitation phenomena supporting the cognitive theory of deception as briefly outlined above. However, a number of studies exist which suggest the opposite, namely, a decrease in ROT and speech disturbances which complements the results of the current experiment (Benus et al. 2006, Vrij & Heaven 1999). A solution to the apparent disparity is offered by Vrij & Heaven (1999) who concluded that lie complexity affects pausing behavior. In their research the authors illustrated that liars made fewer speech disturbances when the lie was easy to fabricate as opposed to a more cognitively complex fabrication. Furthermore, research into prepared and spontaneous lying has shown that anticipated lies carried shorter ROTs compared to truthful utterances while spontaneous lies did not conform to this pattern (O'Hair et al. 1981).

In this study, participants were able to prepare for their deceptive act as they were informed, prior to the interrogation process, that they would be required to conceal knowledge. In addition, 'yes' or 'no' were legitimate answers to the majority of the questions and, therefore, it could be envisaged that the amount of cognitive energy necessary to carry out the deception in the present experiment was minimal. Participants may have resorted to some form of automated responding, akin to a suspect's 'no comment' strategy in PACE (Police and Criminal Evidence Act) interviews as the interrogations progressed. Goldman-Eisler (1968:58-59) has shown that routine and automated speech results in a decrease of pausing behavior and this could provide a viable explanation for the present findings.

Vrij & Heaven (1999) make reference to the attempted control theory in order to account for the decrease in speech disturbances apparent in their study. They argue that in order to present a truthful demeanour people may try to suppress or control behaviours which they associate with lying and consequently expect their target to be associating with lying. This type of behavioural management could lead to an 'overcontrol' of speech resulting in the decrease of hesitation phenomena. Both rationalizations are plausible and may work in tandem; however more empirical research is needed to assess the relationship between behavioural control and speech (Kirchhübel & Howard in press).

Having said all this and when taking a closer look at the experimental design one has to be careful not to come to premature conclusions. The nature of the data tended to reflect short answer responses and speaking turns tended to contain little speech and at times only 'yes' or 'no' responses. There are limitations of measuring tempo related speech characteristics using these types of utterances. Sound prolongation is one of the more obvious factors but at the other end of the scale we might also find syllable shortening both of which would unjustly influence mean SR measurements. The nature of yes/no responses also limit the opportunity for the realisation of hesitation markers and may affect ROT measures due to participants' engaging in automated/routine responding.

Amongst the many factors affecting speech, speaking context and setting have been shown to be influential (Giles et al. 1991). Compared to the Baseline which aimed to create a positive and warm atmosphere, the two interviews posed a more threatening communicative environment. Setting aside the participants' intent to deceive, the interrogation process itself could have contributed to participants feeling intimidated and affronted and may therefore have resorted to speech divergence and limited information sharing. The presence of variability within as well as between participants underlines the fact that deceptive behaviour is individualised, very multifaceted and far from being clear cut, a finding which repeatedly emerges in research on deception (Kirchhübel & Howard 2012).

7   Conclusion and Limitations

The present research highlights the complex nature of deception and underlines the difficulties in locating consistent cues of deceptive behavior. There are a range of factors that affect deceptive behaviour with 'lie complexity' and 'time to prepare for deception' being of most relevance to the present experiment. Differences in research design and analysis methods as well as failure to control for the various confounding variable have led to discrepancies in results. Temporal analysis may be useful for deceptive speech detection but may only apply in specific settings and certainly needs to take into account situational as well as individual factors. Applying the research to a practical setting, caution needs to be employed when attempting veracity judgments based on the temporal characteristics of speech regardless of whether the speech stemmed from formal interviews or polygraph examinations using the guilty knowledge paradigm (Lykken 1998). It is worth emphasizing that more data is in existence which was taken from of a group of truth-tellers undergoing the same experimental procedure. Unfortunately, the deceptive and truthful speech samples are based on a between-subjects design and, therefore, the scope for direct comparison of features is limited; however, temporal speech analysis of the truth-tellers would nevertheless offer additional insight and is planned in future work.

References

1. Benus, S., Enos, F., Hirschberg, J., Shriberg, E.: Pauses in deceptive Speech. In: Proceedings ISCA 3rd International Conference on Speech Prosody, Dresden, Germany (2006)
2. DePaulo, B.M., Lindsay, J.J., Malone, B.E., Muhlenbruck, L., Charlton, K., Cooper, H.: Cues to deception. Psychological Bulletin 129(1), 74–118 (2003)
3. Eachus, P., Stedmon, A.W., Baillie, L.: Hostile Intent in Crowded Places: A Field Study. Applied Ergonomics (2012), http://dx.doi.org/10.1016/j.apergo.2012.05.009
4. Ekman, P.: Telling lies: Clues to deceit in the marketplace, politics and marriage. W. W. Norton, New York (1985) (Reprinted in 1992 and 2001)
5. Giles, H., Coupland, N., Coupland, J.: Accommodation Theory: Communication, Context and Consequence. In: Giles, H., Coupland, J., Coupland, N. (eds.) Contexts of Accommodation: Developments in Applied Sociolinguistics. CUP, Cambridge (1991)
6. Goldman-Eisler, F.: Psycholinguistics. Experiments in Spontaneous Speech. Academic Press, London (1968)
7. Kirchhübel, C., Howard, D.M.: Detecting suspicious behavior using speech: Acoustic correlates of deceptive speech – an exploratory investigation. Applied Ergonomics (2012), http://dx.doi.org/10.1016/j.apergo.2012.04.016
8. Kirchhübel, C & Howard, D. M.: Deception and Speech – a theoretical overview (in press)
9. Lykken, D.: A Tremor in the Blood: Uses and Abuses of the Lie Detector. Perseus Publishing, Reading (1998)
10. Miller, G.R., Stiff, J.B.: Deceptive Communication. Sage, Newbury Park (1993)
11. O'Hair, H.D., Cody, M., McLaughlin, M.L.: Prepared lies, spontaneous lies, Machiavellianism and nonverbal communication. Human Communication Research 7, 325–339 (1981)
12. Vrij, A.: Detecting lies and deceit: pitfalls and opportunities, 2nd edn. Wiley, West Sussex (2008)
13. Vrij, A., Heaven, S.: Vocal and verbal indicators of deception as a function of lie complexity. Psychology, Crime & Law 5, 203–315 (1999)
14. Walczyk, J.J., Roper, K.S., Seemann, E., Humphrey, A.M.: Cognitive mechanisms underlying lying to questions: Response time as a cue to deception. Applied Cognitive Psychology 17, 744–755 (2003)
15. Walcyyk, J.J., Schwartz, J.P., Clifton, R., Adams, B., Wei, M., Zha, P.: Lying person-to-person about live events: A cognitive framework for lie detection. Personnel Psychology 58, 141–170 (2005)

A Detection Method of Temporary Rest State While Performing Mental Works by Measuring Physiological Indices

Shutaro Kunimasa, Kazune Miyagi, Hiroshi Shimoda, and Hirotake Ishii

Graduate School of Energy Science, Kyoto University, Kyoto, Japan
{kunimasa,miyagi,shimoda,hirotake}@ei.energy.kyoto-u.ac.jp

Abstract. In order to evaluate intellectual productivity such as the efficiency of performing mental works, several studies were conducted where specially designed tasks were given. However, the result may not be reflected the actual intellectual productivity because the designed tasks are different from office works. Meanwhile, there are two mental states (work and temporary rest state) in office workers which are changing alternatively during mental work and the ratio of the two states reflects the productivity. If the mental states of the workers can be detected, the productivity can be measured more accurately. In this study, a detection method of temporary rest state while performing mental works by measuring physiological indices has been developed. As the result of the subject experiment, it was found that the detection accuracy was 80.2%. This result shows the possibility to use the physiological indices as one of the mental state detection methods.

Keywords: intellectual productivity, physiological psychology, cognitive psychology, office work, mental work.

1 Introduction

Recently, mental works such as intellectual works have occupied most of office works in companies and have become more and more valuable in our society. Therefore economic and social benefits can be bigger by improving intellectual productivity such as the efficiency and accuracy of performing mental works. In order to achieve this, the evaluation of intellectual productivity is required, and several studies have been conducted. Obayashi et al. have developed specially designed tasks for quantitative evaluation of intellectual productivity [1]. However, a number of tasks used in experiments for the evaluation are different from actual office works, because the tasks have been designed in order for experimenters to collect operation logs easily and accurately. In order to evaluate intellectual productivity in actual office, it is desired to use actual office works. It is, however, difficult to collect and evaluate most of their logs.

On the other hand, Miyagi et al. [2] have revealed that there are two mental states (work and non-work state) in the office workers which change alternatively

D. Harris (Ed.): EPCE/HCII 2013, Part I, LNAI 8019, pp. 142–150, 2013.

during mental work. And, intellectual productivity can be evaluated quantitatively by using the ratio of these two states. In particular, the non-work state has a negative influence on the intellectual productivity.

Meanwhile, physiological indices are supposed to reflect various mental states such as arousal, concentration, anxiousness, stress, relaxation. Thus, there have been several studies as to the detection of mental states by using physiological indices: Miyagi et al. measured brain activity during mental works with Near-Infrared Spectroscopy [3]. Hosseini, S.A. et al. proposed a new system recognizing emotional stress using electroencephalogram (EEG) [4].

In this study, therefore, the authors have aimed at developing a detection method of the non-work state (it is called temporary rest state here and after) by measuring physiological indices such as electrocardiogram (ECG), electromyogram (EMG), around left eye and EEG. If this detection method can be developed, intellectual productivity in office works can be evaluated quantitively because this method requires only measuring physiological indices of office workers, not specially designed tasks.

2 Method

2.1 Participants and Measurement

26 healthy volunteers participated in this experiment who are the ages of 19 to 25 and could operate PC without difficulty and their native language was Japanese. The experimental period was approximately 2 hours. The subjects were instructed to conduct mental tasks and their physiological indices were measured. And based on these indices, their two mental states (work state and temporary rest state) have been detected. The temperature, illuminance, and ambient noise of the experimental room were controlled to $25 \pm 1°C$, 680lx, and $50 \pm 3db$ respectively.

In this experiment, the subjects equipped the instruments, and their ECG, EMG around left eye, EEG have been measured. The position of these electrodes is shown in Fig. 1.

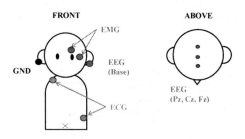

Fig. 1. The position of these electrodes

EEG electrodes were placed on Pz, Cz and Fz according to the international 10-20 system and their midline electrode was placed on left earlobe. ECG electrodes were placed on the left side of the body and the right side of the neck. EMG electrodes were placed on the left temple and upper part of the left eye blow.

2.2   Experimental Design

The experiment consisted of 2 measurements ,where the subjects performed tasks in 3 conditions which were defined as follows:

Task Condtion
> In this condition, the subjects were instructed to perform mental tasks, which require intellectual ability. Therefore, the physiological indices measured in this condition were regarded as that in the work state.

Control Condition
> The subjects were instructed to move their arms and fingers as the same way as the task condition without thinking. In other words, they performed non-mental tasks demanding little intellectual ability. Hence, the physiological data in this condition were regarded as that in the temporary rest state.

Rest Condtion
> In this condition, the subjects were instructed to stop moving, relax, and gaze a black fixation cross without thinking. The physiological data in this condition were also regarded as that in the temporary rest state.

In one of these 2 measurements, the subjects were required to change these 3 conditions in turn as a presented display was switched automatically every 30 seconds as shown in Fig. 2, and these procedures were repeated 5 times. Tasks, figures (squares, triangles, and circles), and a black fixed cross were presented respectively in the task condition, the control condition, and the rest condition. This measurement is called Automatic Switching Measurement (ASM). It was conducted in order to collect the same amount of the data in these 3 conditions.

In the other measurement, a presented display was not switched, and the subjects were instructed to perform tasks for 7.5 minutes by switching these 3 conditions freely. This measurement is called Free Switching Measurement (FSM). It was expected that the subjects changed the work state and temporary rest state spontaneously in this measurement.

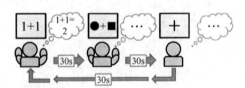

Fig. 2. The sequence of task in automatic switching measurement

5 types of tasks such as 1-digit addition, classification, and text typing were employed in order to confirm the independence of the detection performance on tasks.

2.3   Tasks

5 types of tasks were used which were 1-digit addition, 3-digit addition, classification, block assembling, text typing in the experiment. These tasks are supposed to be relatively similar to office works [1].

1-Digit Addition
  The subjects were instructed to do the sum of two 1-digit integers presented on a PC display in their heads, and type the answer by using a numeric keypad of the PC.

3-Digit Addition
  They were instructed to remember one 3-digit integer and press the enter key. Then another 3-digit integer was presented and they were instructed to do the sum of these two 3-digit integers in their heads and type the answer by using a numeric keypad of the PC.

Block Assembling
  In the case of this task, they were instructed to freely assemble blocks presented on a PC display and name a assembled figure as shown in Fig. 3.

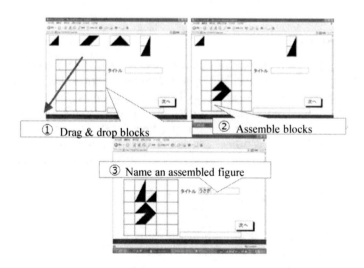

Fig. 3. Block assembling task

Text Typing

They were instructed to type sentences presented on a PC display with a keyboard. The presented sentences were the Japanese proverbs which are well-known in Japan. Owing to this, the subjects whose native languages are Japanese were employed in this experiment.

Classification

They were instructed to look at the amount, date, name of a company in a receipt as shown in Fig.4 and classify it by tapping one of 27 buttons in the classification table on iPad display as shown in Fig.5.

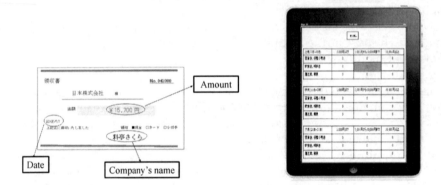

Fig. 4. An example of receipts in classification task

Fig. 5. The classification table on iPad display

2.4   Data Analysis

After each measurement, 6 feature values were extracted every 2 seconds from the measured physiological indices, and these values were divided into the work state group or temporary rest state group by using the operation log of the presented tasks. Finally, Mahalanobis distance between these 2 groups was calculated so that the correct discrimination probability (theoretical value) was calculated. In this study, Mahalanobis distance, D^2, is a generalized measure of the distance between the work or temporary rest state groups. The distance is defined as

$$D_{12}^2 = (n + h - 2) \sum_{i=1}^{p} \sum_{j=1}^{p} w_{ij}^{-1} (\overline{X_{i1}} - \overline{X_{i2}})(\overline{X_{j1}} - \overline{X_{j2}}) \tag{1}$$

where n is the number of samples in work state, h is the number of samples in temporary rest state, p is the number of variables ($p = 6$ in this study.), $\overline{X_{i1}}$ is the mean for the ith variables in work state, $\overline{X_{i2}}$ is the mean for the the ith variables in temporary rest state, w_{ij}^{-1} is an element from the inverse of the within-groups covariance matrix. If the distribution of samples is assumed to be a multivariate normal distribution, the error rate (e) in Mahalanobis discriminant analysis is defined as

$$e = \frac{1}{\sqrt{2\pi}} \int_{D/2}^{\infty} exp(-\frac{u^2}{2})du \tag{2}$$

Then, the correct discrimination probabilities is $1 - e$. Note that the minimum of the probabilities is 50 % .

The method of extracting feature values from physiological indices is described below.

ECG

In this analysis, the high (0.20 to 0.35 Hz) and low (0.05 to 0.20 Hz) frequency wave of heart rate were calculated. In order to calculate these feature values, the Gabor Wavelet transform [5, 6] have been applied among various types of frequency analysis methods because 2 second time window was too short to apply other frequency analysis method. The concrete transform equation is described below;

$$WT(b,a) = \frac{1}{\sqrt{|a|}} \int_{-\infty}^{\infty} f(t)\overline{\psi(\frac{t-b}{a})}dt \tag{3}$$

$$\psi(t) = \frac{1}{\sqrt{2\pi\sigma^2}} e^{\frac{t^2}{2\sigma^2} - i2\pi t} \tag{4}$$

where $1/a$ and b correspond to frequency and time respectively. And $\psi(t)$ is Gabor's function.

EMG around left eye

From EMG around left eye, the intervals of eye blink and saccade eye movement were extracted. Several studies have reported that eye blink and saccade eye movement reflect human higher cognitive process and psychological state [7–9].

EEG

In the analysis of EEG, brain waves of EEG at Fz and Cz were excluded from this analysis because EMG caused by eye blinking affected the brain waves as artifact. And alpha (8 to 13 Hz) and beta (13 to 30Hz) wave at Pz were calculated by the Fourier transform.

3   Result

R waves of ECG of 5 subjects could not be detected properly or the amplitude of these waves have been found too small, so that the measured data of these subjects were excluded from the analysis. And there were 2 cases where a task could not be performed for a fault of experimental PC, so that the measured data when the fault occurred were also excluded.

Table 1 shows the correct discrimination probabilities in ASM and FSM. The average of the detecting performance as to all the presented tasks in these 2 measurements was 80.2% .

Table 1. Correct discrimination probabilities in ASM and FSM

Task	n	Correct discrimination probability			
		ASM		FSM	
		Mean(%)	SD	Mean(%)	SD
1-digit addition	21	85.4	10.7	83.4	10.1
3-digit addition	21	83.4	9.0	82.6	9.5
Block assembling	20	75.5	5.4	78.3	10.3
Text typing	20	71.0	6.1	81.1	8.0
Classification	21	78.5	7.6	79.3	7.7

As shown in Table 1, the accuracy of the proposed method in ASM is significantly lower than in FSM in only the case of text tying task ($p < 0.01$).

4   Discussion

As noted above, the detecting performance as to only text typing in ASM was significantly lower than in FSM. Likely explanations are hinted at by the low mental workload of text typing and the difference between the time length of task condition in the case of ASM and FSM: while subjects were performing text typing, it required them only to look at the presented sentence and type it, not to perform higher cognitive activities (e.g. assembling a sentence, correction in some words, and so on). In addition, they had no trouble in typing words with keyboard because they could operate PC without difficulty. Thus, text typing required lower mental workload than the other tasks, which probably caused the physiological data to change a little and slowly under task condition. Owing to this, the authors consider that in comparison with the other tasks, text typing required longer time length of task condition in order to measure the significant differences between the physiological data under task condition (the work state) and control/rest conditions (the temporary rest state). In the case of ASM, each condition was changed automatically every 30 seconds. The time length of task condition were probably too short for the data under this condition to change significantly. On the contrary, as for FSM, the subjects could change each condition at their own paces. According to the operation logs of this task, most of the subjects remained under task condition for more than 30 seconds (the mean time length of task condition was 59.0 seconds.). The time length was probably long enough for the physiological data under this condition to change significantly. Besides, if the significant differences between the data under task condition and control/rest conditions cannot be measured, the detecting performance becomes low. For these reasons, the accuracy of the proposed method as to text typing in ASM was significantly lower than in FSM.

Based on analysis of variance, no significant differences were found in the results between these 5 tasks in FSM ($F(4, 98) = 2.47, p = 0.435$), while as for ASM, significant differences were found ($F(4, 98) = 2.47, p < 0.01$). Hence, it can be argued that as for FSM there is no dependence of the detection performance

on tasks. This suggests that the experimenter should let subjects perform mental works at their own paces in order to detect their mental states accurately.

As mentioned above, the mean accuracy of the proposed method was 80.2 %. The value is not close to 100%, which is the maximum of the discrimination probability, but 30.2% higher than the minimum of the probability (50%). This suggests that there is still room remaining to improve this method, but there is also the possibility that the work state and the temporary rest state in mental workers can be detected based on physiological indices by using this method.

In this study, the presented tasks were designed in order to collect their operational logs and to evaluate the discrimination probability of the proposed method. However, it is necessary to use actual office works so as to evaluate intellectual productivity in office. In the future, the authors will confirm whether the method can be applied to other tasks and actual office works.

Meanwhile, this study have employed the physiological indices such as EEG, ECG and EMG around left eye, but others such as electrodermogram (EDG) [10,11], cerebral blood flow (CBF) [12] have a possibility to reflect mental states. Therefore other physiological indices should be considered in order to establish more accurate detection method.

5   Conclusion

There are two mental states (work and temporary rest state) in office workers which are changing alternatively during mental works [2]. In this study, the authors have aimed at developing the detection method of these states by measuring physiological indices and conducted a subject experiment.

As the result, the average of the discrimination probability is 80.2 %. This result suggested the possibility that physiological indices could be used to evaluate intellectual productivity such as the efficiency and accuracy of performing mental works. However, the proposed method still cannot be applied to the evaluation of intellectual productivity in actual office works, because the employed tasks were specially designed in order to collect the operation logs in this study. Therefore, it is necessary to consider the detection method available to office works.

Finally, the authors are aiming at developing the more accurate detection method applied to the evaluation of the intellectual productivity in office.

References

1. Obayashi, F., Tomita, K., Hattori, Y., Kawauchi, M., Shimoda, H., Ishii, H., Terano, M., Yoshikawa, H.: A Study on Environmental Control Method to Improve Productivity of Office Workers Development of an Illumination Control Method and its Experimental Evaluation. Human Interface Society 1, 151–156 (2006)
2. Miyagi, K., Kawano, S., Ishii, H., Shimoda, H.: Improvement and Evaluation of Intellectual Productivity Model Based on Work State Transition. In: The 2012 IEEE International Conference on Systems, Man, and Cybernetics, pp. 1491–1496 (2012)

3. Miyagi, K., Kondo, Y., Enomoto, K., Ishii, H., Shimoda, H., Iwakawa, M., Terano, M.: Measurement of Brain Activity with Near-Infrared Spectroscopy during Performance Test for Assessing Improvement of Intellectual Productivity. Human Interface 10, 149–154 (2008)
4. Hosseini, S.A., Khalilzadeh, M.A.: Emotional Stress Recognition System Using EEG and Psychophysiological Signals: Using New Labelling Process of EEG Signals in Emotional Stress State. In: 2010 International Conference on Biomedical Engineering and Computer Science (ICBECS), pp. 1–6 (2010)
5. Omi, N., Morimoto, Y., Yokoyama, K., Mizuno, Y., Takata, K.: Heart Rate Variability Analysis during Long Distance Driving Using Wavelet Transform. Technical Report of IEICE 99, 9–14 (1999)
6. Omi, N., Morimoto, Y., Yokoyama, K., Mizuno, Y., Takata, K.: Application of Wavelet Analysis to Heart Rate Variability. Technical Report of IEICE 97, 47–52 (1998)
7. Forgarty, C., Stern, J.A.: Eye movements and blinks: their relationship to higher cognitive process. International Journal of Psychophysiology 8, 35–42 (1989)
8. Ichikawa, N., Ohira, H.: Eyeblink activity as an index of cognitive processing: temporal distribution of eyeblinks as an indicator of expectancy in semantic priming. Perceptual and Motor Skills 98, 131–140 (2004)
9. Fukuda, K., Stern, J.A., Brown, T.R., Russo, M.B.: Cognition, Blinks, Eye-Movements, and Pupillary Movements During Performance of a Running Memory Task. Aviation, Space, and Environmental Medicine 76, C75–C85 (2005)
10. Bursteinm, K.R., Fenz, W.D., Bergeron, J., Epstei, S.: A comparison of skin potential and skin resistance responses as measures of emotional responsivity. Psychophysiology 2, 12–24 (1965)
11. Umezawa, A., Kurohara, A.: A Comparison of Skin Conductance and Skin Potential as an Index in Electrodermal Biofeedback Studies. Japanese Society of Biofeedback Research 21, 26–36 (1994)
12. Matsumura, K., Sawada, Y.: Cardiovascular responses during two kinds of mental arithmetic tasks. The Japanese Journal of Psychology 79, 473–480 (2009)

Affective Priming with Subliminal Auditory Stimulus Exposure

Juan Liu, Yan Ge, and Xianghong Sun[*]

Institute of Psychology, Chinese Academy of Sciences
sunxh@psych.ac.cn

Abstract. The primacy hypothesis about affection (Zajonc, 1980) holds that positive and negative affective reactions can be elicited with minimal stimulus input and virtually no cognitive processing. This hypothesis challenges the cognitive appraisal viewpoint (Lazarus, 1982), which maintains that affection cannot emerge without prior cognitive mediation. There have been many studies shown that human emotion could be affected by subliminal visual stimulus, so how about subliminal auditory stimulus (SAS)? In this study two pieces of traditional Chinese music were used as SAS, and the unheard music was played in a continuous loop, which was different from the commonly used priming paradigm. 56 undergraduates were randomly divided into two groups; participants in one group were exposed to the subliminal happy music, and in the other group were exposed to the subliminal sad music. A before-and-after self-paired design was used to assess the emotion of all the subjects. During the experiment their galvanic skin response (GSR) and subjective ratings were recorded. The results showed that SAS caused the obviously change on human's GSR, but there was no change found in their subjective ratings of emotional valence (happy-unhappy). A lot of evidence showed that GSR was more sensitive than subjective ratings for the evaluation to current emotion status. The overall results of our study confirmed this perspective. So, we believed that SAS affected people's emotion, and this kind of affective priming wasn't perceived consciously by people themselves.

Keywords: Effective priming, Subliminal auditory stimulus, Emotion, Unconscious.

1 Introduction

The relationship between emotion and consciousness is becoming a research hotspot in psychology. Many scholars have done lots of experiments and found that emotional perception, especially negative emotion perception could occur without conscious awareness. In recent years, numerous relevant studies have been conducted using fMRI and ERP technology. The fMRI and ERP technology are non-invasive method of measuring brain activity during cognitive processing. Psychologists investigate brain activity related to affective changes. However, the results of their studies have often been inconsistent.

---

[*] Corresponding author.

D. Harris (Ed.): EPCE/HCII 2013, Part I, LNAI 8019, pp. 151–157, 2013.

Neuro-imaging studies have shown that emotional stimuli, especially fearful facial expression, elicit strong activation of the amygdale even when the expressions are spatially unattended or backward masked and inaccessible to conscious awareness[1].This functional imaging work is particularly interesting in that the enhanced activation of the amygdala has been activated in response to unconscious threat-related stimuli. This result is consistent with the view that in a binocular rivalry paradigm, even during suppressed periods of binocular rivalry, fearful faces still generate a strong response in the amygdala. Compared with the visible condition, binocular rivalry suppression also eliminated activity to fearful faces whereas amygdala activity was robust in both the visible and invisible conditions [2]. However, there are some studies which do not support the view that perceptual processing of emotional (especially threat) stimuli do not necessarily depend on conscious. On the basis of the fMRI study of Vuilleumier et al, Holmes explores the same problem using event-related brain potential (ERP) technology. In this event-related brain potential (ERP) study, Observers viewed emotional face stimuli, either attentively or inattentively. The experiments showed that visible emotional faces elicited a significantly larger negative deflection starting at 170ms (compared to invisible faces). Therefore, the author believes that emotional processing is dominated by consciousness [3]. Phillips and his colleagues investigated the relation of facial expression perception and conscious with functional magnetic resonance imaging (fMRI). A backward masking paradigm was used. In the psychophysics experiment, the following parameters were established: 30ms target duration for the non-consciously perceived (covert) condition, and 170ms target duration for the consciously perceived (overt) condition. Results of the block-design fMRI study indicated substantial differences underlying the perception of fearful facial expressions: the overt condition (170 ms) generated amygdala activation to fearful faces while in the covert condition (30 ms), the amygdala was not activated to fear [4]. Overall, the above inconsistent conclusions demonstrate that there is debate in cognitive neuroscience whether emotional stimuli can actually be perceived without awareness. Different laboratories have reached different conclusion, the reason is that levels of consciousness are manipulated by different method and stimuli are measured by different standards, whether the subjective threshold method or objective signal detection method.

Existing studies mainly focus on the emotional visual stimuli processing and it is unknown if subliminal stimuli of other sensory channels, such as auditory channel and tactile channel, can evoke emotional reactions. And it is not clear that whether the emotion processing activated by subliminal stimuli from different sensory channels is the same and how they are influenced by consciousness. Thus we study the effect of subliminal auditory stimuli on emotion, using electrophysiological measurement method to explore participants' emotion change activated by two pieces of traditional Chinese music. Music is an abstract symbolic language with no specific references or associations. Nevertheless, its intrinsic pattern and structure convey meaning to our brain [5]. This study will expand the research on emotional perception and consciousness. We predict that affective priming will be activated by subliminal auditory stimuli.

2   Method

2.1 Participants

28 participants (half men and half women, aged 21-27, mean age 23.64 years) re-cruited for this experiment are college students and all of them have normal visual acuity (or corrected visual acuity). All participants reported normal hearing and no history of neurological disease. Participants were non-musicians who had no formal musical training (besides typical school education) and had never learned to play a musical instrument. Participants were asked to sign an informed consent form before commencing testing, and were paid for their participation. The whole test session lasted about 16min.

2.2 Apparatus

The experiment stimuli were presented by Lenovo computer (Intel Pentium 4). Partic-ipants heard the auditory stimuli through headphones. All physiological recordings were performed by a Biopac MP150 system (Biopac Systems Inc., USA).

2.3 Experimental Materials

- **Subliminal Auditory Stimuli**.

The Subliminal sound files were edited by Adobe Audition Software.

a)   The happy song.
The Chinese Folk Symphony 《Spring Festival Overture》 was selected as the sub-liminal happy music. The happy music was masked by a loud sound of mental arith-metic task, and the target sound intensity level was 42 dB higher than the level of masking sound. The song lasted eight minutes. The music continued playing during the whole experiment period. Participants completed mental addition of 1-digit num-ber and 1-digit number in the first two minutes and mental subtraction of 1-digit number and 1-digit number in the last two minutes. In the middle four minutes, partic-ipants rested and kept listening to the subliminal music, the sound intensity level of which was 0db.

b)   The sad song.
The Chinese famous music 《Moonlight on The Pond》 was selected as the subli-minal sad music. The sad music was masked by a loud sound of mental arithmet-ic task, and the target sound intensity level was 37 dB higher than the level of masking sound. The song lasted eight minutes. The music continued playing during the whole experiment period. Participants completed mental addition of 1-digit num-ber and 1-digit number in the first two minutes and mental subtraction of 1-digit number and 1-digit number in the last two minutes. In the middle four minutes, partic-ipants rested and kept listening to the subliminal music, the sound intensity level of which was 0db.

- **The Emotion Self-Rating Scale**.

As shown in Figure 1, the whole length of the emotion self-rating scale is 13cm. The point of "very unhappy" has a coordinate of -6.5, and the coordinate of 0 for "neither unhappy nor happy" and the coordinate of 6.5 for "very happy".

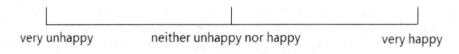

very unhappy   neither unhappy nor happy   very happy

Fig. 1. The emotion self-rating scale

2.4 Procedure and Experimental Design

The experiment was conducted in a sound-proof and electrically shielded cabin. On arrival at the laboratory, participants were told that the study consisted of a mental arithmetic task. Participants were seated in a comfortable self-adjustable chair. The subliminal auditory stimulus (music) was presented through headphones during the whole experiment. Every participant was asked to finish the task for two times, one time without subliminal stimuli and the other time with subliminal auditory music. The experiment lasted about sixteen minutes. Participants did not report experiencing any feelings in response to the primes.

A paired design and a paired analysis were employed in this study. The presentation order is completely balanced. The independent variable was emotional priming, including two levels: no stimuli and subliminal auditory stimuli. The dependent variables used to value emotion in this research were galvanic skin response (GSR) and emotion self-rating results.

3   Results

The key question addressed by our analyses was whether subliminal auditory primes influence participants' emotion.

3.1 The Galvanic Skin Response (GSR)

a)   **Listening to the Happy Music of** 《**Spring Festival Overture**》.
The statistical results of participants' GSR are provided in Table 1.

Table 1. The descriptive statistics of GSR (N=28, hearing happy music)

	GSR	
	M (μmho)	S (μmho)
No Subliminal Stimuli	0.091	0.022
Subliminal Happy Music	0.075	0.018

Paired-Samples T Test was used to explore the impact of sub threshold happy music on GSR. The results showed that there were significant differences, t (27) =2.226, p=0.030*. Obviously, the subliminal music of 《Spring Festival Overture》significantly affect the participants' GSR.

b) Listening to the Sad Music of 《Moonlight on The Pond》.
The statistical results of participants' GSR are provided in Table 2.

Table 2. The descriptive statistics of GSR (N=25, hearing sad music)

	GSR	
	M (μmho)	S (μmho)
No Subliminal Stimuli	0.091	0.022
Subliminal Sad Music	0.077	0.029

Paired-Samples T Test was used to explore the impact of sub threshold sad music on GSR. The results showed that there were significant differences, t (24) =2.269, p=0.037*. Obviously, the subliminal music of 《Moonlight on The Pond》significantly affect the participants' GSR.

3.2 The Emotion Self-rating Results

a) Listening to the Happy Music of 《Spring Festival Overture》.
The statistical results of emotion self-rating are provided in Table 3.

Table 3. The descriptive statistics of emotion self-rating (N=28, hearing happy music)

	Emotion Self-Rating	
	M	S
No Subliminal Stimuli	2.226	1.850
Subliminal Happy Music	2.690	1.928

Paired-Samples T Test was used to explore the impact of sub threshold happy music on emotion self-rating. The results showed that there was no difference, t (27) =1.693, p=0.118.

b) Listening to the Sad Music of 《Moonlight on The Pond》.
The statistical results of emotion self-rating are provided in Table 4.

Table 4. The descriptive statistics of emotion self-rating (N=25, hearing sad music)

	Emotion Self-Rating	
	M	S
No Subliminal Stimuli	1.307	1.384
Subliminal Sad Music	0.842	2.101

Paired-Samples T Test was used to explore the impact of sub threshold sad music on emotion self-rating. The results showed that there was no difference, t (24) =1.5045, p=0.176.

4   Discussion and Conclusions

Subliminal perception is a kind of unconscious perception, people can not consciously perceive. Plenty of studies have found that the level of unconscious processing is relatively low. That is to say, with the influence of unconscious perception, one can process the physical characteristics of the word, without understanding the meaning [6-8]. The research on affective priming has a long history of more than 30 years. The affective primacy hypothesis holds that affective reactions can be elicited with minimal stimulus input [9]. This hypothesis challenges the cognitive appraisal viewpoint, which maintains that affect cannot emerge without prior cognitive mediation [10]. Indeed, the affective primacy hypothesis hinges on the assumption that the simple affective qualities of stimuli, such as good versus bad or positive versus negative, can be processed more readily than their non-affective attributes. The mere exposure paradigm, however, provides only indirect evidence for this contention. Clearly, more direct evidence is needed.

In our experiment, we explored the effect of subliminal auditory music on emotion, and the presentation of subliminal stimuli was different from traditional unconscious stimuli forms. We made the auditory stimuli unheard by an ideal sound-masking solution. In addition, the subliminal stimuli in our experiment persist during the whole experiment time. Comprehensively analyzing the experiment results, we found that subliminal emotional music greatly influenced human's galvanic skin response (GSR), but did not have significant effect on their own feelings. The galvanic skin response seemed to be a reliable measure of emotional intensity when emotion was viewed not as a special type of mental or behavioral state but rather as a description of an individual who was energized, activated, mobilized for emergency. GSRs had been found to be relatively great to words which were emotionally toned, meaningful, conflicting, and tension or fear-arousing[11]. Rankin and Campbell found highly significant differential GSRs (P< .001) in subjects to Negro and white experimenters [12]. Based on the psycho physiological significance of GSR, it was suggested that although all the participants did not hear the emotional music, but they were indeed significantly affected by those subliminal sound. It was apparent that affect could be elicited without the participation of subjects' awareness. More interesting, however, was the fact that the non-conscious priming of affective reactions under certain conditions might be more successful than when it was with subjects' full awareness. What were the differences between conscious and non-conscious priming? The results showed that participants did not feel their mood change but their physiological indexes (GSR) changed obviously. It seemed quite possible that the techniques which may be effectively used to activated emotion. Because emotion elicited by this way would be more natural and more sustainable. Furthermore, this kind of emotion may be more able to influence people's behavior.

References

1. Vuilleumier, P., Sagiv, N., Hazeltine, E., Poldrack, R.A., Swick, D., Rafal, R.D., Gabrieli, J.D.: Neural fate of seen and unseen faces in visuospatial neglect: a combined event-related functional MRI and event-related potential study. Proc. Natl. Acad. Sci. U S A 98, 3495–3500 (2001)
2. Blake, R., Logothetis, N.K.: Visual competition. Nature Neuroscience Reviews 3, 13–21 (2002)
3. Holmes, A., Vuilleumier, P., Eimer, M.: The processing of emotional facial expression is gated by spatial attention: evidence from event-related brain potentials. Cognitive Brain Research 16, 174–184 (2003)
4. Phillips, M.L., Williams, L.W., Heining, M.: Differential neural responses to overt and covert presentations of facial expressions of fear and disgust. NeuroImage 21, 1484–1496 (2004)
5. Miell, D., MacDonald, R., Hargreaves, D.J.: Musical communication. Oxford University Press, Oxford (2005)
6. Richard, L.A., Greenwald, A.: Parts outweigh the whole word in unconscious analysis of meaning. Psychological Science 11, 118–123 (2000)
7. Dehaene, S., Naccache, L.: Imaging unconscious semantic priming. Nature 395, 597–600 (1998)
8. Kouider, S., Dehaene, S.: Levels of processing during non-conscious perception: a critical review of visual masking. Philosophical Transactions of the Royal Society B: Biological Sciences 362(1481), 857–875 (2007)
9. Zajonc, R.B.: Feeling and thinking: Preferences need no inferences. American Psychologist 35, 151–175 (1980)
10. Lazarus, R.S.: Thoughts on the relationship between emotion and cognition. American Psychologist 37, 1019–1024 (1982)
11. [c] Joseph, B., Helen, E.: The Galvanic Skin Response as a Measure of Emotion in Prejudice. The Journal of Psychology: Interdisciplinary and Applied 42, 149–155 (1956)
12. Rankin, R.E., Campbell, D.T.: Galvanic skin response to negro and white experimenters. J. Ab. Soc. Psychol. 51, 30–33 (1955)

Novel Chromatic Pupillometer: Portable Pupillometry Diagnostic System

Peyton Paulick[1], Philipp Novotny[2], Mark Bachman[1], and Herbert Plischke[2]

[1] Department of Biomedical Engineering, University of California Irvine,
2227 Engineering Gateway, Irvine, CA 92697, USA
[2] Generation Research Program der Ludwig-Maximilians Universität München,
Prof. Max Lange Platz 11, 83646 Bad Tölz, Germany

Abstract. This research study explores development of a novel chromatic pupillometer that can analyze the characteristics of a patient's pupil light reflex (PLR). Characteristics of the PLR are not only used to determine retinal function but also have been recently used as a non-invasive diagnostic for a variety of neurological disorders and diseased states. This device is a compact diagnostic goggle that contains both stimulating and recording abilities of the PLR. This paper will discuss the design and function of the prototype as well as present preliminary data on evaluation of a subset of cells within the PLR.

Keywords: chromatic pupillometry, pupil light reflex, ipRGCs, pupillometry, eye tracking, assistive device, portable system.

1   Introduction

The pupil light reflex (PLC) has been of great interest to physicians and scientists alike not only for its ability to represent retinal function, but to serve as a marker for other diseased states [1–5][1], [3], [5]. Researchers are now exploring the pupil light reflex as a diagnostic measure for retinispigmentosa[4], Parkinson's and Alzheimer's disease [6], [7] , optic neuritis [8], diabetic autonomic neuropathy [9], head injury [10], and many others. This thus makes the pupil light response compelling to study and utilized as a non-invasive clinical measure of a variety of diseased states. More recently the importance of the pupil response to specific wavelengths at ranging intensities has been described as a protocol to asses inner and outer retinal function [1], [4], [11]. Due to the recent nature of these studies a combined pupillometry system has yet to become commercially available. Most systems are composed of a light stimulating system and a separate eye tracking system, none of which are portable. Our group is interested in creating one combined non-obtrusive system that is portable and easy-to-wear. This paper will discuss our novel non-obtrusive chromatic pupillometer and some preliminary data evaluating one specific cell population of the PLC: melanopsin-expressing intrinsic photosensitive retinal ganglion cells(ipRGCs).

D. Harris (Ed.): EPCE/HCII 2013, Part I, LNAI 8019, pp. 158–166, 2013.

2   Materials and Methods

The objective for the CPG was to create an all-in-one device to simultaneously stimulate and record the pupil light reflex. The left eye will be illuminated by a stimulating sphere composed of LEDs and the right eye will contain the eye tracking unit to record the pupillary light reflex in response to stimulation. The response of both pupils in normal conditions is identical, regardless of which eye is being exposed to stimulation [15].

The frame of the chromatic pupillometry goggles (CPG) was made from an off the shelf pair of welding goggles with removable eyepiece and an elastic head strap. This pair of goggles is relatively lightweight and comfortable to wear. Each eye frame was fitted with a magnet embedded acrylic ring. Both the stimulating and recording units of the CPG have a magnetic ring base; therefore can be easily connected to the frame of the goggles. This design feature allows for easy transport of the CPG and for components to be interchangeable. Test subjects place the goggles onto the head then both stimulating and recording units can be clipped into place using the magnetic attachment feature.

Fig. 1. A standard pair of welding goggles with removable housing and eyepiece was used as the foundation for the chromatic pupillometry goggles (CPG). Each eye socket was outfitted with anpolystyrene ring embedded with magnets to allow both the stimulating light sphere and the pupil recording components to click on to the eye in a 'plug and play' method.

2.1   Light Stimulator

The light-stimulating unit of the CPG is made of a hollow plastic sphere with an interior coating of titanium dioxide white paint for increased reflectance [16]. Six RGB (Red, Green, Blue) LEDs are mounted on the magnetic polystyrene ring at a 45° angle and sealed within the hemisphere. This design configuration allows for increased uniformity of light dispersion within the sphere. The stimulating sphere is assembled with a connector that will connect the stimulating sphere the RGB controller. As demonstrated in Fig.2c the sphere is easily removed and attached to the frame of the CPG goggles.

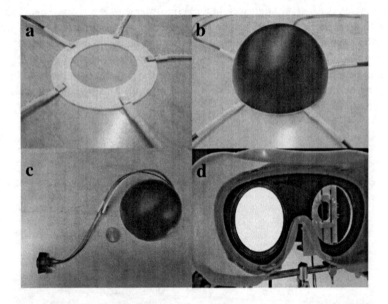

Fig. 2. The CPG light stimulating sphere a) demonstrates the acrylic ring embedded with magnets and the RGB LEDs mounted radially along the ring at a 45°b) the RGB LED array sealed within the hemisphere c) Completed RGB stimulating hemisphere attached with a connector to power and control the LED array d) stimulator fully assembled and attached to the goggle frame. This demonstration is showing a 100 cd/m² blue light stimulation.

In order to control the output of the stimulating sphere to create a specific lighting scheme of interest we will use a RGB (Red-Green-Blue) microcontroller that will execute the lighting sequence. The RGB controller used in this prototype is a 'MS-35' (CONRAD GmbH; Munich, Germany) and is featured in Fig.3. This controller comes with an easy to use graphical user interface (GUI) to send several settings and sequences to the unit via the USB programming cable. Once a specific sequence is set it can be saved to the controller's memory and the USB connection is no longer required. The controller is 8-bit controller thus allows for 256 step setting for the diming/brightness of the LEDs. All three of the colors are controlled independently. The driving voltage for both the microcontroller and the LEDs is 9V DC.

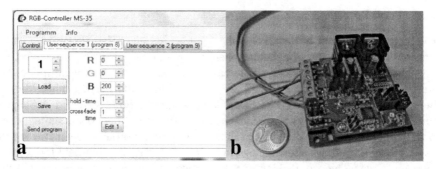

Fig. 3. a) Figure demonstrating the Conrad MS-35 RGB microcontroller interface. Specific protocols can be imported into the user sequence and the intensity of the light controlled by the inputted value. Duration is controlled by the hold-time feature, then a program is sent directly to the microcontroller and subsequently to the light stimulating unit b) Figure of the actual RGB controller with connections for power, ground, and RGB LEDs.

In order to convert the value used in the microcontroller GUI into a photometric measure a calibration of the light emitted from the stimulating sphere must be performed. A spectroradiometer (JETITechnischeInstrumente GmbH; Jena, Germany) was used to characterize the visible range of spectrum produced by our stimulating sphere when driven by a 9V power source. The spectroradiometer was placed approximately 1" from the base of the stimulating sphere, which is the distance the eye will be from the stimulating sphere during testing. The characterization reports values of luminance (cd/m2), radiance (W/sr*m2), dominant wavelength, and color purity. This calibration was repeated at three microcontroller step values, 50, 100, 200) and their results compiled to generate a conversion factor that can translate the 0-255 step value of the microcontroller to photometric measures of luminance and radiance for each color.

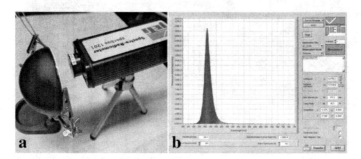

Fig. 4. a) Spectrometer testing setup for evaluation of the different lighting scenarios of the stimulating sphere b) spectrometer data output reporting the color spectrum, luminance, and radiance values for a given stimulation level.

2.2   Pupil Recording

The second component of the CPG is the eye-tracking unit. The eye-tracking unit is mounted similarly to the stimulating sphere using a polystyrene ring with embedded magnets. This allows the entire unit to easily clip on and off the goggle frame. The eye-tracking unit consists of a CMOS C-Cam-2A camera (CONRAD GmbH; Munich, Germany) and four infrared (IR) LEDs (GaAIAs Infrared Emitter IRL 81 A Siemens GmbH; Munich, Germany) all mounted on a vertical and horizontal sliding stage. With this adjustable stage our device can accommodate for different geometries of the patients head and allows allow the eye to be in appropriate viewing field for accurate data acquisition. The eye-tracking unit will connect to an integrated circuit (IC) that will power the IR LEDs and provide all electronics to drive and process the video out signal from the CMOS camera. This eye tracking IC also features a small dial where the intensity of the IR LEDs can me adjusted for maximal visualization of the pupil. This circuit then connects to the eye tracking software (SensoMotoric Instruments GmbH; Teltow, Germany) that will analyze pupil diameter, contraction/dilation velocities, and eye gaze.

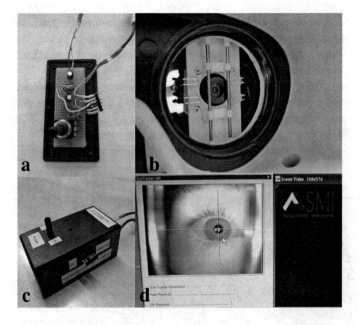

Fig. 5. a) Eye-tracking unit integrated circuit that consists of a voltage regulators, capacitors, resistors, and a potentiometer for adjusting the intensity of the IR LEDs. This circuit connects to power, the eye tracking unit, and the video in on the computer for SMI software to analyze the pupil response b) assembled eye tracking unit showing eye tracking camera, four mounted IR LEDs on the slidablehousing frame c) Eye tracking integrated circuit when sealed in enclosure; IR LED knob for modifying intensity and connectors for the eye tracking unit, video out, and power are visible d) eye tracking software during testing depicting white cross hairs that center on the pupil and place crosshairs that indicate the gazing direction.

2.3   ipRGC Stimulation Method

While the CPG is a versatile diagnostic tool that can execute many light stimulating protocols to activate a variety of cells with the pupil light reflex, our preliminary studies have focused on isolating the function of the ipRGCs. Using the PLR to study the function of the ipRGC can have many valuable clinical applications [3], [12]. An effective evaluation can aid in in determining the level of damage to the rentalphotocoreceptors compared with the retinal ganglion cells, the level at which ipRGCs regulate circadian rhythms in patients with minimal receptor function [13], and lastly determining if a patient has functioning retinal ganglion cells and can thus be a candidate for a retinal prosthesis[3], [14]. The lighting sequence is detailed in Fig. 6 and consists of two main stimulation methods, high intensity red light to stimulate the cones and high intensity blue light to stimulate the ipRGCs.

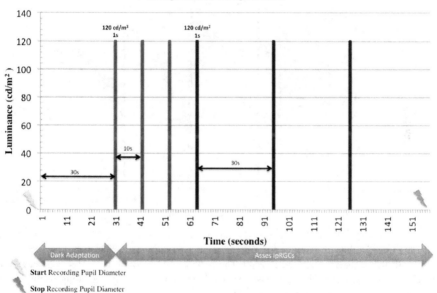

Fig. 6. Protocol used modeled after Park et al[3]findings to isolate the optimal stimulation sequence foripRGC function. This protocol uses a high intensity red light with a one second duration to stimulate the cone cells of the eye and a high intensity blue light to stimulate the ipRGC cells. The total testing time of this protocol is 2 minutes and 36 seconds.

3   Results

Preliminary validation of the pupillometry system has been conducted on ten different patients using the ipRGC protocol to assure the device and all corresponding data analysis protocols are working properly. Patients were between the ages of 25 and 70 with no known ocular or visual problems. The chromatic pupillometer successfully stimulated the pupil light reflex at varying wavelengths and intensities while recording the pupil response. Patients reported the device was comfortable and the testing was simple and non-obtrusive and the testing sequence was not bothersome or too bright that it became uncomfortable.

Fig.7 demonstrates the raw data collected from one patient that was given the ipRGC protocol. This data is unfiltered and no artifact removal has been done. This data demonstrates the validation of the CPG successfully stimulating and recording the PLR.

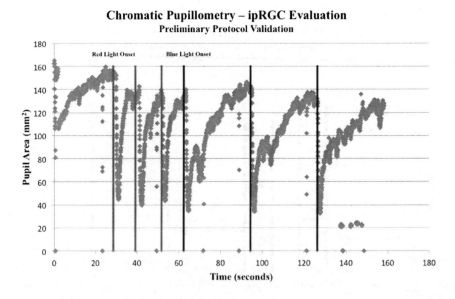

Fig. 7. Figuredisplays the raw and unfiltered pupil area data after stimulating the patients the PLC with the sequencedescribed in Fig.6.The patient blinked right as the test was beginning which explains why there is a decreased in pupil area directly at the beginning of the experiment before the lighting protocol had begun.

4   Discussion

Our group has developed a device for chromatic pupil response measurements to explore the pupil light reflex. This device is easy to use and comfortable for the patient to wear during testing. This compact system houses both the stimulating and the recording hardware for all measurements to be taken. Preliminary testing has demonstrated the repeatability of these measurements and is ready for a larger scale clinical trial to explore the complex PLR and specifically the function of the ipRGCs. The preliminary experiments evaluating the ipRGC and cone function of the pupil light reflex have demonstrated the expected response profiles for healthy PLR. Specifically, high intensity blue light was able to produce a sustained pupil response, presumably a melanopsin driven sustained response, lasting approximately 30 seconds[3], [11] .Comparatively, the cone function assessment using high intensity red light demonstrated a response time (return to baseline) of approximately 10 seconds post stimulation. Our group is interested in conducting a large scale trial evaluating the function of ipRGCs over a wide range of ages to explore for the ipRGCs function changes over time. Moreover our group would like to establish a guideline for healthyipRGC response to use as anindicator for non-invasive diagnostic testing ofipRGC function.

Acknowledgments. The authors of this paper would like to thank Marcel Dickmann for his work on the first prototype of the chromatic pupillometer. While the device presented here is a second generation his work helped lay the foundation for the featured design improvements and usability testing.

References

1. Herbst, Sander, B., Milea, D., Lund-Andersen, H., Kawasaki, A.: Test-retest repeatability of the pupil light response to blue and red light stimuli in normal human eyes using a novel pupillometer. Frontiers in Neurology 2, 10 (2011)
2. Kawasaki, A., Munier, F.L., Leon, L., Kardon, R.H.: Pupillometric quantification of residual rod and cone activity in leber congenital amaurosis. Archives of Ophthalmology 130(6), 798–800 (2012)
3. Park, J.C., Moura, A.L., Raza, A.S., Rhee, D.W., Kardon, R.H.: Toward a Clinical Protocol for Assessing Rod, Cone, and Melanopsin Contributions to the Human Pupil Response, pp. 6624–6635 (2011)
4. Kardon, R., Anderson, S.C., Damarjian, T.G., Grace, E.M., Stone, E., Kawasaki, A.: Chromatic pupillometry in patients with retinitis pigmentosa. Ophthalmology 118(2), 376–381 (2011)
5. Zele, A.J., Feigl, B., Smith, S.S., Markwell, E.L.: The circadian response of intrinsically photosensitive retinal ganglion cells. PloS One 6(3), e17860 (2011)
6. Stergiou, V., et al.: Pupillometric findings in patients with Parkinson's disease and cognitive disorder 72, 97–101 (2009)
7. Fotiou, D.F., Stergiou, V., Tsiptsios, D., Lithari, C., Nakou, M., Karlovasitou, A.: Cholinergic deficiency in Alzheimer's and Parkinson's disease: evaluation with pupillometry. International Journal of Psychophysiology: Official Journal of the International Organization of Psychophysiology 73(2), 143–149 (2009)
8. Shindler, K.S., Revere, K., Dutt, M., Ying, G.-S., Chung, D.C.: In vivo detection of experimental optic neuritis by pupillometry. Experimental Eye Research 100, 1–6 (2012)
9. Dütsch, M., Marthol, H., Michelson, G., Neundörfer, B., Hilz, M.J.: Pupillography refines the diagnosis of diabetic autonomic neuropathy. Journal of the Neurological Sciences 222(1-2), 75–81 (2004)
10. Diego, S., Hospital, L.E.: Quantitative pupillometry, a new technology: normative data and preliminary observations in patients with acute head injury. Technical note. Journal of Neurosurgery 98(1), 205–213 (2003)

11. Gamlin, P.D.R., McDougal, D.H., Pokorny, J., Smith, V.C., Yau, K.-W., Dacey, D.M.: Human and macaque pupil responses driven by melanopsin-containing retinal ganglion cells. Vision Research 47(7), 946–954 (2007)
12. Kardon, R., Anderson, S.C., Damarjian, T.G., Grace, E.M., Stone, E., Kawasaki, A.: Chromatic pupil responses: preferential activation of the melanopsin-mediated versus outer photoreceptor-mediated pupil light reflex. Ophthalmology 116(8), 1564–1573 (2009)
13. Lockley, S.W., Skene, D.J., Arendt, J., Tabandeh, H., Bird, A.C., Defrance, R.: Relationship between melatonin rhythms and visual loss in the blind. The Journal of Clinical Endocrinology and Metabolism 82(11), 3763–3770 (1997)
14. Besch, D., et al.: Extraocular surgery for implantation of an active subretinal visual prosthesis with external connections: feasibility and outcome in seven patients. The British Journal of Ophthalmology 92(10), 1361–1368 (2008)
15. Purves, D., Augustine, G.J., Fitzpatrick, D., Hall, W.C., LaMantia, A.S., McNamara, J.O., White, L.E.: Neuroscience, 4th edn. Sinauer Associates (2008)
16. Winkler: Titanium Dioxide. European Coatings Literature (2003)

Estimation of Operator Input and Output Workload in Complex Human-Machine-Systems for Usability Issues with iFlow

Stefan Pfeffer[1], Patrick Decker[1], Thomas Maier[1], and Eric Stricker[2]

[1] Institute for Engineering Design and Industrial Design, Research and Teaching Department Industrial Design Engineering, University of Stuttgart, Germany
{stefan.pfeffer,thomas.maier}@iktd.uni-stuttgart.de
[2] Center for Patient Safety and Simulation, University Hospital Tuebingen, Germany
eric.stricker@tupass.de

Abstract. Usability studies often use methods focused on product parameters. Test designs are processed in laboratories and evaluation is commonly performed by expert opinions. For validation studies we want to point out the importance of field studies and user and system oriented evaluation. For this purpose we want to present the methodological approach iFlow (information flow) as multiple assessment technique for usability issues in real or quasi-real (simulated) situations. The idea of iFlow is to assess input and output workload via video and audio recordings combined with subjective and objective measurement techniques of workload. In this contribution the iFlow method and an evaluative study in anesthesiology are presented. The added value to already existing methods and approaches is considered in the sensitivity of iFlow to identify situations of overload in a descriptive way. For design interventions it would be helpful to consult the iFlow chart to deduct cause and effect relations.

Keywords: Information Flow, Usability, Input Workload, Output Workload.

1   Introduction

Today the concept of usability is applied in many areas of human-machine-systems (HMS) expanding from its software ergonomic roots [1] to a broad understanding of any kind of interface between biology (human) and technology (cultivated products). In socio-technical-systems usability also considers networking of humans among each other which is mostly deficient in terms of efficient and error-free messaging. Because of the large amount and variety of information flow an operator has to handle in such systems, they are called complex.

An approach to operationalize this complexity in a macroergonomic perspective has been made by Manser [2] via the density of simultaneous and sequential processes in a time line analysis of anesthesia administration. Our methodological approach iFlow transfers this idea into the area of microergonomics, towards the estimation of operator input and output workload as criteria for usability considerations in complex

D. Harris (Ed.): EPCE/HCII 2013, Part I, LNAI 8019, pp. 167–176, 2013.
© Springer-Verlag Berlin Heidelberg 2013

HMS [3]. Figure 1 shows the abstraction of such an HMS, the parameters that determine operator workload in the iFlow approach and the methods we used for assessment at a glance.

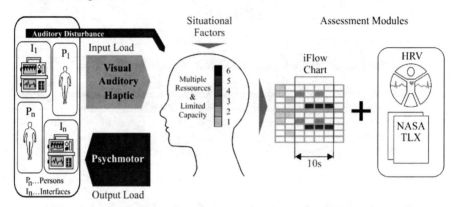

Fig. 1. iFlow model of a complex HMS and connected assessment parameters of iFlow

After a brief summary and discussion of typically used methods for usability assessment in chapter 2 the theoretical background (chapter 3.1) and the procedure of descriptive workload evaluation (chapter 3.2) are described. To show the added value of iFlow to already existing methods and approaches we want to present the results of an evaluative usability study in anesthesiology at the Center of Patient Safety and Simulation (University Hospital Tuebingen, Germany) in chapter 4.

2   Usability Assessment in Complex Human-Machine-Systems

The basic idea of usability engineering has its roots in human factors science. For this reason methods for evaluation arise from this discipline. Usability methods commonly are classified into formative (inductive) and summative (deductive) evaluation [4]. This division regards the method´s operational date – during or after design process. In human factors sciences methods are categorized into analytical and empirical methods [5], regarding the type of procedure. Besides these categorizations there are several other approaches to classify the large variety of methods (e.g. subjective/objective, descriptive/predictive, laboratory/field, qualitative/quantitative, static/dynamic). Each type of method can be beneficial in its own specific way. Human factors researchers have agreed that a multiple method approach would be the best way for usability assessment [6]. In practice it can be found that usability observations show a main focus in product oriented, static laboratory methods with qualitative outcome from subjective expert or user sources. This may be because of benefits regarding resource consumption (users, time, equipment).

Validation can be regarded as special kind of usability study. For example, in medical device design usability has to be validated according to the standards. Therefore the usability of the medical product has to be evaluated with high external validity and documented in a usability engineering file with comparable quantitative data. Hence we recommend that usability validation studies should be user and system oriented, performed under real (field) or quasi-real (simulation) dynamic conditions with quantitative outcome from an ideally objective and theory based assessment. With respect to a multiple method approach, subjective (user questionnaire) and psychophysiological assessment techniques should complete a validation study.

Especially the assessment of dynamic processes under real or quasi-real conditions is necessary for external validity. Moreover usability for validation shouldn´t be fixed only to observation of errors or nearly errors in user trials (product oriented, expert based) and subjective user opinions (product oriented, user based). Rather the assessment approach for validation should be extended and human factors methods for user oriented evaluation should be used more often. For example assessment of mental workload and situation awareness under real or quasi-real conditions could give a view on system usability and human reliability with respect to stressful situations. In the following chapters we want to present the iFlow method as an approach for estimating operator input and output workload and an evaluative usability study in a dynamic, quasi-real (simulated) anesthesiology setting.

3   The iFlow Method

The iFlow method is a descriptive usability assessment approach which is based on data collection of information input and output flows of the operator. This data is extracted of video and audio recordings and has to be transferred into the iFlow chart which is the basis for further evaluation steps along the timeline. The objective of getting quantitative data out of descriptive analyses is achieved by observing the density of input and output information flows (iFlows) by means of action codes similarly to Ekman´s FACS method [7]. This value in turn determines the level of workload. Weighted density analysis is combined with an objective (heart rate) and subjective (NASA TLX [8]) assessment method (see Figure 1).

3.1   Theoretical Background

The iFlow method has been developed on the basis of Wickens´ Multiple Resource Theory (MRT) [9]. It assumes that the external factors of the HMS, i.e., the interfaces have a main influence on operator workload. The theory also considers these external factors in the context of situational disturbance and control variables. The iFlow model (Figure 1) does not include internal factors like the current emotional state of the operator. In MRT input and output modules have disjunctive resource capacities. Hence each input (visual, auditory, haptic) and output (psychomotor) channel should not be overloaded singularly. In addition we want to recommend a limit for input (visual+auditory+haptic) and output load (motor+verbal). The division into input and output workload with regard to the user as sender and recipient of information flow can help to detect bottlenecks in both areas and specify deficits in interface elements of output (e.g. displays) or to interface elements of input (e.g. controls). Like limitations empirically found in anthropometry concerning physical workload (e.g. for raising a weight four times an hour) it would be a landmark for usability engineering to assess the amount of information a human operator can receive, process and turn into safe and efficient actions.

3.2   Workload Assessment Process

The basic idea of iFlow is the evaluation of time-related information density and the descriptive deduction of workload levels. Information flows in all channels of input and out are evaluated with respect to their potential degree of load for the operator. Classes of load have been developed after the VACP model [10].

VACP originally is used in a discreet, function-oriented way to predict workload for visual (V), auditory (A), cognitive (C) and psychomotor (P) channels in cumulated 10s intervals as well as an overall workload rate. Each channel or workload component is described by a 7-point ordinal rating scale (except auditory) [10]. The scales have been extended (second visual scale and kinesthetic scale) and further developed to an interval scale by pair comparison survey among pilots [11]. Also task time required for each task was considered for prediction of workload.

In order to evaluate the density of iFlow we used this basic work and designed new classes for a descriptive and continuous use. Several adaptions had to be made with regard to reliability and objectivity of behavior observation. After a recapitulation of the 7-point scales, ordinal 4-point (input) and 5-point (output) scales were formed with descriptors that are well distinguishable in video and audio recordings (see Table 1). For this reason, action codes have been developed to ensure a correct and consistent allocation of information flows to the classes. The interval scales of Bierbaum et al. (1989) refer to a sample of 20 pilots wherefore we decided to use an ordinal scale (following the order of the interval scale) showing more general applicability. Furthermore, we added the channel of haptics (H) and left cognition descriptors (C) out of account. The psychomotor scale was newly introduced so that a value of 5 (overload) is defined by a multiple task that is performed (two or more actions with different goals at once).

The limit of each workload component is fixed by Bierbaum et al. (1989) to the value that exceeds the maximum on any of the scales. Thus, a value of 8 implies a component overload and those channels can be identified that are associated with overload for each task and in total. We applied this systematization to generate specific limits of workload for input (V+A+H → Limit 8) and output (P → Limit 4) channels with the objective to detect situations of high workload that have an influence on the usability and safe use of the devices. Overload for input and output modalities can be described by adding up all information flows that come up in a continuous T=2-sec interval. Considering all input and output parameters in a socio-technical-system should lead to a higher external validity.

Table 1. Workload scales and limits of input and output referring to Bierbaum (1989)

	VISUAL		
No.	**Description**	**Action Code**	**Weight**
V1	Visual Detection	Gaze <=2s	1
V2	Visual Discrimination	Gaze >2s, Static, Target-oriented	2
V3	Visual Tracking	Gaze >2s, Dynamic, Target-oriented	3
V4	Visual Read, Searching, Orienting	Dynamic, Visually high attentive	4

Input (Limit 8)

	AUDITORY		
No.	**Description**	**Action Code**	**Weight**
A1	Auditory Detection	Digital Signal, Sound	1
A2	Auditory Verification	Auditory Feedback	2
A3	Auditory Decoding	Speech, Semantic Content	3
A4	Auditory Interpretation	Sound patterns, Auditory high attentive	4
	Auditory Disturbance	Background noise (non-directive)	each 1

	HAPTIC		
No.	**Description**	**Action Code**	**Weight**
H1	Haptical Activation	Touch, Hold	1
H2	Haptical Detection	Passive (Pressure), Active (Use Object)	2
H3	Haptical Scanning	Active: Feel out, Haptic Feedback	3
H4	Haptical Interpretation	Passive: Patterns	4

Output (Limit 4)

	PSYCHOMOTOR		
No.	**Description**	**Action Code**	**Weight**
P1	Discrete Actuation, Speech, Walk	e.g. Push Button, Talk, Walk	1
P2	Continuous Adjusting	Unimanual	2
P3	Symbolic Production	e.g. Writing	3
P4	Convergent Multiple Operations	>=2 Extremities, 1 goal	4
P5	Divergent Multiple Operations	>=2 Extremities, >=1 goal	5

4   Evaluative Study in Anesthesiology

To evaluate the possibilities and limitations of iFlow for usability evaluation we examined a critical incident situation in anesthesiology. The anesthesia work system can be classified as complex human-machine-system. For a high external validity in validation studies it would be essential to test the products in context of the socio-technical-system with regard to situational factors (e.g., critical incidents). Because of safety reasons such situations can be produced by simulations. At the Center for Patient Safety and Simulation (Tuepass) it is possible to simulate such critical incidents. Beside the main purpose of crisis resource management the simulation can excellently be used for quasi-real usability studies [12]. Tuepass has four simulation rooms which can be established as operating or intensive care rooms. All devices are functional and the patient is represented via the full-scale simulation doll which has manifold options like pathological and physiological cardiac and respiratory sounds, difficult airway, centrally and peripherally palpable pulses, pupil reaction, chest drainage system etc.

4.1   Test Procedure

We chose an intensive care setting for the evaluation. Eight subjects (consulting and ward physicians) performed a critical incident situation in intensive care. Three cameras video- and audiotaped the observation. The subjects had to wear a bipolar one-channel ECG. After the observation they completed the NASA TLX questionnaire (weighting and rating). The observation lasted 5 minutes for each subject. The scenario began in the intensive care room with a critical incident noticed by the nursing staff and residents. The observation started when the subjects came into the running scenario.

4.2   Data Analysis

The audio and video data were analyzed by means of iFlow and transferred into the iFlow chart. Figure 2 shows a 2:40 min extract of the iFlow chart (subject 1). The iFlow chart consists of 4 sections (input, output, heart rate (HR) and load evaluation). The input and output sections are divided into the workload scale descriptors of Table 1. Descriptor P1 was itemized into P1-T (talk and discrete actuation) and P2-W (walk) for better overview. The information flows were manually extracted of the footage by the action codes. When a descriptor appeared twice in a 2-sec interval the values were added (e.g. 2x auditory decoding → 6). The time bars are coded from bright (value 1) to dark (value 6). The bar graphs in the HR section show the mean heart rate and standard deviation for a 10-sec interval. The graph illustrates the absolute deviation of heart rate in 1/min from the measured resting value of the subject. The load section is divided into input and output load showing the added values for each 2-sec. interval. Those values which exceeded the maximum were marked black. Hashes represent values >9. Sections of reduced video and/or audio data quality are shaded in grey. Accuracy of evaluation is lower in these sections.

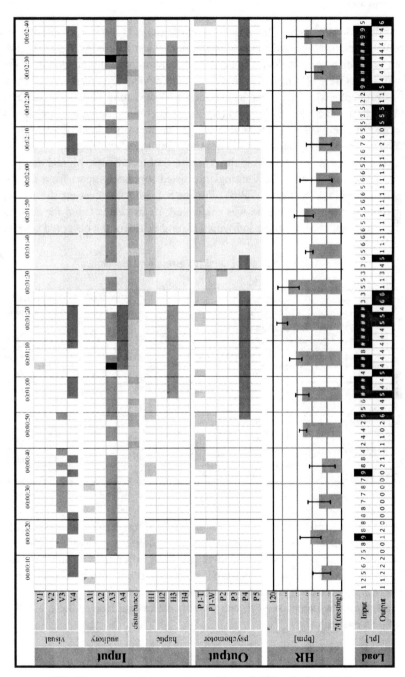

Fig. 2. iFlow chart excerpt (rotated through 90° anti-clockwise)

4.3   Results

Several devices were used in the scenarios by the subjects (patient monitoring system, defibrillator, bag valve mask, ultrasound system, syringe pumps etc.). The analysis did not focus on a specific device but rather on human-machine-interaction in general. The physicians were all familiar with the standard devices they were using in practice. That is probably why no errors in handling and operating occurred. Nevertheless, several near-errors could be observed (e.g., missed commando nearly leaded to shock the subject by defibrillator). In these situations an input overload (iFlow value >=9) could be observed while heart rate did not show any stress evidence.

Table 2 shows the results of the three assessment techniques. Mental and physical demand in original NASA TLX ratings are listed separately apart from the Overall Weighted Workload Score (OWWS). For each 5 min observation the average of iFlow input and output workload was calculated. Heart rate is listed for each subject as percentage deviation from the individual resting value for the observed timeframe.

Table 2. Results of the three assessment techniques

	NASA TLX [pt.]			Workload [pt.]		Heart Rate [1/min]
	Mental Demand	Physical Demand	OWWS	Input	Output	
Subject 1	90	30	65,33	6,83	2,39	+27,2 %
Subject 2	75	60	69,3	5,25	3,69	+49,9 %
Subject 3	65	20	45,67	5,23	1,85	+ 15,7 %
Subject 4	95	15	67,67	5,38	2,77	+38,2 %
Subject 5	85	20	68,3	3,7	1,83	+38,5 %
Subject 6	65	5	35,3	3,24	0,79	+27,6 %
Subject 7	75	10	48,3	4,45	0,77	+15,0 %
Subject 8	90	25	77,6	4,38	0,71	+36,3 %

We set up a correlation matrix (see Figure 3) for iFlow input workload and NASA TLX mental demand (hashes) as well as for iFlow output workload and NASA TLX physical demand (squares) although there are little differences in the constructs of workload. It is visible that the analyzed values by iFlow show dependence to the NASA TLX original ratings of the subjects in the two considered dimensions. OWWS and heart rate show inconsistent results towards the overall load of the subjects in this kind of data analysis.

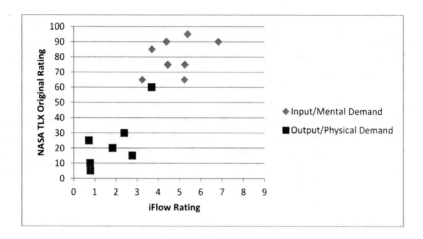

Fig. 3. Correlation matrix of workload parameters evaluated with iFlow and NASA TLX

5   Conclusion

The evaluative study shows both possibilities and limitations of iFlow. The claimed methods´ focus for validation studies (see chapter 2) of user-oriented and system-oriented usability studies performed in real or quasi-real situations under dynamic conditions can optimally be observed by video and audio recordings. The idea to quantify the qualitative video and audio data via action codes is realized by iFlow. In consideration of device design optimizations the strength of iFlow lies in a cause and effect analysis of single overloaded situations. The workload values for input and output channels produced by iFlow have to be considered as values of orientation. Even if not every situation in the evaluative study showed a near-error, these situations of input and/or output overload may potentially lead to an error. Passing just these situations without loss of efficiency or errors would mean a successful validation of the device. Approaches of design should gather interaction phases of overload and underload (monotony) to improve information-design and interaction-design. We provided a theory of action codes keeping objectivity of evaluation and rater reliability in mind (see Table 1). This theory has to be adapted in further steps (e.g. the distinction of auditory interpreted semantic content with and without situation awareness). Another benefit of iFlow is the possibility to document usability evaluations via the iFlow chart and discuss the results together with subjects.

It has to be stated that iFlow can´t and should not be used as single method. Following a multiple method approach iFlow has to be combined with subjective (questionnaires) and objective (psychophysiological) methods. The potential of psychophysiological methods lies in a continuous and time dependent data collection. In further studies we will consider continuous evaluating questionnaires too to get an attribution to specific phases. The chosen 10-sec. intervals show an adequate averaging of heart rate data (see standard deviations in Figure 2) in contrast to the overall heart rate means presented in Table 2.

In further studies it would be interesting to add EEG measurement for interpreting the cognitive readiness of the subjects by analyzing the alpha waves. This would probably give hints for the so far unconsidered module of cognition (C) and could help to deduct subjects´ mental states.

Concluding the added value of iFlow can be described as the possibility to quantify real-time data of human-machine-interactions within context of other process variables embedded in an overall situation considering user and system oriented dimensions of usability. In our evaluative study the calculated input and output workload is correlated with the NASA TLX dimensions of mental and physical demand. This result made us confident that a descriptive evaluation of workload limits as preliminary phases of errors in field studies are within reach.

References

1. Foley, J.D., Van Dam, A.: Fundamentals of Interactive Computer Graphics (Systems Programming Series). Addison-Wesley, USA (1982)
2. Manser, T., Wehner, T.: Analysing action sequences: Variations in action density in the administration of anaesthesia. Cognition, Technology & Work 4(2), 71–81 (2002)
3. Pfeffer, S., Maier, T.: Systematical improvement of an anesthesia workstation considering physical and mental workload. In: Salvendy, G., Karwowski, W. (eds.) Advances in Human Factors and Ergonomics 2012: Proceedings of the 4th AHFE Conference, July 21-25. CRC Press, Boca Raton (2012)
4. Sarodnick, F., Brau, H.: Methoden der Usability Evaluation: Wissenschaftliche Grundlagen und praktische Anwendungen. Verlag Hans Huber, Bern (2011)
5. Stanton, N.A., Salmon, P.M., Walker, G.H., Baber, C., Jenkins, D.P.: Human Factors Methods: A Practical Guide for Engineering and Design. Ashgate, Farnham (2005)
6. Vidulich, M.A., Tsang, P.S.: Mental Workload and Situation Awareness. In: Salvendy, G. (ed.) Handbook of Human Factors and Ergonomics, pp. 243–273. John Wiley & Sons, Hoboken (2012)
7. Ekman, P.: What the Face Reveals: Basic and Applied Studies of Spontaneous Expression Using the Facial Action Coding System (FACS). Oxford University Press (2005)
8. Hart, S.G., Staveland, L.E.: Development of NASA-TLX: Results of Empirical and Theoretical Research. In: Hancock, P.A., Meshkati, N. (eds.) Human Mental Workload, pp. 239–250. Elsevier, Amsterdam (1988)
9. Wickens, C.D.: The structure of attentional resources. In: Nickerson, R. (ed.) Attention and Performance VIII, pp. 239–257. Lawrence Erlbaum, Hillsdale (1989)
10. McCracken, J.H., Aldrich, T.B.: Analyses of selected LHX mission functions: Implications for operator workload and system automation goals. Anacapa Sciences, Fort Rucker, Alabama (1984)
11. Bierbaum, C.R., Szabo, S.M., Aldrich, T.B.: Task Analysis ofthe UH-60 Mission and Decision Rules for Developing a UH-60 Workload Prediction Model, vol. 1: Summary Report. Anacapa Sciences, Fort Rucker, Alabama (1989)
12. Stricker, E., Pfeffer, S., Trick, M., Rall, M., Maier, T.: Standardized research onergonomics, usability and workflow analysis using high fidelity simulation labs. In: Dössel, O. (ed.), Biomedical Engineering, SI-1 (2012) ISSN 1862-278X

Effects of Task and Presentation Modality in Detection Response Tasks

Roman Vilimek, Juliane Schäfer, and Andreas Keinath

BMW Group, Concept Quality, Munich, Germany
{roman.vilimek,juliane.schaefer,andreas.keinath}@bmw.de

Abstract. To assess driver distraction adequately, cognitive workload measurement techniques are necessary that can be used as part of standard in-vehicle testing procedures. Detection response tasks (DRTs) are a simple and effective way of assessing workload. However, as DRTs require cognitive resources themselves, interferences between task modality and DRT modality are possible. In this study, DRT stimuli (auditory, visual, tactile) are varied systematically with secondary task presentation modality (auditory, visual, or purely cognitive tasks). The aim is to infer if different DRT variants remain sensitive to changes in workload even if primary and secondary task convey information using the same presentation modality, thus making resource conflicts likely. Results show that all DRTs successfully discriminate between high and low workload levels in terms of reaction time independent of DRT presentation modality. Differences in discriminability can be found in hit rate measurement.

Keywords: DRT, PDT, workload, driver distraction.

1   Introduction

Driver distraction is in most cases defined as inadequate visual-manual orientation to the driving task. Usability tests in the automotive context typically use eye tracking and defined acceptable thresholds for eyes-off-the-road durations (e.g. [1]). However, in attempts to reduce driver distraction, recent developments in in-vehicle information and communication systems show a trend towards less visual-manual activity. This trend includes technologies like speech interaction that reduces visual-manual demands but may increase cognitive demands. In order to assess the cognitive distraction potential of these new technologies in a suitable way during standard usability testing procedures, a simple continuous method is required which is able to reliably differentiate between different levels of cognitive task demands.

Self-reported measures of workload are based upon the premise that a test participant is able to identify and state the experienced load of a task at hand. Subjective rating scales like the unidimensional Rating Scale of Mental Effort (RSME, [2]) or the multidimensional NASA Task Load Index (TLX, [3]) are in most cases administered directly after task processing and proved to be sensitive to changes in workload. A disadvantage of these methods is their summative and a posteriori

D. Harris (Ed.): EPCE/HCII 2013, Part I, LNAI 8019, pp. 177–185, 2013.

nature. Subjects have to recall at the time of the survey the degree of cognitive workload they experienced during completing a certain task. If tasks are complex like using technical systems, short peaks in cognitive effort can be over- or underrated or even completely forgotten. Therefore, if the objective of a usability test is to evaluate specific aspects of a complex technical system, single use cases need to be isolated to be assessed individually which often makes the procedure more difficult and less realistic.

Physiological measures of workload are an alternative to subjective self-report methods. Several of these have the advantage of high temporal resolution [4]. In order to evaluate workload induced by in-vehicle systems, cognitive workload needs to be tested over rather short task durations. This requirement is met by EEG-based methods, pupillometry, and detection response tasks. Obviously, EEG-based methods are currently hardly suitable for widespread standard usability tests as the technical equipment is not only very expensive, but also time-consuming to set up and obstructive during testing. Pupillometry uses highly sensitive eye tracking equipment that can detect short-term changes in the pupil diameter. Changes in pupil dilation occur in direct response not only to changes in environmental illumination conditions but also to emotional and mental processes. Analyzing these characteristic bursts in pupil dilation can be a valid indicator of mental workload [5]. However, as alterations in lighting conditions or stimulus distance do also affect pupil size, filter mechanisms are needed to eliminate these influences. The Index of Cognitive Activity [6] corrects the pupil signal. Although this is a very innovative way of continuously measuring workload with extraordinarily high temporal resolution, the method and the underlying algorithms are still under validation in various research projects (e.g. [7]).

Detection response tasks (DRTs) are a promising method to evaluate cognitive workload [8-10]. The peripheral detection response task was developed by van Winsum, Martens and Herland [11] using visual stimuli. Subjects have to detect and respond to a stimulus that is presented regularly with slightly varying interstimulus intervals. The method is based on a dual task setting, in which the impairment in one task (the detection response task) is an indication of the workload imposed by another task (e.g. using a technical system). Although research shows that the DRT method is very sensitive to fluctuations of cognitive load, it is currently unclear as to how far different versions of the DRT, i.e. different stimulus presentation modalities, interact with different task modalities of the primary task. Attention and workload models like Wickens' multiple resource model [4] would predict that bottleneck effects are likely to occur if DRT presentation modality and primary task modality overlap. These effects would reduce the usefulness of the DRT method or at least would make adaptions necessary depending on primary task characteristics.

The present experiment compares effects of DRT presentation and secondary task modality in a controlled setting that allows for direct comparisons on the sensitivity of the DRT versions under resource conflicts. Three types of DRTs were evaluated: The standard visual remote peripheral detection response task (RDRT), the auditory detection response task (ADRT) and the tactile detection response task (TDRT). In order to evaluate the sensitivity of each of these DRTs, cognitively loading tasks were deployed in two levels of difficulty: easy (simpler variant with less task demand) and difficult (more complex variant with an increased task demand). This was intended to show whether the DRTs were sensitive enough to detect variations in workload. These cognitive tasks involved visual presentations, auditory presentations or no primary task presentation modality at all (purely cognitive task). The aim of this was to induce resource conflicts between for example the RDRT and the visually presented cognitive task in order to test for robustness of the DRTs.

2   Methods

2.1   Participants

Twenty four participants (12 female) took part in this experiment. The age range was between 21 and 42 years old, with a mean of 29 years (SD=5.17). All participants had normal or corrected-to-normal vision. Three of them were left handed.

2.2   Detection Response Tasks

The experiment was carried out in the Usability Lab at the BMW Group's Research and Innovation Center in Munich, Germany. Participants were seated at a desk with a laptop in front of them in central normal viewing distance. External loudspeakers were also located in front of the participants. All detection response tasks required participants to detect a stimulus and to respond to it via button press. The interstimulus interval randomly oscillated between 3000-5000 ms. Stimuli (auditory, visual or tactile) were presented for 1000 ms. Responses were always given by pressing a button (microswitch) that was attached to the index finger of the dominant hand (see Fig. 1, right side). Upon button press, the stimulus was switched off even if the presentation duration had not yet elapsed. Average reaction time and hit rate (responses within 2 s after signal onset) were recorded as performance indices.

Tactile Detection Response Task (TDRT). A vibrating cell phone motor was attached to the wrist of the non-dominant hand (see Fig. 1, left side). Prior to the beginning of the experiment, participants adjusted the vibration strength within a certain range to a comfortable level.

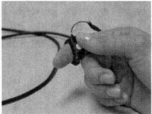

Fig. 1. Left side: Vibrating node attached to the wrist. Right side: Microswitch attached to the index finger of the dominant hand.

Remote Detection Response Task (RDRT). The RDRT was set at approximately 100 cm viewing distance. Four red LEDs were mounted on a black cardboard. These were arranged horizontally and spread symmetrically 11° and 23° from the center point as proposed by [12].

Auditory Detection Response Task (ADRT). Following the procedure of [10], the auditory stimulus was a 1 kHz sinus tone presented via loudspeakers. Participants were asked before the beginning of the experiment to adjust the audio volume within a certain range to a comfortable level.

2.3   Secondary Tasks

All secondary tasks were used to induce cognitive workload in two levels. In order to induce resource conflicts auditory task presentation and visual task presentation were introduced. Additionally, a purely cognitive task was part of the design in order to infer general sensitivity of the DRTs without resource conflict. The performance in the secondary tasks was monitored in order to see if participants were really engaged to a sufficient level.

Auditory N-Back Task. For auditory presentation mode, the n-back task [13] was used. It consists of the aural presentation of single digit numbers (0-9) with a system-paced interstimulus interval of 2.5 s. In the easy condition, the participants just had to repeat out loud each digit immediately after hearing it (0-back). In the difficult condition (2-back) participants needed to recall from memory the digit that was presented two digits before the currently presented numeric value and repeat it out loud while listening to further digit presented.

Visual N-Back Task. The procedure for visual presentation mode followed closely the auditory presentation mode. The n-back task was used with the same difficulty levels (0-back and 2-back). The digits were shown on the laptop monitor, each for 3 seconds without interstimulus interval.

Counting Task. A counting task was implemented that needed no further instruction during task execution than providing a three-digit initial number. Participants were requested to count upwards in steps of two in the easy condition and count downwards in steps of seven in the difficult condition. In this setting no visual or auditory processing load was present while executing the counting task.

2.4   Procedure

Prior to experimentation, participants went through a brief familiarization period in which all tasks were explained to them adequately by the experimenter. Participants adjusted signal levels of the ADRT and the TDRT, as described above. They were instructed to treat all tasks, primary task DRT and cognitively loading secondary task, with the same priority.

To minimize task switching effects, trials were arranged in DRT blocks. Participants performed the current DRT variant with all secondary tasks before starting the next DRT block. DRT variant order was randomized. Each secondary task was repeated three times. Participants were informed that the first trial always served as a training trial and was excluded from further analysis. The experiment took approximately one hour.

3   Results

The experiment was performed in order to evaluate the DRT as a workload assessment technique and to provide information on modality interference effects (resource conflicts) between primary and secondary task if these were based on the same presentation modality. Repeated measures ANOVAs were carried out on the data set for each secondary task in order to identify effects of difficulty level on reaction time and hit rate. Further t-test for each DRT within a secondary task scenario delivers information on the specific sensitivity of the DRT variant in detecting workload differences.

Results for the visual n-back task are shown in Fig. 2. Significant main effects for difficulty level were found for reaction time ($F(1,23) = 32.68$, $p < .05$) as well as for hit rate ($F(1,23) = 13.48$, $p < .05$). T-tests revealed that all of the DRTs proved to be effective and able to differentiate between workload levels. (reaction time: RDRT $t(23) = -3.15$, $p < .05$; TDRT $t(23) = -4.72$, $p < .05$; ADRT $t(23) = -3.41$, $p < .05$; hit rate: RDRT $t(23) = 2.31$, $p < .05$; TDRT $t(23) = 2.90$, $p < .05$; ADRT $t(23) = 3.23$, $p < .05$).

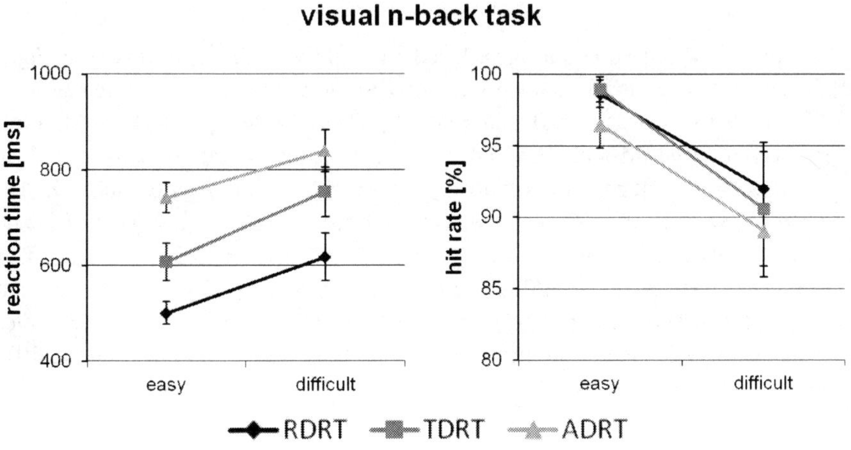

Fig. 2. Mean reaction times (left) and hit rates (right) for the DRTs during visual n-back task

For the auditory n-back task, a similar result pattern was found as can be seen in Fig. 3. Significant main effects for reaction time (F(1,23) = 129.45, p < .05) and for hit rate (F(1,23) = 19.55, p < .05) were confirmed by ANOVA. T-tests again showed significant differences for all DRTs while performing different levels of auditory n-back (reaction time: RDRT t(23) = -6.81, p < .05; TDRT t(23) = -6.67, p < .05; ADRT t(23) = -9.27, p < .05; hit rate: RDRT t(23) = 3.34, p < .05; TDRT t(23) = 4.13, p < .05; ADRT t(23) = 2.45, p < .05).

auditory n-back task

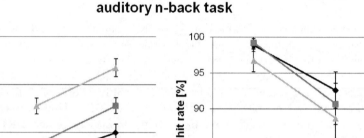

Fig. 3. Mean reaction times (left) and hit rates (right) for the DRTs during auditory n-back

The purely cognitive counting task led to slightly different results (see Fig. 4). While again a significant main effect for difficulty was found for reaction time (F(1,23) = 29.15, p > .05) and hit rate (F(1,23) = 18.44, p < .05), a significant interaction between difficulty and DRT variants on the hit rate dimension indicates differences in the degree of sensitivity of the DRTs in reaction to task levels (F(2,46) = 3.38, p < .05). As can be expected from Fig. 4, t-test analyses led to significant differences on reaction times (RDRT t(23) = -3.25, p < .05; TDRT t(23) = -3.44, p < .05; ADRT t(23) = -2.63, p < .05). When analyzing hit rate results, only TDRT (t(23) = 3.45, p < .05) and ADRT (t(23) = 3.18, p < .05) were able to discriminate between easy and difficult counting task. RDRT did not yield significant differences (t(23) = 1.92, ns).

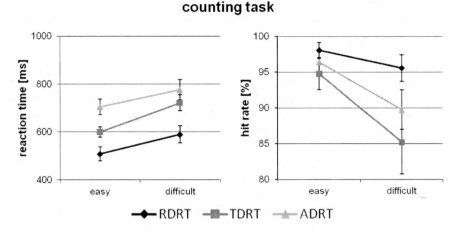

Fig. 4. Mean reaction times (left) and hit rates (right) for the DRTs during counting task

4   Discussion and Conclusion

The aim of the current study was to shed light on the sensitivity of different DRT variants while systematically varying secondary task presentation modality. Participants performed artificial cognitively loading tasks in different difficulty levels that were either presented aurally, visually or that consisted of a purely cognitive task without information presentation during task execution. DRTs under examination included visual remote peripheral, auditory and tactile stimuli detection.

The results strongly indicate that the DRT is a very robust and sensitive method to measure cognitive workload. Surprisingly, no interference effects were found between DRT stimuli presentation modality and secondary task modality. A possible explanation for this result can be that performing detection response tasks requires only little attention resources in itself. Both tasks could then be accomplished in spite of the resource conflict as no critical bottleneck level in task sharing was approached. An alternative explanation can be that the secondary task was cognitively loading but not requiring attentional resources in a level sufficiently high to induce critical modality interference. Future research thus needs to measure the amount of cognitive resource consumption during DRT execution only. Additional experiments should also systematically increase the level of sensory resource competition in the different secondary task modalities to check for interference effects.

All DRTs were basically able to discriminate between different levels of cognitive workload. The research presented here showed equally good results for ADRT, RDRT and TDRT when analyzing reaction times. As this is the dependent variable primarily used in DRT studies, the current study shows that researchers can choose the DRT modality most suitable for their experimental design in terms of avoiding resource conflicts without taking the risk of losing sensitivity. However, the experiment also provided evidence that the RDRT may not equally distinguish levels of workload when using hit rate as dependent variable. Future research should address the circumstances of this finding by focusing more strongly on providing comparable hit rate data in DRT studies.

Several steps need to be undertaken in order to establish DRTs as a suitable tool in driver distraction testing in the automotive context. First, more data is needed in how far DRTs can be used in triple task scenarios with concurrent driving simulation. Using a very simple driving task, [8] was able to show that tests participants are basically able to perform DRTs while driving and concurrently executing naturalistic and artificial secondary tasks. In a next step, data on more complex driving environments will be helpful. Second, a criterion needs to be defined which levels of DRT reaction time deterioration are critical when assessing cognitive driver distraction. Olsson and Burns [14] suggested that hit rates should not be less than 65% and reaction times should not fall below 800 ms. However, any threshold level needs to refer to concrete everyday driving situations in order to obtain ecological validity. A possible baseline for a socially accepted cognitive distraction level could be attention demanding conversations between driver and passenger.

Acknowledgments. The authors would like to acknowledge Otmar Hamm for his kind technical assistance as well as the Institute of Ergonomics team at the Technische Universität München (Klaus Bengler, Antonia Conti and Carsten Dlugosch) for their help in preparing this study and many fruitful discussions.

References

1. National Highway Traffic Safety Association (NHTSA), Department of Transportation: Visual-Manual NHTSA Driver Distraction Guidelines for In-Vehicle Electronic Devices. Report No. NHTSA-2010-0053, NHTSA (2012)
2. Zijlstra, F.R.: Efficiency in Work Behaviour. A Design Approach for Modern Tools. Delft University of Technology, Delft (1993)
3. Hart, S.G., Staveland, L.E.: Development of the NASA-TLX (Task Load Index): Results of Empirical and Theoretical Research. In: Hancock, P.A., Meshkati, N.M. (eds.) Human Mental Workload, pp. 139–183. North Holland B.V., Amsterdam (1988)
4. Wickens, C.D., Hollands, J.: Engineering Psychology and Human Performance. Prentice Hall, Upper Saddle River (2000)
5. Schwalm, M., Keinath, A., Zimmer, H.D.: Pupillometry as a Method for Measuring Mental Workload within a Simulated Driving Task. In: de Waard, D., Flemisch, F.O., Lorenz, B., Oberheid, H., Brookhuis, K.A. (eds.) Human Factors for Assistance and Automation, pp. 1–13. Shaker Publishing, Maastricht (2008)
6. Marshall, S.P., Davis, C., Knust, S.: The Index of Cognitive Activity: Estimating Cognitive Effort from Pupil Dilation. Technical Report ETI-0401. Eyetracking Inc., San Diego (2004)
7. Platten, F.: Analysis of Mental Workload and Operating Behavior in Secondary Tasks while Driving. Dissertation. Chemnitz University of Technology, Chemnitz (2012)

8. Conti, A., Dlugosch, C., Vilimek, R., Keinath, A., Bengler, K.: An Assessment of Cognitive Workload Using Detection Response Tasks. In: Stanton, N.A. (ed.) Advances in Human Aspects of Road and Rail Transport, pp. 735–743. Taylor & Francis Group, Boca Raton (2012)
9. Jahn, G., Oehme, A., Krems, J.F., Gelau, C.: Peripheral Detection as a Workload Measure in Driving: Effects of Traffic Complexity and Route Guidance System Use in a Driving Study. Transportation Research Part F 8, 255–275 (2005)
10. Merat, N., Jamson, A.H.: The Effect of Stimulus Modality on Signal Detection: Implications for Assessing the Safety of In-Vehicle Technology. Human Factors 50, 145–158 (2008)
11. van Winsum, W., Martens, M.H., Herland, L.: The Effects of Speech Versus Tactile Driver Support Messages on Workload, Driver Behaviour and User Acceptance. Report No. TM-99-C043, TNO Human Factors, Soesterberg (1999)
12. Martens, M.H., van Winsum, W.: Measuring Distraction: the Peripheral Detection Task. TNO Human Factors, Soesterberg (2000)
13. Mehler, B., Reimer, B., Coughlin, J.F., Dusek, J.A.: Impact of Incremental Increases in Cognitive Workload on Physiological Arousal and Performance in Young Adult Drivers. Transportation Research Record: Journal of the Transportation Research Board 2138, 6–12 (2009)
14. Olsson, S., Burns, P.C.: Measuring Driver Visual Distraction with a Peripheral Detection Task. Linköping University, Linköping (2000)

Part III

Cognitive Issues in Complex Environments

The Role of Specular Reflection in the Perception of Transparent Surfaces – The Influence on User Safety

Marcin Brzezicki

Faculty of Architecture,
Wroclaw University of Technology,
Prusa 53-55, 50-317 Wroclaw, Poland
marcin.brzezicki@pwr.wroc.pl

Abstract. The perception of transparency in human's build environment consti-
tutes a significant cognitive challenge, also affecting the user's safety. It is
supposed that, apart from the mid-level vision transparency cues, specular reflection is also a key feature of the perceived image taken into consideration by
the visual system. In the paper, this optical phenomenon was observed and estimated based on the author's own method, here called the "pictorial image
analysis", which uses pairs of photographs: unmodified – showing the virtual
image on the building's transparent façade, and modified – devoid of this image. The images were digitally processed to extract the reflection laid over the
undisturbed transmitted image. The results show that evident specular reflection
significantly improves the perception of transparent surfaces, but, in the case of
excess or back-lit panes, it can hardly be used as perceptual cue.

Keywords: transparency perception, mirror-like reflections, building's façade.

1 Introduction

Large scale light-transmitting surfaces have been present in human's build environment since the advent of 19th and 20th century industrialized manufacturing methods.
Smooth, faultless and frameless sheets of glass are difficult to perceive, especially on
a diverse background, because of the high degree of transparency. As a result, perceptual mistakes occur, resulting in people accidentally walking into the transparent pane.
Application of safety standard limits the number of instances of human-pane collision, but this "considerable threat to human safety" [1, p. 74] needs to be addressed.
Measures should be taken to limit or avoid potential accidents and to understand the
phenomenon better.

2 The Cognitive Mechanisms of Transparency Perception

At the mid-level vision stage – while creating the 3-dimensional model of the environment – the visual system recognizes transparency as a "special case of superposition" of surfaces [2, p. 257]. One of the key mechanisms depending on the pane's

D. Harris (Ed.): EPCE/HCII 2013, Part I, LNAI 8019, pp. 189–196, 2013.

absorbance is detecting the difference in transmitted image luminance between the obscured and unobscured portion (called a *reference area*) of the field of view. If the entire field of view is occupied by the pane, no edge is visible (the *reference area* is missing) and this basic mechanism simply ceases to work. In such circumstances, the perception system must rely on other cues for the recognition of transparency.

High-level cognitive processes involved in the perception of transparency are supposed to be based on cues produced by the so-called *optical surface phenomena*. These include: *(i)* specular reflection – generated by glossy transparent materials, thus creating a virtual image, *(ii)* transmitted image distortion, *(iii)* light ray refraction, among others. It is supposed that perception of specular reflection is – apart from the mid-level transparency cues – a key feature of the perceived image that is taken into consideration by the human visual system in the perception of transparency.

3   Specular Reflections and Virtual Images

Specular reflection is formed on the surface of all materials (not only light-transmitting) that have a sufficiently well finished surfaces (the imperfections of the material's surface are smaller than the wavelength of light). In such conditions, uni-directional light reflection occurs and a virtual image is created. Specular reflection could be created on a flat mirror, resulting in an undistorted virtual image (apart from left-right inversion) or on a free-form, ovoid object. The latter case results in a heavily distorted virtual image taking the form of luminance *highlight* – an area of higher luminance, distinctly different than the observed object. The location of those highlights was proven to be an important cue for the visual system in decoding the ovoid shape of an observed object, as shown by Blake & Bulthoff [3, p. 240].

In the case of a transparent material, two phenomena occur simultaneously. Every smooth pane that lets light through without deflection, simultaneously reflects light uni-directionally and provides the conditions for the formation of a virtual image.

An undistorted virtual image of the environment is created upon the flat mirror surface. It conforms to the laws of perspective and is usually perceived as appearing "behind" the mirror, or "inside the object". This is due to an optical illusion (humans perceive light rays as radiating along straight lines).

The image generated by a flat mirror, does not differ from the real image (both cannot be distinguished in the retinal image). The lack of differences causes the virtual image to be further processed by the visual system in the same way as the real image. The formation of a virtual image on the pane of light-transmitting material results in an interesting optical phenomenon – the superposition of two images: a real one transmitted through a pane, and a virtual one formed by the reflected rays. Presumably, the perception system uses this property to identify optical transparency and pane orientation in a 3-dimensional space surrounding the observer [4].

4   Research Tools and Methodology

The presented analysis is based on photographs depicting large-scale panes of light-transmitting material where two overlapping images are perceived in specific case studies. Both the buildings' glazing and the free-standing panes of transparent materials were included in this stage of the research.

The core study was conducted through observation with its results recorded using digital equipment. It was assumed that the image recorded by the digital camera matrix reproduces the instantaneous image perceived by the observer with sufficient accuracy. The main analytical method applied in the paper is called "pictorial image analysis" and is based on a comparison of two photographs: *(i)* unmodified, showing the virtual image on the surface of a transparent material and *(ii)* modified – with the virtual image blocked by the polarizing filter (details below).

4.1   Data Acquisition

The buildings selected for the study were: the Thespian Housing and Office Building (by Mackow Pracownia Projektowa, 2012) and the Silver Forum Office Estate (by Archicom, 2007), both prominent examples of contemporary architecture, recognized worldwide. The Thespian was a nominee for the European Union Prize for Contemporary Architecture – the Mies van der Rohe Award. Twofold images of selected buildings were recorded using a Sony Alfa 100 reflex camera (10 Mpix), 10-20 mm Sigma lens and a polarizing filter. Out of 140 photographs shot on site, 4 most representative series were selected for further digital processing.

4.2   Image Post-processing and Tools of Digital Analysis

The analysis was carried out using the ImageJ post-production software [5] originally developed by the Research Service branch of the U.S. National Institutes of Health for analyzing medical image data. The software offered tools unavailable in other applications, like image calculations (image subtraction and difference) and exact pixel count (using histogram measurement). Image processing occurred in stages, including: *(i)* cropping the selected areas of corresponding recorded images, *(ii)* subtracting or differentiating the images in order to isolate the virtual image, *(iii)* thresholding the image to isolate the areas of the virtual image, and visualize them by color coding, *(vi)* measuring the percentage of façade pixels affected by the virtual image using the histogram function. The individual steps of image processing have been shown in Figure 1.

The individual character of the field study photographs (changing light and point of view conditions) prevented the use of standardized parameters for all processed series. The level of threshold had to be determined individually for every viewpoint in order to achieve optimal virtual image selection. It has to be stated here that in series 3 and 4, the subtraction operation (i.e. subtracting digital numeric value of one image from another image) did not achieve the desired result because of the high pixel values (reaching max. in grayscale) contained within the virtual image areas.

Fig. 1. Steps of image processing e.g. series 1: *(i)* image crop (dashed frame), *(ii)*, *(iii)* image subtraction, *(iv)* image thresholding and color coding (black – façade area, white – virtual image), *(v)* measuring the percentage of façade pixels by using the histogram tool. Pictured building: the Thespian Housing and Office Building (by Mackow Pracownia Projektowa, 2012)

5   Pictorial Image Analysis and Results

In the "pictorial image analysis", a total of four series of images were analyzed. In two of them (series 1 and 2), the virtual image was isolated automatically, using the subtraction or differentiation tool of the ImageJ software and processed according to the above algorithm (see simplified graphical flowchart on Fig. 1). In the other two (series 3 and 4), the virtual image was isolated by tracing the outline based on the borders of the glazed portions of the façade. The results of the analysis are presented on the corresponding figures 2-5.

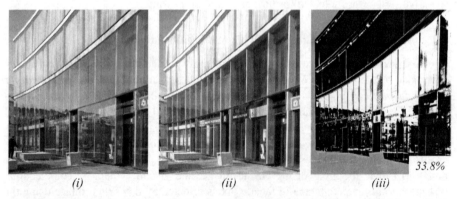

Fig. 2. Pictorial image analysis of series 1: *(i)* unmodified image, *(ii)* modified image with reflection filtered out, *(iii)* image thresholding and percentage calculation. Pictured building: the Thespian Housing and Office Building (by Mackow Pracownia Projektowa, 2012)

In series 1 (see Fig. 2), the virtual image of the surrounding buildings is visible in the lower part of the image, while the upper part of the virtual image is dominated by the reflection of the clear sky. The curvature of the façade makes the virtual image change gradually due to the different position and angle of the observed panes of glass. The glazed area obscured with the virtual image was calculated as 33.8%.

Fig. 3. Pictorial image analysis of series 2: *(i)* unmodified image, *(ii)* modified image with reflection filtered out, *(iii)* image thresholding and percentage calculation. Pictured building: the Thespian Housing and Office Building (by Mackow Pracownia Projektowa, 2012)

In series 2 (see Fig. 3), the virtual image is less prominent and vanishes as the angle of viewing increases (measured from normal). The image is dominated by trees, the reflection of the clear sky that was noticeable in the upper two stories do not affect transparency substantially. The glazed area overlaid with the virtual image amounted to 25.4%.

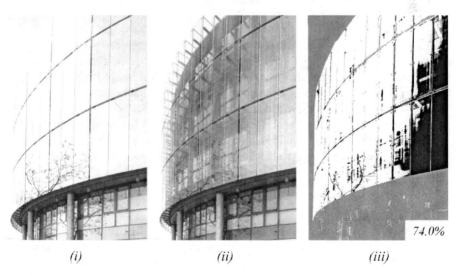

Fig. 4. Pictorial image analysis of series 3: *(i)* unmodified image, *(ii)* modified image with the reflection filtered out, *(iii)* image thresholding and percentage calculation. Pictured building: Silver Forum Office Estate (by Archicom, 2007)

In series 3 (see Fig. 4), the virtual image dominates the whole area of the transparent glazed façade. The substructure of the façade is not visible at all, it can be assumed that nearly the entire glazing is affected by the virtual image. Calculated values confirm this. The glazed area overlaid with the virtual image amounted to 74.0%.

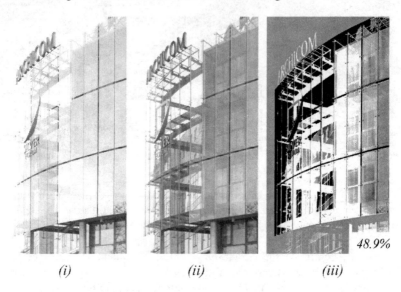

(i)   *(ii)*   *(iii)*

Fig. 5. Pictorial image analysis of series 4: *(i)* unmodified image, *(ii)* modified image with the reflection filtered out, *(iii)* image thresholding and percentage calculation. Pictured building: Silver Forum Office Estate (by Archicom, 2007)

In series 4 (see Fig. 5), a freestanding glazed screen is recorded projecting from the curved façade. The luminous flux balance makes this part of the glazing act differently in terms of optics. Since the panes are backlit, the virtual image is visibly weakened in this part of the façade, while the substructure and the background are visible. The glazed area overlaid with the virtual image amounted to 48.9%.

In all series, the application of a polarized filter in modified images lead to at least partial elimination of the virtual image. The area of glazing affected by the virtual image was calculated (white to black+white pixel ratio) was measured based on the histogram.

6   Discussion

In series 1 and 2 – when bright sunlight illuminated the photographed buildings – the share of the area overlaid with virtual image is smaller in proportion to the overall glazing area. In series 3, the larger share of the virtual image's covered area occurs due to the high luminance of the cloudy sky. Series 4 depicts both phenomena, since the glass panes are partially backlit. These differences in the visual outcome are caused by the difference in lighting conditions at the moment of image recording and allow to study the phenomena of how different lighting scenarios can influence the perception of transparency.

Based on analyzed images, the following possible cognitive mechanisms of transparency recognition based solely on reflection could be identified:

1. *image superposition* – a mechanism based on the local increase of luminance of the transmitted image resulting from the overlap with the virtual image (visible as moderate superposition in unmodified images in series 1 and 2 of 33.8% and 25.9% of area). The object (surface, other building, sky) that is reflected in a transparent pane always has a non-zero luminance. A virtual image resulting from this reflection overlaps with the real image transmitted through the pane. The reflected and transmitted luminous fluxes con-fuse (mix) and, if the luminance of the virtual image overpowers the luminance of the transmitted image, a local increase of luminance is perceived. If the luminance of the virtual image is lower than the luminance of the transmitted image, the visual outcome remains unaffected (no darkening occurs!).

Apart from the moderate superposition of the two images, two perceptual extremes could also be recognized, which lead to the obvious impairment in the perception of transparency:

2. *low luminance or total lack of the virtual image.* In the absence of a filtered out virtual image, the visual system has to rely solely on mid-level cues. In modified images, the most reliable cue – the reference area – is missing. Therefore, the perception of transparency in the modified images of series 1, 2 and 3 is much more doubtful than in series 4, where an evident reference area is present. In optical terms, the glazing projecting on a separate supporting structure works as a screen. Only a part of the background is veiled by the screen, hence obscured and un-obscured parts of the field of view could be compared by the visual system.

3. *excessive luminance of the virtual image.* Excessive luminance of the virtual image blocks the transmitted image totally. The transparent surface is indistinguishable from the mirror surface and its appearance depends on the geometry of the environment surrounding the observer and the luminance of the surface reflected in the pane (the cloudy sky in series 3 and 4 in 74.0%. and 48.9%).

Other issues should be researched in the future, according to the proportion of the virtual image visible on the pane: *simultaneous observation* of a distorted virtual image and an undistorted transmitted one, as well as the conditions of *variable eye accommodation* resulting from different real and apparent distances of the observed objects from the observer.

7   User Safety

Transparency perception is deeply linked with the recognition of invisible barriers, often in the form of a glazed pane. If this process fails, collision might occur. As previously shown in other papers by the author, increasing the human ability to ideally perceive transparent materials could be "fulfilled only by local suppression of transparency" [1, p. 80]. In this context, the above observed phenomena of *moderate image superposition* and *excessive luminance of virtual image* seem to be safe, as the obstruction of the real image by the virtual image sufficiently increases the ability to locate the pane correctly in a 3-dimensional environment surrounding the observer. The *lack of a virtual image* seems to be of real concern here, as this condition removes the mid-level cues by which the visual system can judge the transparent pane's location.

8   Conclusions

The conclusions based on the analysis of four series of images are as follows:

1 The presence of a virtual image significantly improves the perception of transparent surfaces. The absence of this important cue (e.g. in panes with special coatings) results in a decreased ability to recognize transparency and creates hazards for users.

2. In the case of high luminance values of the virtual image, the impression of virtual depth (virtual space, "world behind the mirror") is created. Attenuation of the transmitted image and amplification of the virtual one can lead to spatial disorientation, especially if the observers are to deal with multiple reflections.

3. The virtual image can hardly be used as a perceptual cue in the case of back-lit panes. This is due to the fact that the levels of illuminance on the opposite side of the pane are usually significantly higher than on the observer's side. This imbalance usually results in a visibly weakened virtual image that does not influence the image transmitted through the pane.

The elimination of the virtual image is supposed to impede the perception of transparency to the same extent as the excess of virtual image. The vital role of the virtual image in the process of recognition requires further study and research, possibly enriched with some field studies.

Acknowledgments. The author would like to thank prof. Edward Necka of the Institute of Psychology, Jagiellonian University in Krakow, for sharing his knowledge and research experience.

References

1. Brzezicki, M.: Perceptual mechanisms of transparency recognition as measures of increased human spatial orientation. In: Vink, P., et al. (eds.) Advances in Social and Organizational Factors, pp. 73–82. CRC Press, Boca Raton (2012)
2. Arnheim, R.: Art and visual perception: a psychology of the creative eye. University of California Press (1971)
3. Blake, A., Bulthoff, H.: Shape from sepcularity. Philosophical Transactions of the Royal Society B: Biological Sciences 331, 237–252 (1991)
4. Brzezicki, M.: Symmetry of superimposed facade reflection patterns. Symmetry: Art and Science (1-4), 34–37 (2010)
5. Abramoff, M., Magelhaes, P., Ram, S.: Image processing with ImageJ. Biophotonics International 11(7), 36–42 (2004)

Cognitive Engineering and Emergency Management

Denis A. Coelho

Human Technology Group, Dept. Electromechanical Engineering,
Universidade da Beira Interior, Calçada Fonte do Lameiro, 6201-001 Covilhã, Portugal
denis.a.coelho@gmail.com

Abstract. It is intended with this paper to shed light on the potential of cognitive engineering approaches to advance emergency management. Hence, the paper may inform future research on the problem domain. The paper considers cognitive engineering research paradigms, e.g., Hollnagel and Woods' (2001) cognitive systems engineering and design seeded by immersion in the application domain. The paper concludes with future directions for research in order to fulfil the gaps identified.

Keywords: cognitive systems engineering, disaster management, emergency management, decision-making.

1 Introduction

Global climate change related natural disasters and other events generating emergencies have been steadily increasing over the past years as a consequence of increased pressure on the natural environment and failure to meet the challenges for sustainability. Natural disasters are succeeding at an ever increasing rate with growing costs and human death tolls (UNISDR, 2011). Simultaneously, technological devices for information and communication are becoming ubiquitous, especially considering the wide dissemination of personal mobile phones and smart phones. Alternative forms of managing emergencies have been springing up and shifting, accommodating to a greater or lesser extent, the new possibilities brought about by the influx of information from steadily growing networks, and to the socio-economic context.

Emergencies, whether natural or technological, randomly or wilfully induced, challenge society's capabilities for both planning and response. They require action under risk and time constraints, which are imposed on responding organizations by the environment and thus are largely out of decision makers' control. Moreover, despite steady advances in managing emergencies, these continue to generate highly non-routine situations, requiring managers to generate and execute new plans nearly simultaneously. The resulting activities may then become part of organizational knowledge, increasing the capability of society to respond to future events (Mendonça and Wallace, 2007).

There is growing evidence (Guha-Sapir and Santos, 2012) that it is the poorest of the poor who will take the highest toll when a disaster strikes, and those which are most vulnerable and will often be permanently submersed in poverty as a result of a

D. Harris (Ed.): EPCE/HCII 2013, Part I, LNAI 8019, pp. 197–204, 2013.
© Springer-Verlag Berlin Heidelberg 2013

natural disaster. This has triggered an alternative response to emergencies, especially fostered in poorer regions and territories, fostering informal arrangements that are aimed at increasing community resilience (IEG, 2006). These approaches stand in contrast to formal government supported efforts to increase resilience and deal with emergency creating disasters. Both settings represent the outer limits of a continuum including many intermediate organizational settings, and levels of collaboration between diverse entities. In respect to these shifting settings for emergency management activities, and in order to support them, this paper presents a review of selected studies on cognition considering the activities of emergency management.

Poorly designed emergency management practices and systems may lead to higher rates of operating errors and slow performance. A better understanding of the human cognitive processes can lead to better-designed systems and tools that enable quick and easier intuitive understanding. Emergency situations can be stressful. By understanding how stress affects cognition, these effects can be mitigated through proper planning, training and system design. The key to emergency management success is planning and preparation, so that cognition during the critical phases of actual ongoing emergencies is not impaired by stress, or emotional distress of the decision makers and collaborating agents. Therefore, understanding the cognitive processes in the management of the response to emerging events and critical disasters provides fundamental insight to inform the processes leading to increased preparedness and efficient action.

1.1   Cognitive Engineering

According to Lambie (2001), the concept of cognitive engineering is not fixed and unequivocal, but in its various expressions certain common features are found. Norman (1987) invented the term 'cognitive engineering' to emphasize cognitive aspects of human-machine interaction. Norman (1986) stated:

> *"(...) the aims of cognitive engineering are:*
> *to understand the fundamental principles behind human action and performance that are relevant for the development of engineering principles of design,*
> *to devise systems that are pleasant to use. - the goal is neither efficiency nor ease nor power, although these are all to be desired, but rather systems that are pleasant, even fun: to produce what Laurel (1986) calls 'pleasurable engagement'.*
> *(...) The critical phenomena of cognitive engineering include: tasks, user actions, user conceptual methods and system image. The critical methods of cognitive engineering include: approximation and treating design as a series of trade-offs including giving different priorities to design decisions."*

Aristotle, who claimed that a measure of quality by which a work of fiction could be judged was the extent to which the audience became engaged by the story, first identified the concept of engagement. Laurel applied it to computers, claiming that a sense of engagement with the 'world' of the program that the person is using can be a central factor in determining whether he or she experiences a positive joy. Attaining pleasurable engagement would thus be a means of making a system pleasant to use, although there are other envisaged means.

In parallel to Norman's postulates on cognitive engineering, cognitive systems engineering was developed by Rasmussen, Hollnagel, Woods, etc., and was concerned with systems that were safety critical or complex (Lambie, 2001). As their work developed it attracted attention, because it offered better means to design. This version of cognitive engineering is forward looking to precision and testing of models and representations, rather than backward looking towards its epistemological roots (Coelho, 2002).

1.2   Cognitive Systems Engineering Approach

Emergencies and abnormal occurrences represent critical situations close to the margins of safe operation that challenge the controller operational practices and supervisory systems in place. The joint human and technical system is stretched to accommodate new demands, inevitably putting the joint system's resilience to the test. Emergencies and abnormal situations are hence fertile grounds for stories of resilience, which can stimulate human factors research (Malakis and Kontogiannis, 2011). Resilience represents the ability of a system to adapt or absorb disturbances, disruptions and changes and especially those that fall outside the textbook operation envelope (Woods et al, 2007). Resilience has been defined as a system's capability to create foresight, to recognize, to anticipate, and to defend against the changing shape of risk before adverse consequences occur (Woods, 2005, 2006; Hollnagel, Woods, and Leveson, 2006).

For Dowell and Long (1998), Human Factors (engineering psychology) is largely a craft, the heuristics it possesses being either 'rules of thumb' derived from experiences or guidelines derived informally from psychological theories and findings, with the latter representing the science applied. It has been found increasingly that addressing design problems in Human Factors, Human-Computer Interaction or Computer Supported Cooperative Work, necessitates turning attention away from the research with a psychological, computational or sociological nature (Lambie, 2001). This kind of research aims at universality, and instead one should focus on the problem posed by the target artefact, including the constraint that it meets given requirements.

Dahlman (2001) collected some of the problems, methods of analysis and types of consequent action that have been considered in the area where cognitive engineering acts. Stops, mistakes, stress and performance are the consequences we want to do something about, and which are due to a number of conflicts between the characteristics of human beings and the properties of technology, systems, work, etc. that is handled. Thus there are perception limitations, attention limitations, and so on. In a particular working or use situation these can be identified and understood by using combinations of methods. This understanding can then be used to redesign the design, modify or set up training programs and so on. These actions stand in line with

Woods' (2000) notion of observing people in actual settings and Vicente's (1998) focus on testing alternative proposals. There are theories about perception, attention, information perception and others (e.g. signal detection theory – Green & Swets, 1966) that support the understanding of the situation analyzed. Methods also exist that have been able to produce design guidelines (e.g. Woods, 1995 – display design). Whereas Woods (2000) goes into an introduction of a new technology used in an existing system as the starting point of a process which is geared to deliver design seeds for further development, the process described by Dahlman (2001) steps into a steady state of an existing system. The outcome of the latter process aims at suggesting a new generation system and getting at it with design iterations towards the end of the process.

Despite the large number of methods available, the lack of predictive power was a persistent complaint of engineers about the limitations of typical human factors input into design (Hockey and Westerman, 1998). In his Presidential address to the Human Factors and Ergonomics Society, David D. Woods (1999) claimed that over the previous five decades the profession had been developing and handing over validated guidelines so that others can carry out its professional practice. The process of literal design and "table lookup" was seen by Woods (1999) as an oversimplification that leaves discovery, insight and innovation out of the profession's description of design. He stated ironically that the profession had been "sweeping up at the rear of the parade" ("reacting after-the fact, [...] called in only when others reach impasses, respond to calls for help with 'I can test that ...', miss windows of opportunity [and] best work in the aftermath of surprises"). As a better alternative, Woods (1999) brought forward another perspective, that of complementarity, where research and practice are mutually reinforcing and where field settings are viewed upon as natural laboratories for long term learning. From this perspective, design is seen as "balancing understanding, usefulness and usability".

Hockey and Westerman (1998) acknowledged that measurement in the area of cognitive engineering is complex, claiming that various components of usability – performance, quality and cognitive user costs – are essentially incommensurate. Usability handbooks, such as Nielsen's (1993), refer to crude, context free measures of performance that include time to complete task and number of errors in completing it. These measures, however, can assist in evaluating usability improvements between alternative systems used in the same task and context. On the other hand, subjective assessments refer to concepts such as motivation or satisfaction, but are generally not considered in practice in the methodologies for cognitive engineering. However, Norman (1993) considered the concept of motivated cognitive activity in his writings about cognitive engineering. This concept did not however seem to pass on visibly to research.

2   Phases of Activity in Emergency Management

Emergency management is a mission that can be divided into several phases: work to avoid crises, preparation for crises, operative work, and evaluations after an event.

Emergencies are unpredictable, and the needs for resources and information are difficult to define beforehand. This characterizes the operation of emergency management organizations in crises as dynamic systems, as their states change autonomously and as a result of actions upon it (Brehmer, 1992). The dynamics of the system makes obtaining a complete predetermined plan or task description improbable. In operations, contingency plans only cover a fraction of the types of incidents to be handled: often, opportunistic response and coordination by feedback is used (Smith et al., 2003; Dynes and Quarantelli, 1977). Participants dispersed over a range of organizations and roles, accomplish this by managing a wide range of actions and decision making, such as tracking events as they develop, and constantly modifying plans.

A communication structure is necessary in this type of work, and it provides ground for a culture of norms and practices to grow (Hutchins, 1996). Issues from the represented organizations affect which content is brought up into interaction and how proposed solutions are handled (Keyton and Stallworth, 2003). The relational needs associated with cooperation are compounded with task demands, and go hand in hand with coordination activities (Hutchins, 1996).

The consequence of these interactions and interdependencies is that the cooperative task performance that underlies emergency management must be studied in relation to the social, organizational and technological context (Johansson, 2005) it is performed in.

3   Nature of Cognition in Emergency Management

Cognitive Systems Engineering approaches strive towards explicitly handling issues about how cognition and behaviour is shaped by artefacts in complex interaction (McNeese, 2001; Woods, 1998). This demands an understanding of the processes underlying cognition in human-human and human-computer interaction, with a focus on the external conditions and not on assumed internal mechanisms (Hollnagel & Woods, 2005). Cognitive Systems Engineering frames a view of humans and technology as integrated, joint cognitive systems where the focus is on overall performance. Thus, the complexity in social and organizational constraints and the context of work, situated context (McNeese, 2001) must receive attention. This may be a productive approach in the integration of Geographical Information Systems and other Information and Communication Technology systems in the fields of emergency planning and response. Hollnagel and Woods (2005) have explicated this in a concrete approach that ranges cognition as taking place in a composite system of humans and technology, a joint cognitive system.

As noted by Norman (1990), the aims of cognitive engineering are first 'to understand the fundamental principles behind human action and performance that are relevant for the development of engineering principles of design and second, to devise systems that are pleasant to use'. This definition has engendered many psychological and design studies specifically in human–computer interaction and recently in designing team decision-aiding and training systems (Jones and Mitchell, 1995). Cognitive systems engineering is the integration of human knowledge about task (environment and perception), cognition, and artefact behaviours that can lead to the execution and control of specific tasks at various levels of abstraction (McBride et al., 2004). Cognitive systems engineering is able to capture the human procedural, operational, and structural knowledge about events, activities and behaviours as reasoned through human actions (Zarakovsky, 2004). This provides the main source of knowledge for design of cognitive aids, especially those used in training (Bedny and Meister, 1997). The knowledge required for training can vary along a discrete continuum of the operator's level of expertise, psychological states and traits, and task dimensions (Quarantelli, 1997). From the cognitive systems engineering perspective, the level of expertise is commonly assessed along the dimensions of skill-, rule-, and knowledge-based behaviours known to control the decision-making ability of the human operator (Rasmussen 1986). Implicitly, the levels of expertise allow replicating the human mental model of a computerized system (Ntuen et al., 2006).

4   Conclusion

Research on learning, modelling and decision support in the context of emergency management and increasing resilience, should lead to results with implications for how organizations may identify and respond to unplanned-for contingencies, which is deemed the most critical challenge for cognitive engineering in emergency management. Hollnagel and Woods (2005) argued that the potential for resilience can be measured but not resilience itself. In line with this reasoning, it is concluded that adaptive cognitive strategies improve the potential for resilience in two manners. On the one hand, by providing insights on how adaptations in the form of cognitive strategies are employed to support resilience in cases of safety critical events, and on the other, by the use of these cognitive strategies as foundation blocks in the development of advanced training programs with the aim of cultivating sources of resilience in the emergency management system.

References

1. Bedny, G.Z., Meister, D.: The Russian Activity Theory: Current Applications to Design and Learning. Erlbaum, Mahwah (1997)
2. Brehmer, B.: Dynamic Decision Making: Human Control of Complex Systems. Acta Psychologica 81, 211–241 (1992)
3. Coelho, D.A.: A growing concept of ergonomics, including comfort, pleasure and cognitive engineering – an engineering design perspective. Ph.D. thesis, Dept. of Electromechanical Engineering, Universidade da Beira Interior, Covilhã, Portugal (2002)
4. Dahlman, S.F.: Personal communication (2001)
5. Dowelll, J., Long, J.: Conception of the Cognitive Engineering Design Problem. Ergonomics 41(2), 126–139 (1998)
6. Dynes, R., Quarantelli, E.L.: Organizational Communications and Decision Making in Crises. Disaster Research Center Report 17, Ohio State University (January 1977)
7. Green, D.M., Swets, J.A.: Signal detection theory and psychophysics. Wiley, New York (1966); (reprinted 1988. Peninsula, Los Altos)

8. Guha-Sapir, D., Santos, I.: The Economic Impacts of Natural Disasters. Oxford University Press, Oxford (2012) (in press)
9. Hockey, G.R.J., Westerman, S.J.: Advancing human factors involvement in engineering design: a bridge not far enough? Ergonomics 41(2), 147–149 (1998)
10. Hollnagel, E., Woods, D.D.: Cognitive Systems Engineering. In: Karwowski, W. (ed.) International Encyclopedia of Ergonomics and Human Factors, pp. 1768–1770. Taylor & Francis, London and New York (2001)
11. Hollnagel, E., Woods, D.D.: Joint cognitive systems: Foundations of cognitive systems engineering. CRC Press / Taylor & Francis, Boca Raton, FL (2005)
12. Hollnagel, E., Woods, D.D., Leveson, N. (eds.): Resilience engineering: Concepts and precepts. Ashgate Press, Aldershot (2006)
13. Hutchins, E.: Cognition in the Wild. MIT Press, Cambridge (1996)
14. IEG – Independent Evaluation Group, Hazards of Nature, Risks to Development – An IEG Evaluation of World Bank Assistance for natural Disaster, p. 181. The World Bank, Washington (2006), http://www.worldbank.org/ieg/naturaldisasters/docs/natural_disasters_evaluation.pdf
15. Johansson, B.: Joint Control in Dynamic Situations. Linköping Studies in Science and Technology. Thesis No: 972, Department of Computer and Information Science, Linköpings Universitet, Sweden (2005)
16. Jones, P.M., Mitchell, C.M.: Human–computer cooperative problem solving: theory, design, and evaluation of an intelligent associate system. IEEE Transactions on Systems, Man, and Cybernetics, SMC-15, 1039–1053 (1995)
17. Keyton, J., Stallworth, V.: On the verge of collaboration: Interaction processes versus group outcomes. In: Frey, L.R. (ed.) Group Communication in Context: Studies of Bona Fide Groups, 2nd edn., pp. 235–260. Lawrence Erlbaum Associates, Mahwah (2003)
18. Lambie, T.: Cognitive Engineering. In: Karwowski, W. (ed.) International Encyclopedia of Ergonomics and Human Factors, pp. 22–24. Taylor & Francis, London and New York (2001)
19. Laurel, B.K.: Interface as Mimesis. In: Norman, Draper (eds.) User Centered System Design, pp. 67–85. Erlbaum, Hillsdale (1986)
20. Malakis, S., Kontogiannis, T.: Cognitive Strategies in Emergency and Abnormal Situations Training: Implications for Resilience in Air Traffic Control. In: Hollnagel, E., Pariès, J., Woods, D.D., Wreathall, J. (eds.) Resilience Engineering in Practice – A Guidebook, Surrey, pp. 101–118. Ashgate Publishing Limited, England (2011)
21. Mcbride, M.E., Adams, K.A., Ntuen, C.A., Mazeva, N.: Application of cognitive systems engineering to decision aiding design. In: Proceedings of Institute for Industrial Engineering Research Conference (CD ROM). IIE Management Press, Atlanta (2004)
22. Mendonça, D.J., Wallace, W.A.: A Cognitive Model of Improvisation in Emergency Management. IEEE Transactions on Systems, Man and Cybernetics, Part A: Systems and Humans 37(4), 547–561 (2007)
23. McNeese, M.D.: Discovering how cognitive systems should be engineered for aviation domains: A developmental look at work, research, and practice. In: McNeese, M.D., Vidulich, M. (eds.) Cognitive Systems Engineering in Military Aviation Environments: Avoiding Cogminutia Fragmentosa, HSIAC Press, Wright-Patterson Air Force Base (2001)
24. Norman, D.A.: Cognitive Engineering. In: Norman, D.A., Draper, S.W. (eds.) User Centered System Design, pp. 31–61. Erlbaum, Hillsdale (1986)
25. Norman, D.D.: Stages and levels in human–machine interaction. International Journal of Man–Machine Studies 21, 365–375 (1990)

26. Norman, D.: Things that make us smart - Defending human attributes in the age of the machine. Addison-Wesley, Reading (1993)
27. Ntuen, C.A., Balogun, O., Boyle, E., Turner, A.: Supporting command and control training functions in the emergency management domain using cognitive systems engineering. Ergonomics 49(12-13), 1415–1436 (2006)
28. Quarantelli, E.L.: The Disaster Research Center field studies of organizational behavior in the crisis time period of disasters. International Journal of Mass Emergencies and Disasters 15, 47–69 (1997)
29. Rasmussen, J.: Information Processing and Human–Machine Interaction: An Approach to Cognitive Engineering. North-Holland, Amsterdam (1986)
30. Smith, P.J., Beatty, R., Spencer, A., Billings, C.: Dealing with the Challenges of Distributed Planning in a Stochastic Environment: Coordinated Contingency Planning. In: Proceedings of the 2003 Annual Conference on Digital Avionics Systems, Chicago, IL (2003)
31. UNISDR, Global Assessment Report on Disaster Risk Reduction 2011: Revealing Risk, Redefining Development, United Nations International Strategy for Disaster Reduction (2011), http://www.unisdr.org/we/inform/publications/19846
32. Vicente, K.J.: An evolutionary perspective on the growth of cognitive engineering: the Risø genotype. Ergonomics 41(2), 156–159 (1998)
33. Wickens, C.D., Hollands, J.G.: Engineering Psychology and Human Performance, 3rd edn. Prentice Hall, Upper Saddle River, New Jersey (2000)
34. Woods, D.D.: Towards a Theoretical Base for Representation Design in the Computer Medium: Ecological Perception and Aiding Human Cognition. In: Flach, J., Hancock, P., Caird, J., Vicente, K. (eds.) An Ecological Approach to Human Machine Systems I: A Global Perspective, Erlbaum, Hillsdale (1995)
35. Woods, D.D.: Designs Are Hypotheses about How Artifacts Shape Cognition and Collaboration. Ergonomics 41, 168–173 (1998)
36. Woods, D.D.: W3: Watching Human Factors Watch People at Work. In: Presidential Address, 43rd Annual Meeting of the Human Factors and Ergonomics Society, September 28 (1999), Multimedia Production (Woods, D.D., Tinnaple, D.) at http://csel.eng.ohio-state.edu/hf99/
37. Woods, D.D.: Complementarity and synchronization as strategies for practice-centered research and design. Keynote Speech Presented at the XIVth Triennial Congress of the International Ergonomics Association and 44th Annual Meeting of the Human Factors and Ergonomics Society, San Diego, California, USA, July 29-August 4 (2000)
38. Woods, D.D.: Creating foresight: Lessons for resilience from Columbia. In: Farjoun, M., Starbuck, W.H. (eds.) Organization at the Limit: NASA and the Columbia Disaster, pp. 289–308. Blackwell, New York (2005)
39. Woods, D.D.: Essential characteristics of resilience. In: Hollnagel, E., Woods, D.D., Leveson, N. (eds.) Resilience Engineering: Concepts and Precepts, pp. 21–34. Ashgate Press, Aldershot (2006)
40. Woods, D.D., Patterson, E.S., Cook, R.I.: Behind Human Error: Taming Complexity to Improve Patient Safety. In: Carayon, P. (ed.) Handbook of Human Factors and Ergonomics in Health Care and Patient Safety. Lawrence Erlbaum Associates, Mahwah (2007)
41. Zarakovsky, G.M.: The concept of theoretical evaluation of operators' performance derived from activity theory. Theoretical Issues in Ergonomics Science 5, 313–337 (2004)

Design and Implementation of a Cognitive Simulation Model for Robotic Assembly Cells

Marco Faber, Sinem Kuz, Marcel Ph. Mayer, and Christopher M. Schlick

Institute of Industrial Engineering and Ergonomics of RWTH Aachen University
Bergdriesch 27, D-52062 Aachen, Germany
m.faber@iaw.rwth-aachen.de

Abstract. Against the background of a changing global economy, new production technologies have to be developed to stay competitive in high-wage countries. Therefore, an integrated cognitive simulation model (CSM) has been developed to support the human operator and the assembly process. By making the behavior of the system more intuitive the cognitive compatibility between the operator and the production system is enhanced significantly. The presented CSM faces three different challenges: (1) visualizing the behavior of the system to give the human operator an understanding of the technical systems, (2) cognitive control of a real robotic assembly cell and (3) performing mass simulations in order to evaluate parameters, new assembly or planning strategies or the assembly of new products. Additionally, a graph-based planner supports the cognitive planning instance for realizing complex tasks.

Keywords: cognitive simulation, joined cognitive systems, human-machine interaction, production systems.

1 Introduction

Today the automation of many production systems in high-wage countries is sophisticated and aligned towards a cost-conscious production process. Due to modern automation techniques including manufacturing resource planning algorithms specialized products can be assembled autonomously. Nevertheless, these production systems suffer often from several drawbacks. First, they provide little flexibility in the sense of adopting to both variants of the products and changing conditions of the production environment. In order to stay competitive in a rapidly changing economy it is crucial for companies to anticipate customer specific wishes and to flexibly react, especially in high-wage countries. Wiendahl et al. [1] describes this requirement as the replacement of the era of mass production by the era of market niches. As a result, the product range may increase because of multiple variants of the same product and a growth of the different types of products. These requirements can hardly be satisfied by today's automated production systems as their function is mainly determined by less flexible programs [2]. In addition, production circumstances have to be well defined, i.e. feeding systems are, for example, characterized by a straight consignment and

D. Harris (Ed.): EPCE/HCII 2013, Part I, LNAI 8019, pp. 205–214, 2013.
© Springer-Verlag Berlin Heidelberg 2013

the robustness towards errors in sequence and time is not matured. Against the economic competition, production systems have to address these challenges and need to adopt to changing production factors such as quality, time and cost [2].

Furthermore, the special knowledge and skills of the human operator are not considered enough. In highly automated systems it remains the duty of the human operator to process different kinds of monitoring tasks or intervene, if erroneous states of the production system occur. Due to a large variety in product space, the number of different monitoring tasks and the complexity of a single task increase at the same time. In order to let the operator be able to evaluate the current situation effectively the transparency of the system has to be enhanced. Solving this problem by even more automation is not advisable since this leads to a vicious circle of automation [3], which was introduced by Bainbridge as the "ironies of automation" [4]. Rather, the human operator should be directly considered as an integral part when designing a production system. This leads to joint cognitive systems [5] in which both the technical systems and the operator are regarded as one combined system. Because of the enormous skills of the human operator concerning materials and tools as well as his/her ability to think creatively it is important to consider these aspects.

A sub-project within the Cluster of Excellence "Integrative Production Technology for High-Wage Countries" at RWTH Aachen University focuses on the human-centered design of self-optimizing production systems. These systems are characterized by running continuously through decision cycles: analyzing the current situation, deriving possibly new system objectives, tasks and procedures and adopting the system behavior autonomously [2]. Hence, self-optimizing systems require a flexible and mutable automation, autonomy to manage complex processes without the necessity of manual intervention, and simulated cognition and learning to adopt their behavior. Considering additionally joint cognitive systems, the human operator must be viewed as a part of the production system whose behavior is much more unpredictable than that from a machine so that the mutability of the system also has to cope with that challenge.

For the enhancement of automation, there exists several kinds of simulation models such as, for example, for detecting collisions in robotized assembly processes. With respect to self-optimizing production systems it would also be favorable to be able to investigate their behavior at a higher level of abstraction without the necessity to specify and control real hardware or system emulations. Hence, the cognitive simulation model presented in this paper has been designed and implemented in order to plan and execute assembly tasks while considering the human operator as essential part of the production system.

2   Human-Centered Design of Production Systems

By increasing the level of automation the "ironies of automation" [4] become more prevalent. As a consequence, the human operator may lose the control since he/she has to make more complex decisions although he/she is not involved in the particular fully automated low-level production processes any longer. Rather, the operator has to rely on the automation technique even though he/she might not understand what the machines are doing and which goals they are pursuing. This effect can be compensated by making decisions in the production system that are compatible to the mental model of the human operator [6]. Such joint cognitive systems let the human operator cooperate safely and effectively with the automated machines in order to achieve a maximum of human-machine compatibility. The mistrust against the "new" technique has to be counteracted in the way that the operator is able to build up confidence to the technical system. This can be achieved by establishing a cognitive simulation model of the operator's mental model into the decision process and the behavior of the production system.

Focusing on assembly systems, Mayer et al. have empirically identified several strategies pursued by humans while assembling mechanical components [7,8]. They have shown that the integration of these assembly strategies in terms of production rules in a knowledge base can enhance the transparency of the production system significantly. In particular, the more human-like knowledge is integrated into the knowledge base the less time is needed to anticipate the decisions and movements of robotized systems. As shown by lower prediction times, the human operator is able to understand the technical behavior better and faster leading to a higher confidence in the system. Other studies by Kuz et al. [9] have shown that introducing anthropomorphic movements can further enhance the conformity with the expectations of the operator.

In summary, the studies give insights about how to design a production system so that the human operator is not overburdened by the complexity of its behavioral pattern and mode. Certainly, this knowledge can be applied to simulation models of production systems as well. In the following section, a cognitive simulation model is described that instantiates essential behavior shaping rules of the aforementioned mental model of the human operator and utilize them in order to control a self-optimizing automated assembly cell.

3 Cognitive Simulation Model

The cognitive simulation model (CSM) has been designed to provide a simplified, compatible representation of the mental model of the human operator within the production process in a nondeterministic production environment. Such a model benefits with making the assembly process more transparent for the operator and, finally, giving him the opportunity of understanding the system behavior. Thereby, the model influences both the way of visualizing the process information and controlling robotic assembly actions. It is apparent that the cognitive capabilities of a technical system cannot compete with those of the human operator since the latter one is able to think creatively and to learn extensively from his/her experiences. The human brain appears not to be compatible in a complex production environment. Rather, the CSM should avoid the drawbacks of static and preprogrammed systems by introducing the flexibility of simulated

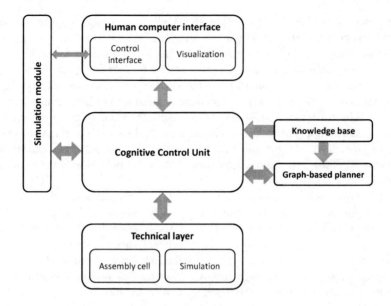

Fig. 1. Architecture of the Cognitive Simulation Model (CSM)

cognitive systems in order to react and adopt to unforeseen and unpredictable changes.

3.1   Architecture

The CSM has a flexible architecture and provides perceptual interfaces for human-computer interaction and technical interfaces for controlling machines as depicted in Fig. 1. Its core component is the so-called Cognitive Control Unit (CCU) which is primarily responsible for planning the action sequences. It is based on the common three layer architecture for robotic applications by Russel and Norvig [10] comprising of a planning layer, a coordination layer and a reactive layer. The CCU requires as input a part list of the final product (e.g. in terms of a XML file) containing only the properties of the components but no assembly order. During the assembly process it acts similar to human cognition by iterating through cycles of analyzing the current situation, planning the actions according to this analysis and performing these actions. Thereby, the system makes use of three different workspaces: New components are fed into the system in the supply area. The final product is built in the assembly area whereas components that are needed later can be stored in the buffer area.

The cognitive functions of the CCU are simulated by the popular cognitive architecture Soar[1]. In contrast to other methods such as neural networks, Soar does not need any training data for instantiation which is favorable especially for dynamic production environments. Instead, the knowledge is encoded in terms of

---

[1] http://sitemaker.umich.edu/soar

Fig. 2. Human-machine interface of the Cognitive Simulation Model (CSM) consisting of the control interface and the visualization of the system state

explicit if-then production rules in the knowledge base statically or dynamically by learning at runtime and forms the basis for making decisions in each cycle of the CCU.

In detail, the knowledge base provides the information for performing assembly steps. Therefore, an assembly step is divided into its basic components by means of the fundamental motions REACH, GRASP, MOVE, POSITION and RELEASE. These motions correspond to the basic elements of Methods-Time Measurement (MTM), a standard method for analyzing and planning human motions in the industrial production. Hence, they should agree with the expectations of a human operator. In addition, the human-like strategies identified in empirical studies by Mayer et al. [7,8] are encoded as production rules which can be activated on demand. Both the fundamental motions according to MTM and the additional rules of the human-like strategies have been chosen because of their relevance for increasing transparency for the human operator.

The technical layer is responsible for controlling an assembly cell and the human-computer interface for interacting with the operator. The simulation module provides an automated access to the CCU for extensive simulations. These three components are described in detail in Sec. 3.2. Finally, the graph-based planner can be used for advanced possibilities in planning the assembly sequences. Its capabilities are described in detail in Sec. 3.3.

3.2 Integration of Simulation and Assembly Control

Due to its flexibility the CSM is qualified for three different areas of application. First, it can be used as a comprehensive visualization of the assembly processes. The control interface, as depicted on the left side of Fig. 2, displays the current motion step of the robot, i.e. which of the MTM operations REACH, GRASP, MOVE, POSITION or RELEASE is currently performed. The state WAIT signals a kind of standby mode in which no other operation can be performed.

This may occur due to missing or wrong components that are not needed for the current assembly process. Furthermore, information about the decisions of the CCU and the current system behavior is displayed including the movements of the components between the assembly and buffer areas.

Besides the control function, the human-machine interface also provides a fully featured visualization of the assembly cell as depicted on the right side of Fig. 2. This virtual simulation serves as a simplified geometric and kinematic representation of the real assembly cell. The user is able to choose an arbitrary point of view to take a look at the scene and observe the behavior of the technical systems easily. However, this module serves only as visualization and does not provide any plausibility checks except that exceeding the reachability distance of the robotic arm would lead to failure messages.

The second field of application is the control of a real robotic assembly cell. For the purpose of evaluation an exemplary assembly cell was developed by Kempf [11] as shown in Fig. 3. It reflects the three different areas of action, namely supply area, assembly area and buffer area. An articulated KUKA robot with six axis is used in combination with a three finger gripper with haptic sensors for assembling components. The supply area is realized by a circulating conveyor belt. In the context of this assembly cell, the CSM is able to control the behavior of the robotic arm in terms of the fundamental motions of MTM [6]. Hence, the robot performs motion sequences as the human operator would do. As a result, the transparency of the behavior of the CCU is transferred to the technical systems. Since KUKA provides an interface for controlling a virtual model of their products, the CSM can also interact with a realistic simulation of an assembly cell in the technical layer.

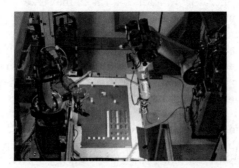

Fig. 3. The robotic assembly cell controlled by the Cognitive Simulation Model (CSM) [6]

The third application of the CSM is found in the area of simulating assembly processes. By decoupling the visualization and the control of the assembly cell, the CSM can be used to perform extensive simulations to evaluate different parameters or assembly strategies. The parameters that can be modified comprise among others the destination system, i.e. the product to be assembled in terms of a part list, and the supply of components. The latter one can be varied in terms of the number of components that the system is provided with in the supply area and the mode of supply which can be random or deterministic by a given list of components in a fixed order. In addition, the knowledge base can be set individually for each run of the simulation. This allows, for example, to compare different human-like assembly strategies in order to find those rules that promise the best support for the human operator. Finally, the initial states of the supply area, the assembly area and the buffer area can be set to enable the simulation of specific situations in the assembly process. The CSM could be used successfully in extensive simulation studies in order to investigate different assembly strategies [12].

Beyond the evaluation of parameters, the CSM can be utilized to test the feasibility of assembling unknown products in consideration of the knowledge integrated into the CCU. This is especially important when introducing rules into the knowledge base that limit the number of valid assembly sequences as there may not remain any feasible sequence. Then, the component could not be built by the CCU and consequently neither by the cognitively controlled assembly cell, although it may physically be possible. Considering the test of a real assembly cell it is possible to use the simulation module in combination with a technical simulation of the cell such as that provided by KUKA. This enables discovering problems in assembling the components physically.

Finally, the simulation environment can also be used to evaluate new planning procedures. One of them is, for example, the graph-based planner that is described in the next section.

3.3   Support by a Graph-Based Planner

During its decision cycles the CCU evaluates all possible assembly actions by making preferences between pairs of actions. Hence, the planning procedure gets the more complex the more competing actions are available that could be performed. This is especially the case when many uniform components could be assembled at the same time assuming that all needed components are available [12]. Because of the RETE algorithm underlying the process of decision making in Soar this leads to exponential worst-case runtime behavior [13].

At the same time, the CCU suffers from being able to look only one step ahead in the assembly sequence, i.e. it cannot plan for more than the currently next step. Hence, the CCU may arrive at a state where it cannot build any further component, for example due to technical restrictions of the gripper. Against this background, the cooperation between the human operator and the robot has been investigated in studies by Odenthal et al. [14]. However, such impasses of the assembly process cannot be detected earlier by the CCU, although the overall goal is to build the final product as autonomously as possible until the human operator has to intervene. Increasing the planning depth of the CCU to a higher level would significantly increase the complexity of planning so that the real-time capability of the CCU is impaired when assembling complex products.

As a tradeoff, an additional planning module utilizing a graph-based representation of the assembly sequences has been developed to support the CCU. It is based on the hybrid architecture of the planner by Ewert et al. [15] in the sense that it is divided into an offline and an online part. In the offline preprocessing procedure, a state graph is generated by following an assembly by disassembly strategy [16]. Thereby, the product is decomposed recursively in all possible separations until only single components remain. The resulting graph contains all valid assembly sequences of the final product and serves as a basis for further planning activities.

During the assembly process, the edges of the graph are rated according to the activated rules in the knowledge base. Thereby, state transitions that violate a rule cause penalty costs. In each decision cycle of the CCU, the current state is located in the graph and the costs for all possible extensions of the current assembly sequence are computed by the application of the algorithm A*Prune [17]. In contrast to the algorithm A* used by Ewert et al., this algorithm returns in addition to the path having the lowest costs also further suboptimal paths up to a specified threshold. Therefore, prefixes of paths having higher costs than the currently best solution are stored in a list and examined later according to their costs reached up to that time. Using the cost information about the best extensions of the current assembly sequence, the CCU is able to make an appropriate choice according to both the global view of the graph-based planner and its own optimization criteria.

Working together with the graph-based planner, the CSM is able to consider more complex optimization criteria in the planning process of the assembly. Possible rules are, for example, following the path with the highest autonomous assembly progress, the highest level of occupational safety or the minimum number of discomfort postures for the human operator.

Although nearly any kind of rule could be integrated into the planner, the planning and decision making component of the CCU still has to react dynamically to unforeseen changes. Furthermore, the graph-based planner reduces the solution space and thereby decreases the processing time, that is used by the CCU to find the optimal next assembly action, by making a preliminary selection of all valid sequences. Since the graph-based planner is designed as an independent module and integrated seamlessly into the simulation model, the CSM is flexible in case of a failure of this component. This might be caused by a timeout indicating that the planner has exceeded a specified time limit or by a loss of connection when the planner runs on a different resource than the CCU. The CCU would then rely on its own knowledge which still leads to a valid but possibly suboptimal assembly sequence.

4   Summary and Outlook

Although today's production systems are sophisticated and efficient, they are not flexible enough to adopt to unforeseen and quick changes of the products as well as the production environment. They usually need a well-defined environment and have to be adjusted manually when unexpected changes occur.

Additionally, the role of the human operator and his/her skills and knowledge are not considered sufficiently.

Hence, a flexible cognitive simulation model (CSM) has been developed which supports the human operator in the production process and is due to its modularized architecture applicable to several scenarios of human-computer interaction. The core of the CSM comprises a Cognitive Control Unit (CCU) based on the cognitive architecture Soar. The CCU acts according to the human cognition, i.e. it constantly runs through cycles of analyzing the current situation, planning the actions and handling. The CCU makes its decision based on human-like strategies, that were identified empirically and consolidated in the knowledge base. By transferring this human-like behavior to the technical systems the cognitive compatibility between the operator and the production system is significantly enhanced.

Besides the control of a real assembly cell, the CSM addresses the challenges of visualizing comprehensively the production process and performing a virtual simulation in order to evaluate new planning strategies or the feasibility of assembling a new product. To support the CCU a graph-based planner has been developed working on a graph-based representation of the possible assembly sequences. Dependent on the activated knowledge it reduces the solution space for the decision procedure of the CCU by making a preselection of the possible next actions. This enables the CSM to consider much more complex and human-oriented strategies than it would be possible otherwise.

In order to enhance the transparency of the technical systems even more, current research addresses the path planning of the robotic movements. By introducing anthropomorphic movements the time needed to anticipate can be reduced leading to a higher confidence of the human operator [9]. Besides that, the principles of the CSM are transferred to whole production networks in order to design them in a similar cognitively compatible way.

Acknowledgment. The authors would like to thank the German Research Foundation DFG for the kind support within the Cluster of Excellence "Integrative Production Technology for High-Wage Countries".

References

1. Wiendahl, H.P., ElMaraghy, H., Nyhuis, P., Zäh, M., Wiendahl, H.H., Duffie, N., Brieke, M.: Changeable Manufacturing - Classification, Design and Operation. CIRP Annals - Manufacturing Technology 56(2), 783–809 (2007)
2. Brecher, C.: Integrative Production Technology for High-Wage Countries. Springer, Heidelberg (2012)
3. Onken, R., Schulte, A.: System-Ergonomic Design of Cognitive Automation. SCI, vol. 235. Springer, Heidelberg (2010)
4. Bainbridge, L.: Ironies of Automation. In: Rassmussen, J., Duncan, K., Leplat, J. (eds.) New Technology and Human Error, pp. 271–283. Wiley, Chichester (1987)
5. Hollnagel, E., Woods, D.D.: Joint Cognitive Systems: Foundations of Cognitive Systems Engineering. Taylor & Francis Group, Boca Raton (2005)

6. Brecher, C., Müller, S., Faber, M., Herfs, W.: Design and Implementation of a omprehensible Cognitive Assembly System. In: Conference Proceedings of the 4th International Conference on Applied Human Factors and Ergonomics (AHFE). USA Publishing (2012)

7. Mayer, M.P.: Entwicklung eines kognitionsergonomischen Konzeptes und eines Simulationssystems für die robotergestützte Montage. PhD thesis, RWTH Aachen University (2012) (in German)

8. Mayer, M.P., Schlick, C.M.: Improving operator's conformity with expectations in a cognitively automated assembly cell using human heuristics. In: Conference Proceedings of the 4th International Conference on Applied Human Factors and Ergonomics (AHFE), pp. 1263–1272. USA Publishing (2012)

9. Kuz, S., Heinicke, A., Schwichtenhövel, D., Mayer, M., Schlick, C.: The Effect of Anthropomorphic Movements of Assembly Robots on Human Prediction. In: Karwowski, W., Trzcielinski, S. (eds.) Advances in Ergonomics in Manufacturing, Boca Raton, FL, USA, pp. 263–271 (2012)

10. Russel, S.J., Norvig, P.: Artificial Intelligence: A Modern Approach, 2nd edn. Prentice Hall, Upper Saddle River (2003)

11. Kempf, T.: Ein kognitives Steuerungsframework für robotergestützte Handhabungsaufgaben. PhD thesis, Aprimus, Aachen (2010) (in German)

12. Mayer, M.P., Odenthal, B., Faber, M., Schlick, C.M.: Cognitively Automated Assembly Processes: A Simulation Based Evaluation of Performance. In: Work: A Journal of Prevention, Assessment and Rehabilitation - IEA 2012: 18th World Congress on Ergonomics - Designing a Sustainable Future, vol. 1, pp. 3449–3454 (2012)

13. Barachini, F.: Match-Time Predictability in Real-Time Production Systems. In: Gottlob, G., Nejdl, W. (eds.) Expert Systems in Engineering. LNCS, vol. 462, pp. 190–203. Springer, Heidelberg (1990)

14. Odenthal, B., Mayer, M., Kabuß, W., Schlick, C.: Design and Evaluation of an Augmented Vision System for Human-Robot Cooperation in Cognitively Automated Assembly Cells. In: Proceedings of the 9th International Multi-Conference on Systems, Signals and Devices (SSD). Institute of Electrical and Electronics Engineers (IEEE), Chemnitz (2012)

15. Ewert, D., Mayer, M.P., Schilberg, D., Jeschke, S.: Adaptive assembly planning for a nondeterministic domain. In: Conference Proceedings of the 4th International Conference on Applied Human Factors ad Ergonomics (AHFE), pp. 2720–2729 (2012)

16. Thomas, U., Wahl, F.M.: A System for Automatic Planning, Evaluation and Execution of Assembly Sequences for Industrial Robots. In: Proceedings of International Conference on Intelligent Robots and Systems, vol. 3, pp. 1458–1464 (2001)

17. Liu, G., Ramakrishnan, K.G.: A*Prune: an algorithm for finding K shortest paths subject to multiple constraints. In: Proceedings of the 20th Annual Joint Conference of the IEEE Computer and Communications Societies, vol. 2, pp. 743–749 (2001)

Evaluation of Advanced Multi-Modal Command and Control Communication Management Suite

Victor Finomore[1], Adam Sitz[2], Kelly Satterfield[3],
Courtney Castle[4], and Elizabeth Blair[1]

[1] Air Force Research Laboratory, 711 Human Performance Wing, Wright-Patterson AFB, OH
[2] Old Dominion University, Human Factors Psychology, Norfolk, VA
[3] George Mason University, Human Factors & Applied Cognition Fairfax, VA
[4] Boston College, Educational Research, Measurement, & Evaluation, Boston, MA
{victor.finomore,elizabeth.blair}@wpafb.af.mil,
{sitzadam,satterkm,castlece}@gmail.com

Abstract. Command and Control (C2) operators function in communication intensive environments that impose a high degree of workload on them, thus resulting in failures of detection or comprehension of messages. To combat these issues, researchers at the Air Force Research Laboratory have developed an advanced network-centric communication management suite that aids C2 operators in their mission called Multi-Modal Communication (MMC). This system provides operators with the tools to manage communication in a single, intuitive, dynamic display that reduces perceived mental workload and aids in decision making and situation awareness. This study set out to evaluate the MMC tool as a communication management suite, which affords participants the ability to detect as well as comprehend the presentation of multiple critical messages. The use of the MMC tool resulted in more detections of critical messages and greater message comprehension, while also lowering ratings of perceived mental workload as compared to traditional communication tools such as radio and chat.

Keywords: Command and Control, Operational Research, Multi-Modal Display Design, Mental Workload.

1   Introduction

Command and Control (C2) operators monitor large volumes of communication data for critical, mission-sensitive, information in order to efficiently plan, direct, coordinate, and control assets. This highly demanding communication task requires C2 operators to simultaneously attend to anywhere from 6 - 15 channels of communication for critical information (Bolia, 2003). A consequence of this situation is that critical information can be lost when C2 operators fail to attend to all relevant communication streams (Ramachandran, Jansen, Barcara, Carpenter, Denning, & Sucillon, 2009). The failure to detect and act upon missed information illustrates the need to improve C2 operator performance in the larger context of military operations.

D. Harris (Ed.): EPCE/HCII 2013, Part I, LNAI 8019, pp. 215–221, 2013.

A more efficient communication interface is required in order to maximizes C2 operators' attention capabilities and avoid the loss of critical information.

To combat these issues, researchers and engineers at the Air Force Research Laboratory have developed an advanced prototype, network-centric communication management suite that aids C2 operators in their mission called Multi-Modal Communication (MMC). This system provides operators with the tools to manage communication in a single, intuitive, dynamic display that reduces perceived mental workload and aids in decision making and situation awareness. As seen in Figure 1, the suite of tools captures, records, and displays radio and chat communications to allow for immediate access and control over all information. In addition, speech intelligibility is increased by spatially separating each of the radio channels to virtual locations around the operator via their headphones (for a more detailed overview of MMC, see Finomore, Stewart, Singh, Raj, & Dallman, 2012).

Fig. 1. Two MMC displays. 1) Spatial location of audio channel; 2) Chat input field; 3) Control buttons; 4) Playback, edit/annotate controls, and flag icon tags; 5) Flagged/Transcribed text; 6) Find control; 7) Keyword highlight.

A number of studies have been carried out using the MMC interface demonstrating participants can detect more critical messages and report lower perceived mental workload when using the MMC tool as compared to radio alone or chat alone (e.g., Finomore, Popik, Castle, & Dallman, 2010; Finomore, Satterfield, Sitz, Castle, Funke, Shaw, & Funke, 2012). However, in addition to message detection, message comprehension is critical for mission success. This study set out to evaluate the MMC tool as a communication management suite, which affords participants the ability to not only detect critical messages but gain better comprehension of these messages to carry out their mission.

2   Method

2.1   Participants

Sixteen participants (7 men and 9 women) ranging in age from 18-31 years (M = 24.5), took part in this study. All participants were tested to ensure normal hearing and normal, or corrected-to-normal, vision. Additionally, all participants possessed prior experience and training with the interface and communication detection task.

2.2   Design

A within-subjects design was employed with four levels of communication modes, more commonly referred to as conditions (Radio, Spatial Audio, Chat, and MMC). When the Radio condition was used, information was only presented via monaural audio, with no accompanying text-transcriptions. The Spatial Audio condition spatially separated each audio channel, so that each one came from one of nine possible virtual spatial locations around the operator. This condition also did not include any text-transcriptions. The Chat condition exclusively featured text-transcriptions, with no accompanying audio component. Lastly, the MMC condition featured both spatially separated audio and text-transcriptions. Additionally, the MMC condition featured the availability of several communication augmenting tools (e.g., audio playback, keyword search, and auto-highlighting).

2.3   Apparatus

Participants were required to monitor information presented via four on-screen communication channels. Two of these communication channels featured random phrases from which participants had to detect messages meeting a predefined rule, while the other two channels presented news stories taken from an online database (Literacyworks, n.d.) of dated news articles, all of approximately similar length, from a local news agency in California. All experimental trials had a fixed duration of exactly five minutes.

For critical phrase detection, both critical and neutral phrases were modified phrases from the Air Force Tactics, Techniques, and Procedures communication brevity document (United States Air Force, 2006). Critical phrases were defined by the presence of an "Eagle" call sign, in addition with the keywords "hostile" and "lead" in a singular phrase (e.g., "Eagle Two Hostile South Lead Group fifty five Miles"). Whereas, neutral phrases did not contain the combination of all three critical keywords: "Eagle," "Hostile," and "Lead". Communication phrases for both channels were updated independently of each other. Critical phrase generation was varied at random over a range of 15-120 seconds, with the restriction that a total of two critical phrases were generated per minute (10 overall critical phrases). Neutral phrases were generated randomly over a range of 8-30 seconds, with the restriction that there were always exactly five neutral phrases generated per channel per minute (50 overall neutral phrases)

The news stories were presented in small segments of 1-2 sentences punctuated by pauses of variable length. Different news article pairings were used in each experimental condition, such that participants were never exposed to any single news story more than once throughout the duration of the study.

2.4   Procedure

All participants took part in the computer-based training, which explained that their task was to monitor two communication channels for critical phrases and two communication channels for the content of individual news stories. Special emphasis was given to the fact that both tasks were of equal importance, such that no special preference should be given to the critical phrase detection component or to the presented news articles. The training (two 30-minute sessions) provided participants with experience with the communication formats, critical phrase detection, and filling out the comprehension questions pertaining to the two news stories.

The four experimental conditions were randomized per participant. Participants were stationed at a computer workstation, where they monitored the four communication channels. For the Radio, Spatial Audio, and MMC conditions participants responded to a critical phrase by verbally repeating the phrase into their headset and in the Chat condition they typed their response. Immediately following each session, participants completed questionnaires consisting of 10 multiple-choice questions with five items corresponding to each of the previous news articles. Individual questions were sampled from the same online database from which the actual news articles originated (Literacyworks, n.d.). Participants were also evaluated in terms of their perceived mental workload via a computerized version of the NASA-TLX (Hart & Staveland, 1988).

3   Results

Performance for the critical phrase detection task was evaluated in terms of participants' number of correct detections and performance for the news articles, in terms of comprehension, was evaluated by means of a computer based questionnaire presented immediately following each trial.

3.1   Message Detection

Mean percentage of correct detection for all communication conditions is presented in Figure 2.

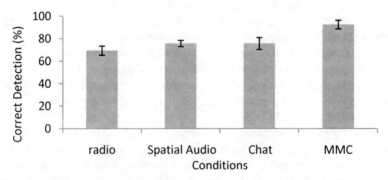

Fig. 2. Percentage of correct detection for all communication conditions. Error bars are ± 1 standard error of the mean across subjects.

Data from Figure 2 were tested for statistical significance by means of a one- way within-subjects analysis of variance (ANOVA). A significant main effect was found for communication format, F (3, 45) = 13.24, p < .01, and a Post Hoc test found that participants detected significantly more critical phrases in the MMC condition (M = 92.5) than Chat (M = 75.6), Spatial Audio (M = 75.6), and Radio (M = 69.4), which were not statistically different from each other.

3.2   Comprehension

Mean reading comprehension scores for both stories are presented in Figure 3.

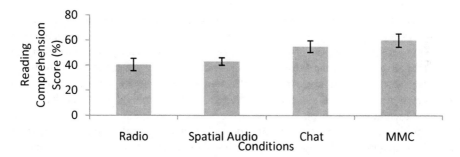

Fig. 3. Mean reading comprehension scores for both stories for all communication conditions. Error bars are ± 1 standard error of the mean across subjects.

A one-way within-subjects ANOVA was performed on the data in Figure 3, which found a statistically significant main effect, F (3, 45) = 5.91, p < .01 for communication condition. Post Hoc tests found that participants scored higher on the reading comprehension questions in the MMC (M = 60.0) and Chat (M = 55.0) conditions, which were not different from each other. Comprehension in both of these conditions was greater than comprehension in the Spatial Audio (M = 43.1) and Radio (M = 40.6) conditions, which were not different from each other.

3.3   Mental Workload

Mean NASA-TLX scores measuring perceived mental workload are displayed in Figure 4.

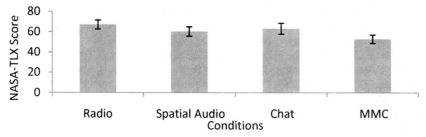

Fig. 4. Mean NASA-TLX scores for communication conditions. Error bars are ± 1 standard error of the mean across subjects.

Data from Figure 4 were tested for statistical significant by means of a one-way within-subjects ANOVA. A statistically significant main effect was found, F (3, 45) = 5.30, p < .01 for communication condition. Post Hoc tests found that participants rated workload the highest for the Radio (M = 67.12) and Chat (M = 63.25) conditions, which were not different from each other but were greater than the MMC (M = 52.94) and Spatial Audio (M = 60.44) conditions, which were not significantly different from each other.

4   Discussion

In this study, participants monitored and responded to the occurrence of critical phrases presented during a 5-minute signal detection task while simultaneously monitoring the presentation of two short news stories. It was hypothesized that the purported advantages of the MMC interface would facilitate greater comprehension of the news stories, while allowing for effective monitoring for critical phrases. In addition, it was predicted the tools developed for MMC would result in decreased scores in mental workload.

As predicted, the use of the MMC tool resulted in a greater percent of correct detections of critical phrases and greater message comprehension, while reducing perceived mental workload compared to traditional communication tools. The MMC tool allows for greater detection and intelligibility afforded through spatialized radio communication as well as the persistent text display of the communication through use of the speech-to-text functionality. This persistent display has been shown to facilitate a better understanding of context since it creates a record that can later be referenced or reread, thus increasing message comprehension (Heacox, Moore, Morrison, & Yturralde, 2004). This combination of tools was developed with the purpose of providing the operator with the flexibility to process information in the manner that optimizes performance.

References

1. Boila, R.S.: Effects of spatial intercoms and active noise reduction headsets on speech intelligibility in an AWACS environment. Proceedings of the Human Factors and Ergonomics Society 47, 100–103 (2003)
2. Finomore, V., Popik, D., Castle, C., Dallman, R.: Effects of a Network-Centric Multi-Modal Communication Tool on a Communication Monitoring task. Proceedings of the Human Factors and Ergonomics Society Annual Meeting 54, 2125–2129 (2010)
3. Finomore, V., Satterfield, K., Sitz, A., Castle, C., Funke, G., Shaw, T., Funke, M.: Effects of the Multi-Modal Communication tool on Communication and Change Detection for Command & Control Operators. Proceedings of the Human Factors and Ergonomics Society Annual Meeting 56, 1461–1465 (2012)
4. Finomore, V., Stewart, J., Singh, R., Raj, B., Dallman, R.: Demonstration of advanced multi-modal, network-centric communication management suite. In: 13th Proceedings of the Interspeech, paper # 1252 (2012)

5. Hart, S.G., Staveland, L.E.: Development of NASA-TLX (task load index): Results of empirical and theoretical research. In: Hancock, P.A., Meshkati, N. (eds.) Human Mental Workload, pp. 139–183. North-Holland, Oxford (1988)
6. Heacox, N.J., Moore, R.A., Morrison, J.G., Yturralde, R.F.: Real-time online communications: 'Chat' use in Navy operations. In: Proceedings of Command and Control Research and Technology Symposium, San Diego, CA (2004)
7. Literacyworks (n.d.) Learning resources: Story archive, http://www.literacyworks.org/learningresources/ (retrieved)
8. Ramachandran, S., Jansen, R., Bascara, O., Carpenter, T., Denning, T., Sucillon, S.: After action review tools for team training with chat communications. In: Interservice/Industry Training, Simulation, and Education Conference (2009)
9. United States Air Force, Air Force Tactics, Techniques, and Procedures 3-1.1, Operational brevity words definitions, and communication standards (U). Nellis AFB, NV (2006)

Evaluating Two Modes of Observational Learning in Cognitive-Spatial Task Training

Nirit Gavish[1] and Michal Shelef[2]

[1] Ort Braude College, Karmiel, Israel
[2] Technion – Israel Institute of Technology, Haifa, Israel
Nirit@braude.ac.il, shelefm@tx.technion.ac.il

Abstract. The focus of the current study was to evaluate the effect of two modes of observational learning, dyad trainer-trainee performance and preliminary observational learning part, on training, as well as the interaction between them. We conducted an experimental study with a 3-D computerized puzzle. Each trainer offered four trainees instruction in solving this puzzle in a 2X2 between-participants design: with or without preliminary observational learning, and with dyad trainer-trainee performance or with verbal guidance only during training (16 trainees in each group). Results demonstrated that the preliminary observational learning resulted in longer training time but better performance in terms of success rates, and that dyad trainer-trainee performance led to shorter training time and did not influence performance. No significant interaction between the two modes was found. The cost-effectiveness matrix that was found in this study can assist in designing guidelines for choosing the appropriate observational learning methods in training.

Keywords: Observational learning, Training, Dyad performance, Cognitive tasks.

1 Introduction

In active learning – the standard means of learning a psychomotor task – the performer learns by doing, acquiring competence by trial and error or practice. In observational learning, a person learns by watching the actions of another person and imitating them (e.g., in a woodworking or cookery class) or mentally recording their effects (e.g., watching the driver from the passenger seat; watching a football game on TV). During learning by observation, the learner is not physically engaged in performing the task, and so can engage his full mental energy on monitoring the other person's actions and responses. Given the great power of human imagination and inferential processes, this method of learning has the potential to be highly effective. Indeed, the value of observational learning has been demonstrated in many studies (e.g., [1-3]), and observational learning has been proved to produce good cognitive representations of skilled actions [4-5].

When an expert in the task serves as the trainer, taking advantage of observational learning may be even more worthwhile. First, observing an expert enables the learner

D. Harris (Ed.): EPCE/HCII 2013, Part I, LNAI 8019, pp. 222–231, 2013.
© Springer-Verlag Berlin Heidelberg 2013

to build up an accurate representation of the task, which may be different from his or her intuitive representation; this representation allows the learner to imitate (either immediately, or later on) the necessary correct actions [3]. As Herrnstein, Loewenstein, Prelec and Vaughan [6] and Herrnstein and Prelec [7] pointed out, in a multiple-alternative space, when the value of alternatives is not known, subjects will stop exploring as soon as they hit an acceptable response, and thus converge to a local optimum. Many complex tasks can be performed in many ways, so demonstrating the best way to complete the task can prevent this convergence. Second, performing a complex task can put a high cognitive load on the novice, preventing him from absorbing the necessary information. Observing an expert can release the cognitive resources needed for focusing on the essential elements of the task [2].

Observational learning can take various forms. One of them is dyad performance. In dyad performance, the trainer and trainee – or, alternatively, two trainees – perform the task together. A variant, triad training, involves either three learners or two learners and a trainer. Shebilske, Regian, Arthur and Jordan [8] tested dyad and performance protocols using a complex computer game called Space Fortress [9]. In the dyad condition, trainees practiced in pairs, each controlling half of the task (performing half of its roles). Despite having only half as much hands-on experience during practice sessions, the dyad trainees performed as well as individual trainees on ten test sessions. Replications of this study have produced similar results of improving training efficiency by reducing training time without sacrificing performance (See [10-15]).

Observational learning can also be part of a two-stage learning process, where the learner first watches an expert performs the task, and only then engages in active practice. As described above, through observation the learner builds an accurate mental representation of the task, which he or she can then imitate during the active-learning phase [4]. As Wouters et al. [2] point out, such learning makes it less likely that novices will adopt inappropriate automated patterns of behavior that are difficult to change. This type of learning paradigm is also in keeping with the strategy of beginning with easier forms of training and progressing to more difficult stages [16] - a strategy widely employed in modern training.

Choosing between different methods to employ observational learning during training requires knowing the effects of each method on the training and the unsupervised performance following it. Employing more than one method requires also being aware of the interaction between the selected methods. The current study explored the use of the abovementioned two modes of observational learning: dyad performance and preliminary observational learning part. The aim was to identify the separate effects of each of these methods on training and performance and the interaction between the two methods. Based on past research on dyad performance protocol [9-15], it was predicted that dyad trainer-trainee performance will reduce training time while performance time will not be affected. It was also predicted, based on research on the benefit of observational learning at the beginning of the training [2], that preliminary observational learning, in which the trainee is usually given enhanced information on the task, will result in longer training time, but better performance. An additional prediction was that combining these two modes of observational learning will achieve the best result: better performance with shorter training time.

The task chosen for this study was a three-dimensional computerized puzzle task, used previously by Yuviler-Gavish et al. [17]. Training and performance in this task was found to be affected by employing different training methods. For example, Yuviler-Gavish et al. [17] demonstrated that training participants in this task with visual guidance in addition to verbal guidance was attractive to both trainers and trainees and demanded less cognitive effort from trainees, but at the same time impaired skill acquisition relative to verbal guidance only. It was hence assumed that the use of different observational learning strategies to train this task will produce significant effects on training and performance.

In the current study, training was performed on the computerized task. The trainers' goal was to teach trainees to solve a puzzle *on their own*, and trainees' performance was evaluated in non-supervised tests on both the computerized task and the real-world version of it. Combinations of two modes of observational learning were examined in a 2X2 design: the first mode - preliminary observational learning (with versus without,) and the second mode - dyad trainer-trainee performance (versus verbal guidance only).

2   Method

2.1   Design

The study used a 2X2 between-participants experimental design with randomized order, where the training variables were with preliminary observational learning (hereinafter, "Preliminary") versus without preliminary observational learning (hereinafter, "No Preliminary"), and with dyad trainer-trainee performance (hereinafter, "Dyad") versus verbal guidance only ("Verbal"). The four conditions were created by combining the four training variables described above. In condition Preliminary-Dyad, trainers demonstrated and verbally explained the task while the trainee watched and listened, until both trainer and trainee felt ready to move on to the active training phase. During the active training, trainers could continue to use both verbal guidance and pointing with the mouse or manipulating objects as needed. In condition Preliminary-Verbal, training in both phases was limited to verbal explanation only; trainers were not given access to a mouse and so could not demonstrate or point. In the two No Preliminary conditions, training began with the active training phase. In condition No Preliminary-Dyad, trainers were allowed to give verbal guidance and point with the mouse or manipulate objects, while in condition No Preliminary-Verbal, they could give verbal guidance only.

2.2   Participants

Ninety-five participants were recruited for the study. Nineteen (12 males and 7 females) received extensive training in the 3-D computerized puzzle task and served as trainers. The 76 trainees, 39 males and 37 females, were evenly distributed among the four experimental conditions (9 males and 10 females in the No Preliminary–Dyad condition, 10 males and 9 females in each of the other conditions). Each trainer trained four trainees, one in each condition, in random order. All participants were undergraduate or graduate students at the Technion - Israel Institute of Technology. Participants' average age was 24.2 (ranging from 20 to 31). None of the trainees had experience with the specific task used in the experiment, and only 17% had any experience with computerized puzzles.

Due to a technical recording problem, training data from three trainees (two of them were trained by the same trainer) and real-world test data from an additional trainee were not available for this analysis. In order to maintain the trainer's repeated-measures analysis design, all other trainees' data belong to these four trainers were not included in the analysis (12 altogether). Hence, the analysis includes only the data of sixteen trainees, 9 males and 7 females, and sixty-four trainees, 30 males and 34 females (8 males and 8 females in the No Preliminary-Verbal condition, 7 males and 9 females in each of the other conditions).

Participants were paid a fixed amount of NIS 40 (about USD 10) per hour. Additionally, trainees could receive a bonus according to their performance in the computerized test phase (either NIS 50 or 100), and trainers received a bonus according to their trainees' performance in this test (ranging from NIS 5 to 60 for each trainee).

2.3   Experimental Task and Setup

The main task required participants to solve a three-dimensional puzzle, called Shuzzle (*http://www.leweyg.com/lc/shuzzle.html;* see Figure 1). In this puzzle, pieces must be moved in a virtual three-dimensional space so as to complete a shape indicated by a wire frame. Horizontal movements are performed by dragging the pieces with the left mouse button. Vertical movements involve dragging the pieces with the left mouse button while pressing a key. Vertical rotation is achieved by dragging with the right mouse button, and horizontal rotation by dragging with the right mouse button while pressing a key.

Each trainer sat in a booth next to his trainee, to enable vocal communication between them and avoid any kind of non-verbal communication (e.g., gestures) that was not tested in this study. A white rectangular plastic divider between the booths prevented trainers and trainees from seeing each other. The trainee used a regular PC with two 19 inch screens, one in the trainee's booth and one in the trainer's booth, so that both trainer and trainee had the same visual presentation. A second computer mouse attached to the computer extended into the trainer's booth, allowing the trainers in the Dyad condition to use the mouse for pointing and manipulating objects.

The test phase also included a real-world version of the puzzle. In the real puzzle, colored pieces must be arranged so as to create a given shape, indicated by a hollow metal model (see Figure 2). The pieces were made from lightweight polypropylene (Delrin); each piece weighed about 40-60 grams.

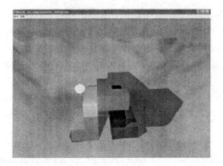

Fig. 1. Top: The computerized 3-D puzzle task. Bottom: The two practice tasks.

Fig. 2. The real-world puzzle task

2.4 Procedure

The experiment had five stages: an initial practice stage; training on the computerized puzzle; two tests, one on the computerized puzzle and one on the real-world version of it; and a subjective evaluation questionnaire.

Participants in all four conditions were first given a brief explanation of the puzzle objective and general information on how to perform the various movements (as noted above). Then, participants completed an initial practice stage consisting of two easy puzzles with two or three shapes (see Figure 1, bottom). During the practice stage, participants could ask questions and the experimenter was permitted to remind participants of the appropriate keys to perform each routine. This stage was included so that the main challenge in the training phase would be the assembly of the three-dimensional object rather than the details of how to handle the puzzle pieces.

Following the initial practice, trainees were informed that their goal in the experiment would be to complete the same puzzle as quickly as possible *on their own* following a training phase. They were told that their payoff would depend on their completion time in the computerized test: The best performer in their respective condition (of 19 individuals) would receive a bonus of NIS 100, and the four runners-up would each get a bonus of NIS 50. The experimental training phase followed. Trainees were then given the two tests – first the same computerized puzzle task they had trained in (Figure 1, top) and then the real-world puzzle version of it (Figure 2).

Participants recruited as trainers gathered at the lab the day before the main experiment. Following the initial practice stage, they performed the main puzzle task on their own three times. Nineteen participants who succeeded in the main puzzle task were invited back the next day. At that point, they were informed that their goal in the experiment would be to train four novice participants, and that they would be rewarded based on the success of the four participants in a non-supervised test. The trainers were instructed about the training protocol for each condition. Each trainer trained one participant from each group, in random order.

Questionnaires were completed after the tests by both trainers and trainees. Each questionnaire included four items to be answered on a scale from 1 to 5; trainers answered the questions separately for each of their trainees. For trainers, the questions were: 1) How easy was it for you to train this trainee? 2) How well did the trainee understand your training, in your opinion? 3) Do you think you succeeded in transmitting the message for the trainee in a clear fashion? 4) How difficult was the task for the trainee, in your opinion? For trainees, the questions were: 1) To what extent was the training understandable? 2) Do you think the trainer succeeded in transmitting the message in a clear fashion? 3) How much did the training help your task performance? 4) Rate the level of task difficulty. After completing the questionnaires, trainers and trainees were thanked, debriefed, and given their bonuses. Trainers' bonuses were based on their trainees' completion times in the computerized test in minutes (COMP) according to the following formula: BONUS = 60- 2.5×COMP, rounded up to the nearest multiple of 5.

3   Results

3.1   Training

Training times, as well as test times, were analyzed using repeated-measures ANOVA, with Preliminary observational learning (Preliminary or No Preliminary) and Dyad Performance/Verbal Guidance conditions as the within-participant variables. The unit of analysis for the repeated-measures tests was the trainer (data from his four trainees were analyzed as repeated-measures).

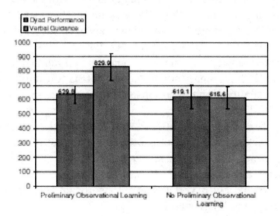

Fig. 3. Mean training time (in seconds) for the four experimental groups. The error bars denote the standard error.

Training time (including the time of the preliminary observational learning) was significantly longer for the Preliminary observational learning condition compared with the No Preliminary condition (Preliminary mean: 734.8 seconds, *SD* = 322.4; No Preliminary mean: 617.4 seconds, *SD* = 309.3; $F(1,15) = 5.32$, $p = .036$, *Partial Eta Squared* = 0.262). In contrast, training time in the Dyad Performance condition was significantly shorter than in the Verbal Guidance condition (Dyad mean: 629.4

seconds, $SD = 282.3$; Verbal mean: 722.8 seconds, $SD = 350.1$; $F(1,15) = 4.9$, $p = .043$, *Partial Eta Squared* = 0.246). The interaction between Preliminary and Dyad/Verbal was not significant ($F(1,15) = 2.09$, $p = .169$, *Partial Eta Squared* = 0.122). See Figure 3. The differences between training time levels in the experimental conditions for the 12 participants that were not included in the analysis were the same as for the analyzed data (showing longer training time for the Preliminary condition compared with the No Preliminary condition: a difference of 183.7 seconds, and shorter training time for the Dyad condition compared with the Verbal condition: a difference of 278.2 seconds).

3.2   Test Performance

Following the supervised training, participants were tested on the same computerized puzzle without the trainer's supervision, then on the real-world version. Failure in the computerized puzzle test was defined as not managing to successfully solve the puzzle within 30 minutes. In the real-world puzzle this time was reduced to 10 minutes, because this test did not include difficult computerized manipulations in order to rotate the shapes or to move them, and thus it could be performed (and was performed) much faster. Success rates were analyzed using Multinomial Logistic Regression with Preliminary observational learning (Preliminary or No Preliminary) and Dyad performance/Verbal Guidance conditions as factors.

For the computerized puzzle test, success rates were significantly higher for the Preliminary observational learning condition compared with the No Preliminary condition (Preliminary mean: 100%; No Preliminary mean: 90.6%, $\chi2(1, N = 64) = 4.33$, $p = .038$). For the Dyad and Verbal conditions, however, they did not differ significantly (96.9% and 93.8%, respectively; $\chi2(1, N = 64) = 0.37$, $p = .541$). See Figure 4. The mean performance time for the Preliminary observational learning condition compared with the No Preliminary condition was not significantly different, probably due to the high variability among participants in the No Preliminary condition (Preliminary mean: 193.3 seconds, $SD = 149.8$; No Preliminary mean: 336.4 seconds, $SD = 506.6$; $F(1,15) = 2.95$, $p = 1.107$, *Partial Eta Squared* = 0.164). Performance time in the Dyad Performance condition was similar to that of the Verbal Guidance condition (Dyad mean: 237.0 seconds, $SD = 342.8$; Verbal mean: 292.8 seconds, $SD = 412.9$; $F(1,15) = 0.30$, $p = .593$, *Partial Eta Squared* = 0.020). The interaction between Preliminary and Dyad/Verbal was not significant ($F(1,15) < 0.01$, $p = .974$, *Partial Eta Squared* < 0.001). See Figure 5.

No significant effects were found for the real-world test. Success rates were not significantly different for the Preliminary observational learning condition compared with the No Preliminary condition (Preliminary mean: 87.5%; No Preliminary mean: 90.6%, $\chi2(1, N = 64) = 0.17$, $p = .685$), and also not significantly different for the Dyad and Verbal conditions (84.4% and 93.8%, respectively; $\chi2(1, N = 64) = 1.49$, $p = .222$). The mean performance time for the Preliminary observational learning condition was not significantly different compared with the No Preliminary condition (Preliminary mean: 115.7 seconds, $SD = 191.1$; No Preliminary mean: 97.7 seconds, $SD = 190.9$; $F(1,15) = 0.15$, $p = 0.707$, *Partial Eta Squared* = 0.010). Performance time in the Dyad Performance condition was also not significantly different compared with the Verbal Guidance condition (Dyad mean: 148.2 seconds, SD = 223.5; Verbal mean: 97.7 seconds, SD = 147.25; $F(1,15)$ = 0.96, p = .344, *Partial Eta Squared* = 0.060). The interaction between Preliminary and Dyad/Verbal was not significant, either ($F(1,15)$ = 0.08, p = .781, *Partial Eta Squared* = 0.005).

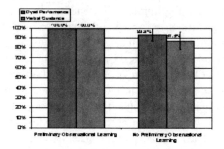

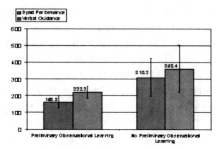

Fig. 4. Success rates in the computerized test for the four experimental groups. The error bars denote the standard error.

Fig. 5. Mean test time in the computerized test (in seconds) for the four experimental groups. The error bars denote the standard error.

3.3   Subjective Evaluation of the Training

In the questionnaires completed after the tests, three significant effects of training conditions were found. Trainers reported that the they succeeded more in transmitting the message, Question 3 for trainers, in the Dyad Performance condition (mean score 1.78 out of 5, SD = 0.49) than in the Verbal Guidance condition (mean score 2.31, SD = 1.15, $F(1,15)$ = 10.87, p = .005, *Partial Eta Squared* = 0.420), and also rated the difficulty of the task for the trainee, Question 4 for trainers, as lower in the Dyad condition (mean score 2.56, SD = 0.88) than in the Verbal condition (mean score 3.03, SD = 1.15, $F(1,15)$ = 7.83, p = .015, *Partial Eta Squared* = 0.343). In addition, trainees felt that the training helped their task performance, Question 3 for trainees, more in the Preliminary condition (mean score 1.09, SD = 0.30) than in the No Preliminary condition (mean score 1.38, SD = 0.55, $F(1,15)$ = 7.64, p = .014, *Partial Eta Squared* = 0.338).

4   Discussion

Observational learning, in which a person learns how to perform a task by watching another person perform the relevant steps, has been shown to be effective in many experimental tasks as well as in everyday life (e.g., [1-3]). It has also been shown that observational learning can produce good cognitive representations of skilled actions [4-5]. Using an expert in the task as a trainer can increase the value of observational learning even more.

Two different modes of observational learning, in an expert-trains-a-novice paradigm, were examined in this study in a 2X2 between-participants design for a computerized 3-D puzzle task. In the first mode, dyad performance, the trainer and trainee perform the task together during the training process (see [8]). In the second, preliminary observational learning, the training starts with a demonstration, and the trainee performs the task only after acquiring a basic knowledge of the necessary steps (see [2], [16]). It was predicted that: Dyad trainer-trainee performance will reduce training time and will have no effect on performance; Preliminary observational learning will result in longer training time but better performance; And that the combination of them will achieve better performance with shorter training time.

Results demonstrated that the preliminary observational learning resulted in longer training time but better performance (in terms of success rates), and that dyad trainer-trainee performance led to shorter training time and did not influence performance, in line with our assumption. However, no significant interaction between the two modes was found. Participants' subjective evaluations were in favor of these two modes. The lack of significant findings for the real-world test in the present research can be a consequence of the preceding computerized test, which eliminated possible differences between conditions. Trainers reported that they succeeded more in transmitting the message in the dyad performance condition, and also rated the task as easier on this condition. Trainees reported that the training helped their task performance more in the Preliminary condition than in the No Preliminary condition.

The findings of this study can assist in designing guidelines for choosing the appropriate observational learning methods in training. A cost-effectiveness matrix was found, in which preliminary observational learning costs additional training time, but improves performance. In contrast, dyad trainer-trainee performance saves training time without sacrificing performance. Designers of training protocols and training systems can choose between these two methods based on training goals. The lack of interaction between the two methods may be due to the current study's limitation or a robust finding, and it is recommended that future research will focus on ways to best combine the two methods. In addition, the transfer of learning to similar tasks should be further evaluated.

The task chosen for this study is a cognitive-spatial task, in which the motor elements are of lesser importance. In addition, the training included a preliminary stage meant to overcome the major motor difficulties that trainees may encounter. Findings from the current study may be limited to this specific kind of tasks, and should be further evaluated using tasks with different characteristics. Another shortcoming of the selected task is that once the solution for the puzzle was discovered, it is easy to perform the necessary steps, and as a result a relatively large variance across trainees was produced, especially for the condition without preliminary observational learning. Taking advantage of a task with a smaller expected variance may ease to reach statistical significance even for the factors which were not found to have significant effect in the current study.

Acknowledgment. This research was supported in part by the European Commission Integrated Project IP-SKILLS-35005.

References

1. Bandura, A., Jeffery, R.W.: Role of Symbolic Coding and Rehearsal Processes in Observational Learning. Journal of Personality and Social Psychology 26, 122–130 (1973)
2. Wouters, P., Tabbers, H.K., Pass, F.: Interactivity in Video-based Models. Educational Psychology Review 19, 327–342 (2007)
3. Wulf, G., Shea, C.H.: Principles Derived from the Study of Simple Skills Do Not Generalize to Complex Skill Learning. Psychonomic Bulletin & Review 9, 185–211 (2002)
4. Bandura, A.: Social Foundation oF Thought and Action: A Social Cognitive Theory. Prentice-Hall, Englewood Cliffs (1986)
5. Carroll, W.R., Bandura, A.: Representational guidance of action production in observational guidance of action production in observational learning: A causal analysis. Journal of Motor Behavior 22, 85–97 (1990)
6. Herrnstein, R.J., Loewenstein, G.F., Prelec, D., Vaughan Jr., W.: Utility maximization and melioration: Internalities in individual choice. Journal of Behavioral Decision Making 6, 149–185 (1993)
7. Herrnstein, R.J., Prelec, D.: Melioration: A theory of distributed choice. Journal of Economic Perspectives 5, 137–156 (1991)
8. Shebilske, W.L., Regian, J.W., Arthur, W., Jordan, J.A.: A dyadic protocol for training complex skills. Human Factors 34, 369–374 (1992)
9. Mane, A., Donchin, E.: The Space Fortress game. Acta Psychologica 71, 17–22 (1989)
10. Arthur, W., Strong, M.H., Jordan, J.A., Williamson, J.E., Shebilske, W.L., Regain, J.W.: Visual attention: Individual differences in training and predicting complex task performance. Acta Psychologica 88, 3–23 (1995)
11. Arthur, W., Day, E.A., Bennett, W., McNelly, T.L., Jordan, J.A.: Dyadic versus individual training protocols: Loss and reacquisition of a complex skill. Journal of Applied Psychology 82, 783–791 (1997)
12. Arthur, W., Young, B., Jordan, J.A., Shebilske, W.L.: Effectiveness of individual and dyadic training protocols: The influence of trainee interaction anxiety. Human Factors 38, 79–86 (1996)
13. Day, E.A., Arthur, W., Shebilske, W.L.: Ability determinants of complex skill acquisition: Effects of training protocol. Acta Psychologica 97, 145–165 (1997)
14. Sanchez-Ku, M.L., Arthur, W.: A dyadic protocol for training complex skills. Human Factors 42, 512–520 (2000)
15. Shebilske, W.L., Jordan, J.A., Goettl, B.P., Paulus, L.E.: Observation versus hands-on practice of complex skills in dyadic, triadic, and tetradic training-teams. Human Factors 40, 525–540 (1998)
16. Yechiam, E., Erev, I., Parush, A.: Easy first steps and their implication to the use of a mouse-based and a script-based strategy. Journal of Experimental Psychology: Applied 10, 89–96 (2004)
17. Yuviler-Gavish, N., Yechiam, E., Kallai, A.: Learning in multimodal training: Visual guidance can be both appealing and disadvantageous in spatial tasks. International Journal of Human-Computer Studies 69, 113–122 (2011)

Symbology Development for a 3D Conformal Synthetic Vision Helmet-Mounted Display for Helicopter Operations in Degraded Visual Environment

Patrizia Knabl and Helmut Többen

German Aerospace Center (DLR) Institute of Flight Guidance, Lilienthalplatz 7,
38108 Braunschweig, Germany
{Patrizia.Knabl,Helmut.Toebben}@dlr.de

Abstract. To increase situation awareness for helicopter pilots in poor visibility symbology for a helmet-mounted display was developed. The symbology comprises the conformal presentation of obstacles, route information and threat areas. In an online survey 48 helicopter pilots evaluated the designs from a user-centered perspective and provided comments and suggestions of improvement. The paper presents selected results of the survey and discusses general aspects associated with the use of conformal symbology and helmet-mounted displays.

Keywords: helicopter operations, degraded visual environment, synthetic vision systems, helmet-mounted display, conformal symbology.

1   Introduction

Degraded visual environment (DVE) is still one of the most challenging and dangerous situations for helicopter pilots. When operating in adverse weather with very poor or no out-the-cockpit visibility spatial disorientation is likely to occur, severely compromising flight safety. Especially in low altitude obstacles like power lines, wind mills and masts quickly become very dangerous to the pilot. This often results in severe accidents, e.g. the recently occurred helicopter collision with a power line in southern Germany [1] and a tower crane in London [2] killing the pilot in both cases.

However, not only poor weather conditions but also surface properties can contribute to a loss of orientation. When operating in desert environment impaired visibility is caused by sand or dust being stirred up by the helicopter's rotor downwash during landing or take-off. This situation is referred to as brownout. Especially in the military field brownout is responsible for multiple incidents and accidents during desert operations. According to the NATO report on Rotary-Wing Brownout Mitigation it is responsible for about 75% of helicopter mishaps within NATO member countries and the largest cause of rotary-wing airframe loss in the US services alone [3].

Given the high accident rate there is an urgent need to provide the pilot with additional information in DVE to reduce spatial disorientation and workload and increase

D. Harris (Ed.): EPCE/HCII 2013, Part I, LNAI 8019, pp. 232–241, 2013.
© Springer-Verlag Berlin Heidelberg 2013

situation awareness. The current paper introduces design solutions on conformal symbology sets for helmet-mounted displays (HMD) and their evaluation from a user-centred perspective. Therefore helicopter pilots assessed the designs in an online-survey.

The aim of the development is to provide an intuitive and well-arranged synthetic presentation of relevant flight information within the pilots' forward field of view that allows for fast and accurate perception of the environment.

2   Theoretical Background

Within the national project ALLFlight the DLR Institute of Flight Guidance is working on diminishing the problem of piloting helicopters in DVE conditions [4]. In contrast to currently existing 2D-symbology sets, DLR is developing 3D conformal symbology for a state-of-the-art wide field-of-view binocular HMD. In general a HMD presents information in a monochrome green colour on a semi-transparent visor in front of the pilot's eye. Binocular refers to the presentation of information to both eyes in contrast to monocular displays where information is only presented in front of the dominant eye [5].

The importance of HMD research for rotary-wing aircraft is crucial inasmuch as pilots are usually trained to keep constant visual contact with the outside world even though visibility is poor. Hence staying eyes-out is essential given that pilots frequently operate in very low altitudes or – in the military context – need to perform nap-of-the-earth missions. Thus information should be presented in a way that it does not keep attention on the head-down instruments overly long and does not require frequent attention switching.

However HMD allow for an increased freedom in movements [5], present symbology superimposed and therefore provide the ability to view instrument information and outside scene simultaneously. As a result scanning times as well as eye accommodation when switching between the instrument information and the external scene are reduced [6]. Nevertheless a detriment that is often discussed regarding superimposed symbology is the cost of clutter. It may obscure information in the outside world [7] and impose difficulties in information processing [8]. Combined with a head-tracker the display content can be changed with respect to the line of sight of the pilot. Therefore it allows a conformal presentation of symbology which was found to mitigate the cost of clutter [9]. Conformal –also called scene-linked [10] - refers to "an object that spatially overlies its far domain counterpart" [11]. For example, if an obstacle is presented on the visor it is positioned in the exact line of sight where the actual obstacle in the outside scene is situated. Hence symbols move, appear and disappear on the HMD according to the orientation and movement of both the head and the helicopter. Conformal symbology supports tasks that require divided attention [12] and facilitates the mental integration of the instrument information and the outside scene [13]. In addition conformal symbology was also found to reduce attentional tunneling [9].

3   Display Concepts

The symbology presented on the HMD is based on information from databases. The concept of ALLFlight foresees the use of sensors as well, but due to the low image quality the sensors are only used to update the database and not to present their imagery directly to the pilot. The symbology designs comprise the conformal depiction of obstacles, route information and threat areas.

3.1   Obstacle Presentation

One display objective is the highlighting of obstacles in the outside scene that would normally be difficult to detect. Since the actual appearance of such obstacles is usually very complex it is indispensable to present the synthetic obstacles in a very simplified yet unambiguous way. Obstacles need to be identified easily and fast with little attention required while display clutter has to be kept to a minimum. Each obstacle category is presented as a standardized icon. At first power line masts and wind mills were implemented.

Different designs for power line masts are proposed. Figure 1 depicts a power line mast as an icon with two cross beams (left image) which illustrates the most realistic presentation. Nevertheless it is currently not possible to accurately present the course of the wires that are connected to the masts according to the database information. It is supposed that the horizontal cross beams might lead to confusion by falsely indicating wire direction information that is actually not true. Thus two alternative designs have been developed, a mast with 4 cross beams pointing in each direction (centered image) and one with a circular design (right image).

Fig. 1. Power line mast with two cross beams (left), four cross beams (centered) and circular design (right)

In addition three different designs for windmills were developed (Fig. 2). First, the most lifelike presentation depicts a windmill with three rotor blades (left image). Again, since the exact position and orientation of the rotor blades cannot be determined, two alternative designs were implemented. One adds a circle around the blades (centered image) and one adds a globe around the blades (right image).

Fig. 2. Windmill with three rotor blades (left), circle (centered) and globe (right)

Moreover it is of interest if pilots need additional information about height and distance relative to the obstacle and if so in what way this information has to be delivered, numerically or graphically. Furthermore information for minimum crossing altitude, vertical range of obstacle depiction and the presentation of visual or auditory alarms are of concern.

3.2   Route Presentation

In general route information is intended to assist the pilot in terms of being a navigational aid but not a precise guidance symbology, e.g. a tunnel-in-the-sky [14].

A route is defined by a sequence of pre-determined waypoints. The waypoints are presented as 3-dimensional circles on the ground (Fig. 3). To make them more apparent they also feature a vertical light beam. This is especially important if the next waypoint is hidden due to a terrain elevation. In addition numerous route points are presented between the waypoints. Route points serve as directional cues to the next waypoint, they are depicted as a 3-dimensional triangle placed on the terrain, are equally spaced, follow the elevation and their size is perspective for better distance estimation. Furthermore the top always points in the direction of the next route- and waypoint.

Fig. 3. Waypoint and route point presentation

3.3   Threat Area Presentation

The threat area symbology is designed to depict prohibited airspace that must not be entered. Three different threat zone presentations were developed (Fig. 4). First, a threat zone is presented by equidistant crosses on the terrain (left image). The crosses are perspective and follow the terrain elevation. In addition the second threat area depiction contains vertical lines arising from these crosses (centered image). When flying alongside the threat zone only the crosses are presented, however if the heading of the helicopter is directed towards the threat zone vertical lines start to arise from the ground and grow taller with decreased distance to the threat zone. Thus the lines rise and fall relative to the flight direction of the helicopter and the resulting severity of the threat. Alternatively a threat zone can be presented as a surface shell, covering the restricted area under a cupola (right image).

Fig. 4. Threat zone with terrain crosses (left), vertical lines (centered) and surface shell (right)

4   Method

An online survey was developed using the open source application LimeSurvey Version 1.91. The survey addressed the target group of helicopter pilots. The link to the survey was distributed to several governmental facilities and private helicopter companies.

First pilots were given a short briefing summarizing the aim and content of the survey. In addition they were informed that their statements are handled confidentially. The survey was anonymous, names or email-addresses did not have to be provided. The questionnaire then contained a section on demographic information as well as sections on the presentation of obstacle information, route information and threat area information. The demographic data section for example contained questions about age, sex, nationality, flying experience and prior experience with HMD and conformal symbology. Within the following sections pilots were shown pictures and simulated in-flight videos of the symbology sets. They were then asked to rate the designs with regard to different aspects and provide open comments or suggestions of improvement. After completing the survey they were thanked for their participation and contact information in case of questions and interest in the results was provided. It took approximately 30 minutes to complete the survey. All questions except for open comments were obligatory to proceed in the survey. Only complete data sets were evaluated, hence every question was answered by each pilot.

The data output was exported into SPSS 20.0. Variables were re-coded in a way that high scores denote a high level of agreement. With regard to the on-going discussion about whether rating scales have to be considered as an ordinal or interval scale of measurement it was decided to pursue the more pragmatic approach and follow the rather common practice by interpreting the rating scales on an interval level of measurement [15].

5   Results

5.1   Participants

48 male pilots participated in the survey. The age of participants ranged from 23 to 62 years (M=43.9, SD=8.2). Nationalities included pilots from Germany, Switzerland, Austria, Israel, USA, Canada, UK and South Africa. 38 were civil, 10 were military pilots. They averaged 1966.4 (SD=1104.1) flight hours on their helicopter most frequently operated and 4769.6 (SD=3273.5) flight hours in total. 24 pilots were IFR-rated. 21 pilots reported having experienced severe spatial disorientation in flight due to DVE once and 10 of them even repeatedly. Furthermore 11 pilots reported having encountered a brownout or whiteout situation in flight once and 23 repeatedly. 13 participants had prior experience with HMD either in real flight or in the simulator averaging 209.3 (SD=315.5) flight hours. In addition 38 pilots had on average 299.2 (SD=352.3) flight hours experience with night vision goggles. Finally 13 participants reported to have already flown with 3D-conformal symbology averaging 221.3 (SD=416.0) flight hours.

5.2   Obstacle Presentation

Repeated Measures ANOVAs and Bonferroni post-hoc tests were conducted to assess differences in ratings between the designs each on a scale from one (strongly disagree) to four (strongly agree).

Power Line Masts

In general there is an overall advantage stated in favor for the mast with two cross-beams. 38 (79.2%) pilots ranked the mast icon with two cross beams as their first preference while six pilots (12.5%) favored the circular design and four pilots (8.3%) the icon with four cross beams. As their second choice, 25 pilots (52.1%) preferred the four-cross-beam icon, 18 (37.5%) the circular design and 5 (10.4%) the mast with two cross beams. In line with the results of the ranking pilots state that they would like to use the design with two beams preferably (M=3.2, SD=0.7) rather than the mast with four beams (M=2.2, SD=0.8) or the circular mast (M=2.2, SD=0.9), $F(2,94)=22.2$, p=.00. Besides participants rated the two-cross-beam design (M=3.6, SD=0.5) to be easier to identify than the four-cross-beam (M=2.9, SD=0.7) and the circular (M=2.8, SD=0.9) design, $F(2,94)=23.2$, p=.00. Furthermore it is rated to be more intuitively understandable (M=3.4, SD=0.6) and less complex (M=1.7, SD=0.6) compared to the four-cross-beam (M=2.7, SD=0.7; M=2.5, SD=0.8) and the circular (M=2.6, SD=0.8; M=2.4, SD=0.8) mast presentation, $F(2,94)=20,8$, p=.00; $F(2,94)=23.5$, p=.00. In addition pilots also indicated that the mast with two cross beams produced the least amount of clutter (M=2.0, SD=0.6) compared to the four-cross-beam (M=2.6, SD=0.8) and circular design (M=2.4, SD=0.8), $F(2,94)=10.2$, p=.00.

Windmills

The three-rotor-blade windmill was ranked first by 29 pilots (60.4%) while 16 (33.3%) preferred the windmill with the circle and three pilots (6.3%) favored the windmill with the globe around the blades. Secondly 30 pilots (62.5%) opted for the windmill with the circle, 15 (31.3%) preferred the regular windmill and three (6.3%) the windmill with the globe. Results on windmill ratings revealed a clear overall advantage for the de-cluttered conventional windmill with the three rotor blades. Hence pilots would like to use the conventional windmill design (M=3.2, SD=0.7) preferably over the windmill with the circle (M=2.8, SD= 0.9) and the windmill with the globe (M= 1.8, SD=0.7), F(1.7, 83.2)=44.9 p=.00. Participants indicated that the conventional windmill icon (M= 3.5, SD=0.7) was significantly easier to identify than the icon with the circle (M=3.3, SD=0.7). However there was also a significant advantage in favor for the circle-design compared to the globe (M=2.6, SD=0.8), F(2,94)=31.2; p=.00. In addition the de-cluttered windmill was rated to be less complex (M=1.7, SD=0.6) and more intuitively understandable (M=3.5, SD=0.7) compared to the circle design (M=2.4, SD=0.8; M=3.3, SD=0.6) and the globe. Here again the circle design is favored over the globe (M=3.3, SD=0.8; M=2.5, SD=0.7), F(2,94)=81.1, p=.00; F(2,94)= 44.3. Ratings also indicated the lowest level of clutter for the conventional windmill (M=1.8, SD=0.6) compared to the circle (M=2.3, SD=0.7) and the globe (M=3.1, SD=0.8), F(1.7, 81.0)=56.8 p=.00.

Presentation of Obstacle-Related Information

Results on the presentation of altitude information revealed that according to 27 pilots (56.3%) altitude should be indicated by a graphical presentation. 17 pilots (35.4%) favored a numerical presentation and only four pilots (8.3%) do not need additional altitude information at all. With regard to the graphical presentation results indicated an overall advantage for presenting an additional altitude marker symbol stated by 42 pilots (87.5%) compared to a brightness coding of the obstacle which was preferred by only 6 pilots (12.5%).

In contrast distance should preferably be indicated by numerical information next to the obstacle stated by 30 pilots (62.5%). Only eleven participants (22.9%) favored a graphical representation while seven (14.6%) do not need to see distance information at all. The numerical information should most preferably be presented below the obstacle (31.3%) or on the upper left side of the obstacle (31.3%).

19 pilots (39.6%) reported that they need information on minimum crossing altitude. The majority of 27 participants (56.3%) stated that obstacles should always be presented independent from vertical range (altitude).

With regard to the presentation of an alarm if the distance to an obstacle is below a certain limit, 26 (54.2%) pilots stated that both a visual and an auditory alarm should be given. 16 (33.3%) participants favored solely a visual alarm, five (10.4%) an auditory alarm and only one pilot (2.1%) stated that no alarm should be given.

5.3   Route Presentation

Waypoints
In general waypoints are rated rather well since 33 pilots (68.8%) indicated that they would like to use the design. Furthermore waypoints were rated to increase situation awareness (85.5%), be easy to identify (83.3%), intuitively understandable (77.1%) and not produce too much clutter (79.2%). In addition 40 pilots (83.3%) reported that the light beam is useful. Only five pilots (10.4%) do not want to see waypoints at all. Nevertheless at least 22 (45.9) pilots agreed to some extent that the presentation is lacking information while on the other hand five pilots (10.4%) do not want to see waypoints at all.

Route Points
The majority of 40 (83.3%) pilots agreed that route points would increase situation awareness and are useful (37, 77.1%). With regard to the design 41 (85.5%) rated them to be easy to identify and 36 (75.0%) to be intuitively understandable. 15 (31.3%) stated that route points produce too much clutter and 9 (18.8%) do not want to see them at all. In the end 32 (66.7%) wanted to use the design

5.4   Threat Zone Presentation

20 (41.7%) pilots ranked the surface shell as their first choice, however 16 (33.3%) pilots preferred the representation with the vertical lines and 12 (25%) pilots the re-presentation with the crosses alone. Secondly 19 (39.6%) pilots favored vertical lines, 15 (31.3%) pilots the crosses and 14 (29.2%) the surface shell.

Participants rated the surface shell to be more intuitively understandable (M=3.2, SD=2.6) than the crosses (M=2.8, SD=0.8), F(2,94)= 6.9, p=.02. However the surface shell was also rated highest for producing too much clutter (M=2.7, SD=0.7) compared to the cross-design (M=2.4, SD=0.6), F(2,94)= 4.5, p=.01. 32 pilots (66.7%) stated that the surface shell might capture too much attention while 17 (35.4%) do not want to see it at all. In contrast 16 pilots (33.4%) agreed that the crosses alone are not noticeable enough. However also 33 participants (68.7%) suspected that the vertical lines might capture too much attention and 19 (39.6%) do not need to see the vertical lines at all. Finally 27 (56.3%) helicopter pilots would like to use the surface shell design, 26 (54.1%) the design with the crosses and 23 (47.9%) the design with the vertical lines.

6   Discussion

In summary the survey dealt with the evaluation of symbology designs that have been developed to increase helicopter pilot situation awareness in poor visibility. The demographic statements endorse the relevance of such a development as the majority of pilots reported about having experienced severe spatial disorientation in flight due to DVE or due to brownout and whiteout. These findings are in accordance with the high incident rates stated in the NATO report [3].

Altogether the survey revealed some very interesting and useful results. First it becomes clear that there is a common interest in the use of such technology not only in the military field but also for civil applications.

This legitimates further research not only to be looking into expensive high-end applications that are primarily designed for the military context but also into the development of feasible low-cost alternatives for civil implementation.

With regard to the design of icons and symbols it becomes apparent that clutter is still the most crucial concern for pilots. This is reflected especially in the results for obstacle ratings where the de-cluttered designs – the mast with two cross beams and the conventional windmill - were rated best. Furthermore the cost of clutter and symbology overload was also the highest concern reflected in the comments. This confirms the fact that staying eyes-out and being able to see the outside scene is essential for helicopter pilots in any circumstances. On the other hand results were less clear for the threat zone designs. In fact the de-cluttered cross-design scored insignificantly lowest. The result can probably be explained by the fact that the cross-design is also the less salient one.

Nevertheless the need for information about altitude and distance as well as the presentation of an alarm becomes very clear in the results. Here a slightly preference to present altitude in a graphical and distance in a numerical way is shown.

In addition it should be briefly discussed that pilot comments repeatedly concerned the change of colour especially for alerts and threat indications. Nevertheless, as mentioned in chapter 2, symbology can only be depicted in monochrome green. Therefore only the coding of brightness is currently an option, otherwise different alternatives such as blinking or highlighting with a frame have to be tested. However the requests for changing color will be taken into consideration for a possible implementation on a head-down display.

Moreover it became clear in the comments that the presentation of power line wires is crucial. However as mentioned in chapter 3.1 wire directions cannot be precisely depicted from database information. Thus as a next step DLR is also investigating the use of helicopter-mounted sensors to provide real-time information updates in the database, for instance by using a modified laser radar (Hellas) developed by Cassidian.

Finally the outcomes of the survey will now be integrated into the symbology design, implemented into the HMD and furthermore tested in part-task simulations and flight trials.

Acknowledgements. The authors would like to thank all colleagues who participated in the workshops and assisted in the development of the questionnaire for their valuable contributions.

References

1. http://www.welt.de (January 10, 2013) Retrieved from Hubschrauber stürzt auf Autobahn – Pilot stirbt, http://www.welt.de/vermischtes/weltgeschehen/article112683378/Hubschrauber-stuerzt-auf-Autobahn-Pilot-stirbt.html

2. AAIB, AAIB Bulletin S1/2013 SPECIAL. Air Accidents Investigation Branch (AAIB), Aldershot, UK (2013)
3. NATO Task Group HFM-162, Rotary-Wing Brownout Mitigation: Technologies and Training. RTO/NATO (2012)
4. Lüken, T., Doehler, H.-U., Lantzsch, R.: ALLFlight - Fusing sensor information to increase helicopter pilot's situation awareness. In: Proceedings of the 36th European Rotorcraft Forum (2010)
5. Velger, M.: Helmet-Mounted Displays and Sights. Artech House, Boston (1998)
6. Yeh, M., Wickens, C., Seagull, F.: Effects of frame of reference and viewing condition on attentional issues with helmet mounted displays. U.S. Army Research Laboratory, Maryland (1998)
7. Yeh, M., Wickens, C., Seagull, F.: Target Cuing in Visual Search: The Effects of Conformality and Display Location on the Allocation of Visual Attention. In: Society, H.F. (ed.) Human Factors, vol. 41(4), pp. 524–542 (1999)
8. Wickens, C.: Attentional Issues in Head-up Displays. In: Harris, D. (ed.) Engineering Psychology and Cognitive Ergonomics, vol. 1, pp. 3–21. Ashgate (1997)
9. McCann, R., Foyle, D.: Scene-linked Symbology to Improve Situation Awareness. In: AGARD Conference Proceedings No. 555. Aerospace Medical Panel Conference on Situation Awareness, pp. 16:1–16:11 (1995)
10. Foyle, D.C., Ahumada, A.J., Larimer, J., Townsend Sweet, B.: Enhanced/Synthetic Vision Systems: Human Factors Research and Implications for Future Systems. SAE Transactions: Journal of Aerospace 101, 1734–1741 (1992)
11. Wickens, C.D., Long, J.: Object versus space-based models of visual attention: Implications for the design of head-up displays. Journal of Experimental Psychology: Applied 1(3), 179–193 (1995)
12. Martin-Emerson, R., Wickens, C.: Superimposition, Symbology, Visual Attention, and the Head-Up Display. Superimposition, Symbology, Visual Attention, and the Head-Up Display 39(4), 581–601 (1997)
13. Wickens, C.: Aviation Displays. In: Tsang, P., Vidulich, M. (eds.) Principles and Practice of Aviation Psychology, pp. 147–200. Lawrence Erlbaum Associates, Mahwah (2003)
14. Alexander, A.L., Wickens, C.D., Hardy, T.J.: Synthetic Vision Systems: The Effects of Guidance Symbology, Display Size, and Field of View. In: Society, H.F. (ed.) Human Factors, vol. 47(4), pp. 693–707 (2005)
15. Bortz, J.: Statistik für Human- und Sozialwissenschaftler, 6th edn. Springer Medizin Verlag, Heidelberg (2005)

Empirical Insights on Operators' Procedure Following Behavior in Nuclear Power Plants[*]

Huafei Liao[1] and Michael Hildebrandt[2]

[1] Sandia National Laboratories, Albuquerque, NM, USA
[2] OECD Halden Reactor Project, Halden, Norway
hnliao@sandia.gov, michael.hildebrandt@hrp.no

Abstract. In nuclear power plants (NPPs), operators are in general expected to strictly (but not blindly) follow symptom-based emergency operating procedures (EOPs) in responding to emergencies. The procedures are highly prescriptive by their nature as their purpose is to enable the operators to restore and maintain plant safety functions without having to diagnose events or the specific causes of process disturbance. However, this does not necessarily imply that operators' procedure following behavior can simply be assumed as a preeminently step-by-step, rule-based activity of reading, understanding and following individual steps without much cognitive effort.

This paper examines the procedure following behavior of NPP control room operators in a large-scale empirical human reliability analysis (HRA) study, referred to as *the US Empirical HRA Study* [1-2]. Observations on challenges that operators experienced in following the EOPs are presented, and their implications for enhancing operator performance and modeling operator behavior under the naturalistic decision making (NDM) framework are discussed.

Keywords: procedure following, emergency operating procedures, nuclear power plant, human reliability analysis, naturalistic decision-making.

1 Introduction

Operating procedures are widely used in hazardous and complex industries, such as nuclear, chemical and aviation industries, to ensure safe operations. By providing instructions and guidance for completing a given task (e.g., what parameters to check, how to interpret observed symptoms, and what actions to take), procedures can enhance human operators' performance and reduce human error (e.g., skipping critical actions), particularly if the task has to be carried out under complicated and stressful conditions. Without such instructions, operators are likely to be distracted by irrelevant and/or trivial detail of an abnormal event, make an incorrect or partial plant status assessment, and fail to acknowledge information and perform actions to address the critical aspects of the event in a timely manner. However, it becomes increasingly evident that operating procedures, including those for maintenance, test and calibration, can also degrade

---

[*] The opinions expressed in this paper are those of the authors and not of the authors' organizations.

D. Harris (Ed.): EPCE/HCII 2013, Part I, LNAI 8019, pp. 242–251, 2013.
© Springer-Verlag Berlin Heidelberg 2013

operators' performance and procedure-related system failures constitute a source of vulnerability of the integrity of complex systems [3-8]. Therefore, to improve reliable operator performance, it is important to understand when and how procedures can negatively impact operators, especially their role in operators' responses to emergencies.

In nuclear power plants (NPPs), symptom-based emergency operating procedures (EOPs) are established to guide operators to respond to emergency conditions. The EOPs are highly prescriptive by their nature in that they are a static model of the tasks that need to be completed to accomplish a certain system goal. In addition, the rules and strategies specified in the procedures to guide operators' activities are mechanistic given that they are based on theoretical and practical knowledge of processes or event sequences that are well analyzed [6-8]. Although the purpose of the EOPs is to enable operators to restore and maintain plant safety functions without having to diagnose events or the specific causes of process disturbance, this does not necessarily imply that operators' procedure following behavior can simply be assumed as a preeminently step-by-step, rule-based activity of reading, understanding and following individual steps without much cognitive effort. This is because, in contrast to the static nature of the EOPs, the processes and operations in NPPs under emergency conditions are quite dynamic. When facing an unusual accident condition (e.g., multiple failures involving complicating factors such as failed sensors) that is not foreseen, analyzed or prepared for, operators' cognitive efforts are needed to compensate for the gap and mismatch between the instructions in the EOPs and the real situation. For example, operators need to understand the underlying logic and basis of the required tasks specified in the EOPs so that they can select appropriate activities from the prescribed instructions when the plant conditions are not fully addressed in the EOPs. In addition, due to the level of detail in the description of the actions to be performed, the EOPs may implicitly call on operators' knowledge, judgment and decisions in interpreting and executing the procedures.

This paper explores NPP control room operators' role in handling emergencies and their interactions with the EOPs based on data collected from a large-scale empirical human reliability analysis (HRA) study, referred to as the US Empirical HRA Study [1-2]. Observations on issues and challenges that operators experienced in following the EOPs are presented, and their implications for enhancing operator performance and modeling operator behavior under the naturalistic decision making (NDM) framework are discussed. Note that the purpose of the US Empirical HRA Study was to evaluate various HRA methods against crew performance in scenarios simulated on a NPP simulator. In order to be able to assess to what extent the HRA methods could predict how operators could fail a scenario, some of the scenarios developed in the study, while plausible, comprised far more difficulties than those modeled in standard HRA and probabilistic risk analysis (PRA) studies. In other words, those scenarios are rare in reality. Thus, most of the observations discussed in this article are unlikely to occur and should not be interpreted as common issues or safety status in current NPPs. Nonetheless, a close look at the observations from the challenging scenarios can shed light on the subtle and complex aspects of operators' procedure following behavior that are not well understood or are even overlooked, and provide useful insights to further improve operator performance and procedure effectiveness.

2   Study Background

2.1   Operator Crews and Simulator

Four licensed operator crews (Q, R, S and T) from a participating US nuclear power plant responded to simulated scenarios developed for the study (see Section 2.2 for scenario description) on the participating plant full-scope training simulator (PWR 4-loop Westinghouse) using the plant's EOPs and related procedures.   There were five members in each crew: one Shift Manager (SM), one Unit Supervisor (US), one Shift Technical Advisor (STA), and two Reactor Operators (ROs).

2.2   Scenarios

The three scenarios developed in the study are briefly described in the following sub-sections (see [1-2] for additional details).   To control for confounded learning effects due to the order of presentation of the scenarios, the scenarios were presented to participating operator crews in different orders.   All crews did not have knowledge of the types of scenarios that they would face before they participated in the study.

Scenario 1: Total Loss of Feedwater (LOFW) Followed by Steam Generator Tube Rupture (SGTR). When all three main feedwater pumps are tripped at the beginning of Scenario 1, only one auxiliary feedwater (AFW) pump can be started to supply feedwater.   However, the feedwater cannot reach the steam generators (SGs) because the recirculation valve for the AFW pump is mis-positioned to be open, which will not be indicated in the control room.   Without feedwater, the ability to remove decay heat from the reactor vessel is severely degraded.   Operators will have to first identify the misleading flow indication and the total LOFW and then enter functional restoration procedure FR-H1 (Response to Loss of Secondary Heat Sink) to start bleed and feed (B&F).

After B&F is initiated, operators are allowed to establish AFW flow to SGs by either closing the recirculation valve or cross-connecting the running AFW pump. At this point, another, unrelated failure occurs: a tube rupture is initiated in the first SG that is fed.   Procedure E-30 (Response to SGTR) provides instructions to terminate the leakage of reactor coolant into the secondary system when a tube rupture occurs.

Scenario 2: Loss of Component Cooling Water (CCW) and Reactor Coolant Pump (RCP) Sealwater. At the beginning of Scenario 2, the Distribution Panel 1201 fails. The feedwater regulation valve on SG A cannot be closed and remains fully open; as a result, the reactor will be tripped either manually or automatically. When the reactor trips, one AFW pump cannot start due to the loss of Panel 1201. In addition, all CCW and charging pumps become unavailable. If operators continue running the RCPs without CCW, they risk RCP seal failure, which can result in a loss of coolant accident (LOCA). It is therefore important that operators identify the loss of CCW and RCP sealwater and then trip the RCPs and start the Positive Displacement Pump (PDP) per instructions in procedures RC-0002 (Reactor Coolant Pump Off Normal) and ES-01 (Reactor Trip Response). The procedure requires the operators to stop the RCPs within 1 minute after loss of CCW. After that period, the risk of seal failure increases.

Note that the failing distribution panel is unrelated to the loss of CCW and RCP sealwater but it increases the complexity of the scenario as the alarms associated with the distribution panel can mask the status of CCW and RCP sealwater.

Scenario 3: SGTR. Scenario 3 is a standard SGTR without other complications. Operators will need to first identify the SGTR and then perform actions in E-30 to respond to the event.

2.3   Data Collection and Analysis

The data on scenario development and crew responses were collected and analyzed by reviewing notes, simulator actions monitor logs, interviews and Video recordings.

3   Observations on Interactions between Operators and EOPs

Significant variability in crew performance was observed, especially for the relatively more difficult scenarios (e.g., Scenarios 1 and 2) where complicating factors such as misleading indicators considerably increased scenario complexity and cognitive demands on operators. Overall, the crews varied in their ability to (1) integrate all evidence to formulate a coherent explanation to account for observed plant symptoms and (2) cope with the difficulties in following EOPs in responding to emergency situations. In the following sub-sections, some observations that were made on the interactions between operators and EOPs are discussed with specific plant conditions and operational contexts. It should be noted that although this section focuses on the issues and difficulties that the crews experienced in following the EOPs, it is not intended to and does not adequately reflect the overall performance quality of the participating crews. Not all of the issues and difficulties led to a significant consequence (e.g., failure of a scenario). In some cases, the crews managed to recover from their errors through recovery measures and compensatory factors.

3.1   Misreading or Skipping Procedure Steps

Misreading or unintentionally skipping procedure steps is an example of slips and lapses that operators make in following procedures. It can occur even when the information in the procedure is clear and unambiguous and when operators use human performance tools such as signing off on completed steps. Such slips and lapses can lead to an incorrect plant status assessment or initiation of incorrect response.

Observation 1: In Scenario 1, when Crew Q followed Step 28 in FR-H1 to stop the third high head safety injection (HHSI) pump, the US misread the reactor coolant system (RCS) subcooling requirement. This error caused a delay of approximately 30 to 60 minutes in stopping the pump. As a result, an excessive amount of water was fed into the faulted SG (water in faulted SG reached the steamline).

Observation 2: In Scenario 1, Crew S skipped the step of stopping the RCPs before they initiated B&F. However, this error was soon corrected by their STA. This indicates that good teamwork is an efficient measure to help prevent operators from committing an error in misreading or skipping a step in the procedure. Hence, this example is, to some extent, related to the observation on communication and teamwork (see Section 3.6).

3.2   Verbatim Procedure Following

Operators may literally follow procedures without understanding the intent of the procedures and observed plant symptoms.

Observation: In Scenario 1, when Crew R became aware of the SGTR, they entered Procedure E-30 to isolate the faulted SG. Since they did not turn off the HHSI pump, the pressure in the faulted SG kept rising and eventually caused the Power Operated Relief Valve (PORV) on the SG to open, and the steam flow released from the lifted PORV caused the RCS pressure to decrease. Although the crew was not aware of the lifted PORV, they detected the steam flow from the faulted SG. However, the crew, solely based on the decreasing RCS pressure, transferred from Step 21 in E-30 to EC-31, which is the procedure for tube rupture in combination with a leak in the reactor coolant system. In this situation, as pointed out by a trainer from the participating plant who reviewed the crew's performance, the crew should have been able to connect the steam flow from the faulted SG to the possibility of an open SG PORV and explain that the decreasing RCS pressure was due to the PORV rather than a primary leakage. Without a good understanding of the intention of Step 21 in E-30 and the plant status, the crew literally followed the procedure to make an inappropriate procedure transfer, which eventually caused the crew to fail the scenario.

3.3   Premature Termination of Plant Parameter Trend Assessment

Observing and assessing plant parameter trends is one aspect of procedure following that is particularly dependent on operators' expectations and evaluations. In an emergency situation, plant parameters change dynamically. There are times when a specific parameter satisfies a procedure step entry criterion before the step entry but then changes in the opposite direction after the step entry. An insufficient trend assessment can cause operators to develop an incorrect mental model of the plant status.

Observation: The same case as discussed above in verbatim procedure following. At the moment when Crew R reached Step 21 in E-30, the RCS pressure was decreasing due to the lifted SG PORV. However, it started to increase only after several minutes. Since the crew only evaluated the trend at the moment when they reached Step 21 in E-30 and stopped evaluating the pressure trend very soon, they did not obtain an accurate picture of the plant status and thus made an inappropriate procedure transfer decision (see discussion above). Had they waited a few more minutes they could have seen the pressure rise again and continued to the next step in E-30 to stop the HHSI pump, which could have reduced the RCS pressure and lead the crew to successfully bring the plant to a stable condition.

3.4   Decisions and Judgments Based on Operator's Knowledge

When facing cognitively challenging situations involving complicating factors, operators need to rely on their knowledge to differentiate expected from unexpected plant behavior and pursue all possibilities for the unexpected behavior. Similarly, under circumstances when there is inadequate procedure guidance, operators need to rely on their knowledge to make judgments and take necessary actions outside procedures.

Observation 1: In Scenario 1, an SGTR was initially masked by the AFW flow fed into the faulted SG. After the AFW flow was stopped per procedural instructions, the water level in the faulted SG kept rising. Since the steamline on the faulted SG had been isolated earlier in the scenario, the steamline radiation alarm, which will normally be triggered during an SGTR event, was not triggered when the SGTR occurred. Therefore, the rising SG level became the main cue for operators to identify the SGTR. When Crew S detected the rising SG level after the AFW flow was stopped, they suspected an SGTR. At the same time, they were also aware that the water level was expected to rise to some extent due to a swelling effect after stopping feedwater flow to an SG. The crew relied on their knowledge to evaluate the plant status and decided that the rising SG level was caused by an SGTR rather than a normal amount of swell. In contrast, when Crew R detected the rising SG level, they, like what they were trained to do, checked radiation levels at the plant as a confirmatory plant parameter for an SGTR. Since, as mentioned above, the steamline on the faulted SG had been isolated, no abnormal radiation activities were initially detected as what would be expected in an SGTR. As a result, the crew concluded that no SGTR had occurred. Operators are trained to check plant parameters (e.g., radiation levels) in diagnosing abnormal events (e.g., an SGTR). The observation on Crew R suggests that operators' knowledge about the processes at the plant is needed in interpreting the plant parameters in connection with the plant condition at that moment. Simply following a standard practice without considering the scenario context led Crew R to make an incorrect judgment. Hence, this is, to some extent, related to verbatim procedure following (see Section 3.2).

Observation 2: In Scenario 1, when Crews Q and S identified the SGTR, they were in FR-H1 to recover from the LOFW that occurred in earlier in the scenario. Although E-30 provides instructions to respond to an SGTR, the crews could not transfer to this procedure because FR-H1 has a higher priority over E-30. However, the crews were aware from their training that they would need to adjust the PORV setpoint of the faulted SG to prevent the PORV from lifting (to avoid releasing radioactive water into the containment). Since Crew Q could not find instructions for adjusting the setpoint in any procedure they were in, they cautiously managed to control the SG pressure below the PORV setpoint by controlling the RCS pressure. In the case of Crew S, after assessing the SG pressure at that moment, which was far below the setpoint, the crew considered that they were not at risk of lifting the PORV and thus decided not to adjust the setpoint. In this example, since FR-H1 does not provide guidance to respond to an SGTR, this case is, to some extent, related to the observation of inadequate procedure guidance (see Section 3.5).

3.5   Inadequate Procedure Guidance

Due to the complex nature of the processes in NPPs, it is difficult to develop EOPs that cover every possible contingency in detail. Operators may feel challenged when there is inadequate procedure guidance, but training can help them handle the gap between the EOPs and the real situations.

Observation 1: In Scenario 1, one crew never suspected that the recirculation valve of the AFW pump was open because checking the valve status was not specified in the EOPs. Although the other three crews checked the valve status, the action was driven by their knowledge from training rather than procedures.

Observation 2: In Scenario 2, one objective was to establish RCP seal cooling with the PDP when CCW and RCP seal injection was lost. Crew S indicated that they knew they needed to start the PDP, but they could not find procedure guidance, which is only provided by ES-01 and procedure POP4. It would be helpful to include the guidance in the POP9 annunciator response procedure on low charging flow.

Observation 3: In Scenario 2, as discussed above, the RCP seal cooling can only be placed in service when the RCP temperatures are below 230° F. Crew R attempted to restore the RCP seal cooling with the POP 9 annunciator response procedure on low charging flow; however, since the procedure assumes a single failure (i.e., low charging flow), the temperature limit of the RCP seals is not specified in the procedure.

3.6   Communication and Teamwork

Crew members have their unique roles and responsibilities at the plant. They sometimes often need to simultaneously work in different procedures in complex dynamic situations. Inefficient communication and task coordination can impact their ability to integrate information distributed across crew members to develop team situation awareness, evaluate the appropriateness of procedure paths, reach team consensus, synchronize on a common strategy, and pursue multiple objectives.

Observation 1: In Scenario 2, one expected response was to restore the RCP seal injection (i.e., RCP seal cooling) to protect the RCP seals. According to procedures, the seal injection can only be started when the RCP seal temperatures are below 230° F. When the third RO of Crew Q reported to the US that the seal temperature limit was exceeded, the RO and the US were working in two different procedures. The communication protocol broke down for some reason and the information was not well internalized by the US. Several minutes later, the US attempted to re-establish the RCP seal injection with a charging pump at Step 6 in ES-01. However, this action was soon stopped by the crew's SM, who recognized the temperature limit. It is interesting to note that although Step 6 in ES-01 specifies the seal temperature limit, the US seemed to ignore the instructions, which could be considered a deviation from the procedure. Nonetheless, good teamwork stopped the evolution of the deviation.

<u>Observation 2</u>: In Scenario 1, when Crew R was in Step 28 in FR-H1 to stop the last HHSI pump to terminate B&F, the procedure required them to evaluate if they had an "active loop". One criterion for an active loop is that natural circulation has been established, which is verified by five criteria. Normally, verification of natural circulation and active loops are the STA's task. When the crew's US and SM incorrectly assumed that they had an active loop, neither did they seek verification from the STA nor did the STA verify the assumption by himself. As a result, the crew decided not to stop the last HHSI pump, which eventually caused the crew to fail the scenario.

<u>Observation 3</u>: It was observed that the crews often held team briefings to share information and discuss plant conditions. The briefings effectively kept the crews aware of the goals of the US, the procedural paths that they were supposed to follow, and the course of actions that they were supposed to take.

4   Discussion and Conclusions

EOPs play an important role in guiding NPP operators to respond to emergency situations. In this article, the operational behaviors of four crews in three simulated emergency scenarios were examined and several observations were made on the issues and challenges that the crews experienced in their interactions with the EOPs. Despite of the small set of scenarios and crew performance data, the observations made in the present study echoed the findings from previous studies [e.g., 8-10]. Given that the previous studies investigated crews from different countries (e.g., Korea and Sweden) with different scenarios, it is reasonable to conclude that the observations from the study can be generalized across the boundaries of countries.

Overall, the observations discussed in Section 3 consist of examples of both slips and lapses in executing intended actions and difficulties in high-level cognitive processes (e.g., situation assessment and response planning). Compared to slips and lapses, which could be soon detected and corrected with compensatory factors (e.g., Observation 2 in Section 3.1), the difficulties in high-level cognitive processes seemed to have caused relatively more serious consequences.

The observations also illustrate the dynamic aspect of operators' procedure following behavior. As discussed in Section 1, the EOPs are a static model of the tasks prescribed for the expected progression of pre-defined accident scenarios. In contrast, the real emergency situations are quite dynamic, involving unexpected complicating factors and uncertainties. In the paradox of using a static model to deal with dynamic situations, an active role of operators is called for to fill the gap between the static and the dynamic. This is in agreement with the conclusions from previous studies [8-10] that operators actively engage in high-level cognitive activities to adequately handle cognitively demanding emergencies even when the EOPs are employed (i.e., operators do not just literally follow the EOPs without much thought in the context of the accident scenarios). Evidence of the nature and extent of cognitive activity required of operators from the study includes:

- Operators need to make decisions and judgments and take extra-procedural actions based on their knowledge when (1) relevant procedures are not entered due to scenario characteristics and (2) some specific aspects of a scenario are not fully addressed by the EOPs (see Sections 3.4 and 3.5).
- When facing uncertainty and unexpected plant behavior, operators need to perform systematic diagnosis activity in parallel to following the EOPs to develop and maintain an accurate mental model of the plant status by pursuing all possibilities and integrating all available evidence to form a coherent explanation to account for multiple symptoms across diverse systems (see Sections 3.2 and 3.3).
- Based on their understanding of plant conditions and the EOPs, operators need to prioritize their goals, monitor plant parameters, and evaluate the feasibility of response plans and applicability of procedures as plant status evolves dynamically (see Section 3.2).

One implication of the observations is that operator performance can certainly be enhanced by improving guidance in the EOPs, adding countermeasures to prevent slips and lapses (see Section 3.1), adhering to work practices (see Section 3.6), and strengthening teamwork (see Section 3.6). More importantly, operators need to be trained to develop high-level cognitive skills such as situation assessment and response planning to compensate for the limitations of the EOPs [11]. One prerequisite for such skills is a good knowledge of the plant processes, components, and systems, and an accurate mental model of how they interact with each other. In addition, operators need to develop a good knowledge of the EOPs, including the intent behind specific procedure steps, the rationale for transitions among procedures, and the response strategies embodied in the EOPs.

Another important implication is that it may be more appropriate to study NPP operators' behavior under a naturalistic decision making (NDM) [12] framework rather than normative decision theories (e.g., [13]). Normative decision theories assume that decision makers make rational judgments defined as the optimal choice among available alternatives by a certain comparison scheme. Although they have been highly successful in describing decision strategies in well-structured settings, their prescriptive validity is questionable for describing NPP operators' behavior in their operational settings for the following reasons. Firstly, as discussed above, situation assessment plays an important role for operators to handle a plant upset; however, this cognition component tends to be neglected by the normative decision theories. Secondly, given the time pressure, uncertainty, limited information, dynamic conditions, and shifting goals and priorities involved in plant incidents, it is not always feasible for operators to conduct a relatively thorough information search to choose among concurrently available alternatives through a deliberate and analytic comparison process as described by rational choice models. Thirdly, operators often resort to their experience to make a rapid decision under difficult situations; however, experience is normally treated as a nuisance variable in normative decision theories. In contrast, NDM is an approach to understand how experienced decision makers use their experience to make decisions in real world settings. Its strength is its emphasis on the role of experience in situation assessment and response planning. In addition, NDM describes how humans make a decision rather than attempt to prescribe how humans *should* make decisions. Hence, this can, with a focus on the observable features of operator performance, improve our ability to model and understand operators' qualitative reasoning behavior when there is a mismatch between procedures and the dynamic reality.

References

1. Forester, J., Liao, H., Dang, V.N., Bye, A., Presley, M., Marble, J., Broberg, H., Hildebrandt, M., Lois, E., Hallbert, B., Morgan, T.: US HRA Empirical Study – Comparison of HRA Method Predictions to Operating Crew Performance in a US Nuclear Power Plant Simulator and an Assessment of the Consistency of HRA Method Predictions, Draft Report (2011)
2. Broberg, H., Hildebrandt, M., Nowell, R.: Results from the 2010 HRA Data Collection at a US PWR Training Simulator. OECD Halden Reactor Project. Halden, Norway (2011)
3. Joos, D.W., Sabri, Z.A., Husseiny, A.A.: Analysis of Gross Error Rates in Operation of Commercial Nuclear Power Stations. Nuclear Engineering and Design 52, 265–300 (1979)
4. Goodman, P.C., Dipalo, C.A.: Human Factors Information System: Tools to Assess Error Related to Human Performance in US Nuclear Power Plant. In: Proceedings on Human Factors Society 35th Annular Meeting, San Francisco, pp. 662–665 (1991)
5. USNRC. Development of a Checklist for Evaluating Maintenance, Test and Calibration Procedures Used in Nuclear Power Plants. NUREG/CR-1368 (1980)
6. Park, J.: The Complexity of Proceduralized Tasks. Springer, London (2009)
7. Grote, G.: Management of Uncertainty. Springer, London (2009)
8. Roth, E.M., Mumaw, R.J., Mewis, P.M.: An Empirical Investigation of Operator Performance in Cognitively Demanding Simulated Emergencies. NUREG/CR-6208, U.S. NRC (1994)
9. Massaiu, S.: Critical Features of Emergency Procedures: Empirical Insights from Simulations of Nuclear Power Plant Operation. Reliability, Risk and Safety: Theory and Applications, 277–284 (2010)
10. Choi, S.Y., Park, J.: Operator Behaviors Observed in Following Emergency Operating Procedure under a Simulated Emergency. Nuclear Engineering and Technology 44, 379–386 (2012)
11. Gustavsson, P., Johansson, B., Hildebrandt, M.: Resilience and Procedure Use in the Training of Nuclear Power Plant Operating Crews – An Interview Study and Literature Review. OECD Halden Reactor Project. Halden, Norway (2011)
12. Klein, G.: Sources of Power: How People Make Decisions. The MIT Press, Cambridge (1999)
13. Schoemaker, P.J.H.: The Expected Utility Model: Its Variants, Purposes, Evidence and Limitations. Journal of Economic Literature 20, 529–563 (1982)

The Impact of Type and Level of Automation on Situation Awareness and Performance in Human-Robot Interaction

David Schuster, Florian Jentsch, Thomas Fincannon, and Scott Ososky

University of Central Florida, Institute for Simulation and Training 3100 Technology Parkway, Orlando, FL 32826
{dschuster,sososky}@ist.ucf.edu, florian.jentsch@ucf.edu, t_fincannon@yahoo.com

Abstract. In highly autonomous robotic systems, human operators are able to attend to their own, separate tasks, rather than directly operating the robot to accomplish their immediate task(s). At the same time, as operators attend to their own, separate tasks that do not directly involve the robotic system, they can end up lacking situation awareness (SA) when called on to recover from automation failure or from an unexpected event. In this paper, we describe the mechanisms of this problem, known as the out-of-the-loop performance problem, and describe why the problem may still exist in future robotic systems. Existing solutions to the problem, which focus on the level of automation, are reviewed. We describe our current empirical work, which aims to expand upon taxonomies of levels of automation to better understand how engineers of robotic systems may mitigate the problem.

Keywords: Human-robot interaction, robot design, situation awareness, automation.

1 Introduction

In highly autonomous robotic systems, human operators are able to attend to their own, separate tasks, rather than having to directly operate a robot to accomplish their immediate task(s). Because this is one of these systems' major benefits, robots are being developed to have high levels of autonomy, so that they can function with as little human intervention as possible [1]. Still, as robots grow in capability, they will continue to need some human supervision and occasional human intervention [2].

Human performance problems in complex and automated systems have been discussed for some time [3] [4]. Sarter [5] was one of the first to broaden the contributing factors to the problem to those beyond automation complacency [6]. For example, Sarter identified a lack of SA as a mediator between high levels of automation and poor performance. Endsley and Kiris [7] found that the out-of-the-loop performance problem affected humans working in highly automated systems. In the out-of-the-loop performance problem, operators who attend to their own, separate tasks can end up

D. Harris (Ed.): EPCE/HCII 2013, Part I, LNAI 8019, pp. 252–260, 2013.

lacking SA when they are called upon suddenly, for example, to recover from auto-mation failures or in response to another unexpected event. The phenomenon of the out-of-the-loop performance problem has been studied in multiple domains, for ex-ample, among pilots where a loss of SA has been observed under conditions of high cockpit automation [8].

In this paper, we describe the mechanisms of the out-of-the-loop performance problem and describe why the problem may still exist in future robot systems. Exist-ing solutions to the problem, which focus on the level of automation, are reviewed. We also describe our empirical work, which aims to expand upon taxonomies of le-vels of automation to better understand how engineers of robotic systems may miti-gate the problem.

2   The Out-of-the-Loop Performance Problem in HRI

A common problem of capable, autonomous robots is poor SA [9]. As we introduced above, lack of SA under conditions of automation failure has come to be known as the out-of-the-loop performance problem [10] and the out-of-the-loop unfamiliarity prob-lem [9]. Further, robustness in robot capabilities remains a challenge to robotics [11]. As new capabilities are developed, robots may be able to perform new tasks, but re-liability may be limited, especially initially. For human operators to take advantage of new robot capabilities, operators must be able to recover from robot failures.

The out-of-the-loop performance problem occurs because of a shift in the impor-tance of information within the environment that is the result of a change in the level of automation. Operators working with high-autonomy automation typically do not need the details of the automation's task to achieve their own goals; in fact, the car-dinal objective of the automation is to off-load the operator of having to obtain and hold detailed knowledge and to perform continuous monitoring. Consequently, high-performing operators can be expected to ignore these details and devote their re-sources to their own task components. Unfortunately, failure of the automation leads to a rapid switch from these details being unimportant to suddenly being of crucial importance to task completion. The result can be very poor SA, especially when the operator's current knowledge overlaps minimally with the knowledge needed to ef-fectively achieve task goals.

This problem is likely to be of continued concern in future robot systems. These systems are designed to offload the human through high autonomy. Additionally, a factor contributing to the out-of-the-loop performance problem, namely, imperfect reliability, is likely present, at least initially. Further, when these robots fail, they may do so in non-obvious ways. Indeed, in such systems, the need for a shift from full autonomy to operator intervention may not be marked by clearly pronounced signals, unlike in many current systems or when an obvious failure occurs in a complete sub-system. It is fairly obvious, for example, when a pilot needs to revert to an alternate method of navigation or control when an instrument in the cockpit goes completely blank or gives a value that is clearly out of the possible range. In this case, a combina-tion of signals in the automation (the blank display or wrong value), combined with the pilot's knowledge and SA, signal that a task previously handled by automation must be performed manually.

In contrast, robot failures may include instances in which a robot provides apparently valid information that is based on incorrect sensing. Although this type of failure may occur in other systems, and robots also fail in obvious ways, a pressing problem is dealing with subtle sensing errors in a system separated from its operator by location and task assignment. That is, the operator and robot are not only in different locations, they also have different roles, making it difficult, impossible, or unnecessary to monitor each action of the robot. These types of failures are not mechanical failures (such as when the robot is stuck and cannot complete the task), but rather failures in robot sensing and intelligence (i.e., the robot completes the task but does so incorrectly). Furthermore, measuring a robot's confidence or meta-awareness of their sensors continues to be a more difficult problem than sensing itself [12]. Consequently, robot mistakes may be detectable only through cross-checking with other data, and failure at lower levels (i.e., sensing) may only have noticeable consequences at higher levels (i.e., decision-making). From the operator's perspective, a shift must take place when a robot fails; what previously did not need to be known by the operator suddenly becomes critically important. To maintain SA, interventions are thus needed to support the operator's information processing under robot unreliability. These will be important considerations for system design so that humans can effectively use the capabilities of future robots.

In summary, SA is an important construct that mediates the relationship between autonomy and performance. We assert that without consideration of other task factors, high levels of robot autonomy will lead to poor SA. Next, we discuss the potential solutions to this problem developed in other systems and how they may apply to human-robot interaction.

3   Potential Solutions

Since there are benefits to automation and operator involvement [10], a solution to the problem of "which agent does what" is needed. The solution should be human-centered and bound to the mission context [13]; it also needs to be applicable to human-robot interaction.

3.1   Selecting a Level of Automation

The degree to which a robot is involved in the task has been called the level of robot autonomy. Autonomy has origins in the Greek word autonomia, which means independence [14]. The United States Department of Defense defines an autonomous weapon system as "a weapon system that, once activated, can select and engage targets without further intervention by a human operator" [15] and an autonomous battlefield entity as one "that does not require the presence of another battlefield entity in order to conduct its own simulation in the battlefield environment" [16].

Extending these definitions to robots, their autonomy is the extent to which the behavior of a robot results from integration of its own sensing [17] and the extent to which it makes decisions not mediated by other entities, in particular, humans [18]. Robot autonomy is generally discussed as a quality integrating the robot's capabilities and authority across a series of tasks [19]. Although autonomy is an intuitive quality of robots, there are few developed quantitative models that describe robot autonomy, and fewer still that specify an operational definition.

Robot behavior can be considered to belong to the broader class of automation. Automation is any "device or system that accomplishes (partially or fully) a goal that was previously, or conceivably could be, carried out (partially or fully) by a human operator" [19]. By considering robot behavior as automation, one can describe the robot's involvement in a particular task as the level of automation.

3.2   *What* Is Automated, Not Only *How Much* Automation

The general case of automation has been widely studied [19]. An early taxonomy applicable to robots was developed by Sheridan and Verplank [20] and expanded upon by Parasuraman, Sheridan, and Wickens [19]. Importantly, their taxonomy expanded upon prior models by including what task is automated in addition to how much automation is used. Under this model, the level of automation for a robot can be described as: (a) the levels of information processing in which the robot participants (i.e., what), and (b) the conditions under which the robot participates in each process (i.e., how much).

The first two levels of this model map cleanly onto Endsley's [21] levels of SA [22]. The first two levels of the model are the two levels of diagnostic aiding [23]. Robots perform the information acquisition stage of diagnostic aiding when they gather relevant information through their sensors. Robots perform the second stage, information analysis, when they integrate multiple pieces of sensor data or when they integrate sensor data with previously stored or externally provided information. Thus, information acquisition is a precursor to information analysis, and a robot that performs both stages operates at a higher level of automation than one that only performs information acquisition. Automation that provides the higher level of diagnostic aiding leads to better decision making [24] and performance [25] in operators while lowering their workload [26].

As discussed, the what of automation has been modeled by Parasuraman et al. [19]. However, much of the applied literature has taken a how much approach to measuring and manipulating the level of automation. Although it is understandably easier to manipulate the presence or functionality of an entire system, research needs to specify the stage as well as the amount of automation. Horrey and Wickens [27] adapted this approach and found that both information acquisition (stage 1 diagnostic aiding) and information analysis (stage 2 diagnostic aiding) lead to better performance than an unaided condition on a battlefield simulation task, with the information analysis aid leading to a greater reduction in errors compared with the information acquisition aid. However, memory probe questions suggested that relevant items were processed more deeply with the lower level of diagnostic aiding [27].

Adding automation of information analysis to automation of information acquisition has been shown to have a greater effect on decisions than automation of information acquisition alone. In a study of anesthesiologists, nurses, and hospital housekeepers, for example, operating room management information was presented as either a command display, which provided recommendations, or a status display, which made decision-relevant information available [24]. When making decisions in subsequent scenarios, participants without either type of aid performed less accurately than random chance. Decision-making, both a cognitive outcome and a performance measure, was improved only by the command display (status displays did not have a significant effect on decision accuracy). Further, incorrect command displays had greater costs associated with them for trust, and users were more likely to follow erroneous recommendations that did not affect safety. From this, Dexter et al. [24] concluded that command displays were preferable, but carry additional costs when their recommendations are incorrect.

Although robot diagnostic aiding may be beneficial to SA, the literature suggests that this relationship is highly sensitive to the presence of unreliability in the robot, and that the two levels of diagnostic aiding may be differentially affected. Performance decreases as the reliability of a diagnostic aid falls [28]. While unreliable information negatively impacts performance, the effect may be stronger for information analysis automation than for information acquisition automation [29] [30].

Sarter and Scroeder [30] found that a diagnostic aid that provided recommendations (information analysis), rather than status information (information acquisition), had a greater performance cost when the automation was not reliable. Rovira and colleagues [29] found that unreliability degraded operator accuracy at three levels of increasingly automated information analysis. Unreliability did not have a significant effect on accuracy in the information acquisition condition, however.

A similar pattern of results was found in an airplane identification task by Crocoll and Coury [31]. In a study manipulating status (acquisition) and recommendation (analysis) information, the group receiving only status information was the least affected by inaccuracy in the automation. In line with this finding, Skitka, Mosier, and Burdick [32] found that introduction of imperfect automation that monitored system state lead to an increase in missed events.

Parasuraman and Wickens provided a cognitive explanation for why lower levels of diagnostic aiding may lead to better SA: "The user must continue to generate the values for the different courses of action. As a result, users may be more aware of the consequences of the choice and of the possibility that the choice may be incorrect because of a faulty automated diagnosis" [33]. This may explain the empirical findings of Horrey and Wickens [27]. When operators perform information analysis, they perform additional processing that may keep them "in the loop". Consequently, the operators' information analysis should lead to better SA during robot unreliability.

Galster, Bolia, and Parasuraman [34] found that performance on a target detection task improved when an information status cue was added, even though this cue was not perfectly reliable. When a higher level of aiding was added in the form of decision suggestion, performance was not improved unless the information status cue was also included. This suggests that under conditions of unreliability, operators may be able to recover from erroneous information provided by information acquisition automation more easily than from information analysis automation. In summary, when reliability is limited, access to lower-level data can help an operator to remain in the loop [35].

4   Discussion and On-Going Research

The out-of-the-loop performance problem affects systems that separate the human from the automation during normal operation but need human intervention if something goes wrong. Future robots will be subject to limited reliability as they deal with the complexity of their operational environments and interact with humans. Because of this, the robot will be dependent upon its human operators for successful performance, just as humans will depend upon the robot to execute mission goals. To ensure that humans do not lose SA, it is imperative that system designers consider how an operator's cognition may be affected by the autonomy and reliability of the robot.

We assert that the levels of information processing at which a robot offers assistance provide an important indicator of how the operator's SA will be affected. In other words, robots that are capable of gathering and integrating information can support higher levels of SA in the human, but only if the robot is able to perform this task reliably. When reliability is very high and unreliability has minimal impact on mission effectiveness, operators are likely to benefit from automation that integrates information and operates independently. Under the more realistic scenario of robot unreliability, it may be more beneficial for the robot to provide less integrated information to support lower levels of SA. Taking this approach could help the human mitigate the effects of robot unreliability.

Because the level of automation is both what and how much, the solution to implementing the right level of automation in a robot system will depend on the information and work needs of the human operator as well as the anticipated reliability of the robot system. It is important to consider these as two separate factors, each contributing to the autonomy of the robot. It may be neither sufficient nor desirable to lower the level of automation. Instead, high levels of automation may be possible by designing the robot to keep the human in the loop through the provision of relevant, low-level information. By strategically selecting what is automated, the robot may be able to perform its assigned functions more independently. In this way, the human will be able to maintain SA while benefiting from a robot capable of independent sensing and behavior.

This is the topic of our current empirical investigation. The purpose of our study is to determine the conditions under which diagnostic aiding contributes to operator SA given limitations of robot reliability, on the one hand, and unaided human task performance, on the other. Diagnostic aids that perform information analysis as well as information acquisition should lead to higher levels of SA than information acquisition alone. However, this relationship has been observed only under cases of perfect robot reliability. We expect the opposite under conditions of imperfect reliability. That is, information acquisition will be more beneficial form of automation than information analysis. By providing lower-level information, the human should remain in the loop. This study will confirm and extend the findings discussed while providing insight into the conditions under which the out-of-the-loop performance problem can be mitigated.

Our ultimate goal is to expand upon the existing understanding of the levels of automation by considering how the type of automation may affect levels of human SA and how that relationship varies as a function of robot unreliability. Ultimately, this may provide a path towards maximizing human SA in human-robot interaction.

Acknowledgements. The research reported in this document/presentation was performed in connection with Contract Number W911NF-10-2-0016 with the U.S. Army Research Laboratory. The views and conclusions contained in this document/presentation are those of the authors and should not be interpreted as presenting the official policies or position, either expressed or implied, of the U.S. Army Research Laboratory, or the U.S. Government unless so designated by other authorized documents. Citation of manufacturer's or trade names does not constitute an official endorsement or approval of the use thereof. The U.S. Government is authorized to reproduce and distribute reprints for Government purposes notwithstanding any copyright notation heron.

References

1. Cosenzo, K., Parasuraman, R., De Visser, E.: Automation Strategies for Facilitating Human Interaction with Military Unmanned Vehicles. In: Barnes, M., Jentsch, F. (eds.) Human-Robot Interactions in Future Military Operations, pp. 103–124. Ashgate, Surrey (2010)
2. Burke, J.L., Murphy, R.R., Coovert, M.D., Riddle, D.L.: Moonlight in Miami: A Field Study of Human-Robot Interaction in the Context of an Urban Search and Rescue Disaster Response Training Exercise. Human-Computer Interaction 19, 85–116 (2004)
3. Norman, D.A.: The 'Problem' with Automation: Inappropriate Feedback and Interaction, not 'Over-Automation'. Philosophical Transactions of the Royal Society of London, Series B, Biological Sciences 327(1241), 585–593 (1990)
4. Wiener, E.L.: Beyond the Sterile Cockpit. Proceedings of the Human Factors and Ergonomics Society Annual Meeting 27(1), 75–90 (1985)
5. Sarter, N.B.: Strong, Silent, and Out-of-the-Loop: Properties of Advanced (Cockpit) Automation and their Impact on Human-Automation Interaction. Unpublished doctoral dissertation, Ohio State University, Columbus, OH (1994)
6. Parasuraman, R., Molloy, R., Singh, I.L.: Performance Consequences of Automation-induced "complacency". International Journal of Aviation Psychology 3(1), 1–23 (1993)
7. Endsley, M.R., Kiris, E.O.: The Out-of-the-Loop Performance Problem and Level of Control in Automation. Human Factors 37, 381–394 (1995)
8. Endsley, M.R.: Direct Measurement of Situation Awareness: Validity and Use of SAGAT. In: Endsley, M.R., Garland, D.J. (eds.) Situation Awareness Analysis and Measurement, pp. 147–173. Lawrence Erlbaum Associates, Mahwah (2000)
9. Wickens, C.D.: Spatial Awareness Biases. Technical report. University of Illinois at Urbana-Champaign, Savoy, Illinois (2002)

10. Endsley, M.R., Kiris, E.O.: The Out-of-the-Loop Performance Problem and Level of Control in Automation. Human Factors 37, 381–394 (1995)
11. Stancliff, S., Dolan, J.M., Trebi-Ollennu, A.: Towards a Predictive Model of Robot Reliability. Technical report, Carnegie Mellon University (2005)
12. Eski, I., Erkaya, S., Savas, S., Yildirim, S.: Fault Detection on Robot Manipulators Using Artificial Neural Networks. Robotics and Computer-Integrated Manufacturing 27, 115–123 (2010)
13. Sierhuis, M., Bradshaw, J.M., Acquisti, A., Van Hoof, R., Jeffers, R., Uszok, A.: Human-Agent Teamwork and Adjustable Autonomy in Practice. In: Seventh International Symposium on Artificial Intelligence, Robotics and Automation in Space, Nara, Japan (2003)
14. U.S. Department of Defense: Autonomy in Weapon Systems. Directive Number 3000.09. Department of Defense, Washington, DC (2012)
15. Autonomy, http://www.etymonline.com/index.php?term=autonomy
16. United States Department of Defense Department of Defense Modeling and Simulation glossary. Directive No. 5000.59-M. United States Department of Defense, Washington, DC (1998)
17. Franklin, S., Graesser, A.: Is It An Agent or Just a Program? A Taxonomy for Autonomous Agents. In: Jennings, N.R., Wooldridge, M.J., Müller, J.P. (eds.) ECAI-WS 1996 and ATAL 1996. LNCS, vol. 1193, pp. 21–35. Springer, Heidelberg (1997)
18. Luck, M., D'Inverno, M.: A Formal Framework for Agency and Autonomy. In: Proceedings of the First International Conference on Multiagent Systems, vol. 1, pp. 254–260. AAAI Press/MIT Press, San Francisco, CA (1995)
19. Parasuraman, R., Sheridan, T.B., Wickens, C.D.: A Model for Types and Levels of Human Interaction with Automation. IEEE Transactions on Systems, Man, and Cybernetics—Part A: Systems and Humans 30(3), 287 (2000)
20. Sheridan, T.B., Verplank, W.: Human and Computer Control of Undersea Teleoperators. Technical report, Man-Machine Systems Laboratory, Cambridge, MA (1978)
21. Endsley, M.R.: Situation Awareness Global Assessment Technique (SAGAT). IEEE 1988 National Aerospace and Electronics Conference 3, 789–795 (1988)
22. Horrey, W.J., Wickens, C.D., Strauss, R., Kirlik, A., Stewart, T.R.: Supporting Situation Asessment through Attention Guidance and Diagnostic Aiding: The Benefits and Costs of Display Enhancement on Judgment Skill. Oxford University Press, Oxford (2006)
23. Wickens, C.D., Dixon, S.R.: The Benefits of Imperfect Diagnostic Automation: A Synthesis of the Literature. Theoretical Issues in Ergonomics Science 8(3), 201–212 (2007)
24. Dexter, F., Willemsen-Dunlap, A., Lee, J.D.: Operating Room Managerial Decision-Making on the Day of Surgery With and Without Computer Recommendations and Status Displays. Anesthesia & Analgesia 105(2), 419–429 (2007)
25. Goodrich, M.A., McLain, T.W., Anderson, J.D., Sun, J., Crandall, J.W.: Managing Autonomy in Robot Teams: Observations from Four Experiments. In: ACM International Conference on Human-Robot Interaction, pp. 25–32 (2007)
26. Manzey, D., Reichenbach, J., Onnasch, L.: Human Performance Consequences of Automated Decision Aids: The Impact of Degree of Automation and System Experience. Journal of Cognitive Engineering and Decision Making 6(1), 57–87 (2012)
27. Horrey, W.J., Wickens, C.D.: Supporting Battlefield Aituation Assessment Through Attention Guidance and Diagnostic Aiding: A Cost-Benefit and Depth of Processing Analysis. Technical report. Aviation Research Lab, Savoy, IL (2001)
28. Madhavan, P., Phillips, R.R.: Effects of Computer Self-Efficacy and System Reliability on User Interaction with Decision Support Systems. Computers in Human Behavior 26(2), 199–204 (2010)

29. Rovira, E., McGarry, K., Parasuraman, R.: Effects of Imperfect Automation on Decision Making in a Simulated Command and Control Task. Proceedings of the Human Factors and Ergonomics Society Annual Meeting 49(1), 76–87 (2007)
30. Sarter, N.B., Schroeder, B.: Supporting Decision Making and Action Selection under Time Pressure and Uncertainty: The Case of In-flight Icing. Human Factors 43(4), 573–583 (2001)
31. Crocoll, W.M., Coury, B.G.: Status or Recommendation: Selecting the Type of Information for Decision Aiding. Proceedings of the Human Factors and Ergonomics Society Annual Meeting 34(19), 1524–1528 (1990)
32. Skitka, L.J., Mosier, K.L., Burdick, M.: Does Automation Bias Decision-Making? International Journal of Human-Computer Studies 51, 991–1006 (1999)
33. Parasuraman, R., Wickens, C.D.: Humans: Still Vital After All These Years of Automation. Human Factors: The Journal of the Human Factors and Ergonomics Society 50(3), 514 (2008)
34. Galster, S.M., Bolia, R.S., Parasuraman, R.: The Application of a Qualitative Model of Human-Interaction with Automation: Effects of Unreliable Automation on Performance. In: Tielemans, W. (chair) The Role of Humans in Intelligent and Automated Systems. North Atlantic Treaty Organization, Warsaw (2002)
35. Johnson, R.C., Saboe, K.N., Prewett, M.S., Coovert, M.D., Elliott, L.R.: Autonomy and automation reliability in human-robot interaction: A qualitative review. Proceedings of the Human Factors and Ergonomics Society Annual Meeting 53, 1398–1402 (2009)

When Stereotypes Meet Robots: The Effect of Gender Stereotypes on People's Acceptance of a Security Robot

Benedict Tiong Chee Tay[1], Taezoon Park[1], Younbo Jung[2],
Yeow Kee Tan[3], and Alvin Hong Yee Wong[3]

[1] Division of Systems and Engineering Management, School of Mechanical & Aerospace
Engineering, Nanyang Technological University, Singapore
[2] Division of Communication Research, Wee Kim Wee School of Communication
and Information, Nanyang Technological University, Singapore
[3] Institute of Infocomm Research, Agency for Science, Technology and Research (A*STAR),
Singapore
bene0006@e.ntu.edu.sg, {tzpark,ybjung}@ntu.edu.sg,
{yktan,hyawong}@i2r.a-star.edu.sg

Abstract. A recent development of social robotics suggests the integration of human characteristics social robots, which allows a more natural interaction between users and these social robots targeting better task performance and greater user acceptance to such social robots. It is interesting to note that the recent successful integration of human characteristics has brought an overarching research paradigm, known as Computers Are Social Actors (CASA) theory which suggests that people react and respond to computers and robots, often similar to the way they treat another social entities. Based on the research paradigm of CASA theory, this study further examined the impact of gender-related role stereotypes on the assessment of a social robot in a particular occupation. Though previous research in social science found that stereotyping makes a significant influence on personal decisions, involving career promotion, development, and supervision, as well as personal competence evaluations, limited insights has been found in HRI research. A between-subject experiment was conducted with 40 participants (gender balanced) at a public university in Singapore to investigate the effect of gender-related role stereotypes on user acceptance of a social robot as a security guard. Largely within our expectations, the results also showed that users perceived the security robot with matching gender-related role stereotypes more useful and acceptable than the mismatched security robot as a second-degree social response.

Keywords: Social Robots, Human—Robot Interactions, User Acceptance, Gender Stereotypes.

1   Introduction

United Nations (UN) projected one out of every five people in the world to be elderly in year 2050 (Population Division UN, 2000). Due to the problems of aging populations and labor shortages in healthcare industry worldwide (World Health Organization,

D. Harris (Ed.): EPCE/HCII 2013, Part I, LNAI 8019, pp. 261–270, 2013.

2006), a rising demand for automation is highly expected. Combining the intention to support independent living for elderly, such demand has pin-pointed the usage of social robots as a potential solution for elderly-care at home. These social robots could provide a wide range of home services involving companion, healthcare, house-chores, and security purposes (Carpenter et al., 2009; Dautenhahn et al., 2005; Groom, 2008; Hudlicka et al., 2009; Ray, Mondada, & Siegwart, 2008). Different from the conventional labor-intensive robots in workplaces such as factory, these social robots at home work closely and frequently interact with other humans and its surrounding environment. As a result, their social skills and abilities become pivotal in their performance indicators. Therefore, recent developments of social robotics have suggested the integration of human characteristics social robots, which allows a more natural interaction between users and social robots targeting better task performance and greater user acceptance to such social robots (Fong, Nourbakhsh, & Dautenhahn, 2003).

Though researchers believe that both robots and users can be mutually benefited from the robots integrating 'human social' characteristics (Breazeal, 2003), it stems also potential pitfalls from their benefits in human—robot interaction (HRI). For example, as suggested by Mori's uncanny valley (Mori, 1970), a user response can be revulsive when they are facing robots that look and act almost, but not perfectly, like a human. Therefore, understanding the motivations by which user comes to accept or reject these 'human social' characteristics on social robots is necessary to avoid a potential user repulsion. Such perceptive of user acceptance requires in-depth understanding of human—robot relationship.

Computer as Social Actors (CASA) theory suggests a fundamental social relationship between human and machines (Nass, Steuer, & Tauber, 1994). Within the research paradigm, researchers found that humans mindlessly provide social responses to machines, including computers, virtual agents (Nass, Moon, & Carney, 1999; Nass, et al., 1994; Reeves & Nass, 1996) and social robots (Lee, Peng, Yan, & Jin, 2006; Tapus, Tapus, & Matarić, 2008), similar to the ways that they treat other humans. The point of departure of this paper is the media equation between humans and social robots as suggested by CASA theory. In other words, people will generally apply social model when they are observing or interacting with autonomous robots (Breazeal, 2003). Based on the media equations, this study aims to understand how human responses towards social robots would be affected by the social stereotypes.

2   Literature Review

2.1   Personifying Robots

Apart from building robots and androids with humanoid appearances, researchers suggested also many other interactive 'human social' characteristics including communicating with high-level dialogue, learning/recognizing models of other agents, establishing/maintaining social relationships, possible learning/developing social competencies, and exhibiting distinctive personality and character, to be integrated on social robots (Fong, et al., 2003). Therefore, in order to maximize payoffs in advocating the most appropriate 'human social' characteristics on robots, researchers tend to apply previous successful examples of human—human interactions in sociology on HRIs.

In sociology, human gender and personality were extensively used to explain a variety of personal difference in abilities, attitudes, and social behaviors (Dunn & Guadagno, 2012; Li & Chignell, 2010; Muscanell & Guadagno, 2012; Streiff et al., 2011; Woods & Hampson, 2010). Likewise, these two traits have also been commonly used to personify robots in social settings (e.g., Edsinger, Reilly, & Breazeal, 2000; Eyssel & Hegel, 2012; Kim, Kwak, & Kim, 2008; Lee, et al., 2006; Powers et al., 2005; Siegel, Breazeal, & Norton, 2009; Tapus, et al., 2008; Woods, Dautenhahn, Kaouri, Boekhorst, & Kheng Lee, 2005). After robots become more and more common to public, they took out certain tasks that were previously carried out by humans. Since then, how robot designers gender their humanoids represents a tangible manifestation of their tacit understanding of femininity in relation to masculinity, and vice versa (Robertson, 2010). The creation of gender is largely based on the vague and unreflexive assumptions about humans' differences in gender.

Since the proposal of CASA theory, researchers are given confidence to rationally apply social concepts in modeling and explaining the nature of human-robot relationship. Some successful applications of social concepts include social role identity and personality attraction rules in explaining user's preference of robot's gender and personality type. Upon successful applications, the genders of robots were found to affect user's preference as well as the task suitability and persuasive power of social robots (Carpenter, et al., 2009; Eyssel & Hegel, 2012; Powers, et al., 2005; Siegel, et al., 2009). Besides, personality of social robots was also found to influence user's preference (Tapus, et al., 2008), perceived enjoyment, intelligence, and social attraction (Lee, et al., 2006) of social robots. Generally, the previous successful examples of gendering robots suggested that people see and understand the traits of robots similar to those on humans (Eyssel & Hegel, 2012; Powers, et al., 2005). Largely, this understanding is drawn from their knowledge in head and can be interpreted in the light of role stereotypes founded in real world.

2.2   Social Role Stereotypes

Asch's (1946) defined stereotype as a gestalt view of personal perception, which emphasized the notion that certain traits, characteristics or prototypes are more 'central' and important in organizing our perceptions of other people than other traits. As early as the age of five, children have already developed an impressive constellation of gender stereotypes. They often use these stereotypes to form impressions of others, help guide their own behavior, direct their attention, and organize their memories (Martin & Ruble, 2004). The process of stereotyping is claimed to be automatic and almost unavoidable (see Bargh, 1999; Devine, 1989). Via the simple and automatic act, a perceiver gains a large amount of 'functionally accurate' information to help them guide their perceptions and responses (Swann, 1984). This information includes the important background characteristics of group members, such as personality traits (Grant & Holmes, 1981; Linville & Jones, 1980), individual beliefs, and values

(Rokeach & Mezei, 1966). Besides, certain identity traits such as age, gender, and race were also consistently found as primary categories in the contents of stereotype labeling (Brewer, 1988; Fiske & Taylor, 1991; Schneider, 2004, p. 96). This information, though not entirely accurate, could guide our responses toward the others (Stangor & Schaller, 2000). It provides an anchor for us to organize our behaviors, including self-protections or communicative patterns, towards others and surrounding. Thus, the information obtained through is essential to our well-being (Fiske & Taylor, 1991).

Particularly, the role stereotypes and its impact in social environment can be specifically highlighted by a substantial amount of occupational stereotypes studies concerning individual differences, such as gender, ethnicity, and personality. General public has particular gender and/or personality stereotypes towards many occupation roles including engineer, police officer, politician, homemaker, and model (Crowther & More, 1972; Garrett, Ein, & Tremaine, 1977; Levy, Kaler, & Schall, 1988; McCauley & Thangavelu, 1991; McLean & Kalin, 1994; Shinar, 1975; Triandis, 1959; Walker, 1958). Since the information of stereotypes help us organize the behaviors and characters of others, it may also impact the nature of social interactions (Bargh, Chen, & Burrows, 1996). Largely found in occupational studies, gender-typing was found influential in personal decisions such as job hiring decisions (Glick, Zion, & Nelson, 1988), personal competence evaluations (Gerdes & Garber, 1983; Goldberg, 1968; Rosen & Jerdee, 1973, 1974a), career promotion, development, and supervision (Rosen & Jerdee, 1974b).

Based on the reappraisal of previous literatures, the purpose of this study is to extend the insights of social role stereotypes from human—human interactions into HRI based on the research paradigm of CASA theory. Though some previous studies have discussed the importance of gender (e.g., Carpenter, et al., 2009; Siegel, et al., 2009) and stereotypical images (e.g., Eyssel & Hegel, 2012; Powers, et al., 2005) in affecting user's perceptions towards social robots, these studies did not fully cover the effect of occupational-gender stereotypes on robot usage in home settings. The objective is to examine the validity and impact of gender stereotypes for social robots in home settings. Based on the insights from studies in occupational field, this study expects social robots that violate their occupational stereotypes will be evaluated less advantageous than those that comply with the stereotypes. Two pre-requisites are required to examine the backlash effect of role stereotypes in HRI. First, it is essential to understand user's role stereotypes of the social robots. The second pre-requisite is the successful recognition of gender manipulation in this study.

3   Methods

3.1   Participants

Forty participants from a public university of Singapore participated in this study (M=22.57, SD=2.25). The participants were randomly recruited from various faculties in the university. Each participant received 10 dollars as a compensation for their time spent for the experiment.

3.2   Experimental Design and Manipulations

The usage of male robots in home-settings is rarely discussed in previous research. Therefore, this study selected a security robot which is a stereotypical male occupation in real world to understand how users change their perceptions in accordance to different genders. This study employs a between-subject experimental design. Twenty participants were randomly assigned to interact with a male security robot and the rest was assigned to the condition of female security robot. The male gendered security was given a typical name of a male, John (Swim, Borgida, Maruyama, & Myers, 1989). Similarly, the female gendered security robot was given a typical name of a female, Joan (Swim, et al., 1989). Besides, the gender was also manipulated with male and female voices provided by the gender ready Windows text-to-speech (TTS) software. On the other hand, the appearance, speech rate, and gesture of the robots remained identical for the male and female gendered robot.

3.3   Experimental Procedures

Participants firstly entered a briefing room and given a brief introduction of the security robot that they are going to meet. After signing on a consent form, they were directed to the experimental room and started their interactions with the security robot. To enhance the flexibility of the experiment, an operator acted as a "wizard" behind the one-way mirror in the wizard-of-oz experimental setting. In the first phase of the interaction, the security robot introduced himself/herself to the participants. On the other hand, in the second phase of experiment, the participants were requested to view a closed-circuit television of four surveillance cameras positioned outside of the experimental room. An alert was triggered when the security robot detected a suspicious intrusion through the CCTV. Followed by the alarm, the security robot asked the participants whether they wanted to zoom in into a specific camera view that detected the intrusion. Later on, the security robot determined the intrusion to be safely resolved after the stranger left the surveillance zone. After the intrusion, the security robot found that the participants left their belongings in the briefing room and left the briefing room unlocked. Therefore, the security robot asked if the participants would like the door to be locked with its tele-remote system. In the last task scenario, the security robot alerted the participants that an electric kettle inside the experimental room was unintentionally left switched on. The participants were given freedom to answer and behave on their own during the experiment. With the different responses from participants, the security answered and behaved differently. After the session, the participants were guided back to the briefing room to answer a set of questionnaire for their post-usage responses.

3.4   Measures

To ensure a successful gender manipulation, participant's perceived gender of the security robot was measured after the experiment. Participants rated their perceived masculinity and femininity of the robots on a 7-point Likert scale.

Similar to any IT implementations, a social robot cannot be well utilized unless it is wholly accepted by its user. Therefore, similar with the study of Ezer, Fisk, and Rogers (2009), this study employed the Technology Acceptance Model (TAM) to study user's acceptance of security robot at home. The measures included perceived usefulness, perceived ease of use, and intention to use (i.e., acceptance). The perceived usefulness was measured with four items, 1) *I think the security robot will be useful in my daily life*, 2) *I think using the security robot will improve the effectiveness of my daily life*, 3) *It would be convenient for me to have the security robot* and 4) *I think the security robot can help me with many things*. The perceived ease of use was measured with three items, 1) *My interaction with the security robot is clear and understandable*, 2) *I find it easy to get the security robot to do what I want it to do*, 3) *I find the security robot to be easy to communicate*. Lastly, participant's intention to use was measured by three items 1) *If given a chance, I plan to use the security robot in near future*, 2) *If given a chance, I think I'll use the security robot in near future*, 3) *If given a chance, I'm certain to use the security robot in near future*. Participants rated their agreement of each statement on a 7-point Likert scale (1=strongly disagree, 7=strongly agree).

3.5   Results

The Cronbach's alpha value for the items measuring perceived usefulness, perceived ease of use, and intention to use, are 0.73, 0.91, and 0.96 respectively. Hence, the scales measuring the three TAM constructs appeared to be reliable (alpha > 0.7). The participants perceived the male gendered robot ($M=5.55$, $SD=0.83$) more masculine than the female gendered robot, $M=3.85$, $SD=1.35$, $p=0.00$, $\eta_p^2=0.38$. On contrary, the female gendered had a higher rating of femininity ($M=4.45$, $SD=1.39$) than the male gendered robot, $M=3.10$, $SD=1.12$, $F(1,38)=11.40$, $p=0.002$, $\eta_p^2=0.23$. Upon the successful recognition of gender, the participants perceived the male gendered security robot ($M=5.79$, $SD=0.82$) more useful than the female gendered security robot, $M=5.09$, $SD=0.90$, $F(1, 38)=6.63$, $p<0.05$, $\eta_p^2=0.15$. Also, participants found the male gendered security robot ($M=5.75$, $SD=0.88$) more acceptable than the female gendered security robot, $M=5.05$, $SD=1.26$, $F(1,38)=4.17$, $p<0.05$, $\eta_p^2=0.10$. However, the difference of perceived ease of use between the male gendered ($M=5.48$, $SD=0.72$) and the female gendered robot was only marginally significant, $M=4.97$, $SD=1.03$, $F(1, 38)=3.40$, $p=0.07$.

4   Discussions

Humans were gifted the ability to recognize and differentiate gender since early childhood. Hence, it is not surprising that the participants are able to recognize the gender of social robots with simple vocal cues in this study.

Upon successful recognition, user's evaluations towards the security robots changes with their perceived gender. Though user's evaluations could happen almost instantaneously, we can see it as a two-step process. First, the stereotype heuristics offer a judgment of task suitability based on the different genders of robots. Secondly, based on the perceptions of task suitability, participants evaluated the security robots. The evaluation of one's task suitability is neither novel in society nor HRI. Similar to the documentation of occupational stereotypes, previous studies in HRI found difference in perceived task suitability for social robots with different genders (Carpenter, et al., 2009; Eyssel & Hegel, 2012; Powers, et al., 2005; Siegel, et al., 2009). The results of this study offer a new insight to further relate these gender stereotypes with user's acceptance of social robots.

Carpenter (2009) found that participants generally preferred female gendered robots working in home settings. The reason may be twofold. First, without specifically illustrated, participants assumed the primary task of home-service robots as doing house chores. As a result, they felt that female gendered robot could be more suitable. The second possibility is that they may simply think that female gendered robot would be more suitable in home-setting environment. The former suggests user's evaluations are task-related; whereas, the latter suggests user's evaluations are environment-related. Largely within our expectations, this study shows that participant's perceived the male gendered security robots working at home to be more useful and acceptable than the female security robots. Hence, the results primarily ruled out the second possibility that user's evaluations of social robots are environment-related. In other words, it suggests gender stereotypes as a key determinant of user's evaluations for social robots working at home.

The contribution of this study has two-fold. Practically, it provides an anchor for robot designers to reduce the large design dimensions by possibly laying their focuses on gender stereotypes. Theoretically, it suggests a transfer of high level social concepts in real world to HRI. *Id est*, it serves as an exploratory study that suggests researchers and robot designers to further explore and apply high level social concepts in HRI. The results are supposed to enhance user's attitudes and acceptance towards this newly developed technology at home.

5   Limitations and Future Work

By and large, gender stereotypes are powerful and influential to user's perceptions and attitudes in HRI. Though the study is ambitious in exploring stereotypes in social robotics, it unavoidably suffers from a couple of limitations. First, though the experiment was conducted with male and female gendered robots, it included only a single role of social robots. Hence, the comparison of gender stereotypes is not exhaustive. One may argue, though unlikely, that the participants preferred a male gendered robot working at home and their preference of robot gender is not task-related. This limitation can be solved by duplicating the experiment with another female-stereotyped role of social robots at home. Secondly, some argue that certain occupations are gender-stereotyped because they call for the traits of male or female (Cejka & Eagly, 1999). Hence, subsequent studies exploring role stereotypes in social robotics may include other stereotyped traits such as personality in their studies.

References

1. Asch, S.E.: Forming impressions of personality. Journal of Abnormal and Social Psychology 41, 258–290 (1946)
2. Bargh, J.A.: The cognitive monster: The case against the controllability of automatic stereotype effects. In: Chaiken, S., Trope, Y. (eds.) Dual Process Theories in Social Psychology, pp. 361–382. Guilford, New York (1999)
3. Bargh, J.A., Chen, M., Burrows, L.: Automaticity of social behavior: Direct effects of trait construct and stereotype activation on action. Journal of Personality and Social Psychology 71(2), 230–244 (1996), doi:10.1037/0022-3514.71.2.230
4. Breazeal, C.: Toward sociable robots. Robotics and Autonomous Systems 42(3-4), 167–175 (2003), doi:10.1016/S0921-8890(02)00373-1
5. Brewer, M.B.: A dual process model of impression formation. In: Srull, T.K., Wyer Jr., R.S. (eds.) A Dual Process Model of Impression Formation, pp. 1–36. Lawrence Erlbaum Associates, Inc., Hillsdale (1988)
6. Carpenter, J., Davis, J., Erwin-Stewart, N., Lee, T., Bransford, J., Vye, N.: Gender Representation and Humanoid Robots Designed for Domestic Use. International Journal of Social Robotics 1(3), 261–265 (2009), doi:10.1007/s12369-009-0016-4
7. Cejka, M.A., Eagly, A.H.: Gender-stereotypic images of occupations correspond to the sex segregation of employment. Personality and Social Psychology Bulletin 25(4), 413–423 (1999), doi:10.1177/0146167299025004002
8. Crowther, B., More, D.M.: Occupational stereotyping on initial impressions. Journal of Vocational Behavior 2(1), 87–94 (1972), doi:10.1016/0001-8791(72)90010-3
9. Dautenhahn, K., Woods, S., Kaouri, C., Walters, M.L., Kheng Lee, K., Werry, I.: What is a robot companion - friend, assistant or butler? In: IEEE/RSJ International Conference on Intelligent Robots and Systems, pp. 1192–1197 (2005)
10. Devine, P.G.: Stereotypes and prejudice: Their automatic and controlled components. Journal of Personality and Social Psychology 56, 680–690 (1989)
11. Dunn, R.A., Guadagno, R.E.: My avatar and me – Gender and personality predictors of avatar-self discrepancy. Computers in Human Behavior 28(1), 97–106 (2012)
12. Edsinger, A., Reilly, U.-M.O., Breazeal, C.: Personality through faces for humanoid robots. Proceedings of the 9th IEEE International Workshop on Paper Presented at the Robot and Human Interactive Communication, RO-MAN 2000 (2000)
13. Eyssel, F., Hegel, F.: (S)he's got the look: gender stereotyping of robots. Journal of Applied Social Psychology 42(9), 2213–2230 (2012)
14. Ezer, N., Fisk, A.D., Rogers, W.A.: Attitudinal and intentional acceptance of domestic robots by younger and older adults. In: Stephanidis, C. (ed.) UAHCI 2009, Part II. LNCS, vol. 5615, pp. 39–48. Springer, Heidelberg (2009)
15. Fiske, S.T., Taylor, S.E.: Social Cognition, 2nd edn. McGraw-Hill, Inc. (1991)
16. Fong, T., Nourbakhsh, I., Dautenhahn, K.: A survey of socially interactive robots. Robotics and Autonomous Systems 42(3-4), 143–166 (2003)
17. Garrett, C.S., Ein, P.L., Tremaine, L.: The development of gender stereotyping of adult occupations in elementary school children. Child Development 48(2), 507–512 (1977)
18. Gerdes, E.P., Garber, D.M.: Sex bias in hiring: Effects of job demands and applicant competence. Sex Roles 9(3), 307–319 (1983), doi:10.1007/bf00289666
19. Glick, P., Zion, C., Nelson, C.: What mediates sex discrimination in hiring decisions? Journal of Personality and Social Psychology 55(2), 178–186 (1988)
20. Goldberg, P.: Are women prejudiced against women? Society 5(5), 28–30 (1968)

21. Grant, P.R., Holmes, J.G.: The integration of implicit personality theory schemas and stereotype images. Social Psychology Quarterly 44(2), 107–115 (1981)
22. Groom, V.: What's the best role for a robot? Cybernetic models of existing and proposed human-robot interaction structures. Paper Presented at the Proceedings of the International Conference on Informatics in Control, Automation, and Robotics (ICINCO) 2008, Funchal, Portugal (2008)
23. Hudlicka, E., Becker-Asano, C., Payr, S., Fischer, K., Ventura, R., Leite, I., von Scheve, C.: Social interaction with robots and agents: Where do we stand, where do we go? 3rd International Conference on Paper Presented at the Affective Computing and Intelligent Interaction and Workshops, ACII 2009, September 10-12 (2009)
24. Kim, H., Kwak, S.S., Kim, M.: Personality design of sociable robots by control of gesture design factors. The 17th IEEE International Symposium on Paper Presented at the Robot and Human Interactive Communication, RO-MAN (2008)
25. Lee, K.M., Peng, W., Yan, C., Jin, S.: Can robots manifest personality?: An empirical test of personality recognition, social Responses, and social Presence in human-robot interaction. Journal of Communication (56), 754–772 (2006)
26. Levy, D.A., Kaler, S.R., Schall, M.: An empirical investigation of role schemata: Occupations and personality characteristics. Psychological Reports 63(1), 3–14 (1988)
27. Li, J., Chignell, M.: Birds of a feather: How personality influences blog writing and reading. International Journal of Human-Computer Studies 68(9), 589–602 (2010)
28. Linville, P.W., Jones, E.E.: Polarized appraisals of out-group members. Journal of Personality and Social Psychology 38(5), 689–703 (1980)
29. Martin, C.L., Ruble, D.: Children's search for gender cues: cognitive perspectives on gender development. Current Directions in Psychological Science (2), 67 (2004)
30. McCauley, C., Thangavelu, K.: Individual differences in sex stereotyping of occupations and personality traits. Social Psychology Quarterly 54(3), 267–279 (1991)
31. McLean, H.M., Kalin, R.: Congruence between self-image and occupational stereotypes in students entering gender-dominated occupations. Canadian Journal of Behavioural Science/Revue Canadienne des Sciences du Comportement 26(1), 142–162 (1994)
32. Mori, M.: The Uncanny Valley. Enery 7, 33–35 (1970)
33. Muscanell, N.L., Guadagno, R.E.: Make new friends or keep the old. Computers in Human Behavior 28(1), 107–112 (2012)
34. Nass, C., Moon, Y., Carney, P.: Are people polite to computers? Responses to computer-based interviewing systems. Journal of Applied Social Psychology 29(5), 1093–1110 (1999)
35. Nass, C., Steuer, J., Tauber, E.R.: Computer are social actors. In: Proceedings of the SIGCHI Conference on Human Factors in Computing Systems: Celebrating Interdependence, pp. 72–78. ACM (1994)
36. Population Division UN. World Population Ageing: 1950-2050 (2000),
    http://www.un.org/esa/population/publications/worldageing195
    02050/pdf/62executivesummary_english.pdf (retrieved February 14, 2013)
37. Powers, A., Kramer, A.D.I., Lim, S., Kuo, J., Sau-lai, L., Kiesler, S.: Eliciting information from people with a gendered humanoid robot. IEEE International Workshop on Paper Presented at the Robot and Human Interactive Communication, ROMAN 2005, August 13-15 (2005)
38. Ray, C., Mondada, F., Siegwart, R.: What do people expect from robots? IEEE/RSJ International Conference on Paper Presented at the Intelligent Robots and Systems, IROS 2008, September 22-26 (2008)

39. Reeves, B., Nass, C.: The media equation: How people treat computers, television and new media like real people and places. Cambridge University Press, New York (1996)
40. Robertson, J.: Gendering humanoid robots: Robo-sexism in Japan. Body & Society 16(2), 1–36 (2010), doi:10.1177/1357034x10364767
41. Rokeach, M., Mezei, L.: Race and shared belief as factors in social choice. Science 151(3707), 167–172 (1966)
42. Rosen, B., Jerdee, T.H.: The influence of sex-role stereotypes on evaluations of male and female supervisory behavior. Journal of Applied Psychology 57(1), 44–48 (1973)
43. Rosen, B., Jerdee, T.H.: Effects of applicant's sex and difficulty of job on evaluations of candidates for managerial positions. Journal of Applied Psychology 59(4), 511–512 (1974a), doi:10.1037/h0037323
44. Rosen, B., Jerdee, T.H.: Influence of sex role stereotypes on personnel decisions. Journal of Applied Psychology 59(1), 9–14 (1974b), doi:10.1037/h0035834
45. Schneider, D.J.: The Psychology of Stereotyping. The Guilford Press, New York (2004)
46. Shinar, E.H.: Sexual stereotypes of occupations. Journal of Vocational Behavior 7(1), 99–111 (1975), doi:10.1016/0001-8791(75)90037-8
47. Siegel, M., Breazeal, C., Norton, M.I.: Persuasive Robotics: The influence of robot gender on human behavior. IEEE/RSJ International Conference on Paper Presented at the Intelligent Robots and Systems, IROS 2009, October 10-15 (2009)
48. Stangor, C., Schaller, M.: Stereotypes as Individual and Collective Representations. In: Stangor, C. (ed.) Stereotypes and Prejudice: Essential Readings, pp. 64–85. Psychology Press, Philadelphia (2000)
49. Streiff, S., Tschan, F., Hunziker, S., Buehlmann, C., Semmer, N.K., Hunziker, P., Marsch, S.: Leadership in medical emergencies depends on gender and personality. Simulation in Healthcare 6(2), 78 (2011)
50. Swann, W.B.: Quest for accuracy in person perception: A matter of pragmatics. Psychological Review 91(4), 457–477 (1984), doi:10.1037/0033-295x.91.4.457
51. Swim, J., Borgida, E., Maruyama, G., Myers, D.G.: Joan McKay versus John McKay. Psychological Bulletin 105(3), 409–429 (1989)
52. Tapus, A., Tapus, C., Matarić, M.J.: User-robot personality matching and assistive robot behavior adaptation for post-stroke rehabilitation therapy. Intelligent Service Robotics 1(2), 169–183 (2008)
53. Triandis, H.C.: Differential perception of certain jobs and people by managers, clerks, and workers in industry. Journal of Applied Psychology 43(4), 221–225 (1959)
54. Walker, K.F.: A study of occupational stereotypes. Journal of Applied Psychology 42(2), 122–124 (1958), doi:10.1037/h0045472
55. Woods, S., Dautenhahn, K., Kaouri, C., Boekhorst, R., Kheng Lee, K.: Is this robot like me? Links between human and robot personality traits. 2005 5th IEEE-RAS International Conference on Paper Presented at the Humanoid Robots, December 5-5 (2005)
56. Woods, S.A., Hampson, S.E.: Predicting adult occupational environments from gender and childhood personality traits. Journal of Applied Psychology 95(6), 1045–1057 (2010)
57. World Health Organization, The World Health Report 2006: Working together for health (2006)

Part IV

Productivity, Creativity, Learning and Collaboration

Effects of Individual Differences on Human-Agent Teaming for Multi-robot Control

Jessie Y.C. Chen[1], Stephanie A. Quinn[2], Julia L. Wright[1], and Michael J. Barnes[1]

[1] U.S. Army Research Laboratory – Human Research & Engineering Directorate
Bldg 459, Aberdeen Proving Ground, MD 21005, USA
{jessie.chen,julia.l.wright2,michael.j.barnes}@us.army.mil
[2] University of Central Florida – Institute for Simulation & Training
Orlando, FL 32816, USA
squinn@ist.ucf.edu

Abstract. In the current experiment, we simulated a military multitasking environment and evaluated the effects of RoboLeader on the performance of human operators (i.e., vehicle commanders) who had the responsibility of supervising the plans/routes for a convoy of three vehicles while maintaining proper 360° local security around their own vehicle. We evaluated whether -- and to what extent -- operator individual differences (spatial ability, attentional control, and video gaming experience) impacted the operator's performance. In two out of three mission scenarios, the participants had access to the assistance of an intelligent agent, RoboLeader. Results showed that RoboLeader's level of autonomy had a significant impact on participants' concurrent target detection task performance and perceived workload. Those participants who played action video games frequently had significant better situation awareness of the mission environment. Those participants with lower spatial ability had increasingly better situation awareness as RoboLeader's level of autonomy increased; however, those with higher spatial ability did not exhibit the same trend.

Keywords: human-robot interaction, intelligent agent, military, individual differences, multitasking.

1 Introduction

Robots are increasingly utilized in military operations, and the types of tasks they are being used for are evolving in complexity [1][2]. In the future battlefield, Soldiers may be given multiple tasks to perform concurrently, such as navigating a robot while conducting surveillance, maintaining local security and situation awareness (SA), and communicating with fellow team members. In recent years, several research efforts have developed intelligent software agents that can assist human operators in managing multiple robots in military tasking environments [3]-[5]. Indeed, a recent report on the Role of Autonomy in U.S. Department of Defense Systems recommended that "increased autonomy can enable humans to delegate those tasks that are more effectively done by computer, including synchronizing activities between multiple

D. Harris (Ed.): EPCE/HCII 2013, Part I, LNAI 8019, pp. 273–280, 2013.
© Springer-Verlag Berlin Heidelberg 2013

unmanned systems, software agents and warfighters—thus freeing humans to focus on more complex decision making" (p. 1) [6]. Such a robotic surrogate agent, Robo-Leader, was developed under the U.S. Army Research Laboratory's Director's Research Initiative Program to support mixed-initiative decision making [3][7][8]. In typical mission situations, RoboLeader would recommend route revisions when encountering environmental events that require robots to be rerouted. The human operators, in turn, can accept the plan revisions or modify them as appropriate.

In the current experiment, we simulated a multitasking environment and evaluated the effects of RoboLeader on the performance of human operators (i.e., vehicle commanders) who had the responsibility of supervising the plans/routes for a convoy of three vehicles (their own manned ground vehicle [MGV], an unmanned aerial system [UAS], and an unmanned ground vehicle [UGV]) while maintaining proper 360° local security around their MGV (Fig. 1). The U.S. Army is currently developing 360° indirect-vision display capabilities to enable vehicle commanders to see their immediate environment via streaming video sent from cameras mounted outside the MGV. In the current experiment, the three simulated vehicles traveled in an urban environment as a convoy and the participants had to decide whether and how the routes for the convoy had to change based on environmental events (e.g., threats present, environmental hazards/obstacles) and/or intelligence reports. The paradigm followed Chen and Barnes [3][7] and there were three levels of autonomy (LOAs): the participants either performed the plan revisions manually (*Manual* condition) or with the assistance from RoboLeader (*Semi-Auto* condition: maintaining vehicle distance/separation only; *Full Auto* condition: vehicle separation + route planning). Concurrently, the participants monitored an indirect-vision display where the environment surrounding the MGV was visible. They were required to report any threats present in their immediate environment (i.e., target detection task).

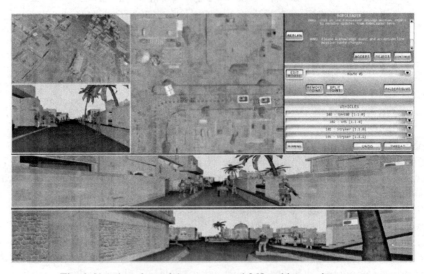

Fig. 1. User interface of the convoy and 360 tasking environment

In the current study, we also sought to evaluate whether -- and to what extent -- operator individual differences in spatial ability, attentional control, and video gaming experience might impact the operator's performance. Significant individual differences in cognitive task performance and interaction with automation have been repeatedly documented in literature [3][9]-[11]. Szalma [12] suggests that individual differences should be considered more frequently in user interface designs and training intervention developments. In fact, based on empirical data, it has been observed that effects due to individual differences in cognitive abilities can sometimes be even greater than effects due to interface design manipulations [13]. Manzey et al. [14] observed significant individual differences in susceptibility to automation bias effects in the multitasking environments they simulated, although the authors did not identify what individual differences factors contributed to the observed behaviors. Previous research has shown that some individuals show more performance decrements than others when multitasking and these decrements may be related to their poorer abilities to control and allocate attention [15]-[17]. These results suggest that individual differences in attentional control seem to play a critical role in determining an operator's overall multitasking performance. Research also shows that individual differences in spatial ability and gaming experience play important roles in determining operators' SA in multi-robot tasking environments [3][7].

2 Method

2.1 Participants

Thirty individuals (21 males and 9 females, mean age 25 yrs) from the Orlando, FL area participated in the study. They were compensated $15/hr for their time.

2.2 Apparatus

A modified version of the Mixed Initiative Experimental (MIX) Testbed was used as the simulator for this experiment [18]. The RoboLeader algorithm was implemented on the MIX testbed and it had the capability of collecting information from subordinate robots with limited autonomy (e.g., collision avoidance and self-guidance to reach target locations), making tactical decisions and coordinating the robots by issuing commands and waypoints etc. [8]. The MGV 360° indirect-vision display emulated the capability currently developed by the U.S. Army Technology Objective (ATO) Improved Mobility and Operational Performance through Autonomous Technologies (IMOPAT). The capabilities of the UGV and the small UAS as well as the behavior of the convoy (e.g., the formation of and the distances among the three vehicles) were simulated based on the concept of the ATO Safe Unmanned Operations in Urban Operations (SOURCE).

A demographics questionnaire was administered at the beginning of the training session. An Ishihara Color Vision Test (with 9 test plates) was administered via PowerPoint presentation. Since the RoboLeader OCU employed several colors to display the plans for the robots, normal color vision was required to effectively interact with the system. A questionnaire on Attentional Control [19] was used to evaluate participants' perceived attentional control. The Attentional Control survey consists of 21 items and measures attention focus and shifting. The scale has been shown to have good internal reliability (α = .88). The Cube Comparison Test [20] and the Spatial Orientation Test [21] were used to assess participants' spatial ability. The Cube Comparison Test requires participants to compare, in 3-minutes, 21 pairs of 6-sided cubes and determine if the rotated cubes are the same or different. The Spatial Orientation Test, modeled after the cardinal direction test developed by Gugerty and his colleagues [21], is a computerized test consisting of a brief training segment and 32 test questions. Both accuracy and response time were automatically captured by the program. Participants' perceived workload was evaluated with the computerized version of the NASA-TLX questionnaire, which used a pairwise comparison weighting procedure [22].

2.3   Procedure

Before the training session, the participants completed the preliminary tests (color vision and spatial) and surveys (demographic and perceived attentional control). Training, lasting about one hour, was self-paced and was delivered by PowerPoint® slides showing the elements of the operator control unit (OCU), steps for completing various tasks, several mini-exercises for practicing the steps, and exercises for performing the experimental tasks. The participants had to demonstrate that they could recall all the steps for performing the tasks without any help. The experimental session immediately followed the training session and consisted of three scenarios, each lasting approximately 30 minutes. During the scenarios, participants tried to get a convoy of three vehicles (his/her own MGV, a small UAS, and a UGV) from point A to point B. The participants were instructed to maintain certain distances among the three vehicles. In each scenario, there were initial waypoint plans for each vehicle when the scenario started, and the participants' task was to modify the plans based on environmental/intel "events" (described later) or based on hostile targets detected by the participants themselves. Simultaneously, the participants had to maintain 360° local security surrounding his/her own MGV by monitoring the 360° indirect-vision display and try to detect targets in the immediate environments. Once a hostile target was detected, the participants "lazed" the target by clicking on the target using the mouse. The "lazed" insurgent would then be displayed on the map. There were civilians and friendly dismounted soldiers in the simulated environment to increase the visual noise present in the target detection tasks. The order of scenarios was counterbalanced across participants.

During the scenarios, there were several events (e.g., intelligence that the human operator received from the intel network or environmental hazards such as fire or road blockages) that would require revisions to the plans for the manned and unmanned vehicles. Once an event transpired, the participants must notice and acknowledge that the event had occurred. In the Full-Auto condition, RoboLeader would recommend plan revisions for the events (by presenting the new waypoints on the map), which the operator could accept, or reject and modify as deemed necessary. In the Semi-Auto condition, the participants modified the waypoints for the lead vehicle (the UAS) when the convoy's route needed to be changed. In the Manual condition, the operator made the revisions manually. In the Semi-Auto and Full-Auto conditions, the distance separations among the vehicles was maintained automatically based on the vehicles' own leader-follower algorithms.

Each scenario contained five SA queries, which were triggered based on time progression (e.g., 3 minutes into the scenario). The SA queries included questions such as "Use the provided paper to identify which areas have encountered the most Insurgents" etc. When an SA query was triggered, the OCU screen went blank, the simulation paused, and the SA query was displayed on the screen. Participants wrote their response to the query on an answer sheet. After participants responded to the SA query, it was removed from the OCU screen and the simulation resumed. There was a two-minute break between the experimental scenarios. Participants assessed their workload using the NASA-TLX immediately after each experimental scenario.

3   Results

A mixed-model ANOVA (within-subject: LOA; between-subject: participants' spatial ability [SpA]) on Target Detection revealed a significant effect of LOA, $F(2, 27) = 12$, $p < .0005$, $\eta 2p = .47$. Post-hoc (LSD) comparisons show a significant increase in Target Detection scores between both Manual and Semi-Auto conditions and Manual and Full Auto conditions (p's $< .05$). There was no significant difference between Semi-Auto and Full Auto conditions.

A mixed-model ANOVA on Situation Awareness (SA) revealed a significant interaction of LOA and SpA, $F(2, 27) = 3.6$, $p = .04$, $\eta 2p = .21$. Participants with lower SpA had increasingly higher SA as the LOA increased; however, those with higher SpA exhibited the opposite trend. Participants who played action games frequently (daily or weekly) had significantly better SA than those who did not, $F(1, 28) = 4.5$, $p = .04$, $\eta 2p = .14$ (Figure 2).

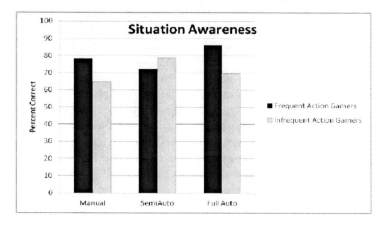

Fig. 2. Effects of gaming experience on situation awareness

A mixed-model ANOVA revealed that there was a significant main effect of LOA on Perceived Workload (NASA-TLX), $F(2, 27) = 24.8$, $p < .0005$, $\eta 2p = .65$. Post-hoc (LSD) comparisons showed that the differences between each pair were all significant (p's $< .05$), with Manual being the highest and RoboLeader being the lowest. All three major dependent measures (target detection, SA, and workload) are graphically summarized in Figure 3.

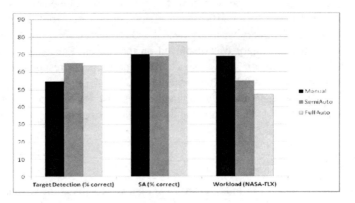

Fig. 3. Major dependent measures

4   Conclusions

In the current experiment, we simulated a military multitasking environment and evaluated the effects of RoboLeader on the performance of human operators (i.e., vehicle commanders) who had the responsibility of supervising the plans/routes for a convoy of three vehicles (their own MGV, a UAS, and a UGV) while maintaining proper 360° local security around their MGV. Results showed that RoboLeader (either semi- or full-auto) enhanced participants' concurrent target detection task performance while reducing their perceived workload (Figure 3). Those participants with lower spatial ability had increasingly better situation awareness as RoboLeader's level of autonomy increased; however, those with higher spatial ability did not exhibit the same trend. Frequent action gamers had significantly better SA of the mission environment than those who did not play action games frequently. This result is consistent with previous findings [3][7][23], suggesting that video game play is associated with greater visual short-term memory and faster information processing, which in turn, may have contributed to game playing participants' superior SA in the current study. These results also support the conclusion of a U.S. Air Force study [24] based on interviews of UAV pilots that gamers' superior SA may be able to translate into superior robotics management performance. These results may have important implications for system design and personnel selection for future military programs [24]-[26]. Future research can investigate training interventions (e.g. attention management) and/or user interface designs (e.g. multimodal cueing displays) to enhance robot operator performance in challenging tasking environments [1][27][28]. Future efforts will also examine the feasibility of implementing RoboLeader-like agent in other military multi-robot missions such as building-mapping and clearing and swarm control.

Acknowledgements. This research was supported by U.S. Army SOURCE Army Technology Objective. The authors wish to thank Daniel Barber, David Adams, and Desmond Solomon for their contribution to this project.

References

1. Chen, J.Y.C., Barnes, M.J., Harper-Sciarini, M.: Supervisory Control of Multiple Robots: Human Performance Issues and User Interface Design. IEEE Trans. Sys., Man, & Cybern.–Part C: App. & Rev. 41, 435–454 (2011)
2. Cummings, M.L., Bruni, S., Mitchell, P.: Human Supervisory Control Challenges in Network-Centric Operations. Rev. Human Factors & Ergon. 6, 34–78 (2010)
3. Chen, J.Y.C., Barnes, M.J.: Supervisory Control of Multiple Robots in Dynamic Tasking Environments. Ergonomics 55, 1043–1058 (2012)
4. Fern, L., Shively, R.J.: A Comparison of Varying Levels of Automation on the Supervisory Control of Multiple UASs. In: Proc. AUVSI's Unmanned Systems North America. AUVSI, Washington, DC (2009)
5. Miller, C., Parasuraman, R.: Designing for Flexible Interaction between Humans and Automation: Delegation Interfaces for Supervisory Control. Human Factors 49, 57–75 (2007)
6. Defense Science Board: The Role of Autonomy in DoD Systems. Undersecretary of Defense, Washington DC (2012)
7. Chen, J.Y.C., Barnes, M.J.: Supervisory Control of Multiple Robots: Effects of Imperfect Automation and Individual Differences. Human Factors 54, 157–174 (2012)
8. Snyder, M., Qu, Z., Chen, J.: Barnes, M.: RoboLeader for Reconnaissance by a Team of Robotic Vehicles. In: Proc. Int. Symp. Collab. Tech. & Sys., pp. 522–530. IEEE, New York (2010)
9. Parasuraman, R., Jiang, Y.: Individual Differences in Cognition, Affect, and Performance: Behavioral Neuroimaging, and Molecular Genetic Approaches. NeuroImage 59, 70–82 (2012)
10. Shaw, T.H., et al.: Individual Differences in Vigilance: Personality, Ability and States of Stress. J. Research in Personality 44, 297–308 (2010)
11. Szalma, J.L., Taylor, G.: Individual Differences in Response to Automation: The Five Factor Model of Personality. J. Exp. Psychology: Applied 17, 71–96 (2011)
12. Szalma, J.L.: Individual Differences in Human-Technology Interaction: Incorporating Variation in Human Characteristics into Human Factors and Ergonomics Research and Design. Theoretical Issues in Ergonomics Science 10, 381–397 (2009)
13. Rodes, W., Gugerty, L.: Effects of Electronic Map Displays and Individual Differences in Ability on Navigation Performance. Human Factors 54, 589–599 (2012)
14. Manzey, D., Reichenbach, J., Onnasch, L.: Human Performance Consequences of Automated Decision Aids: The Impact of Degree of Automation and System Experience. J. Cogn. Eng. & Decision Making 6, 57–87 (2012)
15. Feldman Barrett, L., Tugade, M., Engle, R.: Individual Differences in Working Memory Capacity and Dual-Process Theories of the Mind. Psych. Bulletin 130, 553–573 (2004)

16. Rubinstein, J., Meyer, D., Evans, J.: Executive Control of Cognitive Processes in Task Switching. J. Exp. Psychology: Human Perception and Performance 27, 763–797 (2001)
17. Schumacher, E.H., et al.: Virtually Perfect Time Sharing in Dual-Task Performance: Uncorking the Central Cognitive Bottleneck. Psychological Science 12, 101–108 (2001)
18. Barber, D., Davis, L., Nicholson, D., Finkelstein, N., Chen, J.: The Mixed Initiative Experimental (MIX) Testbed for Human Robot Interactions with Varied Levels of Automation. In: Proc. Army Sci. Conf. US Army, Washington, DC (2008)
19. Derryberry, D., Reed, M.: Anxiety-Related Attentional Biases and Their Regulation by Attentional Control. J. Abnormal Psychology 111, 225–236 (2002)
20. Gugerty, L., Brooks, J.: Reference-Frame Misalignment and Cardinal Direction Judgments: Group Differences and Strategies. J. Exp. Psych.: Applied 10, 75–88 (2004)
21. Ekstrom, R.B., French, J.W., Harman, H.H.: Kit of Factor Referenced Cognitive Tests. Educational Testing Service, Princeton, NJ (1976)
22. Hart, S., Staveland, L.: Development of NASA TLX (Task Load Index): Results of Empirical and Theoretical Research. In: Hancock, P., Meshkati, N. (eds.) Human Mental Workload, pp. 139–183. Elsevier, Amsterdam (1988)
23. Green, C.S., Bavelier, D.: Enumeration versus Multiple Object Tracking: The Case of Action Video Game Players. Cognition 101, 217–245 (2006)
24. Triplett, J.: The Effects of Commercial Video Game Playing: A Comparison of Skills and Abilities for the Predator UAV. Unpublished thesis. US Air Force – Air University (2008)
25. Chappelle, W.L., McMillan, K.K., Novy, P.L., McDonald, K.: Psychological Profile of USAF Unmanned Aerial Systems Predator & Reaper Pilots. Aviation, Space, and Environmental Medicine 81, 339 (2010)
26. McKinley, A., McIntire, L., Funke, M.: Operator Selection for Unmanned Aerial Vehicles: A Comparison of Video Game Players and Manned Aircraft Pilots. Aviation, Space, and Environmental Medicine 81, 336 (2010)
27. Chen, J.Y.C., Haas, E.C., Barnes, M.J.: Human Performance Issues and User Interface Design for Teleoperated Robots. IEEE Transactions on Systems, Man, and Cybernetics–Part C: Applications and Reviews 37, 1231–1245 (2007)
28. Dux, P.E., et al.: Training Improves Multitasking Performance by Increasing the Speed of Information Processing in Human Prefrontal Cortex. Neuron 63, 127–138 (2009)

A Collaborative Multi-source Intelligence Working Environment: A Systems Approach

Peter Eachus[1], Ben Short[1], Alex W. Stedmon[2], Jennie Brown[2],
Margaret Wilson[3], and Lucy Lemanski[3]

[1] University of Salford, Frederick Road, Salford M6 6PU, UK
{p.eachus,b.short}@salford.ac.uk
[2] University of Nottingham, University Park, Nottingham, NG7 2RD, UK
a.stedmon@shu.ac.uk, j.brown@nottingham.ac.uk
[3] University of Liverpool, Foundation Building, Brownlow Hill, Liverpool, L69 7ZX, UK
{margaret.wilson,l.lemansky}@liverpool.ac.uk

Abstract. This research applies a systems approach to aid the understanding of collaborative working during intelligence analysis using a dedicated (Wiki) environment. The extent to which social interaction, and problem solving was facilitated by the use of the wiki, was investigated using an intelligence problem derived from the Vast 2010 challenge. This challenge requires "intelligence analysts" to work with a number of different intelligence sources in order to predict a possible terrorist attack. The study compared three types of collaborative working, face-to-face without a wiki, face-to-face with a wiki, and use of a wiki without face-to-face contact. The findings revealed that in terms of task performance the use of the wiki without face-to-face contact performed best and the wiki group with face-to-face contact performed worst. Measures of interpersonal and psychological satisfaction were highest in the face-to-face group not using a wiki and least in the face-to-face group using a wiki. Overall it was concluded that the use of wikis in collaborative working is best for task completion whereas face-to-face collaborative working without a wiki is best for interpersonal and psychological satisfaction.

Keywords: Collaborative working, intelligence analysis, Wiki.

1 Introduction

Recent intelligence failures, and subsequent reports, have emphasised the need for better ways to organise, manage, and support intelligence analysis (Butler, 2004; 9/11 Commission Report, 2004; Posner, 2005; Murphy, 2006;). A common theme throughout these reports is the need for greater collaboration between the agencies and individuals involved. In the USA projects such as A Space and Intellipedia have been developed to promote and support such collaboration. However, the way in which collaborative work is organised can vary considerably and we need more research to inform decisions on the nature of complex collaborations. For example Convertino et al (2008) investigated the effects of group composition in computer

D. Harris (Ed.): EPCE/HCII 2013, Part I, LNAI 8019, pp. 281–289, 2013.
© Springer-Verlag Berlin Heidelberg 2013

supported collaborative intelligence analysis and found that individuals working with like-minded individuals tended to show and retain greater bias in their analytical judgements than did individuals working in more heterogeneous groups. Neville (2009) has considered the diagnostic errors that can accrue from co-operative working during a friendly fire incident in Iraq. His study illustrated how processes of cooperation can be vulnerable and ultimately fail, particularly when multiple participants are physically distributed and interaction is mediated by communication technologies. In the context of military intelligence analysis Jones et al (1998) have described the use of 'CoRAVEN', an intelligent collaborative multimedia system to support intelligence analysts a forerunner to the more sophisticated Wikis that are now widely available.

The use of collaborative tools such as wikis has also been investigated in the context of intelligence analysis. In this context a wiki is defined as software that allows users to create and edit the content of a document usually via a web browser.Wheaton (2008) studied this extensively both in classroom and real world environments. The findings revealed that Wikis can help to facilitate collaboration to a high degree and that the final intelligence product is often much better than that produced by traditional methods (e.g. face-to-face collaboration).

1.1   A Systems Approach to Collaborative Working

The benefits of collaborative working within the intelligence community appear to be well established (Wheaton, 2008). What is less clear is exactly how collaborative working necessarily leads to a superior intelligence product. One way to examine this problem, and clarify the cognitive and psychosocial factors involved, is to use a systems approach.

Collaborative knowledge building, especially where Wikis or other collaborative software is used can be understood in terms of a system with three facets. The first to consider is the cognitive processes of the individuals involved in the collaborative working. The second aspect of this system is the psychosocial processes that influence group functioning and the third is the group organisation itself. These three aspects of this system will interact and it is this interaction that will lead to the desired collaborative learning. Using this systems approach it is possible to examine in detail how different factors interact to produce new emergent knowledge and this will lead to a greater understanding of collaborative working and its impact on intelligence analysis.

1.2   Accommodation and Assimilation

This systems approach is based on the work of Cress and Kimmerle (2008)who also attempted to describe the learning process itself in terms of the Piagetian concepts of assimilation and accommodation (Piaget, 1970). Although usually considered in the context of individual learning the concepts of assimilation and accommodation can be usefully applied in the understanding of collaborative learning. Working collaboratively involves more than simply sharing information. For example if I give you a recipe and you give me details of a good garage we have exchanged information but no new knowledge has been produced. In collaborative working Cress and Kimmerle (2008) suggest four different types of learning:

- internal assimilation (quantitative individual learning)
- internal accommodation (qualitative individual learning)
- external assimilation (quantitative collaborative knowledge building)
- external accommodation (qualitative collaborative knowledge building).

Together these four types of learning are responsible for the new emergent knowledge that should be a feature of collaborative working.

Where individual knowledge differs from the Wiki (collaborative) knowledge this produces cognitive conflict which people are motivated to reduce, and which Piaget referred to as equilibration (Piaget 1977a). The need for equilibration can be satisfied by a process of internal or external assimilation and accommodation.

Assimilation and accommodation do not only occur internally within the individual, but also externally within the wiki itself. Majchrzak et al (2006) distinguishes between people who simply contribute to a wiki without reference to previous contributions, these are called 'adders'. This type of contribution is assimilated by the wiki which is extended but fundamentally remains the same, as no data reorganisation takes place. The other type of wiki contributor is the 'synthesizer'. These are people who not only add to the existing information, but also reorganise information in a new way by reference to what already exists.

The process of adding information to a Wiki is akin to assimilation and is very common whereas that of accommodation is less so. Accommodation within the Wiki will be shown through the integration of ideas that have already been contributed to produce new ideas. These will show up in the Wiki in terms of the reorganisation of pages or even the rewriting of whole sections.

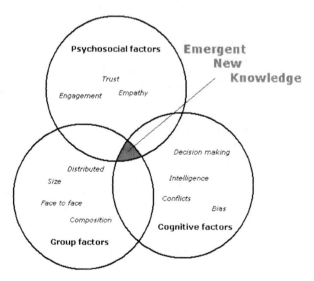

Fig. 1. The interaction of the three facets of the system leads to emergent knowledge

Using this systems approach it is possible to examine in detail how these factors interact to produce new emergent knowledge and this will lead to a greater understanding of collaborative working and its impact on intelligence analysis.

2   Methodology

Design. The aim of this research was to use a systems approach to aid the understanding of collaborative working during intelligence analysis using 'WorkSpace' a dedicated wiki environment . A mixed methodology was used to examine how group functioning influences team sensemaking (Klein et al, 2010) during intelligence analysis. Specifically the study looked at how shared information is assimilated and accommodated by the group to create new knowledge during the analytic process.

WorkSpace has been developed based on the work of Clark (2009) and Heuer and Pherson (2010) and is designed to foster a collaborative environment as well as help analysts use a more structured approach in their work. Collaborative working is supported in WorkSpace via a link that uses IntelliWiki as a platform on which groups of analysts can work together on a given problem. The inputs, (i.e. edits from all collaborating analysts), are recorded by IntelliWiki thus facilitating later analysis when the task is complete.

The task used in this research was derived from the open source IEEE 2010 VAST Challenge, Mini Challenge 1 (http://hcil.cs.umd.edu/localphp/hcil/vast10/index.php) and involved participants analysing multi-source intelligence data, including email and message board intercepts, news reports, web site and blog postings, transcripts from telephone intercepts, and government intelligence reports.

The study compared three different groups working on the same task:

- Group 1: used 'Wiki' + face-to-face contact; referred to as Combo Group, (University of Salford).
- Group 2: used only 'Wiki', without face-to-face contact; referred to as Wiki Group, (University of Nottingham).
- Group 3: used only face-to-face interaction with no access to WorkSpace or any other software apart from a word processor; referred to as F2F Group, (University of Liverpool).

Resource limitations meant that for this initial study we could only test a small number of working groups. However this approach would produce a great deal of valuable quantitative and qualitative data, which would allow the first detailed analysis of the way groups generate collaborative knowledge in a quasi-real world task to be conducted.

It was hypothesised that there would be a relationship between the type of group and the output from the group in terms of both task completion, individual contribution and levels of satisfaction with the task. The following hypotheses were proposed:

- Group 1 (Combo) would perform at the highest level, there would be more evidence of emergent knowledge and this would be produced more quickly and thus contribute to more effective task completion.

- Group 2 (Wiki) would have similar levels of task completion as Combo but would have the lowest levels of interpersonal and psychological satisfaction.
- Group 3 (F2F) would be the worst performers in terms of task completion but would exhibit higher levels of interpersonal and psychological satisfaction than the other two groups.

Participants. Three groups of six 'analysts',(three male, three female), were used at each University location. As this study investigated fundamental issues of collaborative working, the 'analysts' were university students, rather than professional intelligence analysts. The rationale for this was that university students would all be equally 'naïve' in dealing with intelligence problems and therefore this would minimize group problems that might have occurred due to differences in levels of expertise or experience if professional analysts were used.

Materials. Participants were provided with access to a multi-source intelligence database from where they could download the materials for analysis. How and when they chose to access this database was for the group to determine between themselves.

Two questionnaires were developed. The first assessed how well the participants knew each other and their level of computer and Wiki literacy.

The second assessed levels of interpersonal and psychological satisfaction using a modified version of the Survey Instrument (for Virtual Teams), developed to assess relational links in virtual teams by Warkentin, Sayeed and Hightower (1997).

Procedure. The participants were recruited using the procedures determined by the individual University ethics committees. The three groups of participants were asked to attend a briefing session where details of the task, and their involvement were outlined. For Groups 1 (Combo) and 2 (wiki), they were introduced to 'WorkSpace' and the 'IntelliWiki' where they each were to record details of their analysis. The task was explained and they were informed that they had two weeks to complete the task. The rationale for the two week timescale was that this better reflected the way in which wiki construction occurs, (i.e. over a relatively prolonged period). Participants in the Combo and Wiki groups were informed that all work had to be completed online, working either synchronously or asynchronously, using the 'WorkSpace' facility provided. Participants in the Wiki group were also informed that they should not discuss the problem with other members of the group when they were not online. Furthermore, all the participants were told that they should not discuss the task, online or offline, with anyone who was not a member of their group. Group 3 (F2F) met face-to-face according to a timetable they drew up to meet the requirements of a ten hour involvement with the task. All discussions were minuted and recorded using a word processor.

All participants were asked to sign a consent form and also agreed that if they were found to have broken any of the interaction rules they would be required to withdraw from the study and forfeit their payment. This was done to stop participants using the Internet or any other information sources to assist with their analysis.

The Task. The three groups all completed the same task derived from the IEEE 2010 VAST Challenge, Mini Challenge 1 (http://hcil.cs.umd.edu/localphp/hcil/vast10/index.php). Working collaboratively with other members of their group, they used the resources provided to produce a summary of activities that had happened in each country, with respect to the illegal arms dealing. Based on a synthesis of the information from the different report types and sources they were also required to:

- state the situation in each country at the end of the period (i.e. at the end of the information they had been given) with respect to the terrorist act being planned.
- present a hypothesis about the next activities they expected to take place, with respect to the people, groups and countries.

For the Combo and Wiki groups the results of the analysis were presented in the form of a Wiki report submitted in the WorkSpace. The F2F group produced a word processed report in hard copy.

Analysis. The data to be collected was in the form of 'IntelliWiki' transcripts that were recorded in the 'WorkSpace' which included the individual edits of each group member as well as final reports. Data from F2F group was in the form of minutes from their meetings along with a transcript of the audio recordings of their discussion. The emerging individual and collaborative ideas were examined for evidence of accommodation and assimilation as the group progressed towards completion of the task. Using the concepts of adders and synthesisers suggested by Majchrzak et al (2006) the transcripts and minutes were subjected to textual analysis where the main aim was to distinguish between content that was simply added (assimilation) as opposed to content that was the result of integration and reorganisation (accommodation). The data was also examined for evidence of conflict or incongruity and the resultant equilibration. This would support the hypothesis that assimilation and accommodation had contributed to collaborative knowledge building. Because the data from the three locations was being assessed by different research assistants, inter-rater reliability was evaluated before detailed analysis.

3   Results

The results are presented in two parts. The first deals with the social and psychological dynamics of the collaborative working, examining how the participants worked together, group cohesiveness and how they felt about their contribution to the task. In the second part, performance on the task itself is examined looking for evidence of emergent knowledge resulting from the processes of assimilation and accommodation within the three different groups.

Social and Psychological Dynamics - Overall Summary. The groups displayed similar levels of computer and Wiki expertise and had similar relationships before the study began. In the post-test questionnaire for psychological satisfaction the F2F group exhibited significantly higher ratings than the other two groups on all three dimensions as predicted. However there was no significant overall difference between the Wiki group and the Combo group on any of the overall dimensions. Furthermore the Wiki group showed a higher mean, and when looking at individual items this group rated significantly higher than the Combo group on some measures (the reverse was never the case). So our prediction that the Combo group would display higher levels of satisfaction was not confirmed, indeed the data suggests a trend in the opposite direction. However it should be noted that this trend may be due to intra-group conflict within this group as evidenced by the participant comments and therefore any conclusions should be treated as tentative.

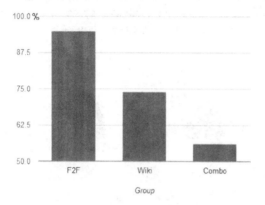

Fig. 2. Psychological Satisfaction Levels in the Three Groups

Analysis of the Task Data – Overall Summary. In the VAST Challenge it is acknowledged that there is no single solution to the task set. Judges will evaluate submitted solutions, make comments and judge what they believe to be the best, rather than, correct, solution. In evaluating the solutions offered by the three groups in this research a similar approach was used.

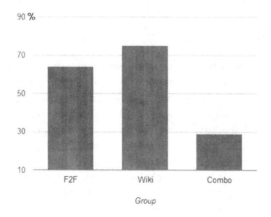

Fig. 3. Comparison of Task Evaluation in the Three Groups

All of the submitted reports were marked using the VAST 2010 sample answer as a basis. A mark was given for each of a possible 96 points about the various groups that were outlined in the VAST answers. The Wiki group scored the highest with 75%, the F2F group next with 64% and the Combo group scored the lowest with just 29%. Overall the Wiki group were better at preserving all of their findings while the F2F group provided a more coherent and structured report.

Analysis of the Wiki Data - Overall Summary. The Combo and Wiki groups who both made use of the Wiki in their collaborative analysis produced data that was highly consistent. The proportions of accommodation and assimilation were found to be very similar and this suggests that the methodology has managed, to some extent, to capture the process of emergent knowledge (see Figure 4).

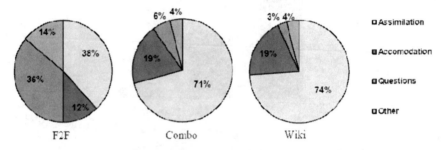

Fig. 4. Charts showing the proportion of each of the coded categories

Comparisons with the group not using a Wiki (i.e. F2F) are interesting in that again similar proportions of accommodation and assimilation are found but within a data set containing much social dross, i.e. the non-task elements that are a feature of face-to-face groups. From this perspective the Wikis are useful tools in that they appear to focus the group on the task and away from the 'social niceties'. This was also apparent as the Wiki group produced the most effective solution to the problem set.

4   Conclusions

The use of Wikis to aid collaborative intelligence analysis, to some extent, has been supported by the findings of this research. Both in terms of effective task analysis, and group satisfaction, people working as part of a group, at a distance, and with no face-to-face contact, communicating via a Wiki, feel they are making a worthwhile contribution to the collaborative effort, are trusted by other group members, and, perhaps most importantly, are most effective at completing the task.

Collaborative intelligence analysis is undoubtedly a highly complex cognitive/social undertaking and this research has demonstrated that Wikis can help in this respect. However, unless the group dynamics of the situation are factored into the collaborative working, then the potential benefits of this approach will be severely curtailed.

References

1. Butler Inquiry Report 2004. Review of Intelligence on Weapons of Mass Destruction: Report of a Committee of Privy Counselors. London: The Stationary Office, 9/11 Commission Report: Final Report of the National Commission on Terrorist Attacks upon the United States. Barnes and Noble, New York (2004); Colombetti, G.: Appraising Valence. Journal of Consciousness Studies 12, 103–126 (2005)
2. Convertino, G., Billman, D., Pirolli, P., Massar, J.P., Shrager, J.: The CACHE Study: Group Effects in Computer-supported Collaborative Analysis. Computer Supported Cooperative Work (CSCW) 17(4), 353–393 (2008); Cress, U., Kimmerle, J.: A systemic and cognitive view on collaborative knowledge building with Wikis. Computer-Supported Collaborative Learning 3, 105–122 (2008); Clark, R.M.: Intelligence Analysis: A Target-Centric Approach. CQ Press, Washington (2009); Heuer, R.J., Pherson, R.H.: Structured Analytic Techniques for Intelligence Analysis. CQ Press, Washington (2010)
3. Jones, P.M., Hayes, C.C., Wilkins, C., Bargar, R., Sniezek, J., Asaro, P., Mengshoel, O., Kessler, D., Lucenti, M., Choi, I., Tu, N., Schlabach, M.J.: CoRAVEN: modelling and design of a multimedia intelligent infrastructure for collaborative intelligence analysis. In: Proceedings of the 1998 IEEE International Conference on Systems, Man, and Cybernetics, San Diego, CA (1998)
4. Klein, G., Wiggins, S., Dominguez, C.O.: Team Sensemaking. Theoretical Issues in Ergonomics Science 11, 304–320 (2010)
5. Majchrzak, A., Wagner, C., Yates, D.: Corporate Wiki Users: Results of a Survey, in. In: Proceedings of the 2006 International Symposium on Wikis, pp. 99–104 (2006)
6. Murphy, P.: Intelligence and Security Committee: report into the London Terrorist Attacks on 7th July 2005 (2006)
7. Neville, M.: You Are Well Clear of Friendlies": Diagnostic Error and Cooperative Work in an Iraq War Friendly Fire Incident. Journal of Computer Supported Cooperative Work 18, 147–173 (2009)
8. Piaget, J.: Piaget's theory. In: Mussen, P.H. (ed.) Carmichael's Manual of Child Psychology, pp. 703–732. Wiley, New York (1970)
9. Piaget, J.: The development of thought: Equilibration of cognitive structures. The Viking Press, New York (1977a)
10. Posner, R.A.: Preventing Surprise Attacks: Intelligence Reform in the Wake of 9/11. Rowman and Littlefield, Lanham, Md (2005)
11. Warkentin, M.E., Sayeed, L., Hightower, R.: Virtual Teams versus Face-to-Face Teams: An Exploratory Study of a Web-based Conference System. Decision Sciences 28(4), 975–995 (1997)
12. Wheaton, K.J.: A Wiki is Like a Room: And Other Lessons Learned From 15 Wiki-based, Open Source, Intelligence Analysis Projects. Accessed from the International and Security Network (2008), http://www.isn.ethz.ch/isn/DigitalLibrary/Publications/Detail/?ots591=cab359a3-9328-19cc-a1d2-8023e646b22c&lng=en&id=50060 (January 2011)

Individual Differences in Cognitive Flexibility Predict Poetry Originality

Ivonne J. Figueroa and Robert J. Youmans

George Mason University
Fairfax, VA 22031, USA
ifiguero@gmu.edu

Abstract. To be successful at creative tasks, people are often required to think flexibly by selectively switching from one cognitive strategy to a more optimal strategy when presented with changing environmental cues [1]. In this study, we measured differences in students' cognitive flexibility, and then examined how well flexibility predicted performance on a subsequent creative task, a Haiku poem. Cognitive flexibility was measured using two variables found in the Wisconsin Card Sorting Task (WCST). Measures of cognitive flexibility predicted the Haiku poem's originality that students created. The results of this study suggest that cognitive flexibility may play an important role in creative writing and in predicting an individual's level of creativity. Implications are discussed.

Keywords: Individual differences, cognitive flexibility, creativity, poetry.

1 Introduction

A major goal of individual difference research is to develop stable measurements of people's traits, and then use those measures to predict differences in subsequent behaviors. Stable individual differences have been detected in peoples' ability to control their attention or hold information in working memory. Differences in these cognitive abilities have been shown to predict how people subsequently perform on vigilance [2], divided attention tasks [3] and attentional failures [4]. Though individual differences in cognitive abilities have been shown to be predictive of basic attention and perception tasks, recent research has the role of individual differences in more complex, higher-order behaviors like *creativity* [5].

Predictably, definitions of creativity vary widely among researchers; previous research has identified motivation [6], expertise [7], and regulatory focus [8] as behaviors that predict creativity. However, when it comes to measuring creative output, many researchers agree (e.g., [9], [10], [11]) that these can be measured along three dimensions: fluency, originality, and flexibility. Fluency is defined as an ability to generate large numbers of ideas, and measures of creative fluency include idea generation tasks that ask people to populate ideas or objects belonging to a particular category [10]. Originality is defined as the ability to generate novel ideas, and measures

D. Harris (Ed.): EPCE/HCII 2013, Part I, LNAI 8019, pp. 290–296, 2013.

of originality include the ability to generate rare or unique ideas within a given category. Finally, flexibility is the number of infrequent cognitive categories that are generated. While none of the three traits are thought to be the sole components of creativity, each trait is thought to represent a part of the multifaceted process that somehow facilitates creative breakthroughs [9], [11], [10].

Cognitive flexibility is defined as the ability to selectively switch from one cognitive strategy to a more optimal strategy when presented with changing environmental cues [1], [12]. Because individuals with high cognitive flexibility are thought to be especially proficient at changing strategies, it stands to reason that individual differences in cognitive flexibility may result in creative behaviors such as *fluency*, *originality*, and *flexibility*. Additionally, recent research has found that individuals who exhibit high flexibility are better at noticing subtle changes in a change blindness tasks [13]. Bilingual children have been able to demonstrate flexible thinking by creating original drawings of non-existent objects [14]. Furthermore, accounting for cognitive flexibility in constructive learning styles resulted in mastery of a subject, or ease of use of the task [15], [16].

The purpose of the present study was to objectively measure an individual's level of cognitive flexibility, and subsequently, to determine if cognitively flexibility predicted performance on an original thinking task, writing a Haiku poem. Although the WCST produces a large number of dependent variables, we utilized only two of the dependent variables that detect flexible thinking [17]. In this study we attempted to directly test whether individual differences as detected using one type of measure, the WCST, predicted creative behavior on a very different type of task, haiku poetry. The hypothesis being tested in this study was that individuals who exhibit a tendency to more easily switch between cognitive mental strategies (i.e., high cognitive flexibility) would produce more creative Haiku poems.

2   Method

2.1   Participants

Forty California State University, Northridge students participated in this study. Ten participants were male and 29 were female of varying ages ($M = 21.28$, SD = 12.8; one participant had incomplete data and was excluded from the analysis). Ethnicities reflected the diversity of the university (White/Caucasian = 7; Hispanic/Latino = 19; African-American/Black = 5; Asian = 6; other = 3). Participants were able to sign up for the study for course credit.

2.2   Materials

Wisconsin Card Sorting Task (WCST). The WCST was used to measure cognitive flexibility. The WCST requires a participant to sort through a deck of cards using three rules: color, shape, and number. Beginning with the first rule, participants must sort ten consecutive correct cards before the sorting rule is switched. Abandoning the sorting rule prior to ten consecutive correct sorts results in a failure to maintain set.

After ten consecutive correct responses, the rule for sorting is changed, and the number of perseverative moves, i.e. the number of moves attempting to sort by the previous, now inactive, rule, divided by the total number of errors yielded the percent perseverative error. The task is complete either if the participant runs out of cards to sort (128 cards), or if the participant completes six correct sorting categories (see [18]).

Haiku Poetry. The Haiku poetry task required participants to write a poem about their favorite season. Participants were given specific instructions about how to write a Haiku poem, which included a brief description of Haiku poetry:

> "Haiku is a form of Japanese Poetry. It often centers around nature. Many Haiku themes include nature, feelings or experiences. A Haiku must "paint" a mental image in the readers mind. Usually they use simple words and grammar. The most common form for Haiku contains three short lines. Haiku Poems don't rhyme; they follow a pattern. The pattern for haiku is the following:
>
> Line 1 = 5 syllables
> Line 2 = 7 syllables
> Line 3= 5 syllables"

Following the description portion, participants were shown a sample Haiku that was written about a rose. In case participants needed additional space, the following instructions were provided:

> "Now it's your turn. Pick your favorite season. That season will be your theme. For what purpose will you write? What mood do you want to convey? Brainstorm words that are about nature. Choose the words that you like from the list. Count the syllables (parts) of the words."

Participants were not required to complete the brainstorming exercise. The instructions shown here were printed at the top of the page. This excluded the sample Haiku poem.

To assess Haiku originality, each word was assigned a number based on the total number of times it was used in all 39 poems. Once every word used was assigned a frequency count, we calculated the average score of each poem. Haiku poems with *lower* scores were most original signifying that less frequent words were used in those poems.

2.3   Procedure

Upon reading the informed consent, participants completed a demographics questionnaire. The WCST or the Haiku were presented in random, counter-balanced order. Prior to writing the Haiku poem, participants were given a description of the goals and rules of a Haiku. No time limit was given to complete the Haiku, but all participants completed the task within five minutes. Before completion of the WCST, the experimenter read a set of instructions that explained the rules, which stated that the only feedback that could be provided was whether the card was correctly, or incorrectly sorted [18]. No time limit was given to complete the task. Following the completion of both tasks, participants were debriefed.

3 Results

Multiple regression analysis was conducted to test if individual differences in cognitive flexibility predict poetry originality. First, the data was checked for *skewness*. Two cases were excluded from the analysis because they were two standard deviations above the mean of both 'failure to maintain set' and 'percent perseverative errors'.

We screened for multicollinearity and there was no correlation higher than 0.55 (VIF = 1.33). The combination of both predictors explained 22% of the variance (adjusted R^2 = .22; $F (2, 33)$ = 5.8, p <.01) indicating that our overall model was predictive of Haiku originality (M = 5.996, SD = 2.02). There was no interaction effect between 'failure to maintain set' and 'percent perseverative errors' ($F (1, 6)$ = .64, $p = ns$). We also identified a significant main effect for each predictor. 'Percent perseverative errors' (M = 12.19; SD = 5.72) significantly predicted Haiku creativity ($t (36)$ = 2.93; $p < .01$) indicating that participants who switched from the old sorting rule to the new sorting rule in less moves wrote more creative Haiku. 'Failure to maintain set' (M = .61; SD = .87) also significantly predicted Haiku creativity ($t (36)$ = -2.98; $p < .01$) indicating that participants who failed to maintain set without being prompted by the experimenter wrote more creative poems. (Figure 1 shows two Haikus, a low and high scoring poem. Also included are percent perservertive score, number of failures, and originality score.)

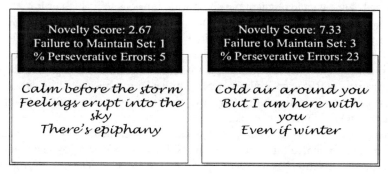

Fig. 1. Example of a low scoring (original) Haiku on the left and a high scoring (less original) Haiku on the right

4 Discussion

The goal of the present study was to determine whether individual differences in cognitive flexibility could predict performance on a creative task, Haiku poetry. We found that participants who exhibit higher levels of cognitive flexibility assessed by the WCST, wrote more original Haiku. Both variables speak differently about how an individual who is cognitive flexible processes information.

The first variable that predicted creative performance, percent perseverative errors, indicated that overall, individuals who took a longer time to switch to the next sorting rule on the WCST, wrote less original Haiku poems. One possibility is that individuals who are more efficient at switching between cognitive strategies, and do not perseverate, are more likely to generate novel, infrequent and original ideas. The relationship between failure to maintain set and originality is more ambiguous. In this case, individuals who broke set in the WCST more often, and thereby performed worse on the WCST, wrote more original Haiku. It is unclear why failure to maintain set, which demonstrates poor performance on the WCST, correlated with creative performance. One explanation for this result could be that individuals who are failing to maintain set, are simply distracted from the task [19] thereby generating infrequently used words as a result of their distracted mindset. Further research is required to determine why a failure to maintain set leads to more creative performance.

One limitation of this study deals with the method chosen to score the originality of the poems. We admit to a certain degree of subjectivity in our measure of originality, but given the challenge of quantifying such a multi-faceted construct we feel that originality scores derived from word infrequency are at least somewhat objectively representative of originality. However, the researchers had to determine if certain words should be grouped together. xFor example, should 'rain' and 'raining' count as the same category? Should *colors* be grouped together (i.e., green, brown, yellow), or should they each be given a frequency score? Future research could combine objective and subjective measures that use inter-rater reliability as a way to determine creativity.

Second, some people might argue about what it means to be high or low along any individual difference dimension, or about the stability of individual difference measures in general. For example, can cognitive flexibility be improved over a lifetime? Can it be enhanced? In fact, research has shown that exercise enhances cognitive flexibility [20], and therefore it might not be safe to assume that cognitive flexibility is a measurement that is not entirely stable. Further research is required that uses other measures of cognitive flexibility (e.g., eye tracking) that can provide insight about why a person is cognitively flexible.

Finally, the results of this study raise questions about the impact of motivation on creativity not accounted for in our predictions. Previous research has linked individual's intrinsic motivation has to creative performance [6], [21]. That is, motivation may be the underlying factor that influences creativity and not cognitive flexibility. In this study, we did not measure motivation, mood, or other emotional traits. However, an argument against the effect of motivation is that individuals who failed to maintain set on the WCST were more creative. It seems inconsistent that a participant failing to maintain set out of boredom would be motivated to write a creative poem. However, we concede that different tasks might motivate people differently. Future research should include measures of mood and motivation in order to determine the effect, if any, of potential mediating variables.

The focus of this study was to assess how individual differences in cognitive processes such as those required in cognitive flexibility predict performance on a subsequent high order task, creativity. The implications extend to fields like Human Factors because it is often necessary to identify individual traits that will result in original and innovative performance. Employers, the military, design products teams, etc., might want to consider having teams who possess a range of complimentary individual differences, one of which will exhibit high levels of cognitive flexibility. Additionally, a heterogeneous team may consist of one focused or persistent member that is paired with a cognitively flexible member, which in turn, would be preferable to two flexible or focused people. Both types of individuals, each with their own level of creativity would work together to create novel, infrequent, and efficient strategies, ideas, or products.

References

1. Scott, W.A.: Cognitive Complexity and Cognitive Flexibility. Sociometry 25, 405–414
2. Shaw, T.H., Matthews, G., Warm, J.S., Finomore, V.S., Silverman, L., Costa, P.T.: Individual differences in vigilance: Personality, ability and states of stress. Journal of Research in Personality 44, 297–308 (2010)
3. Colflesh, G.J., Conway, A.R.: Individual differences in working memory capacity and divided attention in dichotic listening. Psychonomic Bulletin & Review 14, 699–703 (2007)
4. Unsworth, N., McMillan, B.D., Brewer, G.A., Spillers, G.J.: Everyday attention failures: An individual differences investigation. Journal of Experimental Psychology: Learning, Memory, and Cognition 38, 1765–1772 (2012)
5. DeYoung, C.G., Flanders, J.L., Peterson, J.B.: Cognitive Abilities Involved in Insight Problem Solving: An Individual Differences Model. Creativity Research Journal 20, 278–290 (2008)
6. Amabile, T.M.: Motivation and creativity: Effects of motivational orientation on creative writers. Journal of Personality and Social Psychology 48, 393 (1985)
7. Ericsson, K.A., Krampe, R.T.: Institute of Cognitive Science
8. Herman, A., Reiter-Palmon, R.: The effect of regulatory focus on idea generation and idea evaluation. Psychology of Aesthetics, Creativity, and the Arts 5, 13–20 (2011)
9. Amabile, T.M.: The social psychology of creativity: A componential conceptualization. Journal of Personality and Social Psychology 45, 357 (1983)
10. Ward, T.B., Patterson, M.J., Sifonis, C.M.: The role of specificity and abstraction in creative idea generation. Creativity Research Journal 16, 1–9 (2004)
11. De Dreu, C.K.W., Baas, M., Nijstad, B.A.: Hedonic tone and activation level in the mood-creativity link: Toward a dual pathway to creativity model. Journal of Personality and Social Psychology 94, 739–756 (2008)
12. Dennis, J.P., Vander Wal, J.S.: The Cognitive Flexibility Inventory: Instrument Development and Estimates of Reliability and Validity. Cognitive Therapy and Research 34, 241–253 (2009)
13. Youmans, R., Figueroa, I., Kramarova, O.: Reactive Task-Set Switching Ability, Not Working Memory Capacity, Predicts Change Blindness Sensitivity. In: Proceedings of the Human Factors and Ergonomics Society Annual Meeting, vol. 55, pp. 914–918
14. Adi-Japha, E., Berberich-Artzi, J., Libnawi, A.: Cognitive flexibility in drawings of bilingual children. Child Development 81, 1356–1366 (2010)

15. Spiro, R., Feltovich, P.J.: Jacobson, Mi.J., Coulson, R.L.: Cognitive flexibility, constructivism, and hypertext: Random access instruction for advanced knowledge acquisition in ill-structured domains. Presented at the
16. Lowrey, W., Kim, K.S.: Online News Media and Advanced Learning: A Test of Cognitive Flexibility Theory. Journal of Broadcasting & Electronic Media 53, 547–566 (2009)
17. Figueroa, I.J., Youmans, R.J.: Developing an Easy-to-Administer, Objective, and Valid Assessment of Cognitive Flexibility. In: Proceedings of the Human Factors and Ergonomics Society Annual Meeting, pp. 944–948 (2011)
18. Heaton, R.K., Chelune, G.J., Talley, J.L.: Wisconsin Card Sorting Test manual: Revised and expanded. In: Psychological Assessment Resources, Odessa, Florida (1993)
19. Barceló, F., Knight, R.T.: Both random and perseverative errors underlie WCST deficits in prefrontal patients. Neuropsycholgia 40, 349–356 (2002)
20. Masley, S., Roetzheim, R., Gualtieri, T.: Aerobic Exercise Enhances Cognitive Flexibility. Journal of Clinical Psychology in Medical Settings 16, 186–193 (2009)
21. Roskes, M., De Dreu, C.K.W., Nijstad, B.A.: Necessity is the mother of invention: Avoidance motivation stimulates creativity through cognitive effort. Journal of Personality and Social Psychology 103, 242–256 (2012)

A New Behavioral Measure of Cognitive Flexibility

Christian A. Gonzalez[1], Ivonne J. Figueroa[1], Brooke G. Bellows[1],
Dustin Rhodes[2], and Robert J. Youmans[1]

[1] George Mason University, Department of Psychology, Fairfax, Virginia, USA
cgonzal2@gmu.edu
[2] University of California, Santa Cruz, California, USA

Abstract. Individual differences in cognitive flexibility may underlie a variety of different user behaviors, but a lack of effective measurement tools has limited the predictive and descriptive potential of cognitive flexibility in human-computer interaction applications. This study presents a new computerized measure of cognitive flexibility, and then provides evidence for convergent validity. Our findings indicate moderate to strong correlations with the Trail Making Task, and in particular, those aspects of the task most closely associated with cognitive flexibility. Results of this study provide support for the validity of a new measure of cognitive flexibility. We conclude by discussing the measure's potential applicability in the field of HCI.

Keywords: cognitive flexibility, individual differences, user modeling.

1 Introduction

When a user interacts with a system, they bring along their unique skills, biases and abilities. In the past, models of individual differences have been used to predict user behavior [1, 2], however, these models often lack a cognitive component. Conversely, cognitive modeling has been successful in designing, planning and evaluating systems for expert users [3, 4], but typically does not reflect the impact of individual differences in cognitive abilities [5]. *Cognitive flexibility* (CF), defined as an a person's ability to abandon one cognitive strategy in favor of another based on a change in task demands [6], represents one individual difference that may underlie a variety of different user behaviors.

One way to understand the importance of CF is to examine the behaviors that are associated with its absence, namely, *perseveration*. Extreme perseveration is defined as a maladaptive repetition of a particular behavior, and is a well-studied phenomenon in clinical psychology and neuropsychology [7–9]. Outside of clinical populations, more mild perseverative tendencies also naturally occur, and these impact a wide range of everyday activities. Research suggests that CF predicts behaviors ranging from how likely a person is to notice changes in their environment [10] to how creative a poem they are likely to write [11]. Most importantly here, we believe that CF has potential applications towards improving human-computer interaction (HCI).

D. Harris (Ed.): EPCE/HCII 2013, Part I, LNAI 8019, pp. 297–306, 2013.

For example, a recent study [12] found that locating "hard-to-find" features was one of the major sources of frustration during a computer interaction task. Individual differences in CF may explain why some users are more likely to find the sorts of hidden features that others miss because CF predicts an ability to disengage from a specific search or quickly abandon inefficient strategies. Finally, research has identified CF as one of the primary mechanisms of insight when solving problems [13, 14]. Some speculate this is because "it benefits from 'cognitive restructuring' of the problem, enabling the solver to pursue a new strategy or a new set of associations [15]." Overall, how users differ in their approach to problems, and their ability to change cognitive strategies, is relevant to HCI; however, without an effective measure of CF, both its descriptive and predictive potential in HCI will remain limited.

Currently, CF is often measured using two well-established tasks, the Wisconsin Card Sorting Task (WCST) and the Trail Making Task (TMT) [16–18]. In the WCST, the participant's goal is to sort a series of cards according to one of three rules: shape, color, or number. Participants begin unaware of which rule is active, then must learn the sorting rule in response to experimenter feedback, and finally must reacquire a new sorting rule when the old one changes. The WCST variable, 'percent perseverative errors', is most often associated with CF [19]. This variable is a ratio of the number of number of errors attributed to perseveration over the total number of errors made. The TMT assesses flexibility slightly differently. First, a baseline score is obtained in part A where, participants make a 'trail' by connecting an ascending series of numbers. Then, in part B, an additional series of letters is added and participants are required to connect the ascending series alternating between the two. Scores on part B and the difference between part B and part A, are most often associated with CF [18]. In general, the WCST measures errors and the TMT measures increases in time both caused by a lack of CF. However, neither task is really ideal for measuring both: Time on trials when rule switches occur are typically not compared to non-switch trials in the WCST and errors on the TMT are only reflected in increased completion time caused by fixing the error [16, 18]. In addition, both tasks have established themselves as part of neuropsychological batteries used for diagnosing executive dysfunction, but have not seen as wide acceptance as measures of cognitive abilities among healthy populations. By comparison, measures of constructs like working memory capacity, such as the operation span task [20, 21] have been used extensively in individual difference research in a variety of different populations including HCI studies [22, 23].

More recently, self-report methods of CF have been developed. The cognitive flexibility scale (CFS) created by Martin and Rubin [24, 25] measures flexibility in the context of effective communication. However, the CFS approaches the concept of CF differently than behavioral measures by dividing the construct into three areas: awareness of alternatives, willingness to be flexible and self-efficacy in being flexible. The CFS was validated with other measures of communication effectiveness and found to be internally reliable with high test-retest reliability ($r = .83$). A more recent self-report measure, the cognitive flexibility inventory (CFI), builds upon the CFS and extends its utility [26]. The CFI applies to more general life situations and was intended for clinical populations to support cognitive behavioral therapy (CBT) for patients with depression. The authors found that cognitive inflexibility, as measured by the CFI, was associated with more depressive symptoms measured by the Beck Depressive Inventory (BDI-II; $r = -.39$ time 1 and $-.37$ time 2). The CFS and CFI were also found to be highly correlated ($r = .73$ time 1 and $r = .75$ time 2). Overall, the self-report measures of CF suggest that there is a conscious aspect of flexibility related to recognizing alternatives and choosing to act on them. However, there is currently little research comparing results of self-report measures and behavioral measures of CF like the WCST and TMT.

2   A New Measure of Cognitive Flexibility

The goal of this research is to develop a measure of CF that draws from both the WCST and the TMT in order to reliably measure individual differences in flexible thinking in normal populations. By establishing a comprehensive measure of CF, we hope that fields like HCI will be able to assess and incorporate individual differences in CF into predictive and descriptive models of user behavior. Furthermore, in an effort to find consensus between behavioral and self-report measures of CF, we the TMT and the CFS with our measure. The measure presented here is a computerized version of a paper-and-pencil puzzle task developed by the second and last author [27]. In their study, Figueroa and Youmans found that the WCST variable, 'Trials to Complete First Category,' was a significant predictor of puzzle completion time such that fewer trials to complete first category (negatively related to CF) was associated with faster puzzle completion times.

However, as previous work has described [28], the paper puzzle was limited in many ways. The only dependent variable produced was a single puzzle completion time, allowing only for indirect inferences about the specific impact of rule switching on that variable. Unlike the paper-based puzzle, the computerized version presented here (Figure 1) allows for multiple puzzles, manipulation the number of switches per puzzle and measurement of switch and non-switch move times. By administering multiple puzzle trials we were able to assess how the amount of switching per trial impacted each individual. In addition, the possibility of 'dead-ends', a concern with the paper puzzle, was eliminated in the computerized version. Some additional aesthetic differences between paper and computerized versions include: different shapes and colors, a fog-of-war that occludes all tiles except current and previous moves and a nineteen-move path compared to the paper puzzle's twenty-two move path.

In this study, we attempt to further validate our measure of CF by correlating performance with the TMT as well the CFS. We hypothesized that performance on the puzzle task would indicate an individual's cognitive flexibility because participants must maintain an active rule to move quickly through the puzzle on non-switch moves, but must also quickly abandon previous rules in order to make progress on switch moves. As a consequence, perseveration on the previous rule should lead to increased switch move times. Furthermore, we reasoned that if switch costs, the time differences between switch and non-switch moves, were robust [29–31], then puzzle completion times would increase with the number of switches in a given puzzle. Thus, a simple bivariate regression with number of switches predicting completion time would allow us summarize the average effect increasing switches had on each participant's performance. We expected that scores on the TMT B and derived scores would be positively correlated with puzzle performance in terms of both faster puzzle trial completion times and reduced switch cost, and that CFS scores would be negatively correlated with performance.

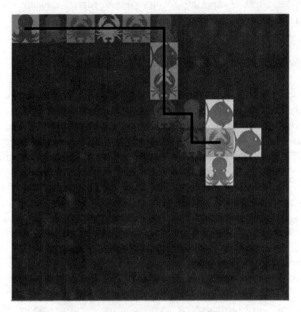

Fig. 1. Screenshot of computerized CF measure

3   Method

3.1   Participants

Twenty-four participants (7 men and 18 women, between 18 and 30 years old, median 19) from George Mason University's undergraduate research pool voluntarily participated for class credit.

3.2   Materials and Procedure

These data were collected as part of a larger study investigating how CF affects internet search. The TMT, CFS and Puzzle were all administered in this order immediately after participants had completed a series of Internet search tasks.

Trail Making Task. Paper-and-pencil-based versions using Reitan's (1955) arrangement of the TMT parts A and B were administered. In part A, participants connected a series of circles numbered 1-25 in order. In part B, participants connected an alternating series of numbers and letters (e.g. 1 to A, 2 to B, 3 to C etc.). Scores on the TMT were in the form of completion times as measured by the experimenter using a stopwatch. Errors were accounted for in terms of time required to correct. Direct scores and derived scores (i.e. B-A and B/A) were used for analysis. Participants always completed part A before part B.

Cognitive Flexibility Scale. Participants completed the 12-item CFS. Items (e.g. "I am willing to work at creative solutions to problems") were scored on a 6-point scale of agreement ("strongly agree" to "strongly disagree"). Higher scores indicated greater levels of flexibility (maximum of 72).

Puzzle. The computerized puzzle was completed in Adobe® Flash®. Participants used a mouse to navigate a 10 x 10 grid of tiles (60x60 pixels each). Each tile had a specific shape, shape color and background color. A "fog-of-war" occluded all moves except those immediately available and participants' previously traveled path, limiting the amount of planning (Figure 1). Of immediately available moves (either two or three depending on the location in the puzzle) there was ever only one correct, legal move, eliminating the possibility of dead ends. In order to make a legal move, participants needed to match their current tile to the desired tile by three different rules: shape, shape color and background color. As participants completed the task, the active matching rule changed and the participant was required to adopt the new rule in order to continue. For example, a participant might make three successive moves by matching by background color, then on the fourth move, no tiles match the background color of the current tile, forcing the participant to abandon the background color matching rule and adopt a new rule based on the tiles available i.e. matching by either shape or shape color. Participants completed the nineteen-move path by always starting from the top-left corner and ending in the bottom-right corner. Each puzzle was randomly generated, with switch moves and order of presentation randomized to mitigate any order effects. Participants completed seven puzzle trials, each containing between two and fourteen switches.

Participants viewed a training PowerPoint and completed three practice puzzles with the experimenter to ensure they fully understood how to navigate the puzzle properly. Before continuing with the experiment, all participants were trained to the criterion that they were able to complete a two-switch, eight-move practice puzzle within thirty seconds. The task and training were run using a Macintosh iMac with a 21.5-inch screen.

The computerized puzzle allowed for the measurement of several different variables. We measured the completion times for each puzzle in seconds, average switch and non-switch move times, and the additive, linear effect of amount of switching on completion times (b). Each participant completed 56 switch and 77 non-switch moves across all seven puzzle trials. Switch moves occurred when the participant switched to a new rule in order to advance. Non-switch moves occurred when they advanced according to the rule in the previous move. Logically, any move that was not a switch move would be non-switch move and vice versa. Switch cost was derived by calculating the difference between average switch and non-switch move times for each puzzle then averaged across trials for each participant. This variable indicates the additional time required to switch rules over and above just making a move. We expected all raw and derived scores to be positively correlated with TMT B, B-A and B/A and negatively correlated with scores on the CFS.

4   Results

After data were screened one outlier, two standard deviations above the mean, was removed. The following analysis was conducted on the remaining twenty-three participants. However, since a participant could have a small b value when fitting a line through a set of highly varied data points, we also accounted for the adjusted R^2 ($\bar{R}^2$) of the line of best fit. For this reason, only b values corresponding to an $\bar{R}^2$ value of .30 or higher were used for analysis. We acknowledge that fitting a linear model over seven data points violates regression assumptions necessary for obtaining linear unbiased estimates, so the reader is encouraged to interpret b values as summary statistics rather than inferential or predictive in any way. After applying the $\bar{R}^2$ cutoff, eight participants were excluded, leaving only fifteen participants analyzable b values. Correlations for this variable are specific to those fifteen participants, but all other variables will refer to the full sample of 23.

Five variables, TMT B, B-A, B/A, Switch Cost and Switch move time violated the assumption of normality (Shapiro-Wilk $p < .05$) required for calculating Pearson product-moment correlations. After performing natural log transforms, all five variables, except TMT B were approximately normal (Shapiro-Wilk $p > .05$). Pearson product-moment correlations were computed between TMT, CF, puzzle dependent variables (DVs) and are shown in Table 1.

Internal consistency of the puzzle trials was assed via Cronbach's alpha ($\alpha = .89$; bootstrap 95% CI [.80, .93]). Three of the five derived puzzle DVs had moderate to strong, significant positive correlations with TMT B and B-A scores providing evidence for convergent construct validity of the puzzle. In addition, five of the seven raw puzzle completion times were significantly correlated with TMT B and B-A. Switch cost was significantly correlated with TMT B scores but not B-A. Interestingly, switch move time was the only DV not significantly correlated with TMT or other puzzle DVs. Average puzzle completion time as well as the six and twelve switch puzzle completion times were significantly positively correlated with TMT A. B/A scores were not significantly correlated with any puzzle DVs. Though generally in the expected direction, correlations between the CFS and TMT and puzzle DVs did not reach significance.

5   Discussion

The goal of this study was to validate a new measure of cognitive flexibility. The high Cronbach's alpha suggests good internal consistency across trials and the strong positive correlations with the TMT provide evidence for convergent validity. Our results

Table 1. Correlations between TMT CFS and Puzzle

	TMT				CFS					Puzzle						
	1	2	3	4	5	6	7	8	9	10	11	12	13	14	15	16	17
TMT A																	
TMT B[1]	0.75**																
B - A[1]	0.34	0.87***															
B/A[1]	-0.25	0.43*	0.81**														
CFS	-0.03	-0.16	-0.23	-0.26													
h (n=15)	0.35	0.64**	0.63*	0.39	0.09												
Avg. Time	0.47*	0.71**	0.65**	0.34	-0.1	0.67**											
Switch Cost[1]	0.33	0.41*	0.37	0.19	-0.02	0.39	0.26										
Switch[1]	0.39	0.36	0.26	0.04	-0.33	0.27	0.32	-0.03									
Non-Switch[1]	0.29	0.55**	0.54**	0.34	0.07	0.60*	0.81**	0.42*	-0.26								
2switch	0.21	0.39	0.40	0.26	-0.34	0.10	0.68**	0.01	0.21	0.51*							
4switch	0.33	0.35	0.28	0.04	-0.31	0.24	0.63**	0.00	0.37	0.38	0.45*						
6switch	0.53**	0.73**	0.63**	0.30	0.13	0.71**	0.84**	0.27	0.02	0.85**	0.36	0.47*					
8switch	0.24	0.54**	0.58**	0.41	-0.09	0.73**	0.81**	0.39	0.25	0.73**	0.40	0.34	0.66**				
10switch	0.40	0.61**	0.55**	0.29	-0.03	0.61*	0.88***	0.33	0.24	0.73**	0.57**	0.50*	0.75**	0.68**			
12switch	0.34	0.55**	0.52*	0.30	-0.05	0.51	0.79***	-0.05	0.44*	0.50*	0.73**	0.29	0.51*	0.66**	0.65**		
14switch	0.48*	0.66**	0.57**	0.24	0.04	0.88***	0.83**	0.41	0.20	0.72**	0.39	0.46*	0.77**	0.60**	0.72**	0.52*	

yielded three major findings. First, the puzzle correlated with those TMT dependent variables most closely associated with CF and executive function, TMT B and B-A, but did not correlate as strongly with TMT A, which has been found to reflect more basic motor and perceptual abilities [18]. Furthermore, the fact that the *b* values, were positively correlated with TMT B and B-A scores is a critical finding. This allows us to better disentangle flexibility from confounding aspects of CF like visual motor abilities (a common criticism of the TMT [18, 32, 33]).

Second, we did not find a correlation between the behavioral measures and the CFS. This suggests that perhaps these measures tap separate aspects of CF[1]. However, this study was too limited in scope to draw defensible conclusions about the overall relationship between behavioral and self-report measures of CF. As Dennis and Vander Wal [26] suggest, more research is needed in this area. A more comprehensive study with a larger sample and a wider range of measures would be better suited to answering this research question.

Third, this study attempted to characterize flexibility in terms of the linear effect of switching on completion time. However, approximately 30% of our sample had an unacceptably low linear fit ($\bar{R}^2$ below .3). This finding may suggest that a segment of the population does not experience a linear additive effect of switching. Perhaps there is a majority of individuals that demonstrate a good linear fit and a range of possible *b* values corresponding to high and low flexibility, and a separate group of individuals that may be distracted, de-focusing their attention or adapting to the task in an unforeseen way. This presents challenges for measurement, but allows for interesting speculation about what sets the 'poor-fit' individuals apart.

Better measures of individual differences like CF allow for the inclusion of cognitive abilities during interaction. Accounting for the flexibility of users with the measure presented here may allow for better prediction of which users are most susceptible to perseverative and ultimately potentially frustrating behaviors, which is a major a concern for designers [12]. Furthermore, cognitive models used in simulations may be able to use data from our measure to predict behaviors of average, high and low flexibility users, identifying what aspects of an interface or task require flexible thinking and how individual differences in flexible thinking may impact performance.

The study presented here highlights only the first step in an effort to bring the study of individual differences in cognitive ability to the field of HCI. The limitations of the human attentional system play a vital role in crafting technologies that are functional and easy to use [36]. Numerous studies have demonstrated that expertise, personality, age and gender may all impact user interactions [34, 35]. However, though the role of cognition in HCI is readily apparent, the role of individual differences in cognitive ability is not. Perhaps the most important principle of design, well-known to many in the field of HCI is 'know the user.' This simple aphorism presents an exceedingly difficult task. Understanding users' cognition and how that may vary across individuals will play a critical role in designing interfaces and experiences for a growing population of users in years to come. We hope that better tools and additional research will lead to a more complete understanding of user behavior and interaction with technology.

---

[1] Anecdotally, Dennis and Vander Wal have unpublished data documenting a similarly null relationship between behavioral and self-report measures of CF.

References

1. Harrison, A.W., Rainer Jr, R.K.: The influence of individual differences on skill in end-user computing. Journal of Management Information Systems, 93–111 (1992)
2. Hong, W., Thong, J.Y.L., Wong, W.M., Tam, K.Y.: Determinants of user acceptance of digital libraries: an empirical examination of individual differences and system characteristics. Journal of Management Information Systems 18, 97–124 (2002)
3. Card, S.K., Moran, T.P., Newell, A.: The keystroke-level model for user performance time with interactive systems. Commun. ACM. 23, 396–410 (1980)
4. Gray, W.D., John, B.E., Atwood, M.E.: Project Ernestine: Validating a GOMS Analysis for Predicting and Explaining Real-World Task Performance. Human-Computer Interaction 8, 237–309 (1993)
5. Olson, J.R., Olson, G.M.: The growth of cognitive modeling in human-computer interaction since GOMS. Human-Computer Interaction 5, 221–265 (1990)
6. Scott, W.A.: Cognitive complexity and cognitive flexibility. Sociometry, 405–414 (1962)
7. Allison, R.S.: Perseveration as a sign of diffuse and focal brain damage. I. Br. Med. J. 2, 1027–1032, contd (1966)
8. Müller, J., Dreisbach, G., Brocke, B., Lesch, K.P., Strobel, A., Goschke, T.: Dopamine and cognitive control: The influence of spontaneous eyeblink rate, DRD4 exon III polymorphism and gender on flexibility in set-shifting. Brain Research 1131, 155–162 (2007)
9. Eslinger, P.J., Grattan, L.M.: Frontal lobe and frontal-striatal substrates for different forms of human cognitive flexibility. Neuropsychologia 31, 17–28 (1993)
10. Youmans, R.J., Figueroa, I.J., Kramarova, O.: Reactive Task-Set Switching Ability, Not Working Memory Capacity, Predicts Change Blindness Sensitivity. Proceedings of the Human Factors and Ergonomics Society Annual Meeting 55, 914–918 (2011)
11. Figueroa, I.J., Youmans, R.J.: Individual differences in cognitive flexibility predict poetry originality. In: Proceedings of the 15th International Conference on Human-Computer Interaction, Las Vegas, Nevada (2013)
12. Ceaparu, I., Lazar, J., Bessiere, K., Robinson, J., Shneiderman, B.: Determining causes and severity of end-user frustration. International Journal of Human-Computer Interaction 17, 333–356 (2004)
13. Beversdorf, D.Q., Hughes, J.D., Steinberg, B.A., Lewis, L.D., Heilman, K.M.: Noradrenergic modulation of cognitive flexibility in problem solving. Neuroreport 10, 2763 (1999)
14. Baas, M., De Dreu, C.K., Nijstad, B.A.: A meta-analysis of 25 years of mood-creativity research: Hedonic tone, activation, or regulatory focus? Psychological Bulletin 134, 779 (2008)
15. Subramaniam, K., Kounios, J., Parrish, T.B., Jung-Beeman, M.: A brain mechanism for facilitation of insight by positive affect. Journal of Cognitive Neuroscience 21, 415–432 (2009)
16. Reitan, R.M.: The relation of the Trail Making Test to organic brain damage. Journal of Consulting Psychology 19, 393–394 (1955)
17. Reitan, R.M.: Validity of the Trail Making Test as an indicator of organic brain damage. Perceptual and Motor Skills 8, 271–276 (1958)
18. Sanchez-Cubillo, I., Perianez, J.A., Adrover-Roig, D., Rodriguez-Sanchez, J.M., Rios-Lago, M., Tirapu, J., Barcelo, F.: Construct validity of the Trail Making Test: role of task-switching, working memory, inhibition/interference control, and visuomotor abilities. Journal of the International Neuropsychological Society 15, 438 (2009)
19. Barceló, F., Knight, R.T.: Both random and perseverative errors underlie WCST deficits in prefrontal patients. Neuropsychologia 40, 349–356 (2002)

20. Turner, M.L., Engle, R.W.: Is working memory capacity task dependent? Journal of Memory and Language. Journal of Memory and Language 28, 127–154 (1989)
21. Unsworth, N., Heitz, R.P., Schrock, J.C., Engle, R.W.: An automated version of the operation span task. Behavior Research Methods 37, 498–505 (2005)
22. Zander, T.O., Kothe, C., Jatzev, S., Gaertner, M.: Enhancing human-computer interaction with input from active and passive brain-computer interfaces. Brain-Computer Interfaces, 181–199 (2010)
23. Wong, A.W.K., Chan, C.C.H., Li-Tsang, C.W.P., Lam, C.S.: Competence of people with intellectual disabilities on using human–computer interface. Research in Developmental Disabilities 30, 107 (2009)
24. Martin, M.M., Rubin, R.B.: A new measure of cognitive flexibility. Psychological Reports 76, 623–626 (1995)
25. Martin, M.M., Anderson, C.M.: The cognitive flexibility scale: Three validity studies. Communication Reports 11, 1–9 (1998)
26. Dennis, J.P., Vander Wal, J.S.: The cognitive flexibility inventory: Instrument development and estimates of reliability and validity. Cognitive Therapy and Research 34, 1241–253 (2010)
27. Figueroa, I.J., Youmans, R.J.: Developing an Easy-to-Administer, Objective, and Valid Assessment of Cognitive Flexibility. In: Proceedings of the Human Factors and Ergonomics Society Annual Meeting, pp. 944–948 (2011)
28. Gonzalez, C., Pratt, S.M., Benson, W., Figueroa, I.J., Rhodes, D., Youmans, R.J.: Creating a Computerized Assessment of Cognitive Flexibility with a User-Friendly Participant and Experimenter Interface. In: Proceedings of the Human Factors and Ergonomics Society Annual Meeting, pp. 1942–1946 (2012)
29. Monsell, S.: Task switching. Trends in Cognitive Sciences 7, 134–140 (2003)
30. Rogers, R.D., Monsell, S.: Costs of a predictable switch between simple cognitive tasks. Journal of Experimental Psychology: General 124, 207 (1995)
31. Kiesel, A., Steinhauser, M., Wendt, M., Falkenstein, M., Jost, K., Philipp, A.M., Koch, I.: Control and interference in task switching—A review. Psychological Bulletin 136, 849 (2010)
32. Crowe, S.F.: The differential contribution of mental tracking, cognitive flexibility, visual search, and motor speed to performance on parts A and B of the Trail Making Test. J. Clin. Psychol. 54, 585–591 (1998)
33. Gaudino, E.A., Geisler, M.W., Squires, N.K.: Construct validity in the Trail Making Test: what makes Part B harder? Journal of Clinical and Experimental Neuropsychology 17, 529–535 (1995)
34. Helander, M.G., Landauer, T.K., Prabhu, P.V.: Handbook of human-computer interaction. North Holland (1997)
35. Aykin, N.M., Aykin, T.: Individual differences in human-computer interaction. Computers & Industrial Engineering 20, 373–379 (1991)
36. Card, S.K., Moran, T.P., Newell, A.: The psychology of human-computer interaction. CRC (1986)

The Roles of Anxiety and Motivation in Taiwanese College Students' English Learning

Mou-Tzu Yang[1], Yi-an Hou[2], Yen-ju Hou[3], and Hsueh-yu Cheng[4]

[1] University of Kang Ning, Taiwan
[2] Kaomei College of Healthcare and Management, Taiwan
[3] Shu Zen College of Medicine and Management, Taiwan
[4] Aletheia University, Taiwan
hycheng@mt.au.edu.tw

Abstract. The study aims to explore the roles of anxiety and motivation in foreign language learning. A total of 141 freshmen at a private university in south Taiwan served as subjects. The research instrument includes the Foreign Language Classroom Anxiety Scale (FLCAS) (Horwitz, Horwitz, & Cope, 1986), Motivation/attitude about foreign language learning (Gardner, 1985), as well as two English scores of Taiwan College Entrance Exam (CEE) and National English Test of Proficiency All on the Web (NETPAW). All available data were processed by SPSS 16 (Statistical Package of Social Science). Findings show the two English scores of CEE and NETPAW, as well as motivation, attitude and motivational intensity are strongly correlated to one another. In addition, motivational intensity is related to score of NETPAW, but anxiety is the best predictor of students' score of NETPAW positively. It's expected that the findings can provide teachers with some hints for more effective foreign language teaching and learning by being aware of students' individual differences.

Keywords: Anxiety, motivation, attitude, foreign language learning, CEE, NETPAW.

1   Introduction

Many learners regard foreign language learning as an anxiety-provoking experience which affects their language performance in one way or another. Hence, the role of anxiety on foreign language learning has been attracting lots of attention from the mid-1970s, in particular, since the early 2000s, there have been a growing number of studies of Asian learners of Japan (Andrade & Williams, 2009; Hashimoto, 2002), China (Hu, 2002; Na, 2007), Taiwan (Cheng, 2002; Chung, 2010; Hou, et al., 2012; Kao & Craigie, 2010; Wu, 2010), Korea (Kim, 2000), even Vietnam (Linh, 2011), the Philippines (Lucas, 2011; Sioson, 2011) and many others. On the other hand, motivation has long been regarded as a key to learning, and is "a major factor in promoting language retention" (Gardner & Lysynchuk, 1990, p.267), while "developing sound attitudes is the first step toward the achievement of bilingualish" (Titone, 1990, p.1). It's believed that to be successful in foreign language learning, learners should have

D. Harris (Ed.): EPCE/HCII 2013, Part I, LNAI 8019, pp. 307–315, 2013.
© Springer-Verlag Berlin Heidelberg 2013

both the "skill" and the "will" (motivation), so to put the two crucial factors together, the study intends to investigate the roles of anxiety and motivation in Taiwanese college students' English learning.

2   Literature Review

2.1   Characteristics of Foreign Language Learning Anxiety

Language anxiety's affect on language learning is two folds: positive and negative. Some consequences caused by language anxiety are proposed below:

Positive Effects. Appropriate tension is normal and necessary. It is suggested that some anxiety can improve performance (Scovl, 1978), positively relate to motivation, and influence both the quality of performance and the amount of effort invested in it. For students with higher self-esteem and strong motivation, anxiety may force them to study harder, arouse their potential and bring about unanticipated better outcome.

Negative Effects. Anxiety's another affect lies in its negative influences on other variables, such as motivation, attitude, and strategy use, as well as in its interfering with language learning process and performance. Findings also show that anxiety is negatively correlated with Field Independence, participation of classroom activities, short-term and long-term memory, TOEFL scores and language achievement (Chung, 2010; Horwitz, et al.,1986; Hou, et al., 2012; Kao & Craigie, 2010; Linh, 2011; Wu, 2010).

2.2   Factors Affecting Language Anxiety

According to Horwitz, Horwitz, and Cope (1986), learning anxiety is "a distinct complex of self-perceptions, beliefs, feelings, and behaviors related to classroom language learning" (p.128), and may occur any time during the learning process. Horwitz, et al. (1986) divided the 33 items of the Foreign Language Classroom Anxiety Scale (FLCAS) into three categories relating to general sources of anxiety, including communication apprehension, test anxiety, and fear of negative evaluation.

Related to the three categories, Chung (2010) defines factors affecting language anxiety as factors dealing with learner, teacher, subject matter, and learning context. Later, in Linh's study (2011), six possible factors contributing to language anxiety are categorized as (1) personal and interpersonal anxieties, (2). learner beliefs about language learning, (3). instructor beliefs about language teaching, (4). classroom procedures, and (6). language testing.

Particularly, an interesting finding was found in Hou, et al.'s research (2012) The study concluded that "Teachers' beliefs have impacts on their students' anxiety about foreign language learning" (p.250). For example, comparing with American teachers, many Chinese teachers tend to emphasize more on the importance of grammar, excellent pronunciation, and immediate error correction. Consequently, Chinese students are more anxious than American students about feeling overwhelmed by the number of rules, being laughed at by other students, and being corrected by teachers whenever they make a mistake.

2.3   Motivation and Attitude toward Foreign Language Learning

Gardner & Lambert (1959) were the first to introduce the integrative-instrumental approach to measuring motivation. Attention was shifted from the study of learner's behavior to the learning process of language learners. It was this shift that gave definition to the field of second/foreign language learning. Integratively motivated learners are those who wish to identify with another ethnolinguistic group, whereas instrumentally motivated learners are those who learn a second/foreign language for utilitarian purposes. Although it has been supported that motivation is the most important factor in second language achievement and proved to be related to attitude and motivational intensity (Hou, 2010), yet some findings failed to find out the relationship between motivation and English achievement (Cheng, 2002). Titone (1990) focused on the role of attitude in second language learning. He indicated that attitudes "strictly tied up with motivational dynamics… work most powerfully, especially in acquiring mastery in a second language (p.2). Furthermore, some findings did find the relationship between attitudes and other variables related to foreign language achievement (Hou, 2010).

3   Methodology

3.1   The Research Questions

The study intends to answer the following research questions:

1. Is there any relationship between Taiwanese EFL college students' foreign language learning anxiety and foreign language learning motivation?
2. Are foreign language learning anxiety and motivation predictive to Taiwanese EFL college students' English proficiency?

3.2   Purposes of the Study

The purposes of the study are to investigate Taiwanese EFL college students' English learning anxiety and motivation as well as the prediction of their English proficiency.

3.3   Research Methodology

A case study and convenience sampling were used for the research methodology. It is the study of a bounded system, which is in a particular circumstance and with a particular problem, and also gives readers 'space" for their own opinions (Stake, 1988). In addition, the subjects included in the sample were "whoever happens to be available at that time" (Gay & Airasian, 2003, p.112).

3.4   Subjects

One hundred and forty-one freshmen from 7 departments at a private university in south Taiwan participated in the study, including 56 male students (40%) and 85 female students (60%). In addition to their English scores of CEE (College Entrance Exam) in 2011 adopted, they took a National English Test in Proficiency for All on the Web (NETPAW), reading part (CEF A2), and filled out a questionnaire dealing with their anxiety and motivation about English learning.

3.5   Data Collection Instrument

The research instruments include questionnaires of Foreign Language Classroom Anxiety Scale (FLCAS), Motivation/Attitude, as well as English scores of College Entrance Exam (CEE) and National English Test of Proficiency All on the Web (NETPAW).

The Foreign Language Classroom Anxiety Scale (FLCAS), designed by Horwitz, Horwitz, and Cope (1986), contains 33 items to be responded to on a five-point Likert scale, ranging from 1 (SD=strongly disagree) to 5 (SA=strongly agree), indicating level of anxiety. Among them, nine items are negatively stated (items 2,5,8,11,14,18,22,28, and 32), which need to be recorded reversely. For easy to read, the questionnaire items were translated into Chinese for students to fill out.

In Taiwan, high school graduates are supposed to have the English proficiency of Intermediate Level (B1), while junior high school graduates, Elementary Level (A2) (LTTC, 2011). Since the average score of the subjects' College Entrance Exam (CEE) is low (M=23.05 out of 100), indicating the CEE is too difficult for most of them, it's appropriate to adopt another test with a lower level, that is Level A2, elementary level. Hence, in addition to students' English scores of CEE in the summer of 2011, their scores of NETPAW (A2) taken in late September that year were used as students' another English performance.

Along with descriptive statistics of mean, standard deviation, and percentages, a Pearson correlation and Regression Analysis were used to answer the research questions. All available data were processed by SPSS 16 (Statistical Package of Social Science). In this study, the significance level was set at $p<.05$.

4   Findings and Results

Findings include the reliability of the questionnaire; descriptive analysis, relationship and regression analysis of students' English scores of CEE and NETPAW, foreign language learning anxiety and motivation. The findings are described below:

4.1   The Reliability of the Research Instrument

The reliability of the questionnaire of Foreign Language Classroom Anxiety Scale (FLCAS), Motivation, Attitude, and Motivational Intensity is Cronbach Alpha =.819,

.858, .824, and .775, respectively. "If a test were perfectly reliable, the reliability coefficient would be 1,00....However, no test is perfect reliable." (Gay & Airasian, 2003, p.141). Hence, the results of the reliability coefficient between .775 and .858 indicate that the research instruments are acceptable and reliable.

4.2 Descriptive Analysis of English Scores of CEE, NETPAW, Anxiety and Motivation

The results reveal that students' English proficiency is not satisfactory and their anxiety level is above average (M=3.08). As for Foreign Language Classroom Anxiety Scale (FLCAS), the top sources of their anxiety come from worrying about the consequences of failing the English class (M=3.54), having to speak without preparation (M=3.51), feeling that the other students speak better (M=3.42), having not prepared in advance when English teacher asks questions (M=3.42), finding themselves thinking about things that have nothing to do with the course (M=3.41), and keeping thinking that other students are better than they are (M=3.41).

In light of students' orientations to learn English, the top five reasons for them to learn English are: "English seems of great importance today" (M=4.17); "To get a better job" (M=4.15); "To travel abroad" (M=4.08); "To pass exam" (M=4.02); "To promote educational and cultural background" (M=3.76). On the other hand, less students are motivated to learn English because they want " To think and behave like an English speaking person" (M=2.62); or "To leave Taiwan and become a member of American society" (M=2.81); or "To be an educated person" (M=3.38). Regarding to students' attitudes toward English learning and culture, they wish they "could speak English fluently" (M=4.18); "English is important, because the people who speak it are important" (M=4.14); "English is an international language, everyone should learn English" (M=4.08); and in addition to English, they "want to learn another foreign language in the future"(M=3.92). As for English learning, they "enjoy listening to English songs and news broadcasts" (M=3.68) and "enjoy speaking English" (M=3.12), but not " enjoy reading English newspapers, magazines, or original publications" (M=2.82); particularly, nor "enjoy writing diary, letters, or compositions in English" (M=2.53).   In addition, for motivational intensity, 85.5% of the students confessed that they "once in a while" actively think about what they have learned in English class" and when their teacher wanted someone to do an extra English assignment, 76.0% of them would only do it if the teacher asked them directly; however, if there were a local English TV station, 73.7% of them would "turn it on occasionally". The individual mean and standard deviation of the research instrument is shown below:

Table 1. Mean and standard deviation of the research instrument

Factor	N	Low	High	Full	M	SD	level
CEE	129	3	50	100	23.05	9.08	CEF A2-B1
NETPAW	113	15	87.5	100	51.84	17.21	CEF A2

Table 1. (*Continued*)

Anxiety	135	1.85	4.15	5	3.08	.51
Motivation	141	1.25	4.94	5	3.60	.52
Attitude	141	1.84	4.53	5	3.49	.44
Motivational intensity	141	1.00	2.80	3	2.10	.34

4.3   Correlation among English Scores of CEE, NETPAW, Anxiety, and Motivation

By using Pearson Correlation analysis, it reveals that the English score of CEE is correlated to the score of NETPAW ($p<.01$) and attitude ($p<.05$). As for the score of NETPAW, it's correlated to anxiety ($p<.01$), attitude ($p<.05$) and intensity ($p<.01$). In addition, motivation, attitude, and intensity are strongly correlated to one another ($p<.01$). All are shown below:

Table 2. Correlation among English scores of CEE, NETPAW, anxiety, and motivation

	CEE	NETPAW	anxiety	motivation	attitude	intensity
CEE	--	.437**	.008	.120	.180*	.073
NETPAW		--	.269**	.093	.166*	.249**
Anxiety			--	-.141	-.106	.074
motivation				--	.784**	.451**
Attitude					--	.500**
Intensity						--

* $p<.05$ ** $p<.01$

4.4   Regression Analysis for Motivation with English Scores of CEE and NETPAW

By Regression Analysis, it's found none of the motivation variables is predictive of CEE scores. But among them, only motivational intensity is predictive of NETPAW score ($t = 2.720$, $\beta = .007$). The findings are shown below:

Table 3. Regression analysis for motivation with English scores of CEE and NETPAW

	CEE		NETPAW	
Variables	t	β	t	β
(Constant)	1.747	.083	1.895	.060
Motivation	-.380	.705	-1.113	.267
Attitude	1.798	.074	1.257	.210
Intensity	-.296	.768	2.720	.007

* $p<.05$ ** $p<.01$

4.5   Regression Analysis for Motivation and Anxiety with English Scores of CEE and NETPAW

However, if anxiety is added, the findings are different. Findings show that none of the variables of both motivation and anxiety is predictive of CEE score, but motivational intensity is no longer predictive of NETPAW score. On the contrary, anxiety becomes the only predictor, of NETPAW scores, instead ($t = 2.957$, $\beta = .004$). The findings are shown below:

Table 4. Regression analysis for motivation and anxiety with scores of CEE and NETPAW

	CEE		NETPAW	
Variables	t	β	T	β
(Constant)	1.514	.133	-1.352	.179
Foreign Language Classroom Anxiety Scale	-.581	.562	2.957	.004
Motivation	-.350	.727	.029	.977
Attitude	1.188	.238	1.007	**.316**
Intensity	.066	.948	1.770	.080

* p<.05   ** p<.01

5   Conclusion and Implication

Some conclusions and implications derived from the study are described below:

5.1   Conclusion

1. The reliability of the research instrument is acceptable (between.775 and .858).
2. The two English scores of CEE and NETPAW are found to be correlated to each other, and motivation, attitude and motivational intensity are correlated to one another, too.
3. Motivational intensity is positively predictive to NETPAW score, but when Anxiety is added, the best predictor of NETPAW score becomes Anxiety, positively. The positive prediction of anxiety to English score is quite different from some other studies which reveal that anxiety is negatively related to foreign language learning (Chung, 2010; Hou, et al. 2012; Linh, 2011).

5.2   Implication

1. Motivational intensity and Anxiety are found positively predictive of students' English learning, so teachers should be aware of the important roles in their learning process, encourage students to put more effort (motivational intensity) and give them appropriate pressure (anxiety).

2. The findings show that suitable evaluation (i.e.NETPAW here) can be used to measure students' real competence and figure out the possible factors related to their learning, so it's suggested that teachers take students' individual differences into consideration and adopt some types of evaluation with good reliability and validity based on students' prior knowledge.

References

1. Cheng, Y.S.: Factors associated with foreign language writing anxiety. Foreign Language Annals 35, 647–656 (2002)
2. Chung, W.Y.: Anxiety and motivation in foreign language learning- a case study. In: The 14th International Conference on Multimedia Language Instruction, December 17-18, pp. 202–216. Kaohsiung, Taiwan (2010)
3. Gardner, R.C.: Social psychology and second language learning: The role of attitude and motivation. Edward Arnold, Baltimore (1985)
4. Gardner, R.C., Lambert, W.E.: Motivational variables in second language acquisition. Canadian Journal of Psychology 13, 266–272 (1959)
5. Gay, L.R., Airasian, P.: Educational Research: Competencies for Analysis and Applications, 7th edn. Merrill Prentice Hall, NJ (2003)
6. Horwitz, E.K., Horwitz, M.B., Cope, J.: Foreignlanguage classroom anxiety. The Modern Language Journal 70, 125–132 (1986)
7. Hou, Y.A.: Multiple Intelligences and foreign language learning- a case study in Taiwan. Whampou Journal 58, 1–30 (2010)
8. Hou, Y.J., Lee, F.M., Hou, Y.A., Chung, W.Y., Cheng, H.Y.: The impacts of teachers' beliefs on students' anxiety about foreign language learning: the east and the West. The International Journal of the Humanities 9(8), 245–260 (2012)
9. Hu, G.: Recent important developments in secondary English-language teaching in the People's Republic of China. Language, Culture, Curriculum 15, 30–49 (2002)
10. Kao, P.C., Craigie, P.: Foreign language anxiety and English achievement in Taiwanese undergraduate English-major students: an empirical study. Hong Kung Journal 61, 49–62 (2010)
11. Linh, N.T.: Foreign language learning anxiety among 1st-year students at FELTE. Thesis of Bachelor degree, Vietnam National University, Hanoi, Vietnam (2011)
12. Lucas, R.I.: English language learning anxiety among foreign language learners in the Philippines. Philippine ESL Journal 7, 3–27 (2011)
13. Na, Z.: A study of high school students' English learning anxiety. The Asian EFL Journal 9(3), 22–34 (2007)
14. Scovel, T.: The effect of affect on foreignlanguage learning: A review of the anxiety research. Language Learning 28, 129–142 (1978)
15. Sioson, I.C.: Language learning strategies, beliefs, and anxiety in academic speaking task. Philippine ESL Journal 7, 3–27 (2011)
16. Stake, R.E.: Case study methods in educational research: Seeking sweet water. In: Jaeger, R.M. (ed.) Complementary methods for research in education, pp. 253–300. American Educational Research Association, Washington (1988)

17. Titone, R.: A psycho-sociolinguistic perspective in EFL Learning: The role of attitude a dynamic factor. 9th Paper Presented at The World Congress of Applied Linguistics. sponsored by the International Association of Applied Linguistics, Thessaloniki, Greece, April 15-21 (1990) ERIC Document Resume, ED 326-073
18. Tobias, S.: Anxiety and cognitive processing of instruction. In: Schwarzer, R. (ed.) Self-Related Cognition Inanxiety and Motivation, pp. 35–54. Erlbaum, Hillsdale (1986)
19. Wu, K.H.: The relationship between language learners' anxiety and learning strategy in the CLT classroom. International Education Studies 3(1), 174–191 (2010)

Impact of Different Course Contents on Working Memory of Elementary School Students

Tai-Yen Hsu[1], Fang-Ling Lin[2], Chih-Lin Chang[2], and Hsien-Te Peng[3]

[1] Department of Physical Education, National Taichung University of Education,
Taichung City, Taiwan
hsu@.ntcu.edu.tw
[2] College of General Education, Hsiuping University of Science and Technology,
Taichung City, Taiwan
fingling@mail.hust.edu.tw, salamen.sa@msa.hinet.net
[3] Department of Physical Education, Chinese Culture University, Taipei, Taiwan
sid125peng@yahoo.com.tw

Abstract. Students tend to have poor learning efficiency when distracted by numerous internal and external factors in class. And there were many evidences demonstrate that students' attention plays a significant role in teaching. Therefore, this study aims to probe into working memory of elementary school students by administering three different courses, including math, physical education (PE), and athletics training courses, to three experimental groups. It compares the impact of the three courses on students' attention. In this study, purposive sampling was implemented to select 36 fifth graders from an elementary school in Taichung City, who were divided into three experimental groups. The data were analyzed based on the correctness of students' responses to attention tasks. The experimental test was employed using display duration of 0.3 and 0.4 seconds, respectively. A Wilcoxon matched-pairs signed-ranks test and Kruskal-Wallis one-way analysis of variance by ranks were conducted to identify the significance of the difference between the experimental groups ($\alpha = .05$). When a substantial difference existed between experimental groups, the researcher implemented a post hoc comparison using a Mann-Whitney U test. The experimental results show that all three groups scored strikingly higher on the post-tests than on the pretests, reaching a significant different ($p < .05$). Moreover, the researcher compared the post-test results and discovered that there was a vast difference between the group receiving the PE course and the one receiving the athletics training course ($p < .05$). When the experimental test was given using a time interval of 0.3 seconds, the difference among the three groups was not statistically significant ($p > .05$). The conclusions of this study were as follows: (1) the implementation of different courses has a significant and impact on the working memory of higher-grade elementary school students; (2) different course contents may influence working memory of students; (3) regular athletic training is helpful in enhancing student attention.

Keywords: attention, training course, working memory, elementary school students.

D. Harris (Ed.): EPCE/HCII 2013, Part I, LNAI 8019, pp. 316–324, 2013.
© Springer-Verlag Berlin Heidelberg 2013

1   Introduction

1.1   Research Background

The attention mechanism plays a very important role in the learning process. School children are often affected by internal and external factors while attending classes. It has to be pointed out that the human attention system is a very complicated process. Attention implies "withdrawal from some things in order to deal effectively with other items of greater importance" [1]. A Taiwan local scholar [2] pointed out that "attention" has three different dimensions:

1. Selectivity: Selective focus on certain aspects of the environment while ignoring other facets.
2. Persistence: Continued focus on certain aspects based on personal choice without being distracted or affected by other stimuli.
3. Attention shift: Shift of focus from one object of attention to another as required.
   We still have a very limited understanding of the complex structure and functions of the brain. Attention plays a key role for the functioning of the brain, while attention deficit negatively affects learning and intellectual abilities and behavioral control [3]. The childhood represents a key stage in the acquisition of knowledge and new information. It is also a major stage of cognitive development. A fully developed cognition is a basic requirement for learning and provides the necessary resources for learning activities [4].

Attention is also a very important processing mechanism of visual information. Key processes such as identification, learning, and memorization all require a high level of attention. Students are often affected by internal and external factors while they attend classes, which in turn have an adverse effect on learning outcomes. When an individual focuses his/her attention on selected stimuli, he/she is able to gain a clear perception and has the proverbial "Sharp eyes and keen ears". On the other hand, he/she takes no notice of stimuli and clues that are not in the focus of attention. Instructors should place special emphasis on the impact of attention during the teaching process and consider the internal and external factors that affect attention in order to aid students in the learning process. This study therefore analyzes the focused visual attention of elementary school students and compares their attention levels before and after classes. It also attempts to determine the immediate impact of their exposure to different curricula on their visual attention levels.

1.2   Research Objectives and Problems

Based on theoretical foundation developed in the previous section, the purpose of this study is an analysis of the focused visual attention of elementary school students and their involvement in different curricula (general curricula such as math, physical education in addition to track and field varsity team training) in addition to a comparison of the different attention levels before and after their participation in different curricula. This should help us gain a better understanding of the impact of different curricula such as math, PE, and track and field varsity team training on the student concentration levels.

1.3   Explanation of Key Terms

1. General Curriculum- Math. According to the Nine-year Integrated Curriculum Guidelines, the goals of the math curriculum should include the instruction of the following new topics: observation and practice, conceptual learning, new calculation methods, and solution of application problems
2. General Curriculum –Physical Education Educators have to provide a suitable environment and teaching materials for physical education curricula and employ appropriate teaching methods based on the psychology of learning, the physical and mental attributes, and unique needs of the students. Educators also have to provide the best possible guidance through purposeful, organized, and planned physical activities to achieve the goals of the physical education curriculum [5].
3. Track and Field Varsity Team Training. Track and field training as referred to in this study includes training activities such as jogging, warm-up activities, body-loosening exercises, Mark exercises, interval running, and short sprints twice a week for 40 minutes each time. The training program focuses on simple activities that put no strain on the muscles.
4. Ratio of correct answers. Percentage of accurate responses to target stimuli of the attention assessment test by the participants in the experiment.
5. Display time. The display time intervals which were employed for the experiment were 0.3 sec and 0.4 sec respectively.
6. Symbol length. Memory capacity and duration are the two main characteristics distinguishing short-term memory from other types of memory. Short-term memory has a very limited capacity (only about six items or symbols can be stored at a time). The symbol length was therefore determined as a six-digit sequence of numbers for this experiment [6].

2   Research Methods

2.1   Test Subjects

We employed purposive sampling techniques to select a sample of 5th graders from elementary schools in Taichung City. The selected test subjects were divided into three groups of 12 students each (a total of 36). We obtained written permission from parents or guardians before using the students as test subjects and conducting the experiments.

2.2   Research Process

We conducted three different experiments for this study in form of visual attention assessments before and after student involvement in classes. The first experiment focused on visual attention levels of general school children before and after their involvement in an activity based-curriculum (Physical education), while the second experiment was centered on student involvement in a passive curriculum (Math). Finally, the third experiment focused on visual attention levels before and after their participation in track and field varsity team training.

We created a software program to assess visual attention levels for this study. The test subjects were asked to familiarize themselves with the software operations for approximately 1 minute. During this practice phase, the test subjects had to identify random six-digit number sequences and enter the information into the software system. To measure their visual attention levels, the students were asked to identify a total of 100 number sequences that randomly popped up on the screen within a time span of 10 minutes. The students were exposed to two series of 100 number symbols each that appeared on the screen for 0.3 and 0.4 sec respectively. The ratio of correct answers served as the main data source for the determination of attention levels.

Upon completion of the pre-class experiment, the test subjects immediately attended PE class for 40 minutes. Right after the class another attention test was administered by following the same procedure as for the pre-class assessment.

2.3   Data Processing

The raw data were recorded in the correct format required for the statistical software. The statistical analysis of the raw data obtained from the experiments was performed with SPSS for Windows 12.0 software.

1. A non-parametric related sample test (Wilcoxon signed-rank test) was conducted to determine the difference between the visual attention levels before and after classes within each group. A comparative analysis of the differences of assessment tests that were conducted before and after classes served the purpose of determining the impact of different curricula on student visual attention.
2. A Kruskal-Wallis one-way analysis of variance by ranks was conducted to determine the difference between the pre-class and post-class attention levels of each group and to compare and analyze the impact of different curricula on the visual attention of the students. If statistical significance was indicated ($\alpha = .05$), a further comparative analysis was undertaken using the Mann-Whitney U test.
3. The differences between different display times (0.4 sec and 0.3 sec) were analyzed by using a non-parametric related sample test (Wilcoxon signed-rank test)

3   Results and Discussion

3.1   The Effect of Class Involvement on the Visual Attention Levels of Elementary School Students before and After Classes

Rueda, Rothbart, McCandliss, Saccomanno, and Posner [7] explored the development of the attention network by employing the attention network test. Their samples included the following age groups: children between 6 and 10 and adults. The results of their research indicate that the alerting network is in a stable state after the age of 10. On the other hand, they were not able to observe any obvious changes in the orienting network. The conflict resolution network enters a stable state after children reach the age of 7. This study is a follow-up of the previous research mentioned above. We focused on the effect of class involvement on visual attention levels of school children. A comparison of the results of the visual attention assessments before and after classes shows that all three groups achieved better scores (higher ratio of correct answers) in the post-class assessment (see Table 1 and 2). However, the groups showed different degrees of improvement based on the type of curriculum. We discovered that indoor classes (Math) were associated with a greater improvement in scores than outdoor classes. This is probably related to the fact that children are less distracted by environmental stimuli than during classes that take place in an open outdoor environment. These results are similar to the findings of other studies. Students are generally more focused in math class than in other classes. A comparison of the two outdoor curricula (PE and track and field training) reveals that members of the track and field varsity team tend to achieve better scores than their counterparts who attend regular PE classes. This is probably related to the fact that members of the varsity team have more physical strength and a better physique than other students. Although they are exposed to the same environmental stimuli as other students, they are less exhausted after their training sessions due to their greater physical strength. Members of the varsity team showed a greater improvement in scores than students who participated in regular PE classes, but their scores were slightly worse than those of students who had attended math classes. We believe that these differences can be attributed to different environmental stimuli in indoor and outdoor areas. To sum up, we firmly believe that the involvement in classes has an immediate positive effect on the visual attention level of elementary school students.

Table 1. The results of the Wilcoxon signed-rank test for the ratio of correct answers on assessments before and after classes (display time=0.4sec) are summarized in the table below (Mean ± Standard error; Unit: %) $^*P<.05$

Unit: %	Pre-class	Post-class	Improvement	Z value	P value
PE	58.72± 8.1	63.13±17.87	4.41	-2.237[*]	.025
Math	71.08±16.53	77.25± 14.33	6.17	-3.061[*]	.002
Track and Field	73.25 ± 13.1	80.60 ± 9.17	7.35	-2.982[*]	.003

Table 2. The results of the Wilcoxon signed-rank test for the ratio of correct answers on assessments before and after classes (display time=0.3sec) are summarized in the table below (Mean ± Standard error; Unit: %)

Unit: %	Pre-class	Post-class	Improvement	Z value	P value
PE	62.53 ±15.58	66.71 ± 15.2	4.18	-2.903[*]	.004

Table 2. (*Continued*)

Math	68.67 ± 4.25	75.95 ± 11.67	7.28	-2.936[*]	.003
Track and Field	71.85 ±14.35	77.97 ± 13.02	6.12	-3.059[*]	.002

3.2   The Effect of the Involvement in Different Classes on the Visual Attention of Elementary School Students

It is evident that visual attention assessments that were conducted before classes for all three groups with display times of 0.3 and 0.4 sec did not show any significant differences, which means that the three groups were homogeneous to begin with. The results of assessment tests that were conducted after the involvement in different curricula (display time = 0.4sec) showed statistically significant differences. A follow-up comparative analysis revealed that students who had been exposed to track and field training scored higher on the attention assessment tests than students who had attended PE class. These results suggest that different curricula have different immediate effects on the visual attention levels of elementary school students.

The results of post-class assessment tests with a display time of 0.3 seconds did not show any significant differences in visual attention levels for all three groups. We therefore shifted our attention to the different degrees of improvement. The post-class tests showed a significant improvement in the ratio of correct answers for all three groups. We went on to subtract the pre-class scores from the post-class scores. Although we did not find statistically significant differences, the results were close to significance. We are therefore still convinced that the involvement in different classes has different immediate effects on the visual attention of school children. Higher attention levels increase the ability of students to detect hints and clues in problems and also lead to a better problem-solving capacity [8].

The results of this study clearly demonstrate that members of the track and field varsity team scored higher in post-training visual attention assessments than students who had attended regular PE classes. This is a very interesting phenomenon since both training and PE classes are activity-based curricula. It is an intriguing question why the participation in these training sessions positively affects visual attention levels. We believe that the main reason for this phenomenon is that long-term athletic training results in greater physical strength compared to students who don't exercise on a regular basis. These students also have a better ability to handle the physical burden of the training curriculum which explains the fact that they score higher on post-class attention assessments and achieve better results than students who participate in regular PE classes. Wu [9]   pointed out that table tennis training has a significant impact on the ability of elementary school students to focus their attention. He also suggests that a medium training regimen produces better results than a light training regimen. Exhaustion from exercise, however, leads to significantly lower attention levels [10]. The results of this study are similar to the findings of numerous past studies. We therefore postulate that different curricula influence the visual attention of elementary school students in different ways.

Table 3. The results of the Kruskal-Wallis one-way analysis of variance by ranks for the ratio of correct answers on assessments before and after classes (display time=0.4sec) are summarized in the table below (Mean ± Standard error; Unit: %)

Unit: %	PE	Math	Track and Field	χ 2 value	P value
Pre-class	58.72±5.22	71.08±4.77	73.25±3.78	4.123	.127
Post-class	63.13±5.16	77.25±4.14	80.60±2.65	6.33[*]	.042
Improvement	4.40±1.10	6.16±1.29	7.35±1.40	1.38	.265

*P<.05

Table 4. The results of the Kruskal-Wallis one-way analysis of variance by ranks for the ratio of correct answers on assessments before and after classes (display time=0.3sec) are summarized in the table below (Mean ± Standard error; Unit: %)

Unit: %	PE	Math	Track and Field	χ 2 value	P value
Pre-class	62.53±4.5	68.67±4.11	71.85±4.14	1.585	.453
Post-class	66.71±4.39	75.95±1.17	77.97±2.32	4.427	.109
Improvement	4.18±.80	7.28±.97	6.13±.99	2.90	.070

3.3   The Impact of Different Display Times on the Visual Attention of Elementary School Students

Gerardi-Caulton [11] employed spatial conflict task to determine the attention and conflict resolution capacity of children. The results of her research show that reaction times decrease with increasing age, while the accuracy rate rises. The differences between spatially incompatible and spatially compatible trials also become smaller, which in turn indicates a better problem-solving capacity. Rueda, Rothbart, McCandliss, Saccomanno, and Posner emphasize the flexibility of attention development in their study[7]. The brain wave data of their experiments suggest that pre-school children who had received attention training exhibited brain wave patterns in the frontal lobe and parietal lobe area that were more similar to adults than those of children who

Table 5. The results of the Wilcoxon signed-rank test for the ratio of correct answers on assessments between different display times are summarized in the table below (Mean ± Standard error; Unit: %)

Unit: %	0.4 sec	0.3 sec	Z value	P value
Pre-class (N=36)	67.68±6.88	67.68±14.84	-.440	.660
Post-class (N=36)	73.66±5.82	73.54±13.91	-.079	.937

didn't receive any training. Shan, Chen, and Su [4] point out in their research that among the attention functions, reaction times are the most sensitive indicator of differences. This is also reflected in the results of this study since we were able to show that identical attention assessment tests with slightly different display times (0.3 sec and 0.4sec) did not produce any significant differences as far as the ratio of correct answers of pre-class and post-class tests are concerned.

4   Conclusion

There is general agreement that attention is comprised of three interrelated networks (orienting, alerting, and executive) and that different brain areas are involved in the attention process. The development of these networks and high-level executive functions are also part of the attention network and are closely related to conflict resolution and inhibition skills. If children exhibit low performance in these areas, it is usually reflected in below average school performance. This study seeks to make a contribution to the research in this field by exploring the connection between attention and learning efficiency. Our results indicate that the involvement in classes has a direct impact on the level of attention and focus during the learning process.

The comparison of the participation in different types of curricula focused on the impact of external stimuli on the student's attention levels. We discovered in our research that no significant differences exist between the pre-class test scores of all three groups. This clearly indicates that the initial attention levels of all participants of the experiments which had been divided into three groups were very similar. After the involvement in different classes, however, it was evident that members of the track and field training group achieved significantly better scores than members of the PE group. We have suggested that this is probably related to the fact that members of the varsity team have a better physique due to their continued participation in a regular training and exercise program. They therefore possess a greater amount of attention resources and abilities which can be employed to effectively suppress environmental distractions and are better equipped to engage in physically taxing activities, which in turn explains why they score higher than their counterparts. Finally, we compared the differences between different symbol display times (0.3 and 0.4 sec). By viewing all participants of the experiment as members of the same sample cluster, we were able to demonstrate that different display times (0.3 and 0.4 sec) have no significant impact on the visual attention levels of elementary school students.

References

1. James, W.: Principles of psychology. Holt, New York (1890)
2. Cheng, C.M.: Cognitive Psychology. Laurel, Taipei (1993) (in Chinese)
3. Lin, C.H., Pei, Y.C., Chung, C.Y., Cheng, P.T., Chen, C.L., Wong, A.M.K.: Event-Related Potentials of Visual Spatial Attention in Healthy Subjects. Taiwan Journal of Physical Medicine and Rehabilitation 33(1), 19–28 (2005) (in Chinese)

4. Shan, I.K., Chen, Y.S., Su, T.S.: Recognition of Facial Expressions: Age and Gender Effects and the Performance of Patients with Aspe Ger's Disorder. Archives of Clinical Psychology 2(2), 76–86 (2005) (in Chinese)
5. Tsai, Z.X.: The Research of Elementary School Physical Education. Wunan, Taipei (1989) (in Chinese)
6. Lin, S.R. (tra): Human performance engineering. (Bailey, R.W.). Laurel, Taipei (1995) (in Chinese)
7. Rueda, M.R., Rothbart, M.K., McCandliss, B.D., Saccomanno, L., Posner, M.I.: Training, maturation, and genetic influences on the development of executive attention. Proceedings of the National Academy of Sciences of the United States of America 102(41), 14931–14936 (2005)
8. Agostino, A., Johnson, J., Pascual-Leone, J.: Executive functions underlying multiplicative reasoning: problem type matters. Journal of Experimental Child Psychology 105(4), 286–305 (2010)
9. Wu, G.H.: Experimental Research of Effect of Soccer and Table Tennis Exercise on Children's Attentional Concentration. Journal of Ningxia University (Natural Science Edition in Chinese) 26(3), 287–289 (2005)
10. Wu, T.F.: The Experimental Research of Relationship Between the Fatigue of University Basketball Athletes and Their Attention. Northeast Normal University, Changchun (2005) (unpublished doctoral dissertation in Chinese)
11. Gerardi-Caulton, G.: Sensitivity to spatial conflict and the development of self-regulation in children 24-36 months of age. Developmental Science 3(4), 397–404 (2000)

Developing Metacognitive Models for Team-Based Dynamic Environment Using Fuzzy Cognitive Mapping

Jung Hyup Kim, Gretchen A. Macht, Ling Rothrock, and David A. Nembhard

Department of Industrial and Manufacturing Engineering,
Pennsylvania State University, USA
{jzk170,gam201,lrothroc,dan12}@psu.edu

Abstract. In this paper, by using Fuzzy Cognitive Mapping (FCM) technique, we developed the metacognitive models for team-based dynamic environment. Preliminary findings from our metacognitive studies provided a possible metacognitive framework in dynamic control tasks [1, 2]. By analyzing metacognition, performance, and communication data between team, we are able to develop the team-based evolving metacognitive models for the dynamic environments using a fuzzy cognitive map. In this research, a human-in-the-loop simulation experiment was conducted to collect communication data, objective performance data (operator on-time action performance), and subjective rating data (retrospective confident metacognitive judgment) from 6 dyads (12 participants). Within the Anti-Air Warfare Coordinator (AAWC) simulation domain, the simulation test bed provides an interactive simulating condition in which the monitoring team must communicate with their team member to defend their ship against hostile aircraft.

Keywords: Metacognition, Team Performance, Human-in-the-loop simulation, Fuzzy Cognitive Map.

1 Introduction

The need to develop more advanced on-the-job training methods has become a growing concern in many industries because people not only work as individuals, but as members of teams. Although advanced technology provides the ability to develop more effective training approaches to novice workers, building effective team training methods is still on-going research area. To address this critical need, this research investigated the different behavior models based on metacognition and communication between team members using Fuzzy Cognitive Mapping (FCM) techniques. FCM is a "mental landscape" of the elements (e.g. actors, values, goals, and trends) in a fuzzy feedback system. FCM can demonstrate the links between causal events of dynamic tasks and human behavior with the change of time. The map lists the fuzzy rules related with events to show causal flow paths like Hasse diagram [3]. The FCM enables job trainers to evaluate trainees' internal learning states, and to help the instructors to choose several possible actions. In this research, we developed a human-in-the-loop simulation, which emulates a computer-based dynamic control task to

D. Harris (Ed.): EPCE/HCII 2013, Part I, LNAI 8019, pp. 325–334, 2013.

identify navigational cognitive behavior in order to collect metacognition and communication data in a team-based training environment. The domain of this simulation test bed is AAWC (Anti Air warfare Coordinator). This is an interactive simulation in which a controller must defend his/her ship against hostile aircraft. Data from the experiment indicated that metacognitive monitoring behaviors which were measured using subjective rating methods showed different patterns between teammates. Role A (executing appropriate actions based on Rules of Engagements (RoE)) showed a significant positive correlation between the metacognition and performance[1] of identification rules while Role B (controlling Defense Counter Aircrafts (DCA) to update the information of unknown hostile aircrafts) was not (Role A: $r = 0.474$, $p < 0.05$; Role B: $r = -0.28$, $p = 0.184$). Since teammates communicated with each other only through the telephone, Role A had to obtain and understand information of unknown hostile aircrafts through the communication with Role B, and this contributed to different metacognitive judgments between teammates [1]. It has been suggested that the key to success in teamwork lies to a great extent in achieving not only successful team cooperation, but also efficient team communication [4]. In this paper, by using FCM techniques and data (metacognition and communication) from the previous team-based AAWC experiment, we develop the team-based metacognitive mapping models in a dynamic control tasks. This work provides understanding on how the communication and metacognitive behavior influence team members.

2   Literature Review

2.1   Metacognition

Metacognition is mainly the mind's ability to monitor and control human cognition. According to the Nelson and Narens's metacognitive model [5], human metacognition is significantly influenced by information flows between "meta-level" and "object-level". The object-level consists of ongoing cognitive processes, such as perception, problem solving, and learning. The meta-level is about a persons' own understanding related to his or her object-level cognition. The information flows between these levels are unidirectional. The information channel from object-level to meta-level is called metacognitive monitoring, while the other channel from meta-level to object-level is called metacognitive controlling. The data entity of the information flows between these levels consists of metacognitive knowledge or meta-memory. The meta-memory is a self-awareness of memory which can reflect how people learn and use their memories. In other words, it is the awareness of one's own cognition. These meta-memories can be transferred to meta-level through the metacognitive monitoring. It is the ability to make accurate accessing the current state of cognitive activities on object-level. By using metacognitive monitoring process, people will produce more effective regulation to improve their learning [6]. After that, the metacognitive control can regulate ongoing cognitive activities such as a decision-making procedure

---

[1] Correct response rate for identifying hostile aircrafts: number of correct responses/ total number of identification tasks for unknown hostile aircrafts.

for using new tactics to solve a difficult problem. In this paper, we focus on the ability to make accurate monitoring judgments for the current state of cognitive activities because accurate monitoring of learning is one of the critical elements in metacognition [7].

2.2   Fuzzy Cognitive Mapping (FCM)

Fuzzy cognitive mapping (FCM) was developed by Kosko in 1986. FCM is an extension of conventional cognitive maps of binary logic set theory. Cognitive maps (CMs) are defined as a type of mental processing composed of a series of modeling decision making in individual mind maps and social political systems. CMs have been studied in various fields due to a strong visual representation of causal relationships and a clear comparison of mental models to reality. However, conventional cognitive maps make knowledge acquisition oppressively burdensome from insufficient decision information, different experts. Hence, a need to represent causal relationships of linguistic quantities becomes very important. FCM can express various degrees of increase or decrease of casual relationships. It is a very powerful tool to represent and compute the "strength of impact" of causal flow paths in dynamic environment. Fuzzy set theory is behind the computational theory of FCM.   Since Lotfi Zadeh published a paper titled "Fuzzy Sets" [8], the various applications using fuzzy sets have been successfully tested in the control engineering distributed networks [9], health care [10], decision support systems [11], and situation awareness for army infantry [12].

3   Method

Our current work focuses on developing the representation of metacognitive mapping model in team-based dynamic control tasks by using FCM technique.

3.1   Dynamic Decision-Making Task Human-In-The-Loop Simulation

The AAWC (Anti Air warfare Coordinator) test bed is interactive simulation in which a controller must defend his/her ship against hostile aircraft.

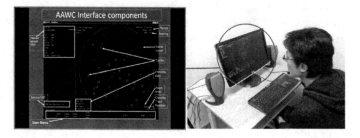

Fig. 1. AAWC interface (left) and experimental setup (right)

A total of 12 male engineering graduate students (age 18 or older) participated with little to no previously established relationships. The experiment was single gender to avoid potential gender interactions in the current study. Participants were voluntary and screened for prior experience with the task domain. The experiment consists of two sessions – a training session and an experiment session. The participants participated in an initial training session (Day 1), which lasted 60 minutes. During this session the participants were trained on the specific skills and provided with feedback on their task. Participants gained experience and understanding of the tasks based on the feedback provided by the instructor. The practice scenario lasted approximately five minutes with a task complexity that was easier than the actual experiment. Based on the result of the pilot test, participants were ready to engage in the actual experiment after they executed the practice simulation for the third time. The participants after being trained underwent an experiment session (Day 2), which lasted approximately 90 minutes. During this session the participants were required to perform certain tasks based on the scenario. In the experiment, four scenarios are developed and events in each scenario have their specific sequence to occur. Each scenario was designed to run 15 minutes long. Freeze occurred randomly between 10 and 15 minutes after the start of the scenario. Once the simulation was frozen, participants required answering retrospective confidence judgment (metacognition) probes. Retrospective confidence judgment comes from metacognitive monitoring processes associated more directly with retrieval [13]. The probes used for measurement are shown below:

- How well do you think you have detected the objects in your airspace?
- How well do you think you are aware of the current overall situation of your airspace?
- How well do you think you are aware of where the overall situation of your airspace is heading?

3.2   Team Selection

Team assignments were determined based on the Big Five Inventory (BFI) as the specific measurement tool for FFM personality conducted on the first of the two days of the study [14]. FFM extraversion formed the basis for dyad membership, wherein dyads were either two introverts (II), or one introvert and one extravert (EI). Each dyad had at least one introvert, also as a part of variance reduction, and that introvert was always assigned to the second of the two task roles (DCA). To construct these dyads, Ward's clustering [15] was used as an iterative pairwise comparison of Euclidean based distances, in order to group participants with similar extravert scores. The remaining introverts were then added to the heterogeneous EI groups, wherein assignments were optimized based on the maximum variance between the levels of extraversion-introversion, while minimizing the variation among the remaining four FFM factors. The result was three distinct teams in each category of dyad. The placement of the extraverts within roles in the dyads did not convey any particular status to either individual within the dyad (e.g., [16, 17]). Both the extrovert or the introvert were responsible to take appropriate actions based on the Rules of Engagement (RoE); where the introverted individual always remained responsible to control

Defense Counter Aircrafts (DCA). This team-based environment provides the condition in which the monitoring team (Roles A and B) must communicate with their team member to defend their ship against hostile aircraft.

3.3   Developing Augmented FCM

By using the communication and performance data between teammates, we defined eleven important behavior concepts (see Section 3.4) that directly relate to the task at hand. Simple FCMs which have bivalent nodes and edges can be addressed based on communication data. Causal edges take values in $\{-1, 0, 1\}$. These simple FCMs additively combine to form new FCMs [3]. The W_i are positive or negative weights for the ith FCM F_i. The weights state the relative value of each FCM in the environment. In this paper, we assume that the weights of any sub-graph of the FCMs are equal and take them as unity: $W_i = 1$. Figure 2 shows an example of the augmented FCM for identification task. F_{ROE} and F_{DCA} are simple FCMs for i^{th} identification tasks in dynamic environment ($i = 1... n$; n = total number of identification tasks).

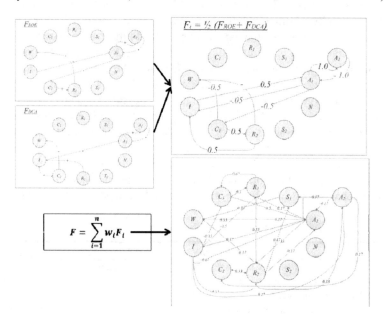

Fig. 2. Procedure for developing Augmented FCM

3.4   Performance Metrics

In this experiment, we collected operator on-time action performance, retrospective metacognitive judgment, and communication data between teammates.

Operator On-Time Identification Performance (OIP): It is defined as the degree of on-time correct action of a dynamic control task. A time window is a construct that specifies the availability of an action opportunity which leads to the required situation

[18]. In our experiment, the main goal is correctly identifying every unknown hostile aircrafts at appropriate times. Here, we only consider hostiles or assumed hostiles. Operator on-time Action Performance is simply calculated by:

$$OIP = CR \times 100 / TW\_id \tag{1}$$

Where:

- OIP: operator on-time identification performance
- CR: number of correct identification responses
- TW_id: total number of time window assigned for unknown identification task

Retrospective Confidence Judgment (RCJ): Participants state their confidence level for their responses before knowing whether they are correct or incorrect. Confidence level ratings are compared to the accuracy of past retrieval. We collected self-rating scores (scale: 1 to 100) during the testing sessions.

Communication Data: The participants for the two roles were kept in separate rooms, thereby eliminating gestural non-verbal communication and other sight related cues. Therefore Role A had to obtain and understand information of unknown hostile aircrafts through verbal communication with Role B. Although, the two monitors are synchronized, no direct communication was available through the computer. Communication metrics were the number of utterances (e.g. Table 1 has 7 utterances; 4 RoE and 3 DCA), word count (e.g. 10 words in the first utterance in Table 1), and duration ([19-21]). For each of the 24 dyad and trial combinations, the audio was transcribed, timed, with words, utterances, and durations determined by two raters. The analysis on communication data between team members provided valuable insight on how to effectively support human cognition within the decision-making process. Based on the communication and performance data between teammates, we developed eleven important behavior concepts that directly relate to the task at hand (see Table 2).

Table 1. Example of Role Dialogue to Complete ID Tasks

Role	Dialogue	Request Type
ROE:	Unknown aircraft number 17, bearing 106, range 21.6 nautical miles.	Call ID (C_1)
DCA:	Yes. I'll send something towards it.	Response ID (R_1)
ROE:	Anything on number 17?	Re-Call ID (C_2)
DCA:	Target 17 is a hostile strike aircraft.	Identification (I)
ROE:	Got it. Thanks.	Re-Affirm ID (A_2)
ROE:	It did not respond to my warnings, so I shot it down.	Shot (S_1)
DCA:	Got it. Thanks.	Response Shot (S_2)

Table 2. Description of Behavior Concept Nodes

Behavior Concepts	Description
Call ID (C_1)	Ask for identification of an Unidentified track Number
Response ID (R_1)	Recognizing the Call ID
Affirm ID (A_1)	Confirming the ID

Table 2. *(Continued)*

Re-Call ID (C₂)	Re-asking for the identification of a unknown aircraft
Re-Response ID (R₂)	Recognizing the Re-Call ID
Re-Affirm ID (A₂)	Re-conforming the ID
Shot (S₁)	Shooting of the Aircraft which poses a potential threat to the ship
Response Shot (S₂)	Confirming the Shot
Wait (W)	Searching the Unidentified or Hostile or Assumed Hostile Aircraft
Identification (I)	Identification action of selected unknown aircraft
Noise (N)	Conversation that have nothing to deal with the task at hand

FCM inferences: After the FCMs were delineated, we could determine the system's steady state by using the auto-associative neural network methods [22]. This method only considers outcomes and dynamics of each node. Following this method, the value of each node (C_i) in iteration (t) can be computed as:

$$C_i^t = f(\textstyle\sum_{j-1}^n C_j^{t-1} W_{ji} + C_i^{t-1})$$

(2)

Where:

- C_i^t : Values of the node i at the end of the iteration.
- C_j^t : Values of the subsequent node j at the beginning of the iteration
- W_{jk}: Corresponding strength of the link from node j to node i
- f: Threshold function that transforms the result of the multiplication. Usually the logistic function that assumes the form $1/(1 + e^{-x})$ is used.

4   Results

4.1   Descriptive Statistics

EI group's OIP performance mean is higher than II group (see Table 3), but there is no significant performance difference between these groups based on the result of ANOVA test ($F = 0.68$, $p = 0.418$). In addition, RCJ means show that there is no significant different between EI and II group ($F = 0.00, p = 0.977$).

Table 3. Metacognition and Task Performance results

Team	Variable	N	Mean	StDev	Minimum	Median	Maximum
EI	RCJ	12	66.00	5.7	40	65	86.75
	OIP	12	45.84	19.82	28.6	42.9	85.7
II	RCJ	12	66.25	22.27	20	70	90
	OIP	12	40.48	10.71	21.4	42.9	50

4.2   Team-Based Metacognitive Models Using Fuzzy Cognitive Mapping (TBM-FCM) in AAWC System

After combining team communication and metacognition data, we are able to construct FCM matrices for each team using the nodes in Table 1. It allows developing different cognitive map patterns between groups by including the union of the causal concepts of the system. Figure 3 and 4 show examples of the augmented TBM-FCM for both EI and II group.

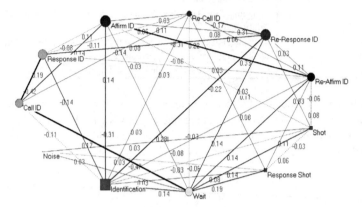

Fig. 3. TBM-FCM for EI Group

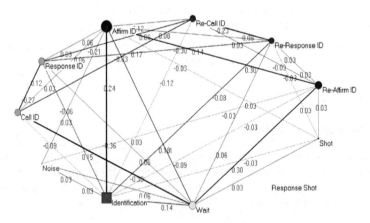

Fig. 4. TBM-FCM for II Group

4.3   Simulation of Steady State for the FCMs

According to the task performance and metacognition data, both groups show either Over-Confident $(RCJ_j > OIP_j)$[*] or Under-Confident $(RCJ_j < OIP_j)$[*] metacognitive behavior during the experiment. Moreover, the communication data reveals that Noise node can cause the misunderstanding between teammates. Hence, we designed two conditions for both metacognition (Over and Under-Confident) and communication status ("Clean" and "Noise") in each group. Based on our experimental data, we are

---

[*] $j = 1,...m$; m = number of dyad and trial combinations.

able to generate three different cases for each group and simulate them until the system reach to the steady state (see Table 4) using equation 2. The values show the effect of communication status and metacognition in the team performance.

Table 4. Steady State Results for the FCMs

	EI			II		
Communication	Noise	Clean	Noise	Noise	Clean	Noise
Metacognition	Over Confident	Over Confident	Under Confident	Over Confident	Over Confident	Under Confident
C_1	0.41	0.38	0.37	0.44	0.40	0.42
R_1	0.455038	0.482606	0.515562	0.533515	0.514912	0.5
A_1	0.556693	0.433616	0.548736	0.536218	0.534958	0.576646
C_2	0.509092	0.571576	0.509636	0.475688	0.472333	0.468993
R_2	0.541461	0.580115	0.529245	0.496961	0.523599	0.498708
A_2	0.569649	0.569476	0.632333	0.545937	0.579218	0.524008
S_1	0.569141	0.547754	0.553558	0.5	0.527899	0.5
S_2	0.523696	0.500000	0.523049	0.500000	0.500000	0.500000
W	0.592464	0.626849	0.617619	0.629986	0.610936	0.609462
I	0.498017	0.518059	0.519041	0.500000	0.500000	0.500000
N	0.521807	0.500000	0.523049	0.500000	0.500000	0.524008

5   Discussion

By using FCM technique and metacognition and communication data from team-based AAWC experiment, we are able to develop the cognitive mapping models in dynamic environment. It shows how the communication noise and metacognitive behavior (over or under confident) influence the different team selection (EI and II group). For example, according to the steady state results (Table 3), EI group shows that the identification task of the unknown aircrafts can be influenced by the unnecessary conversation between teammates (± 0.012). However, it does not have influence on II group (± 0). In addition, for EI group, the under-confident metacognitive behavior increases the frequencies of recognizing the Call ID (R_1) and reconfirming the identification of unknown aircrafts (A_2) as compared to the over-confident judgment condition (R_1: +0.06, A_2: +0.06). However, for II group, under-confident condition decreases frequencies of both R_1 and A_2 as compared to the over-confident metacognitive behavior (R_1: − 0.03, A_2: − 0.02). Our preliminary findings of this study show that FCM technique is useful to understand evolving metacognitive process in terms of the team performance and communication between teammates. The next step of the analysis is identifying the navigational training impact of the metacognitive behavior derived from team-communication.

References

1. Kim, J.H., Macht, G.A., Li, S.: Comparison of Individual and Team-Based Dynamic Decision-Making Task (Anti-Air Warfare Coordinator): Consideration of Subjective Mental Workload Metacognition. In: Proceedings of the Human Factors and Ergonomics Society Annual Meeting. SAGE Publications (2012)
2. Kim, J., et al.: Investigating the effects of metacognition in dynamic control tasks. Human-Computer Interaction. Design and Development Approaches, 378–387 (2011)
3. Kosko, B.: Fuzzy cognitive maps. International Journal of Man-Machine Studies 24(1), 65–75 (1986)
4. Entin, E.E., Serfaty, D.: Adaptive team coordination. Human Factors: The Journal of the Human Factors and Ergonomics Society 41(2), 312–325 (1999)
5. Nelson, T.O., Narens, L.: Metamemory: A theoretical framework and new findings. The Psychology of Learning and Motivation 26, 125–141 (1990)
6. Sussan, D., Son, L.: The training of metacognitive monitoring in children. Columbia Undergraduate Science Journal 2(1) (2007)
7. Perry, N.E., Phillips, L., Hutchinson, L.R.: Preparing student teachers to support for self-regulated learning. Elementary School Journal 106(3), 237–254 (2006)
8. Zadeh, L.A.: Fuzzy sets. Information and Control 8(3), 338–353 (1965)
9. Ndousse, T., Okuda, T.: Computational intelligence for distributed fault management in networks using fuzzy cognitive maps. IEEE (1996)
10. Langan-Fox, J., Langfield-Smith, K.: Team mental models: Techniques, methods, and analytic approaches. Human Factors: The Journal of the Human Factors and Ergonomics Society, 2000 42(2), 242–271 (2000)
11. Xirogiannis, G., Stefanou, J., Glykas, M.: A fuzzy cognitive map approach to support urban design. Expert Systems with Applications 26(2), 257–268 (2004)
12. Jones, R.E.T., et al.: Modeling situation awareness for Army infantry platoon leaders using fuzzy cognitive mapping techniques (2010)
13. Dougherty, M.R., et al.: Using the past to predict the future. Memory & Cognition 33(6), 1096–1115 (2005)
14. John, O.P., Naumann, L.P., Soto, C.J.: Paradigm shift to the integrative Big Five trait taxonomy. Handbook of Personality: Theory and Research, 114–158 (2008)
15. Garson, D.: Cluster Analysis (2008), http://www2.chass.ncse.edu/garson/PA765/cluster.htm
16. Barry, B., Stewart, G.L.: Composition, process, and performance in self-managed groups: The role of personality. Journal of Applied Psychology 82(1), 62 (1997)
17. Barrick, M.R., et al.: Relating member ability and personality to work-team processes and team effectiveness. Journal of Applied Psychology 83(3), 377 (1998)
18. Rothrock, L.: Using Time Windows to Evaluate Operator Performance. International Journal of Cognitive Ergonomics 5(1), 1–21 (2001)
19. Brannick, M.T., Roach, R.M., Salas, E.: Understanding team performance: A multimethod study. Human Performance 6(4), 287–308 (1993)
20. Adams, S.K.: Disciplinarily Hetero- and Homogeneous Design Team Convergence. Virginia Polytechnic Institute and State University, Blacksburg, VA. Doctoral Thesis (2007)
21. Letsky, M.P.: Macrocognition in teams: Theories and methodologies. Ashgate Publishing Company (2008)
22. Reimann, S.: On the design of artificial auto-associative neuronal networks. Neural Networks 11(4), 611–621 (1998)

Proposal of Intellectual Productivity Model
Based on Work State Transition

Kazune Miyagi, Kotaro Oishi, Kosuke Uchiyama,
Hirotake Ishii, and Hiroshi Shimoda

Graduate School of Energy Science, Kyoto University, Kyoto, Japan
{miyagi,oishi,uchiyama,hirotake,shimoda}@ei.energy.kyoto-u.ac.jp

Abstract. Aiming to reveal the mechanism of intellectual productivity variation of office workers, the authors analyzed the behavior of subjective experiment assuming office work, and proposed an intellectual productivity model. The model is a three state transit model assuming "working state", "short-term rest state" and "long-term rest state". A subject experiment was conducted where illuminance on the desk and work motivation were controlled to vary their productivity. The result was analyzed with this model and it is confirmed that the model can explain the productivity variation.

Keywords: intellectual productivity, human modeling, working state, illuminance.

1   Introduction

In office buildings, the energy consumption of lighting and air-conditioning systems account for big percentage of total energy consumption [1]. Therefore many office building have been trying turning down air-conditioning and dimming a light off for saving energy. After East Japan earthquake and the following Fukushima nuclear disaster, the lack of electricity has promoted energy saving policies such activity. On the other hand, many studies have revealed that indoor environment condition affects intellectual productivity and health of office worker [2]. For example, a circadian rhythm lighting which adjusts human circadian rhythm by high illumination light, promotes intellectual productivity [3]. However, it is reported that the effectiveness of indoor environment is also dependent on other factors such as work motivation. In addition, the mechanism of intellectual productivity variation has not been revealed.

In this study, therefore, the authors analyzed the behavior of subjective experiment assuming office work, and proposed an intellectual productivity model. In addition, a subjective experiment was conducted, in which the intellectual performance was controlled by lighting environment and work motivation. With the experiment result, authors discussed the details of the model by comparing the results of the computer simulation based on the model with the experimental results. If this model is completed by the result of experiment, which the authors are planning to conduct for revealing the

D. Harris (Ed.): EPCE/HCII 2013, Part I, LNAI 8019, pp. 335–343, 2013.
© Springer-Verlag Berlin Heidelberg 2013

effect of indoor environment, we can predict productivity without experiment, and optimize the balance between productivity and energy use by the model.

2   Intellectual Productivity Model

2.1   Intellectual Productivity

There are various kinds of office works, and the human abilities for office work also various. But, works which occupy a considerable amount of working time are mental tasks which have standard routine. Therefore, in this model, an intellectual productivity means the performance of less-creative cognitive task such as deskwork or information management tasks.

The working style in real office is seem that office workers devote a given time period for their work. The period would be more than 30 minute or several hours. And workers address their works at their own pace in this period. Therefore, in this study, working style is assumed as above one.

2.2   Time-Series Analysis of Solving Tasks

Aiming to guess the mechanism of work productivity variance, the feature of an experimental result was extracted with time series charts like Figure 1. Its ordinate axis shows the times of answering each problem, when checking receipt task was given. Abscissa axis shows the lapsed time. A receipt checking task is simple and the answering time should be almost same in every receipt. But, the distribution is wide. And there is a tendency that the frequency of problems which need long time is high. For this analysis, the authors assumed that the main process of productivity variance is these short rests to relieve fatigue. In addition, the histograms sometimes have long tail. It suggests that there are two type of rest.

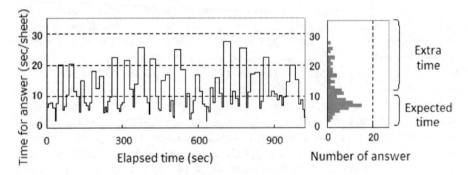

Fig. 1. Time series analysis of answering speed

2.3   Intellectual Productivity Model

Based on above analysis results, the authors had proposed an intellectual productivity model, which is assuming three state transition. Fig.2 shows the concept of this model. The features are as follows;

Fig. 2. Work state model

- There are 3 states, which are "Working state", "Long-term rest state" and "Short-term rest state".
- "Working state" is a state assumed working on a task without trouble. Under this state, the task progresses and MF (mental fatigue) increases.
- "Long-term rest state" is a state assumed conscious rest from several seconds to dozens of seconds. Under the long pause, the task does not progress and MF decreases.
- "Short-term rest state" is a state assumed working on a task with trouble. Under the short pause, the task does not progress and MF increases. This state might be a phenomenon of "Blocking" named by Bills [4].
- State transition probability between the work state and the long pause state is affected by MF.
- State transition probability between the work state and the short pause state is a fixed value.

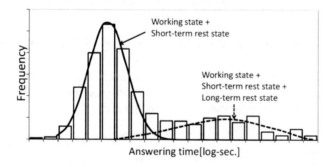

Fig. 3. Histogram of answering time and lognormal distributions

The transition probability is assumed that it is affected with mental fatigue, but it can be treated fixed value in long time scale. It means, these 3 state model could be considered as the superposition of two state Markov Model. It is known that a lognormal distribution is shown when two state Markov model (S1 to S2: p; S2 to S1: q) is assumed. Because of these reason, it is considered that the histogram of the answering time of each problem can be approximated as the sum of two lognormal distributions as shown in Figure 3. The parameters of two lognormal distributions can be calculated by the approximation as shown in Figure 4. At that time, the histogram can be expressed as formula (1) using the parameters.

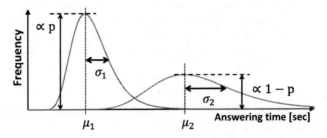

Fig. 4. Lognormal distributions and their parameters

$$f_1(t) = \frac{1}{\sqrt{2\pi}\sigma_1 t} \exp\left[-\frac{(\ln(t) - \mu_1)}{2\sigma_1^2}\right] \cdot pt$$

$$f_2(t) = \frac{1}{\sqrt{2\pi}\sigma_2 t} \exp\left[-\frac{(\ln(t) - \mu_2)}{2\sigma_2^2}\right] \cdot (1-p)t \qquad (1)$$

$$f(t) = f_1(t) + f_2(t)$$

Here, μ_1, μ_2 expresses the averages of lognormal distributions, σ_1, σ_2 expresses their standard deviations, and $p, (1-p)$ express their height ratios.

3   Experiment Focused on Illuminance and Work Motivation

In order to confirm that the model can explain actual productivity variance, the authors conducted a subjective experiment, in which the intellectual performance was controlled by lighting environment and work motivation

3.1   Objective

The first purpose of this experiment was to collect the sample of intellectual productivity variation for simulating with the productivity variation models. The second purpose was to discuss the detail of intellectual productivity variation caused by illumination or work motivation with the model.

3.2   Experimental Method

In this experiment, 24 subjects (male: 22, female: 2, mean age: 26.4) participated. They were given two cognitive tasks and the performance was measured under two illuminance conditions and two work motivation conditions. Two illuminance conditions were prepared which are "Normal illuminance" and "High illuminance" conditions. Under the normal illuminance condition, the illuminance on the desk was fixed to 750 lux, which value is usually used in office. Under the high illuminance condition, the illuminance was fixed to 2,500 lux which is effective to improve arousal level and is expected to improve intellectual productivity [3]. As shown in Figure 5, the illuminance was controlled by task lighting.

Fig. 5. Experimental environment

Two work motivation conditions were also prepared which were "High motivated" and "Low motivated" conditions. Under high motivated condition, the subjects were instructed that extra reward would be paid according to their task performances. Under low motivated condition, they were instructed that this task was not so important and they don't need to conduct it hard.

The prepared cognitive tasks were a receipt classification and one-digit addition. The receipt classification was a cognitive task simulated office work. As shown in the right of Figure 6, twenty seven table cells categorized according to amount of money, date and type of shops was shown on the display of iPad. In this task, one of the cells should be chosen according to the fictitious receipts as shown in the left of Figure.XX. One receipt is usually processed in five to ten seconds. One-digit addition is a task to input the sum of two one-digit numbers on the computer. One addition task is usually solved about one second.

Figure 7 shows the flow of the experiment. The first day was the day for practice. After informed consent to the subject, the procedures of tasks were explained and they made a practice. The 2nd and 3rd day were the days for measuring intellectual productivity variation. On each day, a fatigue questionnaire and a CFF (Critical Flicker Frequency) measurement were conducted, and then four task sets were given to them. Each task sets consists of the receipt classification and the one-digit addition task for 30 minutes and the fatigue questionnaire and the CFF measurement. After the 2nd task set, there was a lunch break and the illuminance condition was changed from that in the morning. In the morning of the 2nd day, the normal illuminance condition was settled while the high illuminance condition was settled in the morning of the 3rd day for the half of the subjects. For the remaining half, the illuminance condition pattern was reversed. In the 1st and 3rd task set, high motivated condition was settled. In other task set, low motivated condition was settled. On the last day, a dummy task set was given to avoid a terminal effect.

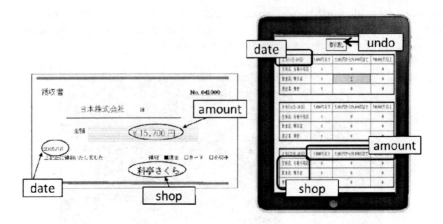

Fig. 6. Image of receipt classification task

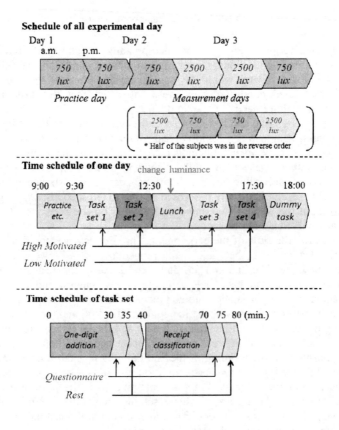

Fig. 7. Experimental procedure

3.3   Results

Experimental Results. Figure 8 shows the results of the task performances. The averages were compared with paired sample t-test. The performance of the receipt classification and the one-digit addition under the high motivated condition was higher than that under the low motivated condition (p<0.01). The illuminance conditions made no difference.

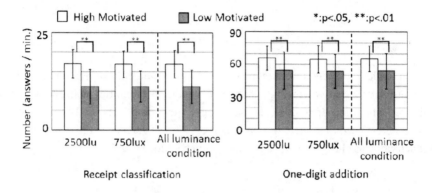

Fig. 8. Task performance of cognitive tasks

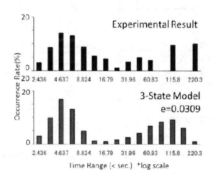

Fig. 9. Comparison of the model simulation and subjective experimental result

Analyzed Results with the Model. Using the concept of intellectual productivity mode, the answering time histogram of experimental data was approximated as sum of two lognormal distributions. five parameters $(\mu_1, \mu_2, \sigma_1, \sigma_2, p)$ in formula (1) was optimized to minimize the error E, which is a quantitative index of reproduction accuracy and it is defined as formula (2).

$$Error\ E = \ \frac{1}{n}\sqrt{\sum_{1}^{n}(Y_{sim\_k} - Y_{exp\_k})^2} \tag{2}$$

For each experimental data, model parameters which made the least Error E were derived with a genetic algorithm method. As a result, it is revealed that most of experimental result is well approximated as shown in figure 9.

3.4   Discussion

Derived model parameters were compared with work motivation condition. As shown in Figure 10, μ_1 and μ_2 in high motivated condition is shorter than them in low motivated condition (p<0.001). It means the time range of short-term rest and long-term rest become shorter in HM condition. This difference is the reason why the productivity was changed with work motivation condition.

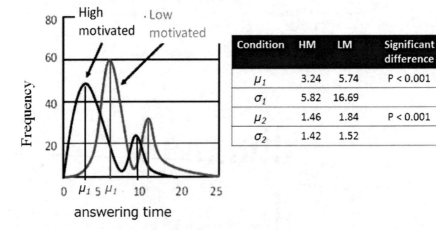

Condition	HM	LM	Significant difference
μ_1	3.24	5.74	P < 0.001
σ_1	5.82	16.69	
μ_2	1.46	1.84	P < 0.001
σ_2	1.42	1.52	

Fig. 10. Comparison of model parameters with motivation condition

4   Conclusion

In this study, the authors have proposed an intellectual productivity model. In this model, there are three state, working state", "short-term rest state" and "long-term rest state" and they transit with probability. Considering with this model suggest that the answering time of cognitive tasks, in which the difficulty of each problem is almost same, approximated a sum of two lognormal distributions.

In addition, a subjective experiment was conducted, in which illuminance on the desk and work motivation were controlled to vary their productivity. As a result, the task performance was improved by high work motivated condition. And this histogram was well fitted with approximated equation. It means the intellectual productivity model can explain productivity variance well. The parameters, which was used for fitting the experiment results, was significantly changed by motivation condition. In the future, it is expected that the mechanism of productivity variance is revealed more detail with this model. And the authors planning a development of evaluating productivity method based on this model.

Acknowledgement. A part of this work was supported by JSPS KAKENHI Grant Number 23360257.

References

1. Lomonaco, G., Miller, D.: Environmental Satisfaction, Personal Control and the Positive Correlation to Increased Productivity. Johnson Controls, Inc. (1997)
2. Brill, M.: Using Office Design to Increase Productivity, vol. 1. Buffalo Workplace Design and Productivity Inc. (1984)
3. Enomoto, K., Kondo, Y., Obayashi, F., Iwakawa, M., Ishii, H., Shimoda, H., Terano, M.: An Experimental Study on Improvement of Office Work Productivity by Circadian Rhythm Light, WMSCI 2008, vol. 6, pp. 121–126 (2008)
4. Bills, A.G.: Blocking: A new principle of mental fatigue. American Journal of Psychology (43), 230–245 (1931)

Promotion of Cooperative Behavior in Social Dilemma Situation - How Group Heuristics, Restriction of Short-Term Memory, and Penalty Promote Cooperative Behavior

Atsuo Murata, Saki Kubo, Naoki Hata, and Takuma Kanagawa

Graduate School of Natural Science and Technology, Okayama University, Okayama, Japan
{murata,kubosaki}@iims.sys.okayama-u.ac.jp

Abstract. The group identity effect in a social dilemma situation might be very important in order to attain cooperation. It is important for organizational managers to make efforts and take measures to enhance cooperative behaviors. First, it was explored how the group heuristics promotes a cooperative behavior in a social dilemma situation. The group heuristics was found to play an important role in a social dilemma situation, and enhance a cooperative behavior. Second, it was examined how the ability of short-term memory affected cooperation. The shorter memory span was found to lead to more frequent cooperative behaviors. An agent whose short-term memory was restricted tended to cooperate more frequently than that whose short-term memory is not restricted at all. In the third experiment, we focused on the effects of penalty and probability of the revelation of defection on the cooperation, and getting insight into how punishment strategy should be used to get rid of social dilemmas and enhance cooperation. The defection (uncooperative behavior) decreased when the penalty to the defection was heavy and the probability of the revelation of defection was low than when the penalty to the defection was light and the probability of the revelation of the defection was high.

Keywords: social dilemma, group heuristics, experimental game theory, cooperative behavior, restriction of short-term memory, punishment model.

1   Introduction

One of the most important features in social interaction is the conflict between the individual motive to maximize personal interests and the motive to maximize collective interests. In many situations, if all attempt to maximize their personal interests, all get worse than when all cooperate to maximize collective interests. Such a behavior might induce a violation-based human error and lead to fatal and crucial accidents. In a variety of social dilemma situations [1], it is necessary to promote cooperative behavior somehow and optimize interests of society or organization. A lot of studies are carried out to enhance cooperative behavior in social dilemma situations [2-4]. Axelrod [3,4] demonstrated that tit-for tat strategy is able to effectively induce cooperative behavior.

D. Harris (Ed.): EPCE/HCII 2013, Part I, LNAI 8019, pp. 344–353, 2013.
© Springer-Verlag Berlin Heidelberg 2013

The prevention strategy of accidents due to violation-based human errors is socially important and paid more and more attention to [5]. In decision making, it is generally impossible for us to perceive and recognize all choices and exactly evaluate their probability of occurrence. We unconsciously use a "heuristic" approach to solve a complicated problem or make difficult decisions, because the time and the cognitive resources usable for such activities are limited. Although Jin et al.[6] tested a hypothesis that common group membership promotes cooperation, they have not verified their hypothesis in the framework of repeated and finite game theory. The condition of cooperation should be examined in the repeated and finite game situations. It is demonstrated that the tit-for tat strategy (First, unconditionally select cooperation, and later on determine a strategy according to the opponent's last selection) is effective for enhancing cooperation under a repeated and finite Prisoner's dilemma situation. This means that only the last behavior of the opponent needs to be remembered. Although such a situation is plausible for people with bounded rationality, it might not be practical to assume that only the last behavior (strategy) is remembered. It is more reasonable to assume that people are more forgiving for more frequent defections even if the short-term memory is restricted. Tit for more tats might be more effective for enhancing cooperation than the tit-for tat strategy. It has not clarified how the restriction of short-term memory affects cooperation. Although there seem to be many ways to elicit cooperative behavior, the punishment (more concretely, the penalty to the defection) must be one of the most effective measures for enhancing cooperation. However, there seem to be few studies on how the punishment to the defective (incooperative) behavior and the degree of penalty can help to enhance cooperative behavior.

First, the group heuristics was taken into account, and it was explored how the group heuristics promotes a cooperative behavior in social dilemma situations. Second, explore the restriction of short-term memory on cooperation under a repeated and finite Prisoner's dilemma situation. Third, simulation experiments were carried out to find the optimal penal regulations condition that can suppress violations (defective behavior).

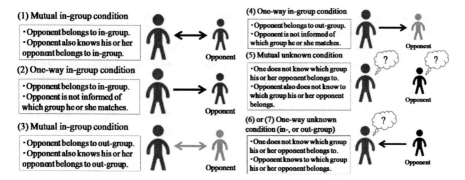

Fig. 1. Explanation of seven types of group heuristics conditions

The paper is organized as follows. Section 2 shows the experimental methods for each of three experiments: (1) how group heuristics affects cooperation, (2) how restriction of short-term memory affects cooperation, and (3) how penalty affects cooperation. Section 3 shows the results of three experiments. Section 4 discuss the results of three experiments, and explore how cooperation should be enhanced. Section 5 summarized and concluded the results.

2   Method

2.1   Experiment1: Effects of Group Heuristics and Restriction of Short-Term Memory on Cooperation

The following hypothesis was verified in this study: We prefer to cooperate with in-group (we-group) members because we generally expect reciprocal responses from in-group, but not from out-group (they-group). In short, we tend to expect reciprocity to exist within in-group, but not within out-group. Therefore, a person facing a social dilemma situation tends to cooperate more frequently with an in-group member than with an out-group member.

The following experiment was conducted to verify the hypothesis above and identify the condition for promoting cooperative behavior in such a social dilemma situation. The participants were ten undergraduates aged from 22 to 24 years. The following seven conditions were selected (see Fig. 1):

(1)Mutual in-group condition
(2)One-way in-group condition
(3)Mutual out-group condition
(4)One-way out-group condition
(5)Mutual unknown condition
(6)One-way unknown condition (in-group)
(7)One-way unknown condition (out-group)

The participants were divided into two groups. In the condition (1) above, each member of the group was informed that he or she belonged to the in-group, and the partner was also told that he or she was gaming with the in-group member. Under the condition (2), each member was known that he or she belonged to the in-group, but his or her partner did not know with which group member he or she played. Under the condition (5), the participant was not provided with the information of opponent, and the opponent also did not have any information of the participant with whom he or she played. Under the conditions (6) and (7), the participant was not provided with the information of opponent, and the opponent had information on which group he or she played with. For each condition, the participants were required to conduct a game of 20 matches.

First, the participants were provided with virtual money x (x=2,000 yen). In each match (trial), the participants were required to carry out the following decision making. The participants made decision on how much (from 0 to 100 yen) they provide their opponent with (This amount is represented by y). This was subtracted from the initial amount, and simultaneously the participants obtained twice the amount which was given by their opponent (This amount is represented by z). The advantage per one match (trial) equaled the amount $2z-y$. The cooperative rate per one match (trial) was calculated as $y/100$.

2.2   Experiment2: Effects of Restriction of Memory on Cooperation

A computer simulation was carried out to explore the restriction of short-term memory on cooperation under a repeated and finite Prisoner's dilemma situation. The restrictions of short-term memory were past two, four, six, and eight trials. The computer agents (players) with the restriction of short-term memory above repeated a finite Prisoner's dilemma game.

(1) restriction condition (1/2): If the opponent selects cooperation at least one time within past two trials, the player selects a cooperative behavior.
(2) restriction condition (2/4): If the opponent selects cooperation at least two times within past four trials, the player selects a cooperative behavior.
(3) restriction condition (3/6): If the opponent selects cooperation at least three times within past six trials, the player selects a cooperative behavior.
(4) restriction condition (4/8): If the opponent selects cooperation at least four times within past eight trials, the player selects a cooperative behavior.

2.3   Experiment 3: Effects of Penalty on Cooperation

The person-agent simulation was run according to the following condition and procedure. The probability of punishment for the defective behavior was set to as follows:
   Model A: 10%, 20%, and 30%
   Model B: 20%, 40%, 60%, and 80%
Two types of penalty conditions (light and heavy) were used. Four types of agents represented by the mixture percentage of ((A) completely cooperative strategy, (B) completely defective strategy, and (C) tit-for-tat strategy) were used as follows:
   ((A), (B), and (C))=(1:1:1)
   ((A), (B), and (C))=(1:1:8)
   ((A), (B), and (C))=(1:8:1)
   ((A), (B), and (C))=(1:1:8)
A total of 56 combinations of probability of punishment, penalty, and mixture percentage of agent's strategy were carried out for all participants. For one condition, a total of 30 trials were conducted. The display used in the experiment is demonstrated in Fig.2.

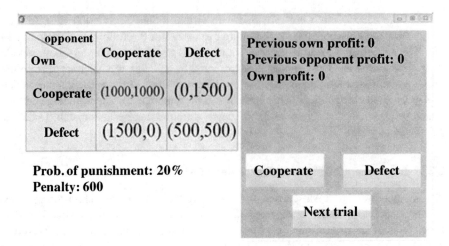

Fig. 2. Display used in Experiment 3

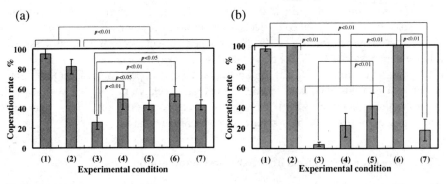

Fig. 3. Cooperation rate compared among seven experimental conditions. (a) first trial, (b) last trial

3   Results

3.1   Experiment1: Effects of Group Heuristics on Cooperation

In Fig.3(a), the cooperative rate at the first trial is compared among seven experimental conditions above. The corresponding cooperative rate at the final trial (20-th repetition) is compared among seven conditions in Fig.3(b).   The condition (3) led to lower cooperative rate, and the condition (1) led to the highest cooperative rate. The conditions (5), (6), and (7) also did not enhance cooperation. The awareness of belonging to the same group (that is, group heuristics) tended to promote cooperative behavior. In a social dilemma situation, the group heuristics seems to play an important role, and enhance cooperative behavior. In conclusion, consciousness of in-group membership might help to promote actively mutual cooperation.

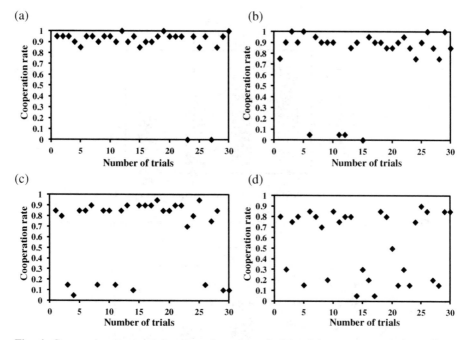

Fig. 4. Cooperation rate as a function of number of trials. ((a) memory restriction: 1/2, (b) memory restriction: 2/4, (c) memory restriction: 3/6, (d) memory restriction: 4/8).

3.2   Experiment2: Effects of Restriction of Memory on Cooperation

In Fig.4(a)-(d), the cooperation rate is plotted as a function of number of trials. The cooperation rate was the least dispersive for the 1/2 restriction condition. The cooperation rate for the 1/2 restriction condition was the highest, and ranged from 0.85 to 0.95 except for two data points corresponding to the cooperation rate of 0.   Unlike the 1/2 restriction condition, the cooperation rate for the 4/8 restriction condition never became 0. The cooperation rate for the 4/8 restriction condition was on the whole less than 0.9 and the most dispersive. In Fig.5, the cooperation rate is compared among the restriction conditions of short-term memory.

3.3   Experiment3: Effects of Penalty on Cooperation

As a result of simulation experiments (person vs. agent (computer)), the probability of punishment (penal regulation) affected the cooperative behavior (See Figs.6 and 7). The higher (heavy) penalty tended to enhance cooperation. Even if the expected values of profit were equal, heavy penalty functioned so that the in-cooperative behavior can be suppressed. Moreover, it was demonstrated that the higher (heavy) penalty (when the probability of violation (in-cooperation) closure is not taken into account) can suppress such in-cooperative (defective) behavior. However, it must be noted that there exists an interactive effect between penalty and probability of punishment.

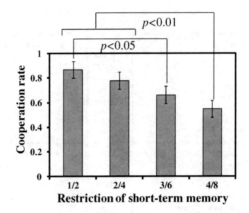

Fig. 5. Cooperation rate as a function of restriction condition of short-term memory

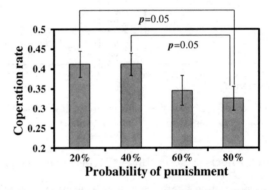

Fig. 6. Cooperation rate as a function of probability of punishment

While, for the lower (light) penalty condition, the lower probability of punishment helped to promote cooperation, the probability of punishment does not necessarily enhance the cooperation for the higher (heavy) penalty condition.

4   Discussion

4.1   Experiment1: Effects of Group Heuristics on Cooperation

As shown in Fig.3 (a) and (b), it tended that the cooperation rate differed between the first and the last trials. The cooperation rate of (3) mutual out-group condition, (4) one-way out-group condition and (7) one-way unknown condition (out-group) got lower at the last trial than at the first trial. Although the cooperation rate of (6) one-way unknown condition (in-group) was by far lower than that of (1) mutual in-group condition and (2) one-way in-group condition at the first trial, this was nearly equal to that of (1) mutual in-group condition and (2) one-way in-group condition at the last trial. These results are indicative of the necessity of exploring the change of cooperation rate with time (evolution of cooperation rate over time) in order to clarify how the group heuristics promote a cooperative behavior.

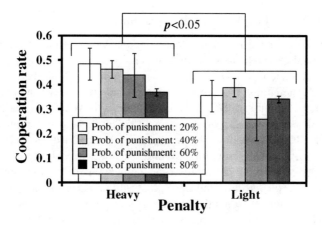

Fig. 7. Cooperation rate as a function of penalty and probability of punishment

As a whole, the condition (c) led to the lowest cooperation rate, and the condition (1) led to the highest cooperative rate. The conditions (e) and (g) also did not enhance cooperation. The condition (f) also enhanced the cooperation especially at the latter half of the experiment. The conditions (a), (b), and (c) are common in that at least one person belongs to the in-group. The awareness of belonging to the same group (that is, group heuristics) tended to promote a cooperative behavior even if one of the two persons belonged to the in-group. This suggests that the consciousness of belonging to the same group might be effective for promoting a cooperative behavior. The in-group might lead to the encouragement of team work. Therefore, we can infer that the consciousness of in-group (group heuristics) leads to the enhanced team work that is regarded as essential for reducing human errors and accidents.

4.2   Experiment2: Effects of Restriction of Memory on Cooperation

It is demonstrated that the tit-for tat strategy (First, unconditionally select cooperation, and ever since determine a strategy according to the opponent's last selection) is effective for enhancing cooperation under a repeated and finite Prisoner's dilemma situation [2,3]. This means that only the last behavior of the opponent needs to be remembered. Although such a situation is plausible for people with bounded rationality, it might not be practical to assume that only the last behavior (strategy) is remembered. It is more reasonable to assume that people are more forgiving for more frequent defections even if the short-term memory is bounded and restricted. As tit for more tats might be more effective for enhancing cooperation than the tit-for tat strategy, we assumed that the more retained duration of short-term memory might induce more cooperation.

As shown in Figs.4(a)-(d) and 5, the shorter memory restriction led to higher cooperation. Contrary to the prediction above, cooperation was enhanced when the short-term memory restriction was shorter. The longer short-term restriction can be regarded as more forgiving strategy such as tit-for-more tats which is generous to more defections of the opponent player.

4.3   Experiment3: Effects of Penalty on Cooperation

The heavy penalty tended to enhance cooperation. Although the expected values of profit were equal for both light and heavy penalty conditions, heavy penalty functioned so that the uncooperative behavior can be suppressed. However, as shown in Fig.7, it must be noted that there exists an interactive effect between the penalty condition and the probability of the revelation of defection. While, for the light penalty condition, the lower probability of revelation of defection helped to promote cooperation, the probability of revelation of detection did not necessarily enhance the cooperation for the heavy penalty condition. While the lower probability of revelation of defection helped to promote cooperation for the heavy penalty condition, the probability of revelation of detection did not necessarily enhance the cooperation for the light penalty condition. It seems that the severity of penalty works more strongly for the promotion of cooperation than the probability of revelation of defection.

The results seem to be contradictory at a glance. It might be misunderstood that the heavy or light penalty is constant irrespective of the probability of revelation of defection. This was not true of this experiment. If the value of heavy or light penalty is constant irrespective of the probability of revelation of defection, the corporation rate should increase with the increase of probability of revelation. This was not observed, and the value of heavy or light penalty was different for each value of probability of revelation of defection. As mentioned above, the values of light or heavy penalty were determined according to the probability of the revelation of detection, and the types of agents represented by the mixture percentage of ((a) completely cooperative strategy, (b) completely defective strategy, and (c) tit-for-tat strategy). Thus, throughput the experiment, the values of light or heavy penalty were not constant for each value of probability of the revelation of detection. The value of penalty differed according to the probability of the revelation of detection even if the penalty condition was the same (light or heavy).

4.4   General Discussion-How Cooperation Should be Enhanced

On the basis of separate discussion of each experiment, the enhancement strategy of cooperation will be summarized from the viewpoints of group heuristics, restriction of short-term memory, and punishment.

We originally expected that the cooperation is promoted only when both in-group players also know that the opponent also belongs to the in-group. We also assumed that the players allocated to the conditions (2) and (6) do not try to maximize collective interests, and cooperation is not facilitated eventually. However, even under such conditions other than (1), the corporative behavior was found to be gradually promoted. This means that at least one-way in-group condition eventually leads to the reciprocal cooperative behavior. In the framework of repeated and finite game theory, at least one-way in-group condition seems to lead to the reciprocal cooperative behavior. The stereotype that in-group members are reliable, honest, and cooperative must effectively work for deriving a cooperative behavior irrespective of the group heuristics condition of the opponent.

It must be noted that the consciousness of in-group membership does not necessarily induce positive aspects (in this study, the enhanced cooperation). As pointed out by Murata [5], such consciousness sometimes leads to groupthink, and induces serious accidents such as a NASA space shuttle explosion accident. Therefore, future work should explore both positive and negative aspects of group identity effect or in-group heuristics systematically. In a social dilemma situation, the group heuristics principle seems to play an important role, and enhance a cooperative behavior. In conclusion, the consciousness of in-group membership by at least one player might help to promote actively mutual cooperation.

We regarded such a generous strategy which forgives the opponent player's multiple defections by extending the retain duration of short-term memory as an important factor to enhance cooperation in our society. Although this generosity to the opponent's more defections was assumed to promote reflection of the opponent player's defective strategies and be necessary for enhancing cooperation, contrary to this assumption, it was demonstrated that such a system never led to the predicted performance. As Axelrod [2,3] demonstrated that the tit-for-tat strategy was the most effective among a variety of strategies, forgetting (forgiving) only one past defection of the opponent player (tit-for tat) seems to lead to enhance more cooperation than the willingness to forgiving more past defections of the opponent player. The behavioral strategy that takes into account not multiple past decisions of the opponent but the nearest past decision leads to more cooperative behavior, which indicate the forgetting of past behaviors without being affected by past defections is essential for eliciting mutual cooperation .

The low probability of the revelation of defection led to a higher value of penalty. The higher probability of the revelation of defection led to a lower value of penalty. As the risk seems to be mainly prescribed not by the probability of the revelation of defection but by the value of penalty in the range of this experiment, the cooperation rate tended to increase with the decrease of probability of revelation of detection and with the increase of penalty. Due to this, the cooperation rate tended to increase with the decrease of probability of revelation of defection. It seems that the participant paid emphasis not on the probability of the revelation of defection but on the penalty itself to assess the risk, and felt more risky when the penalty was heavier.

References

1. Komorita, S.S., Parks, C.D.: Social Dilemmas. Westview Press (1996)
2. Axelrod, R.: The Evolution of Cooperation. Basic Books (2006)
3. Axelrod, R.: The Complexity of Cooperation. Princeton University Press (1997)
4. Taylor, M.: The Possibility of Cooperation. Cambridge University Press (1987)
5. Murata, A.: Human error management paying emphasis on decision making and social intelligence –Beyond the framework of man-machine interface design. In: Proc. of Fourth International Workshop on Computational Intelligence & Applications, pp. 1–12 (2008)
6. Jin, N., Yamagishi, T.: Group heuristics in social dilemma, Japanese Journal of Social Psychology, Vol. Japanese Journal of Social Psychology 12(3), 190–198 (1997)

User Requirement Analysis of Social Conventions Learning Applications for Non-Natives and Low-Literates

Dylan Schouten[1], Nanja Smets[2], Marianne Driessen[3], Marieke Hanekamp[3],
Anita H.M. Cremers[2], and Mark A. Neerincx[1]

[1] Faculty Electrical Engineering, Mathematics and Computer Science, TU Delft, Netherlands
{D.G.M.Schouten,M.A.Neerincx}@tudelft.nl
[2] TNO Soesterberg, Soesterberg, Netherlands
{Nanja.Smets,Anita.Cremers}@tno.nl
[3] CINOP, Den Bosch, Netherlands
{MDriessen,MHanekamp}@cinop.nl

Abstract. Learning and acting on social conventions is problematic for low-literates and non-natives, causing problems with societal participation and citizenship. Using the Situated Cognitive Engineering method, requirements for the design of social conventions learning software are derived from demographic information, adult learning frameworks and ICT learning principles. Evaluating a sample of existing Dutch social conventions learning applications on these requirements shows that none of them meet all posed criteria. Finally, Virtual Reality is suggested as a possible future technology improvement.

Keywords: Social conventions, adult education, ICT learning, low-literates, non-natives, situated cognitive engineering, virtual reality, mixed reality.

1   Introduction

In current society, people are expected to be independent, self-directed problem solvers: they should either be able to solve their own problems or at least know where to go for help. For non-native citizens and people of low literacy, this can be hard. They lack knowledge and language skills required for satisfactory participation in society, possibly combined with low self-efficacy, little social engagement and poor security awareness. These people would benefit from ICT support to acquire and apply the relevant social convention knowledge and skills in their neighbourhood.

Becker and Mark (1998) define social conventions as the normative rules of conduct in a social system, which are adhered to by group members even when acting otherwise is possible. The envisioned support distinguishes between norms-and-rules and language aspects.

First, the 'norms and rules governing social participation' aspect indicates knowledge of the appropriate and accepted ways to act in modern society, including behavioral rules and guidelines for interacting with other people. For the non-native demographic, cultural difference can make these rules unclear; for the low-literate demographic, information density and complexity can surpass their ability to cope.

D. Harris (Ed.): EPCE/HCII 2013, Part I, LNAI 8019, pp. 354–363, 2013.

Second, the 'language' aspect of social conventions refers to the ability to effectively communicate in and participate in modern society. In particular, this project is interested in the communication problems incurred by situated language complexity mismatches, where the complexity of the language used exceeds the level participants are comfortable with. For the non-native demographic, a certain degree of language acquisition might be useful, though the primary focus will be on improving effective communication; for the low-literate demographic, effective learning could focus on increasing comfort and reducing shame in indicating low literacy.

As a first step in the development of computer support for social convention learning, this paper has two main research questions: Are existing social conventions learning applications well-suited for teaching non-natives and low-literates? And in what ways can they be improved?

This study will use the situated Cognitive Engineering (sCE) method (Neerincx & Lindenberg, 2008), which integrates human factors knowledge into the technology development process; figure 1 shows a schematic overview of the sCE methodology. The following sections will follow the 'boxes' shown in the figure: Sections 2 to 4 set the foundation (describing operational demands, human factors and technology) while Section 5 provides a requirements analysis (specification) and a corresponding first evaluation of current applications.

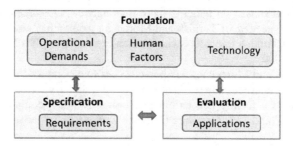

Fig. 1. Situated Cognitive Engineering method (Neerincx & Lindenberg, 2008)

2   Operational Demands

Literacy is measured on a continuous scale, ranging from 0 to 500. In the Netherlands, five levels have been defined: level 1 (0 and 225) indicates that a person is low-literate (Steehouder & Tijssen, 2011). The Organisation for Economic Co-operation and Development indicates level 3 as the minimum level required for active participation in a knowledge-based society ('functional literacy'). This level is the international benchmark, and it is associated with economic independence and increased participation in society and life-long learning (Murray, Kirsch & Jenkins, 1997).

There are currently 1.1 million level-1 low-literate people between the ages of 15 and 65 living in the Netherlands; this number is quite stable. (Houtkoop et al, 2012). 69% of these low-literates are native citizens. Low literacy does not imply a lack of ICT skills: Many low-literates have computer and Internet experience at home and at work. Only about 6% of the labor force has 'never used a computer before'. (Houtkoop et al, 2012).

A 'non-native citizen' is 'a person of whom at least one parent was born abroad' (Keij, 2000). In 2011, 20.6% of the Dutch population consisted of non-native citizens: 9.2% western migrants, 11.4% non-western. The subset of western migrants has grown by 11.8% since January 2000, owing mostly to immigration; non-western migrants have increased by 34.8%, largely due to natural population growth (Gijsberts, Huijnk & Dagevos, 2012).

Within the context of this study, extra attention is afforded to two specific subgroups: the non-native 55+ elderly, and non-western 45+ migrant women. Currently, 4% of all 55+ elderly living in the Netherlands fit the 'non-native'-description (7% in 2025). This group will run a high risk of social isolation over the next decade: their retirement imply loss of social contacts and income, exacerbating the existing problems caused by low education and a poor grasp of the Dutch language (Mertens & van der Zwet, 2009). Furthermore, the non-native elderly show a relatively high degree of depression and social seclusion, yet take less advantage of healthcare services like home care. Factors at play here are both different wishes and perceived needs regarding healthcare (den Draak & de Klerk, 2011) and a cultural focus on informal care by relatives; coming generations of migrant children are expected to put less stock in the notion of 'caring for elderly relatives' (Mertens & van der Zwet, 2009).

About 155.000 non-western 45+ women were found living in the Netherlands in 2006, and this number is growing. Turkish and Moroccan 45+ women perform less paying work and subsist on benefits more than native 45+ women (den Draak & de Klerk, 2011). Over 80% of Turkish and Moroccan women has no degree, and around 66% of elderly Turkish and Moroccan women are functionally illiterate (Mertens & van der Zwet, 2009).

73% of Turks and Moroccans has home access to a computer, 47% of Turks/ Moroccans lacks an internet connection at home, 18% regularly uses a computer at work, and 43% indicates 'feeling like an outsider' when ICT and computers are discussed (91%, 16%, 50% and 17% for native Dutch citizens) (Bijl & Verweij, 2012).

3   Human Factors

Adult Learning Principles. Merriam (2010) outlined four major theoretical frameworks of adult education that jointly offer an encompassing overview of the attributes of adult learning: andragogy, self-directed learning, transformative learning and situated cognition.

The theory of andragogy distinguishes six characteristics: adults are self-directed learners (1), driven by real-life problems (2), internal motivations (3) and societal roles and demands (4), who want to know why they should learn anything they are told to learn (5) and possess accumulated life experience to draw on (6). These characteristics offer clear and simple guidelines for adult education (Knowles, 1984).

Self-directed learning is a theory of adult education that is based on adult learners willingly engaging in learning of their own choice (Tough, 1971). Self-directed learning is connected to informal learning, which distinguishes between three learning styles: formal learning is structured and standardized, non-formal learning is structured but unstandardized, and informal learning is both unstructured and unstandardized

(La Belle, 1982). While self-directed learning can be found in instances of every learning style, it is most often encountered during informal learning.

Transformative learning involves altering frames of reference. Illeris (2010) contrasts transformative learning with assimilative learning (which keeps frames of reference intact) and accommodative learning (which involves restructuring frames of reference). Transformative learning requires the learner to engage in critical self-reflectivity. Mezirow (2000) offers a ten-step list to describe the process of transformative learning, from 'a disorienting dilemma' to 'a reintegration into one's life on the basis of conditions dictated by one's new perspective'.

The main notion of situated cognition is that the context in which the knowledge is presented is as much a part of learning as the information content: context includes the physical learning location, the tools used and their method of use, and the social interactions (Brown, Collins & Duguid, 1989). Studies have also suggested that affective dimensions and emotions form an important element in the context of learning (Merriam, 2010).

Applying these four frameworks to the problem definition outlined earlier, a number of attributes necessary for social conventions learning programs can be derived:

1. There is no 'the adult learner', and no single curriculum can fit every student. A successful social conventions learning program must be adjustable to take different learning styles into account, offering guided 'teacher-directed' options and self-directed 'student-directed' ones.
2. Social conventions learning can be a volatile, culturally charged topic. A social conventions learning application needs to recognize and ameliorate this volatility, by using non-confrontational language and examples and demonstrating cultural awareness.
3. Brown, Collins & Duguid (1989) suggest that knowledge is influenced by the learning environment; as such, learning should take place in an environment as close to the learners' real-life environment as possible. A social conventions learning application must be able to create such an environment.

ICT Learning Principles. Richards's (2005) topology of meaningful ICT learning activities describes three characteristics vital to ICT-learning: the provision of and dissemination of information, the possibility and facilitation of worldwide communication, and the element of interactivity.

'The provision of and dissemination of information' refers to the notion that ICT learning offers a wide range of media and information types. This breadth of possibility makes it easier to adapt elements of a learning application to individual learners' preferences. Low-literates, for instance, could benefit from an implementation focusing on audio/video and simple text, while language-specific subtitles and cultural elements such as avatar ethnicity and dress style could be provided for the non-natives. Additionally, use of the Internet allows learners to look up and access self-chosen materials, supporting self-directed learning from home.

The availability of constant worldwide communication allows teachers and students to stay in contact beyond traditional regulated classroom hours. This opens up venues for directed, personalized support, which is vital in ICT-learning: Nielson (2011) reports high rates of failure in at-home language learning without proper support. Furthermore, it can be argued that the near-total dissemination of ICT use in Dutch society (van Deursen and van Dijk, 2011) has made 'the proper usage of ICT communication tools' an important social skill. As it's suggested that non-natives may be restricted in their home access to ICT and the subsequent user experience (Driessen et al, 2011), an ICT-based social conventions learning application could serve a dual purpose in acquainting the users with ICT communication norms.

The element of interactivity, finally, links ICT learning to notions of experiential learning (Kolb, 2001). Barak (2006) divides learning into four aspects – contextual, active, social and reflective – and reports that the use of ICT enhances the contextual and active parts of learning, tying the interactivity of ICT learning applications to both experiential learning and situated cognition.

One example of ICT learning that demonstrates the effectiveness of interactivity is in educational games. Playing digital games is seen as a form of experiential learning (Kiili, 2005), and Doshi (2005) claims that using gaming to teach skills allows students to fit otherwise abstract concepts into their daily lives. Additionally, educational games offer other benefits to learning: games are a conduit to experiential learning, games create and enhance engagement in students, games promote cooperation, and games could help students in digesting complex subject matter (Fengfeng, 2008).

Next to the experiential learning note, games are known for inducing engagement, immersion (Ermi & Mäyrä, 2005) and flow and fiero (Cornelissen et al, 2012). Both Dickey (2007) and Warren et al (2008) report that games induce intrinsic motivation in players. Gaming has also been shown to promote cooperation among school children (Facer et al, 2004).

The following ICT learning principles can be derived for the current project:

1. A successful social conventions learning program should be adaptable to the target audiences as much as possible. ICT's relative wealth of different media can and should be used to take the requirements of the target demographics into account.
2. Support is important in self-directed learning: study results indicate that proper use of support is necessary for success in self-directed learning (Nielson, 2011) and social conventions learning (Driessen et al, 2011).The use of ICT in this support seems a natural fit.
3. A successful social conventions learning program should be interactive, offering lesson plans and examples tailored to the target demographics' real-life situations and incorporating principles of experiential learning and situated cognition.
4. Gaming principles should be used to enhance motivation, immersion and flow.

4   Technology

Existing Social Conventions Learning Applications. The first literature review focused on applications for our main demographics: non-natives and people of low literacy. There is a specific class of social conventions learning software that is tailor-made for these groups: naturalization and integration courses that focus on both language learning and culture and participation (Driessen et al, 2011) and often handles both topics simultaneously. The investigation focused on seven Dutch naturalization software packages:

- **EHBN** is an older naturalization package that has been around since the 1990's. The website claims that it uses a 'CD-ROM program', and that the 'entire course is now web-based'. Targets non-natives and is intended to support naturalization. (Dutch national social conventions (DNSC), Dutch language learning level A2)
- **IJsbreker Plus** is a language learning naturalization aid for non-natives. It combines independent online work with book exercises and classroom teaching: the website claims to offer a 'strong mix of learning types'. (DNSC, level A2)
- **ETV.nl** and **Oefenen.nl** are two websites that offer a large selection of training programs: ETV.nl acts as a webshop, while Oefenen.nl hosts the training software. Offered are language learning segments aimed at low-literates and naturalization courses aimed at non-natives. (DNSC, various levels)
- **KNS Examen** is the website of the official Knowledge of Dutch Society naturalization exam. **KNS Examentraining** is an online training exam. The KNS Examen targets non-natives. (DNSC, level A2)
- **Naar Nederland** is 'the official self-study guide for the Dutch naturalization exam'. The method works with a DVD, several books and online practice software; the complete package is offered in 18 languages. (DNSC, level A1)
- **Nu in Nederland** is an online social conventions learning package that prepares students for the official KNS exam. It uses the eight main 'themes' of the KNS exam as a guideline, and claims to work with 'texts, questions, hyperlinks, movies and exam questions'. (DNSC)
- **Samen op pad** is a free online learning package focused on language learning and naturalization. It uses highly simplified Dutch to increase accessibility for low-literates and non-natives. Uses video-supported multiple-choice questions and interactive Dutch-language matching exercises. (DNSC, undefined levels)
- **Thuis in Nederlands** is a multimodal teaching method aimed at older female migrants, using a mix of classroom book learning, practical assignments and roleplay and e-learning (including VR environment called the Virtual Neighbourhood). Has an additional language learning track called 'Klaar voor de Start'. (A1 level)

Envisioned Technology. Virtual Reality (VR) seem to provide opportunities to support social conventions learning. Huang, Rauch and Liaw (2010) describe VR as 'a combination of 3D graphics and input devices that manages to create immersion in an interactive virtual environment', which is already wide-spread. VR-supported learning seems to outperform other types of e-learning: interactive virtual environments allow students to see and directly interact with one another, creating a sense of social presence (Monahan, McArdle & Bertolotto, 2008). VR learning can confer greater feelings of physical and social presence and situatedness (Huang, Rauch & Liaw, 2010) and allows for intuitive, natural interaction possibilities, making it interesting for social conventions learning purposes.

5   Requirements Analysis

Based on the demographic information and the human factors principles for adult learning and ICT learning, seven high-level user requirements were derived:

— **Req 1:** The application should offer and / or support different learning styles.
— **Req 2:** The application should be multi-modal, offering content in multiple concurrent ways.
— **Req 3:** The application should use learning materials and contents that are closely related to the learner's physical environment and real-life experiences.
— **Req 4:** The application should use non-confrontational language and content and demonstrate cultural awareness.
— **Req 5:** The application should employ real interactivity to engage the learners.
— **Req 6:** The application should employ principles of interactive gaming, like flow and fiero, to engage the learners and promote intrinsic motivation.
— **Req 7:** The application should possess built-in support options.

The evaluation of the existing social conventions learning applications is presented in Table 1 with a summary of application attributes:

— **Target groups:** the intended target demographic(s) for this application: non-natives (non-nat) and/or low-literates (low-lit).
— **Goal: social conventions:** whether or not the application teaches social conventions.
— **Goal: language**: whether or not the application teaches language skills (including language levels taught).
— **Method(s)** employed by this application: books, websites, CDs, and classroom learning.
— **Req 1 to Req 7** indicate the seven requirements listed above.

Table 1. Evaluation of existing applications on attributes and criteria

Method/ Criterium	EHBN	IJs-breker plus	EVT.nl	KNS examen	Naar Nederland	Nu in Nederland	Samen op pad	Thuis in Nederlands
Target groups	Non-nat.	Non-nat.	Non-nat; low-lit.	Non-nat.	Non-nat.	Non-nat.	Non-nat; low-lit.	Non-nat.
Goal: social conventions	Yes.	Yes.	Yes.	Yes.	Yes.	Yes.	Yes.	Yes.
Goal: language	Yes: level A2.	Yes: level A2.	Yes: level unclear.	Yes: level A2.	Yes: level A1.	No.	Yes: level unclear.	Yes: level A1.
Method(s)	Book. CD. Web.	Book. Web. Class.	Web.	Books. Web.	Books. DVDs. Web.	Web.	Web.	Book. Web.
Req 1	No.	Yes.	No.	No.	Yes.	No.	No.	Yes.
Req 2	Yes.	Yes.	No.	No.	Yes.	No.	Yes.	Yes.
Req 3	Yes.	Yes.	Yes.	Yes.	Unclear.	Yes.	Yes.	Yes.
Req 4	Yes.	Yes.	Yes.	Yes.	Unclear.	Yes.	Yes.	Yes.
Req 5	Unclear.	Yes.	No.	No.	Yes.	No.	Yes.	Yes.
Req 6	No.	No.	No.	No.	No.	No.	No.	Yes.
Req 7	No.	Yes.	No.	No.	Yes.	No.	No.	No.

Table 1 shows that none of the applications meet all requirements. While most applications fulfill the demands for situatedness and non-confrontational content, the application of gaming principles and fully integrated support is rare. The IJsbreker Plus, Naar Nederland and Thuis in Nederlands applications each meet six out of seven requirements: it therefore seems plausible that these applications could be adapted to better fit this study's demands, although the specific nature of this adaptation is as-of-yet undetermined.

In general, there proves to be a mismatch between the existing technology and the obtained operational demands and human factors knowledge (see Figure 1). VR technology has some attributes that can help significantly in fulfilling the listed requirements. VR's main advantages lie in inherent multimodality, enhanced situatedness, greater possibilities for real interactivity and positive aspects of the gaming experience.

6   Conclusion

This paper investigated the current state of social conventions learning applications. Requirements were derived from theoretical frameworks in the fields of adult education (i.e., andragogy, self-directed learning, transformative learning and situated cognition) and ICT learning (interactivity, communication, information, engagement, immersion, flow and fiero. Seven requirements were derived from these frameworks: adaptability, multi-modality, situatedness, non-confrontationalness, 'real' interactivity, use of gaming principles and integrated support. An evaluation of current social conventions learning applications using the derived requirements revealed that none satisfy every requirement. Virtual Reality technology might help to better address the user requirements, by (among other things) making unwritten rules explicit and by taking away anxiety through repeated exposure and practice.

Acknowledgement. This publication was supported by the Dutch national program COMMIT (http://www.commit-nl.nl/).

References

1. Becker, B., Mark, G.: Social Conventions in Collaborative Virtual Environments. In: Proceedings of Collaborative Virtual Environments (CVE 1998) (1998)
2. la Belle, T.J.: Formal, nonformal and informal education: a holistic perspective on lifelong learning. International Review of Education 28(2), 159–175 (1982)
3. Bijl, R., Verweij, A.: Measuring and monitoring immigrant integration in Europe (2012), http://www.scp.nl
4. Brown, J.S., Collins, A., Duguid, P.: Situated Cognition and the Culture of Learning. Educational Researcher 18(1), 32–42 (1989)
5. Cornelissen, F., Neerincx, M.A., Smets, N.J.J.M., Breebaart, L., Dujarding, P., Wolff, M.: Gamification for astronaut training. In: SpaceOps, Stockholm (2012)

6. van Deursen, A.J.A.M., van Dijk, J.A.G.M.: Trendrapport Computer en Internetgebruik 2011. Een Nederlands en Europees perspectief. Universiteit Twente, Enschede (2011)
7. Dickey, M.D.: Game design and learning: a conjectural analysis of how massively multiplayer online role-playing games (MMORPGs) foster intrinsic motivation. Educational Technology Research and Development 55(3), 253–273 (2007)
8. Doshi, A.: How gaming could improve information literacy. Computers in Libraries 26(5), 14–17 (2005)
9. den Draak, M., de Klerk, M.: Oudere migranten (2011), http://www.scp.nl
10. Driessen, M., van Emmerik, J., Fuhri, K., Nygren-Junkin, L., Spotti, M.: ICT Use in L2 Education for Adult Migrants: A qualitative study in the Netherlands and Sweden, JRC 59774 (2011)
11. Ermi, L., Mäyrä, F.: Fundamental Compontents of the Gameplay Experience: Analysing Immersion. In: Proceedings of DiGRA 2005 Conference: Changing Views – Worlds in Play (2005)
12. Facer, K., Joiner, R., Stanton, D., Reid, J., Hull, R., Kirks, D.: Savannah: Mobile gaming and learning. Journal of Computer Assisted Learning 20, 399–409 (2004)
13. Fengfeng, K.: A case study of computer gaming for math: Engaged learning from gameplay. Computers & Education 51, 1609–1620 (2008)
14. Gijsberts, M., Huijnk, W., Dagevos, J.: Jaarrapport integratie 2011 (2012), http://www.scp.nl
15. Houtkoop, W., Allen, J., Buisman, M., Fouarge, D., Van der Velden, R.: Kernvaardigheden in Nederland: Resultaten van de Adult Literacy and Life Skills Survey (ALL). In: Uitgave Expertisecentrum Beroepsonderwijs (2012)
16. Huang, H.M., Rauch, U., Liaw, S.S.: Investigating learners' attitudes toward virtual reality learning environments: Based on a constructivist approach. Computers and Education 55, 1171–1182 (2010)
17. Illeris, K.: Characteristics of Adult Learning. International encyclopedia of education 1, 36–41 (2010)
18. Keij, I.: Standaarddefinitie allochtonen (2000), http://www.cbs.nl
19. Kiili, K.: Digital game-based learning: Towards an experiental gaming model. Internet and Higher Education 8, 13–24 (2005)
20. Knowles, M.S.: The Adult Learner: A Neglected Species. Gulf, Houston (1984)
21. Kolb, D.A., Boyatzis, R.E., Mainemelis, C.: Experiental Learning Theory: Previous Research and New Directions. Perspectives on cognitive, learning, and thinking styles 1, 227–247 (2001)
22. Merriam, S.B.: Adult Education - Adult Learning, Instruction and Program Planning (2010)
23. Mertens, H., van der Zwet, R.: Het versterken van de maatschappelijke participatie van oudere migranten (2009), http://www.movisie.nl
24. Mezirow, J.: Learning to Think Like an Adult: Core Concepts of Transformation Theory. Learning as transformation: Critical perspectives on a theory in progress, 3–33 (2000)
25. Monahan, T., McArdle, G., Bertolotto, M.: Virtual reality for collaborative e-learning. Computers & Education 50, 1339–1353 (2008)
26. Murray, T.S., Kirsch, I.S., Jenkins, L.: Adult Literacy in OECD Countries: Technical Report on the International Adult Literacy Survey. US Department of Education (1997)
27. Neerincx, M., Lindenberg, J.: Situated cognitive engineering for complex task environments. In: Schraagen, J., Militello, L., Ormerod, T., Lipshitz, R. (eds.) Naturalistic Decision Making and Macrocognition, pp. 373–390

28. Nielson, K.B.: Self-study with language learning software in the workplace: what happens? Language Learning & Technology 15(3), 110–129 (2011)
29. Richards, C.: The design of effective ICT-supported learning activities: exemplary models, changing requirements, and new possibilities. Language Learning and Technology 9(1), 60–79 (2005)
30. Steehouder en Tijssen, Opbrengsten in beeld; Rapportage Aanvalsplan Laaggeletterdheid 2006-2011. CINOP, Den Bosch (2011)
31. Tough, A.: The Adult's Learning Projects: A Fresh Approach to Theory and Practice in Adult Learning (1971), http://allentough.com/
32. Warren, S.J., Dondlinger, M.J., Barab, S.A.: A MUVE Towards PBL Writing: Effects of a Digital Learning Environment Designed To Improve Elementary Student Writing. Journal of Research on Technology in Education 41(1), 113–140 (2008)

An Intellectual Productivity Evaluation Tool Based on Work Concentration

Hiroshi Shimoda[1], Kotaro Oishi[1], Kazune Miyagi[1], Kosuke Uchiyama[1], Hirotake Ishii[1], Fumiaki Obayashi[2], and Mikio Iwakawa[2]

[1] Graduate School of Energy Science, Kyoto University, Kyoto, Japan
{shimoda,oishi,miyagi,uchiyama,hirotake}@ei.energy.kyoto-u.ac.jp
[2] Eco-solutions Company, Panasonic Corp., Kadoma, Japan
{obayashi.fumiaki, iwakawa.mikio}@jp.panasonic.com

Abstract. The authors have proposed a concentration time ratio as a new evaluation index of intellectual productivity, which had been difficult to be quantitatively evaluated, with a concept of concentration on target task, and a measurement tool has been developed based on the index. In addition, a subject experiment was conducted with the tool in which the illumination conditions were changed. As the result, it was found that the index was not affected by learning effect and the difference of intellectual productivity by changing the illumination conditions could be evaluated quantitatively with the index.

Keywords: intellectual productivity, office environment, task and ambient light, work concentration.

1 Introduction

Energy saving is one of the countermeasure of increasing greenhouse gas emission caused by increasing worldwide energy consumption. After East Japan earthquake and the following Fukushima nuclear disaster, most of nuclear power stations have been shut down in Japan and we are suffering from lack of electricity. The government has promoted energy saving policies such that the temperature of air-conditioning system in the summer should be 28 degree Celsius and office lightings should be partially turned off [1]. However, the drop in productivity of office workers caused by the energy saving may extend their labor time and this may consume more energy.

On the other hand, recent studies have indicated that improvement of office environment may improve the intellectual productivity of office workers [2]. However, the method which evaluates office productivity objectively and quantitatively has not been established yet. There have been mainly two methods to evaluate the improvement of intellectual productivity caused by the change of office environment. One is subjective evaluation methods [3] and another is quantitative methods based on cognitive task performance [4]. The subjective evaluation method directly asks the change of their work performance to the office workers by the change of work environment.

D. Harris (Ed.): EPCE/HCII 2013, Part I, LNAI 8019, pp. 364–372, 2013.
© Springer-Verlag Berlin Heidelberg 2013

It is therefore difficult to quantify the improvement of the productivity. On the other hand, in case of the task performance-based method, they conduct specially designed cognitive tasks in each work environment and the change of task performance is measured. It is however difficult to accurately evaluate the change of intellectual productivity by the change of work environment because the performance is greatly influenced by learning effect.

In this study, therefore, a new evaluation index and its measurement tool have been proposed based on a concept of work concentration and a subject experiment was conducted with the index to confirm its effectiveness.

2   Concentration Index

When they perform intellectual work, it can be assumed that they performed it with transiting "working state", "short-term rest state" and "long-term rest state" as shown in Figure 1 [5]. In the short-term rest state, they unconsciously stop the work for a short time. In the long-term rest state, however, they consciously stop working to take a break or think other things for a long time. This state transition is affected by such as their work motivations, their fatigues, work contents and work environment [5]. Considering that concentration means a work state where their cognitive resources are assigned to a target work, it can be assumed that the working state and the short-term rest state are a concentrated state while the long-term rest state is a non-concentrated state as shown in Figure 1. And the intellectual work can be performed more when the time ratio of the concentration state among the total labor time is high. This means that the intellectual productivity can be measured by the concentration time ratio.

Based on the model in Figure 1, when they perform a task in which problems with uniformed difficulty are given continuously, the histogram of the answering time of each problem can be approximated as the sum of two lognormal distributions as shown in Figure 2. The left lognormal distribution expresses the sum of working state and the short-term rest state, while the right distribution includes not only working state and the short-term rest state but also the long-term rest state.

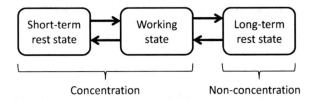

Fig. 1. Work state model

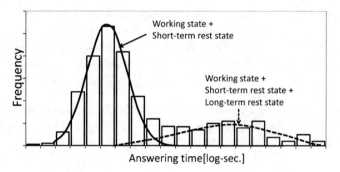

Fig. 2. Histogram of answering time and lognormal distributions

When giving a cognitive task to an office worker and the histogram of the answering time of each problem is drawn, the parameters of two lognormal distributions can be calculated by the approximation as shown in Figure 3. At that time, the histogram can be expressed as formula (3) using the parameters.

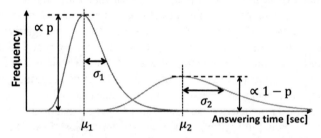

Fig. 3. Lognormal distributions and their parameters

$$f_1(t) = \frac{1}{\sqrt{2\pi}\sigma_1 t} \exp\left[-\frac{(\ln(t) - \mu_1)}{2\sigma_1^2}\right] \cdot pt$$

$$f_2(t) = \frac{1}{\sqrt{2\pi}\sigma_2 t} \exp\left[-\frac{(\ln(t) - \mu_2)}{2\sigma_2^2}\right] \cdot (1-p)t \qquad (1)$$

$$f(t) = f_1(t) + f_2(t)$$

Here, μ_1, μ_2 expresses the averages of lognormal distributions, σ_1, σ_2 expresses their standard deviations, and $p, (1-p)$ express their height ratios. When they concentrate the target task, the expected time of $f_1(t)$ distribution is an average answering time. Therefore the average answering time in concentration state can be expressed as formula (2).

$$\overline{CT} = \exp\left(\mu_1 + \frac{\sigma_1^2}{2}\right) \qquad (2)$$

Because total time in concentration state can be expressed as $N \cdot \overline{CT}$ where they answer N problems when performing the task, the concentration time ratio, CTR, can be expressed as formula (3) where total task performing time is T_{total}.

$$CTR = \frac{N \cdot \overline{CT}}{T_{total}} \tag{3}$$

Since the task performance (answering speed) is improved as repeating the problem solving by learning effect, it is difficult to evaluate the intellectual productivity by the task performance. The concentration time ratio proposed in this study however is not affected by the learning effect because it only expresses the time ratio of concentration state in the total task performing time.

3   Development of Concentration Measurement Tool

In order to find the concentration time ratio proposed in chapter 2, cognitive tasks should be given to office workers, the answering time of each problem should be measured and the parameters of two lognormal distributions should be calculated by approximating the histogram of the answering time. In this chapter, a design of the cognitive tasks and an analysis tool will be described.

3.1   Design of Cognitive Tasks

The cognitive task requires some conditions such that (1)they can continuously answer problems with their own paces, (2)the difficulty of each problem is unified, and (3)their solving strategy is not changed. And since the office work mainly requires linguistic ability such as document preparation and calculation ability such as accounting operations, the cognitive task should require these abilities. It is sure that creative works such as creating new ideas are important among many kinds of office works, however, most of the actual office works are typical and regular works. In this study therefore a word classification task and a mental calculation task have been designed.

Word Classification Task

The word classification task is the task where a given word on a sheet of paper is required to be classified into one of 27 categories by sorts of character, the first vowel and meaning category. Since the word is given in Japanese, the sorts of character are hiragana, katakana and kanji. The first vowels include "i", "u" and "o". The meaning categories are creature, proper noun and artificiality. As shown in Figure 4, the words are given as a bunch of papers where one word is written on each sheet of paper. They are required to answer the proper category by pressing one of 27 buttons on the display of iPad. The answering time of each problem is measured by the iPad and recorded into a server computer connected by the network.

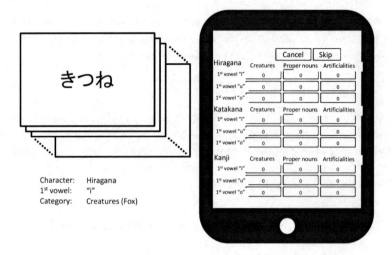

Fig. 4. Word classification task

Mental Calculation Task

In the mental calculation task, two-digit number is first shown on a display of a PC and they are required to memorize it, then another two-digit number is shown after pressing enter key. They are required to do a sum of two numbers in their heads and input the answer with a numeric keypad. After input the answer, pressing enter key moves to the next problem. The answering time of each problem is measured by the PC and recorded into the server computer.

3.2   Analysis Tool

With the recorded answering time, the parameters of two lognormal distributions are calculated by approximation as the histogram of answering time with EM (Expectation Maximization) algorithm [6], and then the concentration time ratio is calculated by the fomula (2) and (3). In other words, the parameters are estimated to maximize its probabilistic expectation as the histogram can be expressed as an approximation of two lognormal distributions. When estimating the parameter with the EM algorithm, the convergent conditions are; (a) μ_1 should be close to mode value of the histogram and (b) $\mu_1 < \mu_2$ and $\sigma_1 < \sigma_2$.

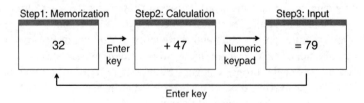

Fig. 5. Mental calculation task

4   Evaluation Experiment of Illumination Environment

4.1   Objective

The objective of the experiment is to confirm that the proposed concentration time ratio can evaluate the influence of intellectual productivity by change of illumination environment.

4.2   Experimental Method

Two illumination conditions were prepared which are (i)ceiling lighting (5,000K, 750 lux on the desk), and (ii)a combination of task lighting(6,000K, 650 lux on the desk) and ceiling lighting(3,000K, 100 lux on the desk). Here and after (i) is called 'Ambient' condition while (ii) is called 'T&A' condition. Although the intensity of illumination of both conditions is 750 lux on the desk, the energy consumption of T&A condition is only 46% of that of Ambient condition. As shown in the right picture of Figure 6, it is expected to concentrate on the target task in T&A condition because the area except the desk is dark and it eliminates surrounding visual noise. The other environmental conditions were controlled as shown in Table 1.

Figure 7 shows the experimental procedure. It was conducted for three days with changing the illumination conditions. 19 male subjects (ages of 20-55) participated in the experiment. 10 out of 19 subjects joined the group A-T&A-A in which the illumination conditions were Ambient, T&A and Ambient for each day respectively, while other 9 subjects joined the group T&A-A-T&A to keep the counterbalance. The actual measurement of the concentration time ratio was conducted in task set 1 and 2 at least two hours after lunch to avoid post-lunch dip. Task set 3 was conducted as a dummy task to avoid a terminal effect. The subjects were instructed not to take caffeine such as green tea and coffee during the experiment.

(a)Experimental environment(Ambient condition)   (b)T&A condition

Fig. 6. Experimental environment

Table 1. Other environmental conditions

Temperature	Humidity	CO_2 density	Sound noise
$25 \pm 1°C$	20-40%	Under 800ppm	Under 55dBA

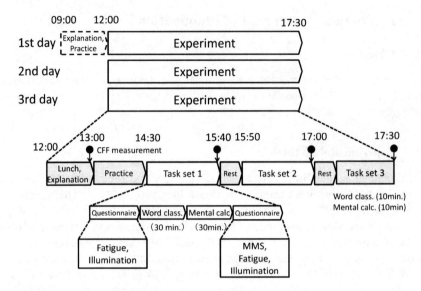

Fig. 7. Experimental procedure

4.3   Results and Discussions

Figure 8 shows the task performance of the word classification task for each group on each day. As shown in the figure, the learning effect was clearly found for both groups. The change of intellectual productivity by the change of illumination condition could not be evaluated from this result. This tendency was also found in the mental calculation task.

The concentration time ratios were tried to be calculated by the analysis tool mentioned in chapter 3, however, a few of them could not be calculated because the parameters of lognormal distributions could not be found by EM algorithm. In the following analysis therefore they are omitted. The same analysis as Figure 8 was done for the concentration time ratio and it was found that there was no significant difference between the results for each group on each day. This means that the concentration time ratio is not affected by the learning effect. Figure 9 shows the comparison of the concentration time ratios under two illumination conditions for each task.

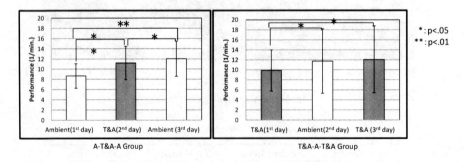

Fig. 8. Task performance of word classification task

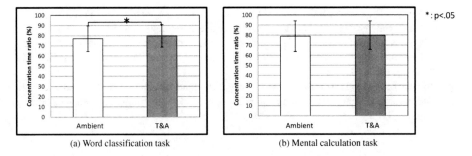

Fig. 9. Comparison of concentration time ratios of illumination conditions

In the word classification task, the concentration time ratio under T&A condition was 2.7% higher than that under Ambient condition (p<.05). In the mental calculation task, the concentration time ratio under T&A was also higher however there is no significant difference.

As the result of the above, it was found that the concentration time ratio proposed in this study has a possibility to evaluate the change of intellectual productivity quantitatively by the change of work environment without the learning effect.

5   Conclusion

In this study, the authors have proposed concentration time ratio as a new evaluation index of intellectual productivity from the view point of concentration on the target work, and have developed a measurement tool based on the index. In addition, a subject experiment was conducted to evaluate it where 19 subjects participated for three days. As the result, it was found that the concentration time ratio was not affected by the learning effect and it could evaluate the difference of intellectual productivity quantitatively by the change of illumination conditions. However there were a few cases in which concentration time ratios could not be calculated by the developed tool. The algorithm and the tool should be improved in the future.

Acknowledgement. A part of this work was supported by JSPS KAKENHI Grant Number 23360257.

References

1. Japanese Industrial Standards Committee: General rules of recommended lighting levels, JIS Z 9110:2011 (2011)
2. Brill, M.: Using Office Design to Increase Productivity, vol.1, Buffalo Workplace Design and Productivity Inc. (1984)
3. Akimoto, T., Tanabe, S., Yanai, T., Sasaki, M.: Thermal comfort and productivity - Evaluation of workplace environment in a task conditioned office. Building and Environment 45, 45–50 (2010)

4. Throme, D.R., Gensor, S.G., Sing, H.C., Hegge, F.W.: The Walter Reed Performance Assessment Battery. Neurobehavioral Toxicology and Teratology 7, 415–418 (1985)
5. Miyagi, K., Kawano, S., Ishii, H., Shimoda, H.: Improvement and Evaluation of Intellectual Productivity Model based on Work State Transition. In: Proceedings of IEEE-SMC
   2012, pp. 1491–1496 (2012)
6. Bilmes, J.: A Gentle Tutorial of the EM algorithm and its Application to Parameter Estimation for Gaussian Mixture and Hidden Markov Models. International Computer Science
   Institute (1998)

Author Index